ARCHITECTS OF POLITICA

This work offers a set of extended interpretations of Madison's argument in Federalist X of 1787, using ideas from social choice theory and from the work of Douglass North, Mancur Olson, and William Riker. Its focus is not on social choice theory itself, but on the use of this theory as a heuristic device to better understand democratic institutions. The treatment adapts a formal model of elections to consider rapid constitutional change at periods when societies face social quandaries. The topics explored in the book include Britain's reorganization of its fiscal system in the eighteenth century to prosecute its wars with France; the Colonies' decision to declare independence in 1776; Madison's argument about the "probability of fit choice" during the Ratification period of 1787–8; the argument between Hamilton and Jefferson in 1798–1800 over the long-run organization of the U.S. economy; the Dred Scott decision of 1857 and the election of Lincoln in 1860; Lyndon Johnson and the "critical realignment" of 1964; and Keynes's rejection of the equilibrium thesis in 1937 and the creation of the Bretton Woods institutions after 1944.

Norman Schofield is the William Taussig Professor of Political Economy at Washington Univesity in St. Louis. He has served as Fulbright Distinguished Professor of American Studies at Humboldt University Berlin in 2003–4, a Fellow at the Center for Advanced Study in the Behavioral Sciences at Stanford in 1988–9, and Sherman Fairchild Distinguished Scholar at the California Institute of Technology in 1983–4. Professor Schofield is the author of *Mathematical Methods in Economics and Social Choice* (2003), *Multiparty Government* (coauthored with Michael Laver, 1990), and *Social Choice and Democracy* (1985). He received the William Riker Prize in 2002 for contributions to political theory and is co-receipient with Gary Miller of the Jack L. Walker Prize for the best article on political organizations and parties in the *American Political Science Review* for 2002–4.

POLITICAL ECONOMY OF INSTITUTIONS AND DECISIONS

Series Editor

Stephen Ansolabehere, Massachusetts Institute of Technology

Founding Editors

James E. Alt, Harvard University
Douglass C. North, Washington University, St. Louis

Other books in the series

Alberto Alesina and Howard Rosenthal, *Partisan Politics, Divided Government, and the Economy*
Lee J. Alston, Thráinn Eggertsson, and Douglass C. North, eds., *Empirical Studies in Institutional Change*
Lee J. Alston and Joseph P. Ferrie, *Southern Paternalism and the Rise of the American Welfare State: Economics, Politics, and Institutions, 1865–1965*
James E. Alt and Kenneth Shepsle, eds., *Perspectives on Positive Political Economy*
Josephine T. Andrews, *When Majorities Fail: The Russian Parliament, 1990–1993*
Jeffrey S. Banks and Eric A. Hanushek, eds., *Modern Political Economy: Old Topics, New Directions*
Yoram Barzel, *Economic Analysis of Property Rights*, 2nd edition
Yoram Barzel, *A Theory of the State: Economic Rights, Legal Rights, and the Scope of the State*
Robert Bates, *Beyond the Miracle of the Market: The Political Economy of Agrarian Development in Kenya*, 2nd edition
Charles M. Cameron, *Veto Bargaining: Presidents and the Politics of Negative Power*
Kelly H. Chang, *Appointing Central Bankers: The Politics of Monetary Policy in the United States and the European Monetary Union*
Peter Cowhey and Mathew McCubbins, eds., *Structure and Policy in Japan and the United States: An Institutionalist Approach*
Gary W. Cox, *The Efficient Secret: The Cabinet and the Development of Political Parties in Victorian England*

Continued on page following Index

ARCHITECTS OF POLITICAL CHANGE

Constitutional Quandaries and
Social Choice Theory

NORMAN SCHOFIELD

Washington University in Saint Louis

CAMBRIDGE
UNIVERSITY PRESS

CAMBRIDGE UNIVERSITY PRESS
Cambridge, New York, Melbourne, Madrid, Cape Town, Singapore, São Paulo

Cambridge University Press
40 West 20th Street, New York, NY 10011-4211, USA

www.cambridge.org
Information on this title: www.cambridge.org/9780521832021

First published 2006

Printed in the United States of America

A catalog record for this publication is available from the British Library.

Library of Congress Cataloging in Publication Data

Schofield, Norman, 1944–
Architects of political change : constitutional quandaries and social choice theory /
Norman Schofield.
p.   cm. – (Political economy of institutions and decisions)
Includes bibliographical references (p.) and index.
ISBN-13:   978-0-521-83202-1 (hardback)
ISBN-10:   0-521-83202-0 (hardback)
ISBN-13:   978-0-521-53972-2 (pbk.)
ISBN-10:   0-521-53972-2 (pbk.)
1. Political science – Economic aspects.   2. Social choice – Political aspects.
3. United States – Politics and government – Philosophy.   4. Constitutional
history – United States.   5. Elections – Mathematical models.   I. Title.   II. Series.

JA77.S37   2006
320.97301–dc22   2006004120

ISBN-13   978-0-521-83202-1 hardback
ISBN-10   0-521-83202-0 hardback

ISBN-13   978-0-521-53972-2 paperback
ISBN-10   0-521-53972-2 paperback

Contents

Contents

List of Tables and Figures

TABLES

FIGURES

Preface

Four decades ago, William H. Riker published *Federalism: Origin, Operation, Maintenance* (1964). Riker's motivation in writing this book came from a question that he had raised in his earlier book, *Democracy in the United States* (1953) about the origins of Federalism in the United States. His argument was that only an outside threat could provide the motivation to politicians to give up power by joining the Federal apparatus. His later book, *The Theory of Political Coalitions* (1962), also attempted to answer the question why plurality rule in the U.S. electoral system seemed to be the reason for both minimal winning coalitions and the two-party system. A further book, *Positive Political Theory* (with Peter Ordeshook, 1973), attempted to develop the theory, available at that time, on two-party elections. The convergence result presented in that volume was later shown to depend on unrealistic assumptions about the dimension of the space of political decisions. Later, using the so-called "chaos theorems," Riker returned to the historical questions that had earlier intrigued him and suggested that manipulability and contingency were features of democratic systems (Riker, 1982, 1986, 1996).

Riker's work provides the motivation for this book and for a companion volume (Schofield and Sened, 2006). The formal theory of elections and coalitions, together with empirical analyses of elections in Britain, the United States, Israel, the Netherlands, and Italy, makes up that coauthored volume. This present volume addresses many of the historical questions raised by Riker, using as a conceptual basis the formal electoral model presented in the companion book. This model is only briefly described in the Introduction, and somewhat more extensively in Chapter 8. However, the focus here is not on "social choice theory" itself, but rather on the use of this theory as a heuristic device to better understand democratic institutions.

The essays included in this book were written over a number of years. Obviously, I owe a great debt to William Riker. I considered it a great honor to be the recipient of the Riker prize from Rochester University, in acknowledgment perhaps of some of the earlier versions of this work. Douglass North pressed me to apply the formal reasoning to more general topics than elections. I hope he finds the result of interest.

I received very helpful comments on the versions of these essays presented at the Hoover Institution, Harvard, Yale, MIT, and ICER, Turin. The notions of quandary, of the Atlantic Constitution, and of a "factor coalition" came about from discussion with Andy Rutten. The idea of "dynamic stability" developed out of long conversations with Gary Miller. Chapter 6 is adapted from work (Miller and Schofield, 2003) coauthored with Gary. Chapter 5 is partly based on work with Kim Dixon, and material used in that chapter was collected by Alexander Fak. Imke Kohler kindly made available her research on Truman and McCloy, and this I found helpful in the discussion in Chapter 7, on the founding of the World Bank and of the Marshall plan. I am indebted to Alexander, Andy, Gary, Imke, and Kim, and to my colleagues at Washington University in St. Louis, particularly Andrew Martin, John Nachbar, Douglass North, John Nye, Robert Parks, and Andrew Rehfeld. Iain McLean, who has written extensively on Condorcet and on applying "rational choice theory" to British politics, kindly listened to earlier versions of aspects of the argument. I thank James Alt, Keith Dowding, Robert Goodin, Manfred Holler, Margaret Levi, Carole Pateman, Maurice Salles, and Albert Weale, who were editors associated with earlier versions of these essays. The original versions of the chapters were typed by Alexandra Shankster, and many of the diagrams were drawn by her and by Diana Ivanov. Cherie Moore, Robert Holahan, Ekaterina Rashkova, and Tsvetan Tsvetkov provided further assistance.

I appreciate the support of the National Science Foundation (under Grants SBR-98-18582 in 1999 and SES-0241732 in 2003) and of Washington University. The Weidenbaum Center at Washington University provided support for the completion of the manuscript. A year spent at Humboldt University, Berlin, under the auspices of the Fulbright Foundation, as distinguished professor of American Studies, gave me the opportunity to develop the formal model that provides the theoretical foundation of the current volume. Finally, Scott Parris, chief editor in economics at Cambridge University Press, exercised great patience during the period of more than a decade that it has taken to complete this work.

—Norman Schofield, December 27, 2005, Saint Louis, Missouri

I

Constitutional Quandaries and Social Choice

1.1   INTRODUCTION*

[I]t may be concluded that a pure democracy, by which I mean a society, consisting of a small number of citizens, who assemble and administer the government in person, can admit of no cure for the mischiefs of faction. A common passion or interest will ... be felt by a majority of the whole ... and there is nothing to check the inducements to sacrifice the weaker party. ... Hence it is that such democracies have ever been spectacles of turbulence and contention; have ever been found incompatible with personal security, or the rights of property; and have in general been as short in their lives, as they have been violent in their deaths.

A republic, by which I mean a government in which the scheme of representation takes place, opens a different prospect.

The two great points of difference between a democracy and republic, are first, the delegation of the government, in the latter, to a small number of citizens elected by the rest; secondly, the greater number of citizens and the greater sphere of country, over which the latter may be extended.

It may well happen that the public voice pronounced by the representatives of the people, will be more consonant to the public good, than if pronounced by the people themselves ...

If the proportion of fit characters be not less in the large than in the small republic, the former will present a greater option, and consequently a greater probability of a fit choice.

As each representative will be chosen by a greater number of citizens in the large than in the small republic, ... the suffrages of the people ... will be more likely to centre on men who possess the most attractive merit. ...

The other point of difference is, the greater number of citizens and extent of territory which may be brought within the compass of republican, than of democratic government; and it is this ... which renders factious combinations less to be dreaded in the former, than in the latter. ... Extend the sphere, and you

* This chapter is partly based on a talk presented at the Conference on Constitutional and Scientific Quandaries, at the International Center for Economic Research, Turin, June, 2005.

take in a greater variety of parties and interests; you make it less probable that a majority of the whole will have a common motive to invade the rights of other citizens ...

Hence it clearly appears, that the same advantage, which a republic has over a democracy ... is enjoyed by a large over a small republic – is enjoyed by the union over the states composing it.

—James Madison, *Federalist X*, 1787

This book may be thought of as an extended interpretation of Madison's argument, using ideas from the work of Douglass North, William Riker, and Mancur Olson, and aimed at developing "social choice" approaches to the evolution of society. As I suggest at the end of the book, I see this research program as continuing the work of Madison's contemporaries, Condorcet and Laplace.

North's early work with Thomas (North and Thomas, 1970, 1973, 1977) attempted an economic explanation of the transition from hunter/gatherer societies to agriculture. Later, he proposed a "neoclassical theory of the state," wherein contracts with "Leviathan" set up a system of property rights and taxes (North, 1981). His later work has focused on institutions and how they change as a result of incentives, knowledge, and beliefs (North, 1990, 1994, 2005). One of his most persuasive pieces is his work with Weingast (North and Weingast, 1989) on Britain's Glorious Revolution in 1688 and how this transformed Britain's ability to manage debt, fight wars (particularly with France), and develop an empire.

Riker's earliest work was on American Federalism, particularly the logic underlying the need for Union in 1787 (Riker, 1953, 1964) and the stability of parties as coalitions (Riker, 1962). After working for a number of years on rational choice theory (Riker and Ordeshook, 1973), Riker returned to American political history, to interpret key events in terms of "heresthetic" (1982, 1984, 1986, 1996). Riker coined the word *heresthetic* from the greek αιρετικοζ, meaning "able to choose." His book, *Liberalism against Populism* (1982), argued that social choice theory implied that populism, in the sense of existence of a "general will" was vacuous. At best, all democracy could hope for was the liberal capacity to remove autocrats.

Much of Olson's work attempted to grapple with understanding how some societies are successful and others much less so. In his early book, Olson (1965) used the idea of the prisoner's dilemma to suggest that cooperation may fail as individuals pursue their selfish ends (through strikes, revolutions, etc.) and indirectly constrain economic growth. Later, Olson

(1982a, b) used this argument to provide a "declinist" explanation of why stable democracies such as Britain and the United States appeared less vital (in the 1980s) than the newer democracies of the post–World War II era (such as France, Germany, and Japan).

In this book I attempt to construct the beginnings of a theory of democratic choice that I believe can be used as a heuristic device to tie together these differing historical accounts. The basic underlying framework is adapted from social choice theory, as I understand it, on which I graft a "stochastic" model of elections. This model is an attempt to extend the Condorcetian theme of electoral judgment. I shall argue that its logic was the formal principle underlying Madison's justification for the Republican scheme of representation that he made in *Federalist X*. While this logic does not imply a general will in the sense of Rousseau, it does suggest that Riker was overly pessimistic about the nature of democracy. On the other hand, the social choice framework suggests that democracy, indeed any polity, must face difficult choices over what I call chaos and autocracy. These difficult choices are the *constitutional quandaries* of the subtitle of this book. The historical choices that I discuss often involve a leader or theorist—*an architect of change*, either in the realm of politics or economics—who interprets or frames the quandary troubling the society in a way that leads to its resolution.

1.2 BALANCING RISK AND CHAOS

Figure 1.1 is intended as a schematic representation of the formal results of social choice theory. This figure is replicated in Chapter 2, where a more detailed discussion is provided of its interpretation. This figure is intended as a theoretical construct whose purpose is to suggest the relationship between the many differing results of the theory. The vertical axis denotes the "axis of chaos." The theorems of social choice, from the earliest result by Arrow (1951) to the later work on spatial voting theory (McKelvey and Schofield, 1986, 1987) imply that as factionalism increases, then utter disorder can ensue. The term *chaos* was introduced to describe the possible degree of disorder by analogy to *mathematical chaos*, which was used to characterize a deterministic dynamical system, f, with the feature that for almost any pair of outcomes x, y in the state space, X, there exists a trajectory (see Li and Yorke, 1975)

$$x \rightarrow f(x) \rightarrow f^2(x) \rightarrow \ldots f^t(x) = y. \qquad (1.1)$$

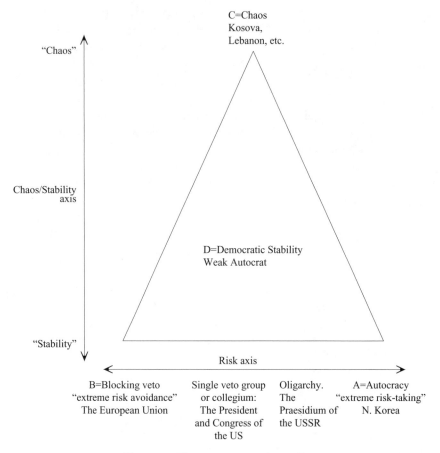

Figure 1.1. Chaos or autocracy in a polity.

For a voting rule, with specified voter preferences and an initial point x, let $f(x)$ be the set of alternatives that beat x. More generally, we can think of the set, $f(x)$, as the set of alternatives that can come about from x, as determined by the social rule. The idea of *social chaos* is that there are conditions under which, starting from almost any x, it is possible to reach almost *any* possible outcome $y = f^t(x)$ by reiterating the social rule. When the set Y that can be reached is large, in a formal sense, then we can call Y the *chaotic domain*, $Chaos(f)$. In contrast, we can identify the *core* or *social equilibrium*, $Core(f)$, as a singularity of f, where y is in $Core(f)$ if and only if $f(y)$ is empty. An element y of $Core(f)$ may be an attractor of f, that is, a single outcome with $y = f^t(x)$, which results from any x, after some number of iterations of the rule.

4

The *social chaos theorem* sets out the conditions for existence or otherwise of the social equilibrium and for the situation where the chaotic domain becomes almost the whole of X. For example, for any voting procedure, f, without a dictator, oligarchy, or collegium[1] able to control, or at least restrict, social choice, then, as the dimension of X increases, so does the extent of voting chaos.[2] For a general social rule, f, Schofield (1985a) formally defines $Chaos(f)$ in terms of local cycles of the rule and then shows that the union of $Chaos(f)$ and $Core(f)$ is non-empty. Thus, if the rule has the property that $Chaos(f)$ is empty, then $Core(f)$ must be non-empty. The theoretical problem for democratic theory is that if $Chaos(f)$ for the social rule, f, is non-empty, then there may be no social equilibrium. However, as discussed at length below, it may be the case that democratic power resides in veto groups. Since a veto group is a collegium in some limited domain of policy (namely a subset of X), then $Chaos(f)$ will be empty, and the social chaos theorem will not apply.

Note however that chaos, as I interpret it, is not just a property of voting procedures. For a society where the social rule, f, is war rather than voting, then I suggest that the chaotic domain, $Chaos(f)$, is likely to be a large subset of X. For less violent methods, the chaotic domain will typically depend on the heterogeneity of preferences in the society. These results do not imply that democracies are necessarily chaotic, but they do suggest that they can be.[3] Throughout this book I shall use the term *chaos* somewhat loosely, to refer to a social situation where there is

---

[1] Chapter 2 gives more detail on this assertion. Roughly speaking, a voting rule is characterized by a family of winning coalitions, D, say. A *dictator* is a single agent who belongs to every winning coalition and is also winning. An *oligarchy* is a group that belongs to every winning coalition and is itself winning, while a *collegium* is a group of voters that belongs to every winning coalition in D, but need not be winning.

[2] Chapter 8 discusses the similar results on chaos in different domains. For social choice, the chaos theorem is presented for a voting rule D, with specified voter preferences. If D is collegial, in the sense that there is a collegium, then the core, $Core(f)$, of the social rule, f, will generally exist. If D is non-collegial, then there is an integer, $w(D)$, called the "chaos dimension," which characterizes D in the following sense: If the dimension of the space, X, exceeds $w(D)$, then the chaotic domain, $Chaos(f)$, of the social rule, f, will be almost the whole of X. What I call the *social chaos theorem* is the result of a long sequence of results by Plott (1967), Kramer (1973), McKelvey (1976, 1979), Schofield (1978, 1980, 1983), McKelvey and Schofield (1986, 1987), Banks (1995), Saari (1996), and Austen-Smith and Banks (1998, 1999).

[3] There has been much debate about the applicability of the social chaos result to democratic theory. See, for example, Riker (1980, 1982, 1984, 1986), Hammond and Miller (1987), and the essays in Ordeshook and Shepsle (1982).

reason to believe that it is impossible to determine, even in general terms, where the social trajectory will go.

When war, or intense and unrestrained conflict, dominates, then we can expect chaos, as in Kosova, in Lebanon during the civil war, and in Iraq at the present time. For a pessimist like Hobbes, it was obvious that any society could fall into chaos, unless mitigating institutional devices were constructed. The quote from Madison's *Federalist X* suggests that Madison certainly viewed direct democracy as subject to chaos. Indeed, in his other writings, he used the phrase "the mutability of the law" in commenting on the possible choices of the legislature. I take his comments to mean that he considered that legislative bodies such as the House and Senate were subject to a degree of disorder—possibly not the complete disorder of chaos. It should be noted that the chaos theorem refers to situations where individuals with specific and heterogeneous preferences come together in either war or assembly and are in conflict over an *outcome*. Thus a legislative assembly can be understood as a direct democracy, and consequently can exhibit chaos, as suggested by the social choice results. Madison was very clear that representative democracy involves the choice of a *person*, and he obviously believed that the voters in the Republic could make a sound choice for the Chief Magistrate if their judgments were not contaminated by preferences. One purpose of this book is to explore the nature of social choice when it depends on judgment rather than simply individual preferences.

The rationalizability of social choice may hold when an electorate makes a specific and limited choice, particularly in a binary situation of yes or no. For example, the negative referenda votes in May and early June 2005 in France and the Netherlands over the European Union (EU) Constitution, while unexpected, cannot be seen as truly chaotic, because they were one-off events. However, the frantic responses by the political leaders of the EU may have elements of considerable disorder. At the same time, there are many institutional devices within the EU that are designed to control disorder.

The effect of these institutional "equilibrium" devices are well understood from the point of view of social choice theory. They all force "rationality" by concentrating power in various ways. This is shown in Figure 1.1 by the power characteristics of the decision rule, f, along the *risk axis*. The work on social choice by Arrow (1951) considered a very strong rationality axiom. Using this he showed that if this rationality property is to be satisfied then the most extreme form of power concentration, namely "dictatorship," is a *necessary* condition in the case that individual preferences are unconstrained. Less extreme forms of power concentration include existence of an "oligarchy," or "collegium," or multiple veto groups. Because a "dictator" can make any choice "he" deems fit, and such a degree of power concentration almost never occurs in a polity, I shall use the term *autocrat* for one who controls the levers of power of the polity and has at least the ability to declare war without being constrained by some form of political veto. Clearly, Saddam Hussein was not a dictator in the formal sense, but he certainly was an autocrat. Similarly, I use the term *oligarchy* for a group who, if they agree, have "autocratic" powers. A *collegium* is a group without full autocratic powers, but who must all agree before the exercise of such power to pursue war or other endeavors. A *veto group* is one with collegial power within a specific restricted domain of policy. Obviously there can be many veto groups in any complex society.

Figure 1.1 presents my hypothesis that autocrats are likely to be extreme risk takers. To some degree, this is an empirical assertion. One only need make a list: Genghis Khan, Attila, Philip II of Spain, Napoleon, Hitler, Stalin. Kennedy's book, *The Rise and Fall of the Great Powers* (Kennedy, 1987) argued that great nations tend to over-exert themselves in the military realm, and through lack of fiscal caution, bring about their own demise. If we translate this argument by regarding the lack of fiscal caution as an element of risk taking more generally, then Kennedy's logic certainly seems valid for Philip II and Napoleon, and possibly for the leaders of the USSR during the cold war. Kennedy also argued that it applied to the United States in the post–World War situation. Table 2.1 in the next chapter gives the relevant data on military spending for the United States and USSR up until 1991 and suggests that there was little indication of this risk-preferring military incaution by the United States until that date. Whether the same inference is valid today is another question entirely.

On the risk axis, an autocrat is likely to be much more risk taking than an oligarchy. I also suggest that an oligarchy will tend to be more risk taking than a collegium. It is difficult to precisely differentiate between an oligarchy and a collegium. An example of an oligarchy is the Praesidium of the Soviet Union. All members of the Praesidium must agree, in principle, for a choice to be made, but if they do, then no decision-making body can override them. A possible example of a collegium is the U.S. President together with his cabinet, in a situation where the majority parties of the House and Senate are in line with the president, and agree with his policy initiatives. The more general situation, of course, is where the President may veto Congress, and Congress may, in turn, counter his veto, with a supermajority. Thus the U.S. executive and Congress, regarded as a unit, can be interpreted as having collegial power. Because the Congressional counter-veto requires a supermajority, only very extreme situations can lead to chaos as a result of presidential/congressional interaction. Note, however, that the President and Congress together do not comprise an oligarchy, since there are obvious policy domains in which Congress and the President may concur but are blocked by state legislatures.

Because Congress may be factionalized, it can, as Madison expected, exhibit what he called *mutability*—a degree of disorder or incoherence in the laws that are passed. My understanding of the U.S. Constitution is that it has a precise design to allow the presidential veto to overcome congressional mutability. Of course, if there is a well-disciplined majority party in Congress, then it can act as a collegium, thus ensuring stability of some kind. However, it is certainly possible for Congress to become factionalized, leading to the collapse of the collegium. One instance of this was the presidential election of 1844 and its aftermath, as discussed in Chapter 5. Because of the actions of Southern Democrats in blocking the candidacy of the New York Democratic, Martin Van Buren, the Northern and Southern wings of the Democratic party split, and Northern Democrats voted with Northern Whigs to suspend the gag rule, forbidding discussion of the issue of slavery in the House. This factionalization led eventually to a realignment of the party structure in the election of 1860.

Madison, of course, was concerned that the President would gain autocratic power, and to avoid this, the Congressional counter-veto was devised. However, even with the counter-veto, the President does have some autocratic power, and I shall use the term *weak autocrat* to characterize his power. It is evident that there is a tendency for U.S. presidents to display the degree of risk preference that characterizes autocrats. I judge that Congress will generally be risk-averse, which is why, I believe, power to declare war resides in Congress. Even when Congress and the President are aligned, then one would still expect the Presidential risk preference to be muted by Congressional risk avoidance.

On the other hand, Congressional risk avoidance has the effect of delaying the resolution of fundamental constitutional quandaries. Typically, a *quandary* can only be faced if there is a risk-taking leader capable of forcing resolution. Without such a leader, the result can be the opposite of chaos, namely "gridlock." An illustration of this is given in Chapter 6, in the discussion of the passage of Civil Rights legislation in 1957, while Johnson was leader of the Senate (Caro, 2002). Decisions in the Senate could be blocked by the filibuster, and this could only be overcome by "cloture." This rule required "support from two-thirds of those present and voting to impose cloture. This meant that a minority coalition of one-third plus one of those present and voting could prevent a vote" (Rohde and Shepsle, 2005). First, as leader of the Senate, and later as president in 1964, Johnson was a risk taker able to persuade the collegium (of one-third plus one) of Southern Democrats to lift its block.

Rohde and Shepsle (2005) go on to observe that "as a consequence of a huge upsurge in filibusters in the decade following the civil rights revolution, Rule 22 was amended in 1975, changing the requirement to an absolute standard—sixty votes—to close debate [in the Senate]." Obviously a group of forty-one senators has blocking power, and the change in the rule has reduced the collegial veto power of such a minority.

As I discuss in Chapter 4, and as indicated by the aforementioned quotation, Madison developed an argument in *Federalist X* that derived from Condorcet. This led him to expect that the election of the president could be assumed to be characterized by a high "probability of a fit choice." In constrained situations where we may assume that judgments predominate and voters evaluate the options in a clear-sighted fashion, then their choice of Chief Magistrate may indeed be well formed in this way. For this reason I locate the weak autocrat in Figure 1.1 at a position where the risk taking of the autocrat is balanced by the risk avoidance of Congress, as well as by judgment of the electorate. It would be natural to assume that electoral judgment will generally be risk avoiding. However, there are situations where a society feels threatened in some fashion and may exhibit a degree of risk preference. It seems to me that the current situation with regard to the United States and Iraq is unusual, precisely because the electoral judgment has seemed to be much more risk preferring than is common. As the true risks of the current siuation become apparent, this risk posture may change.

It is important for my interpretation of electoral judgment that when the "preferences" of the electorate are muted by judgments, then their choice of the Chief Magistrate need not be subject to the chaos results. Whether this is an entirely valid argument is a somewhat delicate matter. Madison hoped that, because the election of the Chief Magistrate involved the selection of a person, rather than an option (as in the passage of a law), judgment rather than preference or interest would predominate. To argue this formally requires analysis of an electoral model where judgment and preference are both incorporated. In this book, I present the tentative outline of such a model. It is of course entirely possible that beliefs or

9

judgments in the electorate can be transformed in a chaotic fashion. Many of the illustrations of belief transformation presented in this book suggest that while the transformations are highly contingent, they are associated with changes in what I call a *core belief*. A *core*, in social choice theory, is an unbeaten alternative. By analogy, a *core belief* is a belief that has general acceptance in the society.

As Figure 1.1 indicates, at the opposite end of the risk spectrum from autocracy is the situation of extreme risk-avoiding blocking groups. Veto groups are like collegia but with power in a limited domain. As indicated earlier, social choice theory implies that veto groups induce stability, so the effect is the opposite of chaos. A good illustration is provided by the veto power that French farmers have over changes in the EU Common Agricultural Policy (CAP). Obviously French farmers, together with their agrarian allies in Germany and the new members of the EU, such as Poland, have a great deal to lose if the CAP is reorganized. CAP is only one instance of a variety of protectionist, risk-averse mechanisms that several veto groups have been allowed to deploy in the expanding European polity. As Table 2.3 in Chapter 2 indicates, the consequence seems to be that the core polities of France, Germany, and Italy in Europe have stagnating economies. As of August 2005, the estimates of growth by the Organisation for Economic Co-operation and Development were less than 2 percent (1.8 percent in France, 1.1 percent in Germany, and less than zero in Italy) with unemployment roughly 10 percent (about 8 percent in Italy, 10 percent in France and 11.6 percent in Germany). With risk aversion comes high saving, low imports, high trade surplus, and an appreciating euro. This will be increasingly exacerbated as the population structure ages. These facts compare with growth and unemployment of 3.6 percent and 5.0 percent respectively in the United States and 1.7 percent and 4.8 percent, respectively in Britain.

The "non" in France and "nee" in the Netherlands in May and June 2005 may have been induced by voter irritation at the apparent incompetence of the EU institutions, and it is reasonable to infer that these referenda were based on electoral judgment. The problem is that, outside Britain, almost every group, except possibly teenagers and students, has a veto over changes in crucial aspects of the social contract, particularly over unemployment and retirement benefits. Without doubt, it is much more comfortable to live in Europe rather than in the United States. The degree of risk avoidance could be reduced, but only by institutional mechanisms that are more risk preferring. The political institutions of the EU (the Commission, Council of Ministers, European Parliament, the rotating President of the EU) all appear to be risk averse. The negative referenda have induced some degree of disorder into the Council of Ministers, because the policy arena is now much more like a zero-sum game than before, with ministers arguing over "rebates,"and agricultural subsidies. Although the CAP budget has fallen over the last few years, from 70 percent of the EU budget to 40 percent, its effect is to distort agricultural trade, harming farmers in less-developed countries. It is unclear at present whether or how this EU quandary will be resolved. What is interesting is that the Labour Party in Britain, though recently chosen by a proportion of only 35 percent of the British electorate (much reduced from its support in 2001) still controls 55 percent of parliamentary seats. Unlike a party leader in the same situation in a polity based on proportional representation, Blair, as leader of the party, has the power to engage in a fairly risky strategy against the other party leaders in the EU polities, directed at transforming the CAP. This is consistent with the view that leaders of polities based on proportional representation tend to be risk averse, while leaders chosen through plurality electoral methods are more likely to be risk seeking.

Social choice theory suggests that the EU quandary could be resolved by the selection of a weak autocrat, such as a popularly elected EU president. However, to satisfy Madison's fears of autocracy, it would be necessary for the electoral choice to be based on the judgments of voters rather than their preferences. It is difficult to see how a Europe-wide election could have an information base that would be sufficient to support such a social choice based on judgment.

With this preamble in mind, I shall attempt to formulate a Madisonian model of election of the Chief Magistrate, President, or political leader, that is in principle applicable to any democratic polity. The model will involve both judgment and preference. Variations of the basic model can then be interpreted in terms of a pure Condorcetian model of judgment, or belief aggregation, as well as a pure, potentially chaotic model of preference aggregation.

1.3   PREFERENCES AND JUDGMENTS

For the formal electoral model I shall assume that individuals have preferences that can be represented as functions on some "policy" space X. This space characterizes both voter interests and possible eventualities. In many of the examples, I argue that X conceptually derives from the societal deployment of the three factors of land, labor, and capital. Because the factors are bounded at any time, we may more conveniently regard X as two dimensional. In empirical applications, for example, surveys nearly always indicate that voters conceive of a conflict between the requirements of capital and labor. What I term the *labor* axis is often derived from beliefs about civil rights or religion. A third non-factor dimension may involve attitudes toward war. In some cases the social attitudes with regard to war are attributable to the desire for territorial expansion. Obviously this notion of factor dimensions is a heuristic device, but it does allow me to represent fundamental constitutional problems in a diagrammatical form.

The interests or beliefs of the population or "electorate," N (of size n), are described by a set $\{x_i\}$ of "ideal points," one for each "voter," $i = 1, \ldots, n$. An individual's ideal point in the space, X, is used to describe or represent that voter's interests. In electoral models the ideal point can be obtained from a survey. Whether we view x_i as representing preferences or beliefs is immaterial.

The set of options, S, of size s, is a set $\{z_j\}$, each one being a point in X.

In the situation of an election, each element of S is a declaration of intended or proposed policy. There is one for each candidate, j.

While it is usual to conceive of each z_j as simply a point, we can easily allow z_j to involve various possibilities associated with differing probabilities of occurrence.[4]

In the simplest model, the "latent utility," u_{ij} of voter i for candidate j has the form

$$u_{ij}(x_i, z_j) = \lambda_{ij}(x_i) - A_{ij}(x_i, z_j) + \theta_j^\mathsf{T} \eta_i. \qquad (1.2)$$

Here $\theta_j^\mathsf{T} \eta_i$ models the effect of the sociodemographic characteristics η_i of voter i in making a political choice. That is, θ_j is a k-vector specifying how the various sociodemographic variables appear to influence the choice for option j. Thus $\theta_j^\mathsf{T} \eta_i$ is simply the influence of i's sociodemographic characteristics on the propensity to choose j.

The term $A_{ij}(x_i, z_j)$ is a way of representing the "preference disagreement" between the interests of voter i and the jth option. In particular $A_{ij}(x_i, z_j)$ may be some function of the distance between x_i, the preferred

---

[4] In principle we can construct a more general model where beliefs are probabilities of outcomes, so the possible states are lotteries. This provides no technical problem, since we can put an appropriate topology on this extended state space. The topology I have in mind is a fine topology taking into account differentiability. See Schofield (1996, 1999a,b) and Schofield and Sened (2006).

position (or ideal point) of voter i, and z_j, the declared policy of candidate j, according to some appropriate metric. In the standard electoral model, where X is a policy space, it is assumed that $A_{ij}(x_i, z_j) = \beta \|x_i - z_j\|^2$ is the Euclidean quadratic loss (with $\beta > 0$) associated with the difference between the two positions. We can, however, conceive of $A_{ij}(x_i, z_j)$ much more generally. In the general case z_j will involve a lottery across different possibilities, and different individuals could evaluate these various possibilities in heterogeneous ways.

The model is stochastic because of the implicit assumption that

$$\lambda_{ij}(x_i) = \lambda_j(x_i) + \varepsilon_j \text{ for } j = 1, \ldots, s. \tag{1.3}$$

Here $\{\varepsilon_j\}$ is a set of possibly correlated disturbances and $\lambda_j(x_i)$ is the perception by a voter, i, with beliefs or interests, x_i, of the "valence" of the option presented by the candidate j. (See e.g., Ansolabahere and Snyder, 2000; Groseclose, 2001). This valence is a way of modelling the non-policy *judgment* by voter i of the quality of candidate j.

In the general model, the probability, Pr, that voter i chooses option j is

$$\rho_{ij} = \Pr[u_{ij}(x_i, z_j) > u_{ij}(x_i, z_k) \text{ for all } k \neq j]. \tag{1.4}$$

Previous versions of this model have assumed that the valence components $\{\lambda_j(x_i)\}$ are all zero and have usually asserted that all candidates would converge to an "electoral mean" when they attempt to maximize their expected vote shares. In the discussion of this model given in Chapter 8, it is argued that, in the situation where the candidate valences differ, this mean voter theorem will only hold when a particular necessary condition is satisfied. The condition depends on the valence differences between candidates, on the coefficient β that specifies the importance of policy, and on the variation of the distribution of voter ideal points, denoted as ν^2. Further, the greater the stochastic variance (or uncertainty) of the disturbances, then the easier it is for this condition to be satisfied. In contrast, high electoral variation will tend to produce divergence of candidate positions. The upshot of this analysis is that empirical situations can be found where convergence in candidate positions is very unlikely to occur. Schofield and Sened (2006) give examples from a number of polities based on proportional electoral systems where extreme divergence of party positions is explained by this model.

We can apply this model in various ways. First, consider the pure preference-based "non-stochastic" or deterministic case, $\varepsilon_j \to 0$, where valence is zero. As noted earlier, a very extensive literature has shown that if decision making is binary (pitting options one against another) and based on majority rule, or more generally on a non-collegial voting mechanism, then "chaos" or disorder can ensue as long as the dimension of X is sufficiently large. The formal results show that chaos can be prevented by requiring that there be a collegium or veto player. Chapter 2 discusses this possibility in the context of an analysis of decision making in Britain in the seventeenth and eighteenth centuries. The outcome in this situation of a collegium, oligarchy, or autocrat may be a *core* or institutional equilibrium. In the absence of a core, and if the dimension of X is sufficiently low, then the set of probable outcomes will be restricted, and I shall use the term the *heart* of the institution to refer to this set of possible outcomes.

In the stochastic situation, with $\varepsilon_j \neq 0$, it is necessary to focus on the "beliefs" or judgments of the participants.

In the case that $\beta \to 0$, then this is a situation of pure "belief aggregation." Individuals will choose among the various options with probability determined by the valence judgment that they have made. I suggest that the final decision is often the consequence of what I call a *belief cascade*. As more individuals decide that option z_s, say, is superior, then other voters will in turn be swayed to form a judgment in favor of z_s. I use the term *architect of change* for an agent, s, who is able to trigger this change in the social situation by providing a plausible argument for the option z_s.

In the more general case with $\beta \neq 0$, the valences $\{\lambda_j(x_i)\}$ and therefore the choices will depend on $\{x_i\}$. It may be the case that different and opposed belief cascades are generated in the population. For example, in Chapter 5, I suggest that Lincoln's arguments about the significance of the Dred Scott decision generated opposing belief cascades in the northern and southern electorates.

More generally, suppose that there is information available to some subset M of the electorate which is consistent with the judgment

$$\lambda_s > \lambda_{s-1} > \ldots > \lambda_1 \qquad (1.5)$$

by the members of M. Then it will be the case that, for every voter i in M, the subjective probabilities will be ranked

$$\rho_{is} > \rho_{is-1} > \ldots > \rho_{i1}. \qquad (1.6)$$

It follows that the majority rule preference within the set M will choose candidate s with option z_s with greater probability than candidates $s - 1$, $s - 2, \ldots, 3, 2, 1$. If M is itself a majority under the electoral rule (or is a winning coalition of more than half the electorate) then candidate s will win. When an alternative such as z_s wins in this fashion, then it will be sustained by a belief (or set of related beliefs) held by a winning coalition. By analogy with the idea of a core, or unbeaten alternative, I use the term *core belief* to refer to this common belief held by such a set of voters.

Condorcet in his *Essai* of 1785 argued essentially that a core belief would tend to be a correct belief.[5] A statement and proof of this result, known as *Condorcet's Jury Theorem*, is given as a short appendix to Chapter 8. The demonstration is given for the case where only judgments are involved, but it is obvious that the result holds in some weaker sense when both interests and judgments are relevant, as long as interests do not predominate. I argue in Chapter 4 that Madison had a version of this argument in mind when he wrote about the "probability of a fit choice" for the President in *Federalist X*. Of course, because interests may intrude in the calculation of a fit choice, we cannot assert, as did Condorcet, that the choice is necessarily superior.[6] Notice also that the electoral rule (such as deployed in the Electoral College) may define a coalition as winning even though it does not comprise a majority. Recent literature has considered extensions of the Jury Theorem when individuals have private information and the decision problem is one of common value, so that all individuals would agree over the correct choice if they had full information.[7] The societal decisions considered in this book have the characteristic that both preferences and beliefs in the society are heterogeneous. I do not attempt to present a full theory of such situations. Instead I hope to combine elements of social choice theory and the theory of elections to present a set of concepts that I feel can be useful in understanding democratic choice.

---

[5] Roughly speaking, the theorem asserts that, in a binary choice situation, the probability that a majority selects the true outcome will be greater than the probability that a typical individual will select the truth. Rae (1969) and Schofield (1972a, b) used a version of the theorem to argue that majority rule would be "rationally"chosen by an uncertain society as a constitutional rule. The theorem depends on the condition of voter (pairwise) "independence," which is a very strong assumption, and unlikely to be satisfied. Recent work by Ladha (1992) and Ladha and Miller (1996) has attempted to extend the theorem to include correlated choice. Empirical techniques also allow for modelling correlated choices (Schofield et al., 1998; Quinn, Martin, and Whitford, 1999).

[6] Schofield (1972a) noticed the connection between Madison's argument and a version of the Jury theorem. Recently various authors have developed the theme of the "wisdom of crowds" and how they might be swayed (Gladwell, 2000; Ball, 2004; Surowiecki, 2004).

[7] Recent work includes Austen-Smith and Banks (1996, 2005), Ladha (1996), Fedderson and Pesendorfer (1997), McLennan (1998), and Martinelli (2003).

Thus the *core belief* underpins the selection of the option *s*, with the greatest valence. I also use the notion of *the heart of the Constitution* to refer to the configuration of beliefs that form the foundation for social choice at each point in time. A *constitutional quandary* is a situation of great uncertainty in the electorate. In the formal model, this is associated with significant stochastic variance and relatively insignificant valences. According to the standard electoral model all candidates should converge to the electoral center. Another way of expressing this is that the candidates should be risk averse. However, this assertion only holds true if the electoral variation is relatively small. If electoral preferences are very heterogeneous then candidates should rationally adopt very different positions.[8] We might say, for a situation with very great uncertainty, that these candidates for the attention of the electorate are *prophets of chaos*. Sometimes, out of this cacophony of voices, there is one who can overcome the barriers to clear perception and present a sensible way to interpret the quandary. Naturally, this does not always happen. I suggest that a polity will prosper when it is both open to the arguments of such an *architect of change* and able to evaluate the opposing arguments. The *evolution of the Constitution* is due to this continuous process of argument, shifting beliefs, and changing valences.

This model is applied in Chapter 6 to suggest that the changing valences of parties in the United States is due to the influence of activists on candidate positions. This accounts for what I call a *structurally stable dynamic*, involving a slow rotation of party positions in what I consider to be a fundamental two-dimensional policy space based on economic factors and civil rights (Miller and Schofield, 2003). There is some evidence that a two-dimensional policy space is also relevant for Britain (Schofield, 2005a), though I suggest that the second dimension may be derived from, or sustained by, beliefs that were appropriate during the period of the British Empire. While my discussion largely focuses on Britain and the United States, it is the larger question of the evolution of what I call the *Atlantic Constitution*[9] that forms the narrative of this book.

[8] Schofield and Sened (2006) show for example why the combination of stochastic and electoral variation leads to many small, radical parties in Israel. Chapter 6 applies a version of this model to presidential elections in the United States.

[9] Bailyn (2005) argues that all the polities on the Atlantic littoral are connected through a common history It seems natural to refer to the *Atlantic Constitution* as the set of political, economic, and social beliefs common to these polities.

1.4   THE "INSTITUTIONAL NARRATIVE" OF THE BOOK

Here I shall briefly sketch the narative scheme that I shall use, based on the ideas of social choice and on the notion of factor coalitions forming in the policy space. Rogowski (1989) earlier made use of the assumption from economic theory that there can be assumed to be three factors of production: land, labor, and capital. External and internal features may grant advantages to particular coalitions of these factor "interests." For example, the United States in the late 1700s could be characterized as abundant in land, with both labor and capital relatively scarce. Principal imports were manufactures, intensive in capital and skilled labor. Thus protection in the form of tariffs would necessarily benefit capital and "industrial labor." In contrast, since land was abundant, this economic interest, together with "agricultural labor," would benefit from free trade. Consequentially, the political conflict between the commercial Federalist Party and the agrarian Jeffersonian Republicans, at the election of 1800, can be interpreted in factor terms. However, some of the elements of the controversy of that time can only be understood with respect to earlier factor conflicts in Britain, in the period from 1688.

North and Weingast (1989) had argued that the creation of the Bank of England in 1694 provided a method of imposing credible commitment on Parliament. The dilemma facing any government of that time was that war had become more expensive than government revenue could cover. Consequently, governments, or monarchs, became increasingly indebted. Risk-preferring, or war-loving, monarchs, such as Philip II of Spain or Louis XIV of France, were obliged to borrow. As their debt increased, they were forced into repudiation, thus making it more difficult in the future to borrow. Since the Bank of England "managed" the debt in Britain after 1694, there was an incentive for Parliament to accept the necessary taxation and to avoid repudiation. However, it was clear after 1688 that William III would pursue the war with France with great vigor and cost. Contrary to the argument of North and Weingast, this escalating debt could, in fact, force Parliament to repudiation. Until 1720, it was not obvious how Parliament could be obliged to commit to fiscal responsibility. How this was done was through the brilliant strategy of Robert Walpole, first "prime" minister.

The fundamental problem was that the majority of members of both Commons and Lords were of the landed interest. The obvious method of funding government debt (which had risen to 36 million pounds sterling by 1713) was by a land tax. Indeed the land tax raised approximately 50 percent of revenue. War weariness had brought in a Tory government in 1710, and the obvious disinclination of the Tory landed gentry to pay increasing land taxes forced up the interest rate on long-term government debt from 6 percent to 10 percent (Stasavage, 2002). In some desperation the government created the South Sea Company in 1711. After Queen Anne died in 1714, and the Hanoverian, George I, became sovereign, increasing speculation in South Sea Company stock, and then the collapse of the "bubble" in September 1720 almost bankrupted the government. Walpole stabilized confidence in the company by a swap arrangement with the Bank of England. In April 1721, Walpole, then Chancellor of the Exchequer and First Lord of the Treasury, began his scheme to stabilize government debt by instituting a complex system of customs and excise. By restricting imports, mostly foodstuffs and land-intensive commodities, this system had the effect of supporting the price of the scarce commodity, land. From 1721 to 1740, these excise taxes and customs raised an increasing share of government revenue. As Brewer (1988) has described, the system required a sophisticated and skilled bureaucracy. The Walpole device had many effects. Firstly, it ushered in a long period of Whig dominance (at least until the 1800s). Protection of land remained in place until the repeal of the Corn Laws in May 1846. As McLean (2000) has described, the repeal was effected by Robert Peel, leader of the Tories (or conservatives), together with Wellington in the Lords, against the interests of the majority of their party. Famine in Ireland made it obvious to Peel and Wellington that unless food prices were lowered social unrest could lead to civil strife. The Walpole "bargain" of 1721 essentially created a compact between the "commercial" Whig interests and both Whig and Tory "landed" interests. By supporting land prices, the bargain led to increased investment in agriculture and (possibly counter intuitively) the decline of the agricultural labor force. Increased food prices may have reduced the real wage of industrial labor (Floud and McCloskey, 1994). Although agricultural output increased in Britain, the population grew even more rapidly, and Britain became increasingly dependent on food imports, particularly from the United States.

Jefferson was well aware of the implications of the Walpole bargain. His reading of the works of Henry St. John, Viscount Bolingbroke, led him to believe that the land-capital bargain led to corruption, as well as the filling of Parliament by placemen. In fact, Bolingbroke's arguments against Walpole were, to some degree, invalid, since the compact did make it possible for Britain to manage its debt, fight its wars, and create an empire.

Bolingbroke's logic was, however, valid for the United States. Hamilton's attempt in 1793 to re-create Walpole's system would have necessitated both a land tax and tariff protection. Since U.S. imports were primarily manufactures, a tariff would protect the scarce factor (capital) associated with these imports. In Jefferson's view, this would have disadvantaged the landed interest. By creating an agrarian coalition, essentially of the Southern slave-owning landed interest and western free farmers, Jefferson created a long-lasting compact under which the United States became the food supplier for Britain. Just as the Walpole compact persisted until 1846, so did Jefferson's agrarian coalition survive until 1860. At that point, the southern demand for expansion to the Pacific destroyed the Jeffersonian-Jacksonian democracy.

The aftermath of the Civil War created a new coalition of commercial interests and industrial labor, as represented by the presidential victory of the Republican, McKinley, over the populist Democrat, William Jennings Bryan in 1896. From this perspective, U.S. politics in the period 1896–1960 can be interpreted in terms of a single factor dimension—*capital*—since we can regard the interest of land to be generally in opposition to capital. Thus, for the period from 1896 until the 1930s, the inclination of Republicans for the preservation of a hard money or gold standard rule was in opposition to the need for available credit in the agricultural sector.

In the 1960s, agitation for greater civil rights brought the labor axis into prominence. L. B. Johnson's positioning on this axis contributed to his great electoral victory in 1964, but also opened the way for the Republican Party to adopt an increasingly conservative position on the social dimension and gain political control in the southern states (Miller and Schofield, 2003).

In Britain, since 1846, all these factors have played a role at various times. For example, McLean (2002) has observed that the success of the Reform Bill, under the Conservative, Disraeli, in 1867, depended on beliefs about Empire. For industrial labor, "Empire" meant the opportunities for emigration and a better life in the Dominions of America, Canada, and South Africa. By using the rhetoric of "Empire," the conservatives could hope to appeal to working-class voters. In fact, such rhetoric was an important aspect of Thatcher's electoral success in the 1980s. Indeed, recent empirical analysis of electoral beliefs in Britain (Schofield, 2005a) make it clear that in addition to the usual economic (or "capital") axis, it is necessary to employ a second "social" axis. This axis incorporates "civil rights," but is also characterized by attitudes to the European Union. The responses of Conservative Party members of Parliament to a questionnaire on this topic suggest that they are strongly opposed to the incorporation of Britain within the European Union. In other words, political beliefs that were founded on an economic rationale dating back more than one hundred years are still relevant, in a somewhat different form, today.

This narrative suggests that preferences, or interests, on economic factors, or dimensions, play an important role in political decisions. However, the manner in which these interests are transformed into beliefs is, to a considerable degree, still a matter of conjecture. Indeed, how these beliefs take political expression seemingly depends on the perceptions and strategies of political leaders such as Walpole, Peel, Disraeli, Franklin, Washington, Madison, Jefferson, Lincoln, or Johnson.

It has been a long-standing controversy whether political economy is best described by the concepts of "equilibrium" or "chaos" (Austen-Smith and Banks, 1998, 1999). In his later work, after 1980, Riker saw chaos as a fundamental property and focused on key "contingent" events in United States political history, like the ratification of the U.S. Constitution in 1787–8, or the onset of the Civil War in 1860–1.

The brief description of British and U.S. political history offered here suggests that neither equilibrium nor chaos is an accurate description of social choice. Instead, there can be long periods during which the political economic equilibrium is quite stable. However, equilibria can be destroyed and dramatically transformed at key historical periods, as previously described. Denzau and North (1994) have adopted ideas from evolutionary theory in biology (Eldredge and Gould, 1972) and from the notion of "informational cascades" (Bikhchandani, Hirschleifer, and Welch, 1992) and proposed the concept of "punctuated social equilibrium." As they suggest, this idea is an analogue in the social realm of Kuhn's notion of scientific revolution (Kuhn, 1962). At least intuitively, the notion of punctuated social equilibrium would seem relevant to the puzzle of the collapse of the Soviet Union that so intrigued Olson. Indeed, it is entirely possible that the apparent relative decline of the United States and Britain (which seemed so obvious to Olson in 1982 and Kennedy in 1987) has been reversed, as the underlying political economic equilibrium has been transformed in these two countries since 1980.

The chapters in this volume address these central questions, raised by North, Olson, and Riker. Chapter 2 provides a more detailed overview of the differing political economic equilibria in Britain and the United States. In particular, the chapter discusses how Walpole's "equilibrium" or balancing of Whig and Tory interests set the scene for British imperial expansion, and gave ammunition to Jefferson in his campaign against Hamilton. This chapter introduces some of the basic social choice ideas used later. The "institutional" narratives of Chapters 3, 4, and 5 consider the constitutional transformations in the United States in the key periods of the Revolutionary War, 1776–1783; the formation of the two-party system in 1787–1808; and the period 1857–1861 leading up to the Civil War. More specifically, Chapter 3 focuses on the nature of the British threat to the Colonies, as expressed in the Quebec Act of 1774, and the need for French aid before the Declaration of Independence. Chapter 4 discusses the period from the ratification of the Constitution in 1787 to the election of Jefferson in 1800. The chapter emphasizes the influence of Condorcet on both Madison and Jefferson. Chapter 5 develops the idea of a constitutional quandary, prior to an institutional transformation, and examines the election of Lincoln in 1860 in the context of the Dred Scott decision by the Supreme Court in 1857. Chapter 6 argues that the theoretical accounts posing chaos against centrist equilibrium miss the underlying feature of dynamic stability, in the United States in particular. This chapter, based on Miller and Schofield (2003), suggests that political parties in the United States slowly cycle in the two-dimensional policy space that was created in the period just prior to the Civil War. In certain periods (such as 1896–1920) the principal axis is one of land/capital. However, in the more general situation, which has held from 1964 to the present, a second dimension—*the social axis* (a mirror of the free labor/slave axis)—is also necessary for understanding political change.

The electoral model suggests that the kind of analysis performed by political leaders such as Franklin, Madison, Jefferson, Lincoln, and Johnson transforms social uncertainty into the much more amenable aspect of risk. Thus plurality, or majority decision making, allows such risk-taking political agents to create solutions to dangerous political quandaries. It is for this reason that I use the term *architect of change* to refer to such agents of political transformation.

Chapter 7 addresses the problem facing Keynes prior to the creation of the Bretton Woods Scheme after World War II. Economic uncertainty could induce a retreat to totalitarianism, as in the 1930s. The chapter suggests that Truman was the "architect of change" who facilitated the creation of the "uncertainty-reducing" institutions that helped promote world economic growth after 1945. In the 1970s, new quandaries over the balance of economic logic and political expediency again became particularly relevant. The declinist arguments of many "prophets of chaos," including Olson, Kennedy, and others, proved, however, to be unwarranted.

One of the themes of this book is the contrast between equilibrium (whether economic or political) and chaos. Chapter 8 attempts to survey the theoretical arguments for one side or the other. As Chapter 2 suggests, equilibrium can always be attained by the imposition of a dictator or autocrat. Indeed, as Arrow's Theorem (Arrow, 1951) implies, a strong form of equilibrium-inducing rationality can only be induced by dictatorship. As I have indicated, social choice theory suggests that factional chaos may occur if the underlying dimension of the political-economic world is sufficiently high and there are no institutional controls. Chapter 8 argues that beliefs need to be incorporated into formal models of societal decision making and provides an outline of how the stochastic electoral model introduced earlier can be generalized. The chapter suggests that there is a parallel between science, regarded as a truth-seeking device, and social choice and gives examples of how the resolution of a quandary, whether scientific or social, may reside in the overcoming of a core belief that acts as a barrier to resolution. An appendix to Chapter 8 gives a short proof of the Condorcet Jury Theorem.

The narrative presented here suggests that when beliefs rather than simply preferences or interests are relevant, then representative democracy can maintain a kind of structural stability balanced between chaos and the rigidity of permanent equilibrium. While the evolution of the developed Atlantic polities may be structurally stable, it is also true that social change in many parts of the world appears to be fundamentally chaotic. A very brief Chapter 9 suggests that in a world of interconnection and technological change, it is this likelihood which forms the constitutional quandary that these Atlantic polities currently face.[10]

---

[10] To put this formally, I suggest that typically the chaotic domain, $Chaos(f_{dev})$ is relatively limited for the social choice rule in developed polities, though it may change over time. In many less-developed polities the set $Chaos(f_{nondev})$ is large with respect to possible outcomes, and it is the linkage between these two sets that creates the quandary.

2

Power and Social Choice

2.1 INTRODUCTION*

Mancur Olson's book, *The Rise and Decline of Nations* (1982a), used ideas from his earlier *Logic of Collective Action* (1965) to argue that entrenched interest groups in a polity could induce economic *sclerosis*, or slow growth. These ideas seemed relevant to the perceived relative decline of the United States and Britain during the 1970s. Five years later, Paul Kennedy's *The Rise and Fall of the Great Powers* (1987) proposed a more general "declinist" argument, that a great power such as the United States would engage in fiscal irrationality through increasing military expenditure, thus hastening its own decline. Neither of these two declinist arguments seem applicable to the situation of the new millennium. Olson's last book, *Power and Prosperity*, published posthumously in 2000, attempted a more general theoretical analysis of the necessary and sufficient causes of prosperity and growth. For Olson, only "securely democratic societies" could be conducive to long-lived individual rights to property and contract, but democracy itself need not be sufficient for the protection of rights. This chapter attempts to further develop Olson's logic on the connection between prosperity and liberty, by exploring insights derived from Riker's interpretation of U.S. Federalism (Riker, 1964), from the contribution of North and Weingast (1989) to neo-institutional economic theory, and from recent work on war and fiscal responsibility by Ferguson (1999, 2001, 2004) and Stasavage (2002, 2003).

The logic of economic growth is fairly well understood. In the absence of a well-defined system of property rights and the rule of law, economic

---

* This chapter is based on Norman Schofield, "Power, Prosperity and Social Choice: A Review," *Social Choice and Welfare* 20 (2003): 85–118, reprinted by kind permission of Springer Science and Business Media.

growth, if it can be made to occur at all, will splutter or induce extreme inequalities that may rend the society apart. The full apparatus of property rights, law-based contracts, and relatively free and open markets we call *capitalism*. It is the argument of this chapter that capitalism can be the engine of growth. Indeed, experience over the last two hundred years suggests that it is the only known reliable engine of growth. However, without the control mechanism that we call *democracy*, capitalism can become cancerous, leading to cycles of expansion and collapse.

The appropriate links, or inter relationships, between capitalism, the engine of growth, and democracy, the mode of control, are subtle. They have been explored by political economists for more than three hundred years. Recent formal advances over the last sixty years in both economic and political theory suggest how precisely the engine and the control system should be linked, so as to avoid collapse into chaos. The design of democratic capitalism is essentially a problem of social engineering. When the relationship between the economy and the polity is poorly designed, then the causes of the erratic behavior of the engine are examined by those perceptive individuals we may call "prophets" of chaos. The redesign, or recalibration of the engine, and its control, as well as the relationship between them, is carried out by those we could call "social engineers." However, since the design change typically involves transformation in the institutions of the political economy, I use the metaphor *architects of change*.

I first illustrate the problem of political economy for different cases around the world and then discuss the arguments of a number of prophets of chaos, including Olson and Kennedy. I shall then go on to outline the historical development of various solutions by architects of change, first in Britain, then the United States. I shall attempt to show how these various solutions all derive in one way or another from fundamental principles of social choice theory.

2.2   THE WORLD TODAY

Economic growth can occur in the absence of a full system of property rights and free markets. One has only to think of China, which steadily attains economic growth over 8 percent. Control is exercised by an oligarchy, determined to stay in power and resist, by force, any tendency to democracy.

In periods in the past, particularly in the 1930s, the propensity for uncontrolled capitalism to collapse into chaos made such command systems very attractive. If one considers the balance between the possible chaos of capitalism and the order maintained within an oligarchy or dictatorship, it is easy to see why many would prefer order. In fact, the logic of such a choice depends on the empirical evidence. As Keynes (1936) clearly saw, it is also the case that people in a democracy might prefer the order possibly induced by dictatorship to the chaos of the market.[1] This dilemma stimulated Keynes' thoughts on how capitalism could be restructured at the global level to lessen the chances of chaos. At least since the end of the 1970s, the Atlantic democracies in Europe and North America have mitigated the possibility of economic chaos. This in turn means that the people of China, when they compare the advantages of their own economic command system to those of a more democratic capitalism, are likely, increasingly, to prefer the latter. Moreover, the growing inequality will, in all probability, increase their demand for greater openness in their political life. This, in turn, will make it more difficult for the oligarchy to exert control. One troubling aspect of this may be the attempt by the oligarchy to refocus the demands of their people toward territorial expansion. It is also likely that, without democratic control, the spurts of regional economic growth will exacerbate social tensions within China itself. It is because of the likelihood of territorial expansion or internal chaos that I view the kind of uncontrolled economic growth exhibited in China at present to be potentially dangerous.

At least the local freeing of regional markets accompanied by political oligarchy in China has led to economic growth. In contrast, the Soviet Union, under Gorbachev, tried a different strategy of opening up the polity to some extent, allowing greater freedom of expression and movement. The idea was obviously based on the hope that political freedom might trigger a greater degree of economic growth than had been possible within the rigid command economy. Western advisers after 1990 concentrated on the attempt to put in place a system of property rights and law-based contracts, while stressing the opening of the market. In the 1990s, a rather unusual electoral system led to fragmented parties, and increased power for the president. At the same time, concentration of crucial economic power and resources created an economic oligarchy.

---

[1] It is interesting that Keynes (1936) in emphasizing uncertainty implicitly rejected the logic of probable belief that he had set out in his *Treatise on Probability* (Keynes, 1921). Although it is not often emphasized, Karl Popper's scientific philosophy (Popper, 1935) gave an argument against induction as well as Keynes's theory of probable belief. It seems that the chaotic events of the 1930s induced both Popper and Keynes to reject certainty. See Chapter 7.

At present, President Putin is engaged in a kind of economic civil war with this oligarchy for political control. There seems little chance that real democracy will develop in Russia without considerable delay. Although economic growth has began to occur, it has been concentrated in the extractive industries of oil, diamonds, and minerals. Such growth may lead to greater inequality, social unrest, decreased life expectancy, epidemics, and so on. The fact that the events of September 11, 2001, have made Russia and the United States allies against terrorism, seems to have enhanced Putin's power. It is true that autocratic power may induce stability; however, once power is obtained, it may become very difficult for democracy to take root.

An imbalance between the economy and the polity can also kill economic growth even in societies that outwardly appear democratic. Japan is an interesting case in this regard. After the postwar "reforms," Japan seemed to have a fully functioning democracy. However, as I shall argue more fully below, the essential component of democratic control is that it occurs through a competitive polity, which utilizes the diverse beliefs of the electorate. For whatever historical reasons, Japan's polity is controlled by a single party, the Liberal Democratic Party (LDP). The party is a coalition of factions, whose leaders comprise an oligarchy. To fund the factional competition, the factions have formed alliances with various banks and companies. The nature of these political-economic alliances has allowed the economic agents to expand into property or production. Because the factional alliance has been able to extract capital cheaply from the electorate, through the post office, capital was effectively subsidized. This meant that the true cost of the risk of capital expansion was not appreciated. The property collapse of the early 1990s was simply a manifestation of this political manipulation. While something similar may have been the cause of the savings and loan debacle in the United States, the difference in the U.S. case was that the economic agents were forced eventually to face the consequences of their risk taking. In Japan, in contrast, the political factions still depend on the banks and companies for financial support. Consequently, the oligarchy cannot bring itself to force the banks to face the true costs. It is probable, of course, that the costs are large enough to bankrupt the entire financial system. Even so, the outcome is a kind of economic disease. The financial links between Japan and other countries in Asia have meant that Japan's disease is infectious. Economic problems in Malaysia, Indonesia, the Philippines, and so forth, induce greater social unrest, and make whatever democratic institutions there less viable.

The lesson from Japan is that whenever the political system is insufficiently competitive and open, then corruption flourishes. Competition entirely within the political apparatus may be insufficient to deter corruption. Corruption may, over many years, induce a kind of low-level cancer of the economy. Italy, for example, would usually be considered a competitive democratic society. Until 1992, the conventional wisdom would have been that, if anything, Italy was too competitive, in the sense that governments were highly unstable and of brief duration. It was seldom noticed that all Italian governments included the dominant Christian Democratic Party, the DC (Mershon, 2002). By shifting coalition partners, the DC was able to stay in power, bribing parties like the Liberals and Social Democrats with powerful ministries. This had little apparent effect on economic growth, but the hidden side effects were incessant corruption, inefficient government, and growing budget deficits.

Only a vigorous effort by a radical group of magistrates was able to expose the degree of corruption. Most of the parties in existence prior to 1993 have collapsed in political convulsions. Changes in the electoral law in the 1990s, from a pure system of proportional representation (PR) toward one with mixed PR and plurality, have led to a new political system based on two coalitions of parties, the Olive Branch ("Ulivo") and the House of Liberty ("Casa delle Liberta"). Although Italy's unemployment, at 8.4 percent, is not as high as that of France (10.0 percent) or Germany (9.6 percent), its budget deficit, at 4.4 percent is much higher than the other members of the EU.

In Israel, there has been no dominant party or coalition of factions. The electoral system is based on PR, and a dozen parties are represented in the Knesset. Competition between the two major parties, Labor and Likud, is keen. Governments dominated by the two parties have oscillated, with Likud in power after 1988 and after 1996, and Labor in power under Rabin in 1992 and under Barak in 1999. However, from 1988 on, a key pivotal party has been the smaller Sephardic party known as Shas. Controlling the balance of government, Shas was able to extract powerful ministries, first from Netanyahu and later from Barak (Schofield and Sened, 2006). In the last election, Sharon, leader of Likud, formed a coalition with Labor (offering Peres the foreign ministry). The Oslo agreement with the PLO, negotiated while Rabin was Prime Minister after 1992, had come apart, and Israel has been riven with violence. Until the formation of the Likud–Labor coalition of Sharon and Peres, it seemed that factionalism would prevent any significant move toward a peaceful resolution. Recently, however, Sharon has shown his risk-taking ability by pulling back from Gaza, despite the opposition of both settlers and members of his own party. This may give the Palestine state the opportunity to develop democratic institutions.

Some of the current challenges facing the EU were briefly discussed in Chapter 1. At present, the focus is on economic union, ushered in with the euro in January 2002, as well as the inclusion of the other European polities of Hungary, the Czech Republic, Slovakia, Cyprus, and possibly later Turkey, or even Israel. The East European countries have, in general, made great strides toward democratic capitalism in the past decade, but the EU is primarily concerned with the problem of free mobility of labor into the EU. In some sense, this is a question of full enfranchisement, with all social and economic rights, of the population of the new member states. Indeed, this question only serves to highlight the difficulty of political control that the EU faces.

Although political leaders such as Chirac, Schröder, and Blair, for example, differ on how they see the final form of the EU, it will probably be a federation, rather than a full federal union such as put in place in the United States circa 1788. One problem is that each of the member states devised somewhat different modes of political control after World War II. Britain has always had a plurality electoral system, dominated by two large parties with opposing ideas about the proper relationship between the individual and the state. In the 1970s, the intense degree of competition this engendered between the parties may have contributed to the high degree of social conflict—between labor and management for example. As has been argued in the past (Duverger, 1954, 1984), plurality rule seems to force parties to offer differing solutions to difficult problems. This in turn forces the electorate to make a choice. In Britain in 1979, the electorate chose Thatcher, and this led directly to a restructuring of the economy: inefficient public industries were privatized and the labor market was made much more free. This strategy did have extreme costs for some, particularly in coal mining and shipbuilding, but it did make Britain's economy more efficient.

Other countries in Europe have based their electoral systems on PR. Theory suggests that PR polities will emphasize coalitional cooperation, sometimes called "consociationalism." In any case, labor–management relations in the core EU states were much more peaceful in the 1970s and 1980s than they were in Britain. However, the cost of cooperation can be a lower emphasis on adaptation. While this is obviously a great oversimplification, theory provides a plausible explanation why the EU members of continental Europe typically have labor markets that are somewhat less flexible and maintain greater state intervention in the economy than either Britain or the United States. This feature is also a characteristic of the larger political economy of the European Union. By itself, the degree of state intervention simply reflects, in some sense, the average risk posture of the European electorate. However, the EU institutions are not democratic in nature. Parliament, though elected, has little power, other than budget approval. Decisions are made in a complex bargaining arrangement between the appointed Council of Ministers and the appointed bureaucracy of the Commission.

The diverse opinions of the European electorate are only reflected, indirectly, through negotiations within the Council of Ministers, and in bargaining between EU heads of state. No institutional apparatus is available for electoral opinions to be sampled directly. Olson's (2000) analysis suggests that politicians are inadequate to the task of controlling the economy, if they are not subject to electoral control.

To be more specific, this is the logic of democracy: Although the electorate may be highly diverse, and probably not fully informed, it is the case that wise choices for the economy can only be made by aggregating these diverse opinions through a sophisticated democratic apparatus. By *sophisticated democratic apparatus*, I mean one that presents the electorate with a full range of possible options, as well as a full range of likely outcomes of these choices. Not all electoral systems are capable of this sophistication. For example, if bargaining is an endemic feature, then a wide range of options will not be discussed in the political arena. In the same way, if there is a dominant party that becomes used to the exercise of power, or there is a powerful bureaucracy habituated to the restriction of policy choices, then political discourse will be too limited to engender wise choices.

Obviously this creates a paradox for the happy exercise of political choice. On the one hand, it is advantageous to have multiple parties, offering diverse options to an electorate. On the other, the electoral response must be clearly interpretable to all, so that the choice once made can be seen to be both legitimate and intelligible. How these two seemingly incompatible requirements can be met is one challenge facing the exercise of political choice.

A second related problem for democracy is the balance between the constraints imposed on government and the ability of politicians to perceive problems and offer solutions. The appropriate balance has to do with the flow of information between the electorate and politicians. Obviously, weakening competition provides politicians with the opportunity to engage in self-serving activity, such as the kind of corruption that has been prevalent in Japan and Italy. Moreover, politicians have a tendency to obfuscate serious economic and political problems, leading possibly to eventual crisis situations. Questions of information turn on freedom of expression and inquiry. Most important perhaps, all polities must deal with uncertain futures, and therefore with questions of how to deal with risk. Sophisticated democracies have devised institutional means to balance differing risk postures and to weigh short-term benefits against long-term development.

Many of these difficulties of political choice were perceived with varying degrees of clarity by political theorists or practitioners of the past; we might consider Thomas Hobbes, Robert Walpole, Adam Smith, David Hume, James Madison, Alexander Hamilton, and, indeed, Abraham Lincoln.

In the rest of this chapter, I outline what I believe can be learned about how best to construct political institutions, using the ideas of social choice theory to understand the dilemmas of chaos and risk.

2.3   DEMOCRATIC DILEMMAS

Hobbes's argument of 1651 was that the state—Leviathan—was necessary to prevent the chaos made likely by people's propensity to resort to force. Underlying this conception of society is the notion of a zero- or constant-sum game. By relinquishing some of their freedom to an autocrat who alone can exercise force, a people can free themselves, perhaps, from chaos.

Keynes's argument of 1936 has many Hobbesian features. For Keynes, chaos could come about not from the exercise of force, but from speculation in the market place. Rejecting the equilibrium view derived from Adam Smith and Marshall, Keynes provided a rationale for the excessive "exuberance," and then collapse, of the market. He accepted a limited equilibrium hypothesis for certain exchange markets, but asserted that "a somewhat comprehensive socialization of investment will prove the only means of securing an approximation to full employment" (Keynes, 1936: 378).

Although Hobbes and Keynes focused on different aspects of the role of the state (the political realm and the economic realm), both acknowledged, in a sense, the logic of the exchange of freedom for the gift of security, the avoidance of risk.

30

Implicitly, both theories require that the state be endowed with power sufficient to exercise its part of an "equilibrium" contract. Implicitly, in the Hobbesian view, the state should be powerful enough to defeat any anarchic agent in its domain. For Keynes, economic chaos could only be mitigated by an agent commanding sufficient resources to stabilize speculative markets. The greater the volatility of a market—the greater the flow and value of transactions—then the greater the economic resources needed to control this volatility. Keynes saw that the great quandary facing decision makers at the end of World War II was how to exercise sufficient resources to stabilize world markets and exclude the possibility of a recurrence of the Depression. As it was, the institutional devices put in place under Bretton Woods, and then the Marshall Aid program, as well as the later devices of the 1960s, were insufficient to prevent the monetary and trade disorder of the 1970s. Since the 1980s, political leaders have refrained from the Keynesian attempt at global risk management. Fortunately, technological change and greater market sophistication have prevented the chaotic collapse that Keynes feared. Various alliances, such as the EU and NAFTA can be seen as regional attempts at risk avoidance and partial market control. Nonetheless Keynes's fears are still relevant.

Neither Hobbes nor Keynes dealt fully with the consequences of an unchained Leviathan. Many prophets of chaos have, of course, taken the position contra Keynes—that the legitimization of government intervention in the economy will necessarily lead to excessive manipulation. Even in a democratic milieu, a political party in power may manipulate for its own ends, attempting to engineer economic growth in the short run so as to ensure re-election. To some extent, the huge literature on this topic underestimates the capacity of electorates in developed countries to see the costs of such manipulation and reject those responsible. Nonetheless, the balance between the preservation of liberty in the populace, and the appropriate degree of power available to government, is a delicate one.

Arguments can be made that the correct balance should privilege liberty. Keynes was very much aware of some of the subtleties of the appropriate balance. Experience of the 1930s suggested to him that if the state shows itself incapable of limiting economic chaos, then the electorate will voluntarily choose dictatorship. As he wrote, "Authoritarian state systems ... seem to solve the problem of unemployment at the expense of efficiency and of freedom" (Keynes, 1936: 381).

In essence, Keynes proposed a compromise: by sanctioning limited government intervention to limit economic disorder, the choice between dictatorship and "order" on the one hand and liberty and "chaos" on the other could be avoided.

The danger of dictatorship, of course, is that the process by which a dictator comes to power will engender risk taking. The biographies of the dictators of the twentieth century suggest strongly that only arrogant and ruthless men can come to positions of such extreme power. As they gather the power of the state, and necessarily limit economic freedom, they curtail, as Keynes saw, the efficiency of their economy. Because such dictators are obliged to seek greater resources, they will do this not simply through domestic economic growth, but by military expansion. This creates a dilemma for other liberty-preserving, democratic states.

A dictator, in his ascent to power, will have learned that risk taking pays off. In foreign adventures, he will be guided by the same risk posture. In democracies, risk taking may or may not pay off, but in general, political leaders will not be as extremely risk taking as their dictatorial opponents. Thus Hitler, for example, seemed able to force his generals to take extreme risks in the early stages of World War II, to the consternation of both French and British political leaders. Hitler believed that the German success by May 1940 would force French capitulation, as well as British acquiescence to German domination of Europe.

Such a situation creates a quandary for any democracy. Because ordinary people in a democracy will tend to be risk avoiding, at least when it comes to military adventure, so will their leaders. But if a democracy faces an adversarial dictatorship, then risk avoidance by the democracy's leaders will only engender further aggression by the dictator. The dilemma facing Britain in May, 1940 illustrates this dilemma. As Lucaks (1999) and Jenkins (2001) have both noted, Hitler had offered to let Britain be, thus preserving its empire, as long as the political leaders in Britain acquiesced to Hitler's conquest of the continent of Europe. At that time it was unknown whether many of Britain's army, stranded in France, could be saved. In the war cabinet, Halifax, with support from Chamberlain, pressed Churchill to acknowledge the German conquest of Europe, and to negotiate for the preservation of the Empire. Although it was obvious that France would soon capitulate and Italy would join the Axis powers, Churchill not only refused to acquiesce, but on France's surrender to Germany ordered the sinking of the remnant of the French fleet at Mers-el-Kebir, near Oran, Algeria. Such risk taking by Churchill may well have seemed irrational to Halifax. Nonetheless, Churchill's judgment over the "honesty" of Hitler and the probable eventualities proved to be correct. Every democracy must deal with this risk dilemma.

My reading of Hamilton's arguments at the time of the constitutional debate in the thirteen states in 1787–8 suggests that he was well aware of the necessity that the federal bargain between these thirteen states deal with risk appropriately by devising mechanisms "to increase ... external force and security" (Freeman, 2001: 197).

Hamilton's arguments in the *Federalist* were based on a number of almost axiomatic points. First, even republics can be addicted to war. So, a federal union was necessary to restrict the possibility of conflict between the states. Second, such a union could more effectively counter outside threats from Imperial powers such as Britain, France, and Spain. Third, an important element of the ability to counter threat is the development of an efficient economic system—a common currency—and provident fiscal mechanisms to raise government revenue. Fourth, Hamilton argued in *Federalist IX* that Montesquieu regarded a confederate republic "as the expedient for extending the sphere of popular government and reconciling the advantages of monarchy with those of republicanism" (Freeman, 2001: 198).

For Hamilton, republicanism meant the exercise of the "science of politics" to distribute power through "legislative balances and checks" (Freeman, 2001: 197). This argument, taken together with James Madison's in *Federalist X* and *Federalist LI*, suggested that representatives of the republic would tend to make wise choices. Although it is not clearly articulated in the writings of Hamilton and Madison, the "wise" choices of the representatives are understood to be those made in times of peace. I suggest that the reference to "monarchy" in *Federalist IX* refers to the necessity of the concentration of power, and thus of the tendency to take risk, in the presence of threat of war.[2]

Although Hamilton was later reviled for his alleged predilection for monarchy, he was, in fact, aware of this democratic dilemma of risk. While democracy depends on the dissemination of power in normal times, it may require the capacity to concentrate decision-making capacity in times of danger. The particular institutional form of the United States may indeed provide a solution to this dilemma of power.

The intuitions of Hamilton and Madison in this regard depended on their reading of history, particularly British constitutional history. To

---

[2] In fact, in *Federalist XI*, Hamilton went on to argue that Europe had for too long been "mistress of the world," and that union would permit the creation of an "American system" able to "dictate the terms of the connection between the old and the new world."(Freeman, 2001: 208). This remark is discussed further in Chapter 4.

better understand their appreciation of this dilemma, and how it relates to an interpretation of the present, I discuss later the development of the British polity in the early modern period, and then compare it with the evolution of U.S. economic and political institutions. Before doing this, however, I consider Kennedy's arguments on the inevitable decline of empire.

2.4   THE LOGIC OF EMPIRE

We may follow North and Weingast (1989) and Weingast (1997a,b) and date the initiation of the British Empire in the period 1688 to 1694, with the Glorious Revolution and the foundation of the Bank of England.

Kennedy (1987) sees the rise from 1688 and fall of the British empire over a three-hundred-year span (until, say, 1957) to be an example of a certain inexorable logic of empire.

To illustrate his more general argument, consider the growth of the Spanish empire from the accession of Charles of Hapsburg to the throne of Castile and Aragon in 1516. In 1519 he was elected Holy Roman Emperor, as Charles V. From his mother, Charles inherited Naples, Sicily, Sardinia, and the South American domains. From his father, he held the Netherlands, part of the Duchy of Burgundy, and from his grandfather, Maximillian, Austria and the Tyrol. After Charles's abdication in late 1555 in the Netherlands, his son Philip II become sovereign over an empire extending from the Moluccas in East Asia to New Spain, in what is now California. Until his death in 1598, Philip had to contend with war with France and Britain, as well as the Ottoman Empire. Against the great naval victory of the Hapsburg Holy League over the Ottomans at Lepanto in 1571 must be set the disaster of the failure of the Armada against England in 1588.

The increasing cost of incessant warfare bankrupted Spain. Parker (1998) suggests that war in Germany in the 1540s cost 1 million ducats annually, in the Netherlands in the 1550s about 2 million ducats annually, and in Flanders in the 1590s about 3 million ducats annually. In 1557, 1560, 1575, and 1596, Philip II was forced to reschedule his debts, essentially admitting the treasury was bankrupt. In 1560, the debt was 29 million ducats, and by 1574 it had risen to 81 million ducats (at least fifteen years' total annual revenue). Kennedy implies that these spiraling costs forced Spain, after Philip II, to cede its dependencies; the Netherlands were granted independence in 1648, while Naples, Sardinia, Piedmont, and the Southern Netherlands were ceded to Austria in 1714. Even though Spain took in tribute from South America (of the order of 2 million ducats annually under Philip II), its economy was insufficient to cover the costs of maintaining the empire (at least in Europe). In 1701, the Hapsburg dynasty was replaced by the Bourbons. Through the eighteenth century Spain lost further territory in the Americas, including Santo Domingo and Trinidad (and then Louisiana in 1802, after it had been ceded to Spain by France in 1763). In 1808, Napoleon forced the Bourbon line to abdicate.

Although the empire was immense at its greatest extent, internal economic contradictions brought about a slow demise over two hundred years. Indeed, economic historians, when they enquire why Latin America has never followed its northern neighbor into prosperity, suggest that the inefficient institutions that hinder growth in the southern continent derive from those of Spain (Haber, 1997).

As a second example, consider the Ottoman Empire which we can regard as founded in 1453, at the conquest of Constantinople by Mehmet II. The Ottomans took Athens in 1456, Belgrade in 1521, and Rhodes in 1522. However, Suleymain died on campaign with his troops in Hungary in 1566 without ever taking Vienna. Cyprus was captured in 1570, but this only led to the great defeat of Ottoman naval power at Lepanto in 1571. The long decline of the Ottoman Empire made possible Greek independence and the autonomy of Moldavia, Wallachia, and Serbia in 1830. Indeed, Russian troops occupied Istanbul in 1833 to preserve it from a rampaging Egyptian army. By 1854, the empire was obliged to borrow from London, and in 1875 it declared bankruptcy (Goodwin, 1999).

Kennedy suggests that the French empire in the modern sense, dates from 1661 when Louis XIV took full control of the French government. Between 1660 and the end of the War of Spanish Succession in 1713, French government debt had increased by a factor of seven (Kennedy, 1987: 106). Indeed, by 1770, after two more major wars against Britain, French government debt was of the order of 1.8 billion livres (about 75 million pounds sterling). Norberg (1994), for example, estimates French government expenditure to be 442 million livres (about 18 million sterling) in 1763, against income of 425 million livres. Increasing debt incurred increased interest rates (nearly 7 percent). Although income had increased to 470 million livres in 1788, this was inadequate to service the much greater debt resulting from French involvement in the American Revolutionary War (by then the debt was of the order of 3.6 billion livres, or 150 million pounds). It is probable that the difficulty of dealing with this debt caused Louis XVI to call the Estates General in 1789, indirectly bringing about the French Revolution.

After the Terror, and the creation of the Consular Triumvirate, Napoleon restructured the French fiscal apparatus. Nonetheless, the financing of his wars in Europe was generally carried out not through taxation, but from spoils (Schom, 1997). Thus, the risk taking of the sovereigns of France led inevitably to the financial crisis of 1789, and hence the revolution. The aftermath of the revolution brought to power an even greater risk taker—Napoleon—who, in pursuing great rewards, brought about a great disaster.

One point that Kennedy does not emphasize is that the British incurred much greater debt than did France in the prosecution of war in the eighteenth century. Brewer (1988) shows that British debt of 17 million sterling (about five years' government revenue) in 1697 had increased to 243 million sterling (twenty years' revenue) by 1784. According to Norberg (1994: 375), the average interest rate on British debt was about 3.8 percent. Indeed, after the American War, Pitt was able to increase taxes, retire some of the debt, reducing debt service from 76 percent to 50 percent of government revenue. Unlike France, Britain, from 1783 on, was in no danger of succumbing to bankruptcy and dictatorship.

As a military historian of World War I, Kennedy is intrigued by the escalating cost of the arms race between the powers that took place prior to 1914. He charts both the relative decline of industrial power of Britain, vis-a-vis Germany, Russia, and the United states, as well as the great increase of military and naval personnel, and thus the relative cost, for the European powers. However, Ferguson (1999) questions Kennedy's inference that the increasing war burden contributed to Britain's decline from hegemonic power. First, the increase of Germany's annual military expenditure between 1894 and 1913 was 57 million sterling (over 150 percent) in comparison to the British increase of 39 million sterling. In line with my reasoning, Germany's leadership was oligarchic, or even dictatorial, and was seemingly much more risk preferring than were the political leaders in Britain. Total government debt for Britain fell in this period, from 655 million sterling to 625 million, while German debt rose from 419 million to more than 1 billion.

As a percentage of national product, Britain's debt was only 28 percent, compared with Germany's 44 percent, France's 86 percent, and Russia's 47 percent (Ferguson, 1999: 127). It is true that the First World War was an unmitigated, and expensive, disaster for all the powers. Expressing total war expenditure in dollars (and as a proportion of 1914 national income) we obtain the following: Britain, 45 billion (409 percent); Germany, 32 billion (266 percent); France, 30 billion (500 percent); Russia,

12 billion (172 percent); Italy, 13 billion (780 percent); and the United States, 36 billion (100 percent). It is not at all surprising that the twenty years after World War I proved economically difficult as the combatants attempted to deal with the huge debts incurred.

From 1933 to 1938, increasing military expenditure repeated the pattern prior to 1913. German and Soviet expenditure (in dollars) rose from 450 million (Germany) and 700 million (USSR) in 1933 to 7.4 billion (Germany) and 5.4 billion (USSR) in 1938. For Britain, the increase was from 333 million to 1.86 billion. The vastly expensive war of 1939–1945 left Britain, Germany, and France exhausted and essentially bankrupt. Even by 1960, after the success of post-war Marshall aid in restructuring the European economies, the U.S. GNP was still approximately twice that of Britain, Germany, France, and Italy, combined.

Writing in the late 1980s, Kennedy saw the relative economic decline of the United States in the period 1960–1980 as presaging the absolute loss of American hegemony in the global economy. Between 1960 and 1980 the U.S. share of world product fell from 26 percent to 21.5 percent, while that of the European Economic Community fell from a similar proportion to 22.5 percent. Japan's rose from 4.5 percent to 9.0 percent, while that of the Soviet Union fell slightly from 12.5 percent to 11.4 percent. Implicit in Kennedy's analysis was the empirical generalization that empires choose to expend resources on military adventures, weakening their economy, thus hastening bankruptcy and their own demise. This hypothesis seemed compatible with the increase of the U.S. Federal deficit from about 60 million dollars in 1980, to more than 200 billion dollars in 1985, as a result of the increase in defense expenditure and the cut in taxes under Reagan (Kennedy, 1987).

Although Kennedy was aware of the difficulties that the Soviet Union faced in the 1980s over feeding its population, it was little suspected at that time that the USSR was approaching bankruptcy. Kennedy's own figures suggest why the bankruptcy occurred. Estimating USSR military expenditure in 1980 at $144 billion and GNP at $1.2 trillion gives a rate of over 10 percent. Table 2.1a compares United States and USSR military expenditure during the 1980s. These figures suggest that Kennedy's imperial hypothesis was relevant to the Soviet Union, but not to the United States, at least until 1991. The beginning of the collapse of the USSR, and the loss of its empire in Eastern Europe, can be plausibly related to the hidden bankruptcy resulting from excessive military expenditure. Table 2.1b shows the extreme drop in Russian military expenditure in the 1990s.

Table 2.1a. *A Comparison of U.S. and Soviet Military Expenditure,*
1984–1991

Year	Military Expenditure (as % of GNP)		Military Expenditure (as % of government expenditure)		Military Expenditure (per capita in) 1994 dollars)	
	USSR	US	USSR	US	USSR	US
1984	13.0	6.2	50.2	26.4	1321	1388
1985	13.1	6.4	50.0	25.7	1327	1466
1986	12.8	6.6	46.9	27.1	1329	1318
1987	12.9	6.3	45.9	27.2	1315	1496
1988	12.7	6.0	46.6	26.2	1352	1452
1989	11.5	5.8	43.5	25.5	1219	1428
1990	11.0	5.5	43.1	23.5	1117	1363
1991	10.3	4.9	NA	19.6	951	1189

Kennedy's arguments on relative U.S. economic decline are also implausible. His figures of $11,360 for U.S. GNP per capita in 1980, com-
pared with $13,590 for West Germany and $11,730 for France are mis-
leading because they are based on current exchange rates. In contrast,
Figure 2.1 presents estimates of GDP per capita in constant 1985 dollars, using purchasing power parity (PPP), for six of the OECD countries.
Although economists like to focus on the annual rate of increase of total GNP, Figure 2.1 suggests that the appropriate basis for comparing
growth is increase in GDP per capita per annum in real PPP terms. By this

Table 2.1b. *A Comparison of U.S. and Russian Military Expenditure,*
1992–1999

Year	Military Expenditure (as % of GNP)		Military Expenditure (as % of government expenditure)		Military Expenditure (per capita in) 1999 dollars)	
	Russia	US	Russia	US	Russia	US
1992	8.0	4.8	28.0	21.1	491	1360
1993	7.5	4.5	35.4	19.9	419	1280
1994	8.3	4.1	25.7	18.8	406	1200
1995	5.8	3.8	22.1	17.4	271	1130
1996	5.4	3.5	26.7	16.5	246	1070
1997	6.0	3.3	30.9	16.3	274	1060
1998	4.6	3.1	17.9	15.8	196	1030
1999	5.6	3.0	22.4	15.7	239	1030

Source: World Military Expenditures and Arms Transfers, U.S. Arms Control and Disarma-
ment Agency, 1994 and 2002.

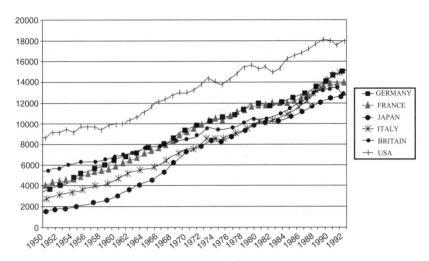

Figure 2.1. Estimates of GDP per capita (in 1985 dollars) for six OECD countries, 1950–1992. *Source*: The graph is based on purchasing power parity using data from World Development Indicators and the Organisation for Economic Cooperation and Development (OECD) (http://www.oecd.org/linklist).

measure, all the OECD economies grew at approximately the same rate. The U.S. growth, from about $8,000 to $18,000 during a forty-year period, gives an average annual increase of $250 per capita. The per capita figures for Germany, France, and Britain are $312, $250, and $180, respectively, compared with $340 for Japan. Obviously, differing average real income increases imply changing relative economic power. However, Figure 2.1 does not seem consistent with the existence of an absolute U.S. decline. The six economies represented in Figure 2.1 all exhibit a plateau in per capita income. The level of the plateau is presumably determined by social, political, and economic institutional features—such as the degree of labor mobility, stock market sophistication, debt structure, and so forth. The U.S. plateau in 1990 is approximately $3,500 higher than that of Germany or Japan. In fact, further growth by the United States in the 1990s suggests that the U.S. plateau is higher than is indicated by Figure 2.1.

Kennedy may well have based his argument on the extraordinary economic and political problems of the 1970s. These problems may have been induced by governments believing in a Keynesianism that Keynes himself would not have accepted. There seems very little theoretical basis to the notion that, by playing with money aggregates, a government could permanently adjust inflation/unemployment combinations. In the early 1970s, the weakening restrictions of the gold standard, and the international flow of dollars, gave governments the opportunity to experiment with inflation/unemployment ratios conducive to re-election. Such an act by government violates the medieval "fiduciary" relationship between the sovereign and the people, proscribing the debasement of the coinage.

Goodhart and Bhansali (1970) were perhaps the first to note that inducing an electorally optimal "short-run" combination of inflation and unemployment along the so-called Phillips curve, would also probably trigger inflationary expectations. As Brittan later observed: "Over a run of political cycles the short-term Phillips curve will drift upwards ... democratic myopia and economic time lags will land the economy with an excessive rate of inflation" (Brittan, 1978: 172).

A whole host of prophets of chaos studied the deleterious economic effects of governmental electoral "rationality" (Nordhaus, 1975; Mac Rae, 1977; Tufte, 1978; Alt, 1979; Brittan, 1983). One of the most interesting arguments of that time was due to Beer (1982). He postulated that in polities with first-past-the-post (or plurality) electoral systems (such as Britain and the United States), the decline of party identification would permit small groups in the polity to be unconstrained in their "rent seeking" claims. Because plurality electoral procedures magnify vote swings, relatively small groups could blackmail the government. It was certainly true that, in Britain, competition between different labor groups became intense during the 1970s. With inflation approaching 25 percent on occasion, weakly organized groups, such as nurses or university teachers, lost economic ground rapidly. The chaos theorems of McKelvey (1976, 1979) and Schofield (1978) seemed to provide a formal explanation of the disorder of the time.

In arguments somewhat similar to those of Olson (1982a, b), the theorists of "consociational" or "corporatist" democracy (Lijphart, 1969; Lehmbruch, 1979; Crouch, 1985) argued that democracies with strong socialist or social democrat parties, and encompassing labor unions, should be able to manage political bargaining more effectively than the liberal market economies (such as Britain and the United States). Recently, Garrett (1998) compared the "consociational democracies" with the polities based on plurality, to see which of them proved less adept at maintaining economic growth in the so-called global world economy of the 1990s. Table 2.2 adapts information for 1980–95 taken from his book.

The four consociational/corporatist polities all have quite powerful socialist/social democrat parties that have been in office at least some time during the 1980s. (Garrett also includes Finland and Norway in this first

Table 2.2. *Twelve Democratic Polities: 1980–1995*

Country[a]	Union[b]	G[c]	B[d]	E[e]	U[f]	I[g]	M[h]
Corporatist							
Sweden	83	67	−8.0	1.9	1.8	8.2	10.0
Denmark	74	62	−3.0	3.1	8.3	6.5	14.8
Austria	46	52	−3.8	2.4	3.2	3.5	6.7
France	10	53	−4.6	1.9	9.0	7.0	16.0
Average		59	−4.9	1.9	5.7	6.4	12.0
Mixed							
Belgium	55	56	−6.0	2.0	10.9	4.8	15.7
Italy	34	54	−9.1	1.9	10.3	10.8	21.1
Germany	31	49	−3.0	2.1	7.6	2.9	10.5
Netherlands	23	54	−3.3	1.6	9.6	2.9	12.5
Average		53	−5.4	1.95	9.6	5.4	15.0
Liberal							
UK	38	43	−5.6	2.0	9.5	7.6	17.1
Canada	32	48	−6.2	2.6	9.2	6.4	15.6
US	15	34	−2.9	2.5	6.7	5.4	12.1
Japan	25	34	−0.9	4.2	2.5	2.5	5.0
Average (with Japan)			−3.9	2.85	7.0	5.5	12.5
Average (without Japan)			−4.9	2.4	8.6	6.5	15.1
Overall Average		51	−4.7	2.2	7.4	5.8	13.2

[a] The countries are grouped according to percentage share of left wing cabinet portfolios over 1980–90.
[b] Union = Percentage trade union membership in 1990.
[c] G = Government spending as percent GDP, 1991–5.
[d] B = Budget balance, deficit (−) or surplus (+) as a percent of GDP, 1991–5.
[e] E = Economic growth, per annum, average 1980–90.
[f] U = Unemployment, average percent, 1980–90.
[g] I = Consumer price inflation, average percent, 1980–90.
[h] M = Misery index = U+I, average 1980–90.
Source: adapted from Gerald Garrett *Partisan Politics in the Global Economy* (1998), by permission of Cambridge University Press.

category, but places France in the second "mixed" category.) In this second mixed category, the left has controlled, on average, less than one quarter of the cabinet positions during the 1980s. In the four liberal/plurality polities, the left was out of power in the 1980s. Nonetheless, Table 2.2 is suggestive. There does seem to be a tendency for governments of corporatist democracies to absorb a greater share of GDP, and to run budget deficits. Unemployment in the 1980s in the Scandinavian democracies tended to be lower than in the OECD as a whole, while growth was somewhat lower and inflation somewhat higher than in the United States, say.

Table 2.3. *Twelve Democratic Polities: August 2005*

Country[a]	B[b]	E[c]	U[d]	I[e]	M[f]
Corporatist					
Sweden	+0.8	1.4	7.1	0.6	7.7
Denmark	+1.8	0.8	5.4	1.6	7.0
Austria	−2.0	2.0	5.6	2.4	8.0
France	−3.0	1.8	10.0	1.6	11.6
Average	−0.6	1.5	7.0	1.6	8.6
Mixed					
Belgium	−0.5	1.4	12.3	3.1	15.4
Italy	−4.4	−0.2	7.8	2.0	9.8
Germany	−3.5	1.1	11.6	1.9	13.5
Netherlands	−2.2	−0.5	6.7	1.6	8.3
Average	−2.7	0.6	9.6	2.2	11.8
Liberal					
UK	−2.9	1.7	4.9	2.0	6.9
Canada	+1.2	3.3	6.9	1.9	8.8
US	−4.1	3.6	5.0	3.2	8.2
Japan	−6.1	1.3	4.4	−0.2	4.6
Average (with Japan)	−3.0	2.5	5.2	1.7	7.1
Average (without Japan)	−1.9	3.0	5.5	2.1	8.0
Overall Average	−2.1	1.5	7.3	1.9	9.1

[a] The countries are grouped as in Table 2.2.
[b] B = Budget balance deficit (−) or surplus (+) as a percent of GDP for previous year.
[c] E = Economic growth, as percent change in GDP, over previous year.
[d] U = Unemployment, average percent, over previous year.
[e] I = Consumer price inflation, average percent over previous year. Because the "deflation" of −0.2% for Japan is an economic "bad," it is interpreted as + 0.2% in computing the misery index.
[f] M = Misery index = U+I, average, previous year.
Source: OECD. http://www.oecd.org/linklist.
This table updates the one in Norman Schofield, "Constitutional Political Economy: Rational Choice Theory and Comparative Politics," *The Annual Review of Political Science* 3 (2000).

Fairly clearly, the table suggests that the predictions of the prophets of chaos of the 1970s and early 1980s were confounded by the events of the late 1980s and early 1990s. The "liberal" polities of the United States and Britain did not fall into a stagflationary trap, forced by their electoral systems to attempt to keep unemployment down and inflationary expectations up. I emphasize the differences between Table 2.2, for the 1980s, and Table 2.3, which presents similar economic data for

August 2005. Inflation is obviously not a problem for the developed economies at present.

Indeed *deflation* (falling prices) has begun to be a serious problem in Japan. Average unemployment has tended to fall from the 1990s to the present, in the liberal polities, though it has recently risen somewhat in the United States. In Germany, Italy, and France, unemployment rose during the 1990s and has stayed high. Budget deficits in the countries in the EU were required to be below 3 percent but in France, Germany, and Italy, the deficits are 3.0 percent, 3.5 percent, and 4.4 percent, respectively. Japan, meanwhile, has been running a budget deficit of about 6 percent, while the deficit for the United States has increased to 4.1 percent. It is possible that France, Belgium, Germany, and Italy have high unemployment figures because of the EU requirement of low budget deficits, and the imposition (through the monetary discipline of a single currency) of low inflation. Because their unemployment rates have been high since at least 1994, it is more likely that these figures are due to structural features of the political economy. In line with Garrett's argument, the three social democratic/corporatist polities (Sweden, Denmark, and Austria) have all managed to maintain low inflation, moderate unemployment, and reasonable growth. However, Tables 2.2 and 2.3 suggest that there is some evidence for a version of Beer's hypothesis involving the relationship between the state and interest groups.

To avoid the kind of economic chaos of the 1970s, it could appear rational to build up the apparatus of the state bureaucracy. This can create an interest group whose purpose becomes misdirected toward the maintenance of its own power. An enormous literature (e.g., Niskanen, 1971) has focused on this problem. Some versions of this theory emphasize the involvement of government in this manipulation. For example, in polities based on PR, the necessity of bargaining between multiple factions may force government to become subject to veto power exercised by groups controlled either by labor or capital. In theory, such veto groups could extract surplus from the economy, thus lowering economic growth and hurting every member of the society in the long run. I return to this point in the next section.

The break up of the Soviet Union in the 1990s opened the way for the expansion of the EU to the east, but also seemingly made the United States the sole global power. French outrage at this turn of events led Hubert Vedrine, the French foreign minister, to call the United States "a 'hyperpower'—the 'country that is dominant or predominant in all categories—attitudes, concepts, language and modes of life'" (quoted in Safire, *New York Times*, June 10, 2001).

This turn of events, resulting from the demise of the Soviet Union in 1989, may be similar in some ways to the collapse of France in 1789. In the eighteenth century, France had fought a sequence of global wars against a fiscally superior power, Britain. The collapse into the chaos of revolution after 1789 brought about the rise of Napoleon and a last grasp at empire. This failed, and France entered a long period of slow decline. The political collapse of the Soviet Union after 1989 was, by Kennedy's thesis, the consequence of the fiscal inefficiency of its economic system. Unlike France in the eighteenth century, it was not so much debt resulting from participation in a world war, but the Soviet Union's attempt to compete militarily with the United States. The superior economic and political institutions of the United States allowed it to outspend the USSR in the arms race of the Cold War. The inferior "institution" of the USSR was, fundamentally, the structure of its autocratic polity. Indeed this had the same design flaw of French political institutions in the eighteenth century.

It is my contention that there is also a close parallel between the evolution of political and economic institutions in Britain from 1688 to 1789, and in the United States from, say, the post–Civil War period, circa 1878, until the end of the Cold War in 1989. The "fiscal efficiency" constituted in Britain in the eighteenth century was a necessary cause of Britain's ability to prosecute the imperial wars against France and Spain. It was the creation of this fiscal war machine that led to the collapse of Napoleonic France in 1815 and opened the way to British hegemony during the nineteenth century. History, of course, does not repeat itself, and there is no way of knowing whether Putin's Russia will attempt a final imperial thrust, or whether the United States will maintain its "hyper-puissance" throughout the twenty-first century. However, we can make some guesses about the rise to hegemony of Britain and the United States by considering the origins of British fiscal efficiency in the seventeenth and eighteenth centuries, and comparing them with the structuring of the institutions of the U.S. political economy after 1787.

2.5 SOCIAL CHOICE THEORY: AUTOCRACY AND RISK

For Olson, the key feature of a society is the degree of concentration of power. Markets can, of course, exist in the presence of an oligarchy, as the case of China, today, illustrates. However, oligarchs are likely to use, or pervert, markets for their own ends, and attempt to weaken rights to property, and so forth. Olson also emphasizes the likelihood that when power is even more highly concentrated in the hands of an autocrat—like Stalin in the USSR—then capital (and labor) will be confiscated from the subjects of the autocrat. This will certainly destroy the incentives for productive activity in the economy, and hinder growth. As I have suggested above, the autocrat will tend to be risk preferring and utilize the confiscated resources for purposes that are ill suited to growth. The arguments of Kennedy and Olson are, in this regard, compatible. Just as with Philip II of Spain, in the sixteenth century, the kings of France and then Napoleon in the eighteenth century, and Hitler and Stalin in the twentieth century, autocrats will lead their subjects into disaster. Even societies that are democratic, at some phase, may fall into autocracy out of fear of economic chaos, just as Keynes perceived. In earlier times, chaos was more likely to be induced by factional disorder; it was this likelihood that prompted Hobbes to argue for the necessity of a powerful sovereign. The establishment of the Protectorate in Britain, under Oliver Cromwell in 1653, can be seen as such a "fall" into the autocracy that Hobbes discussed. Olson's theoretical arguments, taken together with Kennedy's historical studies, suggest that extreme concentration of power in autocracy, or dictatorship—the seeming opposite of chaos—can lead to excessive risk taking, then decline, and finally collapse.

Another alternative, proposed in the previous section, is that certain polities can become subject to veto power exercised by groups, controlled either by labor or capital. As Buchanan and Tullock (1962) suggested many years ago, such a design is likely to lead to lengthy and inefficient negotiations over policy. We may characterize such a design as "extreme risk avoidance."

Figure 2.2 offers a diagrammatic representation of these interpretations in terms of two axes—stability and risk. An "efficient" polity is one that escapes, in some way, the dangers of chaos, the risk taking of autocracy, and the risk avoidance of multiple veto group bargaining.

I first use some ideas from social choice theory to elaborate on the implications of Figure 2.2. As in many of the following chapters of this book, I assume that there are at least three fundamental dimensions characterizing social policy: land, capital, and labor. By "land," I refer to the distribution of land in the society. "Labor" is shorthand for the distribution of social rights, including enfranchisement and religious tolerance. "Capital" means the revenue/tax structure and the "balance" of creditors and debtors in the economy. These three dimensions have been used by

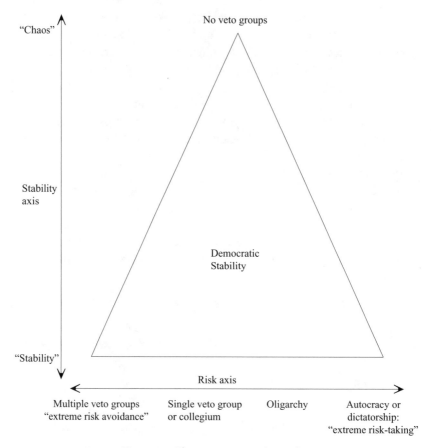

Figure 2.2. Chaos or autocracy in a polity.

Rogowski (1989) to study conflict in a political economy. I elaborate on Rogowski's analysis in the chapters that follow.

The "decisive structure" refers to the distribution of power. Typically, the sovereign and a coterie of great landowners or aristocrats form either an oligarchy or collegium. If an oligarchy, then this group belongs to every winning coalition, and is itself winning. In such a situation, the oligarchy can control social choice in certain domains, such as war. It is of course possible that the sovereign and aristocratic elite disagree: for example, Hoffman and Rosenthal (1997) and Rosenthal (1998) model bargaining between sovereign and elite over the advantage of war. As we have seen, however, the choices made by such an elite oligarchy are unlikely to be advantageous for long term growth.

If the elite group is a collegium, belonging to every winning coalition but not itself winning, then it essentially has a strong veto and can siphon all surplus toward itself. Such a characterization might describe a situation where the elite forms alliances with different social groups to raise taxation for purposes of war, and then repudiates the implicit contracts. To give a very simple example of the possibilities, consider a situation with five factions $\{A, B, C, D, E\}$ in Parliament, and let K represent the sovereign. If K alone is winning (or decisive), then the situation is one of extreme autocracy, as indicated by the right hand vertex of Figure 2.2. At the opposite extreme, on the left vertex, is the case where all the factions, and the King, are necessary for a decision—the case of extreme risk avoidance. On the other hand, if the King is powerless, and any coalition of three factions $\{A, B, C\}$, say, is winning or decisive, then the so-called Nakamura (1979) number is three.[3] The theoretical analyses of Schofield (1984a) and Strnad (1985) show that, in this case, an equilibrium (a "core") can be guaranteed only in one dimension. In two dimensions, a core will generally not exist, and in three dimensions, chaos, or complete disorder, can ensue (Schofield, 1985a).

Suppose, on the other hand, that every coalition of the three factions requires the inclusion of K to be decisive. Then K is a collegium (and has a unique veto). The Nakamura number is infinite, and a core is always guaranteed.[4] Theory implies that K can extract all surplus.

Although Figure 2.2 is an extreme simplification of a complex social choice problem, it can be used to illustrate some of the problems of chaos or risk discussed above. Recent events in Serbia, Bosnia, Kosova, Lebanon, Afghanistan, Iraq, and Palestine all suggest that chaos is a real possibility when there are powerful opposing interests and no institutional check or balance to political conflicts. In the Soviet Union prior to 1989, power was concentrated in the Politburo and the elite of the communist party. Depending on the degree of concentration, policy making could be risk taking (as it appeared to be under the rule of Stalin) or much more risk averse (as it probably was under Brezhnev). My interpretation of current

---

[3] The Nakamura number, v, is three because there are three separate winning coalitions – $\{A, B, C\}$, $\{C, D, E\}$, and $\{A, B, E\}$, – with nobody in common. The smaller the Nakamura number, the more likely chaos will occur. An equilibrium is guaranteed whenever the dimension is no more than $v - 2$. In this example, disorder can occur in two dimensions but not in one.

[4] K is now in every single winning coalition, so it is impossible for a family of winning coalitions to have nobody in common. By "convention," the Nakamura number is, in this case, said to be infinite. However, chaos cannot occur.

events in Japan is that the existence of multiple veto groups within the LDP, the bureaucracy, and big business make it almost impossible to deal with the intractable economic problems.

Inference drawn from the study of the PR polities of the EU suggests that their characteristic of multiple veto groups (such as farmers) prevents necessary policy changes, with respect to agriculture and labor mobility, for example. However, certain EU institutions such as the Commission, may act as collegia in specific policy domains. Thus the change to the Euro as a common currency in January 2002 may have risk-taking characteristics.

It is my contention that the necessity of devising institutional rules in order to balance stability and risk was apparent to the architects of change in their analyses of the constitutions of Britain and the United States. Hobbes (1651), of course, perceived the importance of the stability dimension. My interpretation of the argument of Alexander Hamilton and James Madison in particular suggests that the second risk axis was also understood in some form.

To examine how stability and risk may be balanced, in the context of the underlying social choice theory represented by Figure 2.2, let us abstract from the political history of Britain in the early modern period. Suppose, in contrast to the above example of five factions $\{A, B, C, D, E\}$ and sovereign, K, that each coalition of three factions needs to include K in order to be decisive. However, suppose further that the entire parliament $\{A, B, C, D, E\}$ is also decisive, against the sovereign. In this case there is no collegium, but K can be termed a *semi-collegium*. Such a decisive structure results in what may be named an *apex game*. The Nakamura number is now four.[5] A core is always guaranteed in two dimensions, but not in three. In three dimensions, the game is no longer chaotic, but will result in an outcome that depends on bargaining between the King and the factions. The next section provides a brief interpretation of the evolution of British constitutional history in the seventeenth and eighteenth centuries to make the point that the British polity evolved toward an apex game. In brief, the ability of Parliament and its allies in the 1640s to

[5] To see this, note that there is a family of four winning coalitions – $\{A, B, C, K\}$, $\{C, D, E, K\}$, $\{A, B, E, K\}$, and $\{A, B, C, D, E\}$ – with nobody in common. Thus $v = 4$, and stability is guaranteed in two dimensions, while disorder (or the lack of equilibrium) can occur in three dimensions. As indicated in the text, chaos can occur, but it requires four dimensions. Note that in chapter 1, I used the term "weak autocrat" for the United States president. The distinction between the king and president resides in the federal nature of the U.S.

overwhelm Charles I showed that it could be decisive, although at great cost. Events after 1649 indicate that without a semi-collegium, Parliamentary behavior was indecisive or chaotic. Oliver Cromwell, as Lord Protector, made clear the danger of autocracy. The constitutional challenge that had to be faced after the Restoration of Charles II in 1660 was how to avoid the twin dangers of autocracy and chaos. I develop the argument of North and Weingast (1989) that the "Glorious Revolution" of 1688 formalized the structure of the apex game, but that political equilibrium was not attained until about 1721. What I call Walopole's *Whig equilibrium* was sustained for a long period of Whig dominance, and indeed endured until at least the end of the Napoleonic wars in 1815. In fact, this fundamental equilibrium was maintained until the repeal of the Corn Laws in 1846.

The maintenance of this equilibrium enabled Britain to establish its commercial empire and ushered in the industrial revolution. In turn, the basis of Britain's increasing military power in this political equilibrium provided the context for the constitutional argument in the United States from 1787 on.

2.6 SOCIAL CHOICE IN BRITAIN: 1625–1776

I now provide a brief interpretation of British constitutional developments from 1625 on, attempting to use the social choice ideas just introduced. There is general acknowledgment that the fiscal problems of Charles I were crucial for the constitutional changes that occurred in the seventeenth century. However, what triggered the changes to come had partly to do with Charles's apparent threat against Scotland.

As Davies has observed, Charles I "incensed the nobility (of Scotland) by the famous Act of Revocation (1625), which re-annexed all the church and crown lands that had been alienated since 1542" (Davies, 1959: 86). Charles followed this up in 1637 by attempting to force a Book of Common Prayer on Scotland. The subscribers to the Covenant "swore to resist to the death these . . . innovations which were unwarranted by the word of God, contrary to the Reformation and to acts of parliament, and tending to the re-establishment of popery and tyranny" (Davies, 1959: 88).

To raise an army to put down what he saw as rebellion, Charles called Parliament in 1640. Just as in France in 1789, so in England in 1640 this Parliament, under the leadership of Pym, refused to vote the required subsidies. Charles dissolved Parliament on May 5, 1640.

Charles's attempts to raise money from the city of London, and then from the Kings of Spain and France, proved fruitless. The success of the Scots in their invasion caused the great peers Essex and Warwick to demand the recall of Parliament, and this Long Parliament first met in November 1640. Instead of playing on the hostility between Lords and Commons, Charles attempted to impeach five members of the Commons for encouraging a foreign (Scots) army to invade England. The Lords refused these articles when they were presented, and instead Charles entered the Commons with his supporters. The House of Commons, however, was uncowed.

The first Civil War concluded with Charles's surrender to the Scots in 1646. The second Civil War of 1646–8 ended with his trial and beheading, on January 30, 1649. Many causes, including both religious conflict and disagreement over fiscal arrangements, have been proposed for the Civil War. In fact, disagreements over land (the Scottish annexation), capital (debts and finance), and labor (religion), and the existence of multiple and overlapping factional interests suggest that the politics of England and Scotland were truly chaotic in the 1640s.

As commander of the New Model Army, Oliver Cromwell gradually took on the role of autocrat. His defeat of a Scottish army at Preston in August 1648 was followed by his invasion of Ireland in August 1649, at the head of an army of twelve thousand. The prize was land, for after defeating the Irish, two thirds of the land of Ireland changed ownership.

After the execution of Charles I, the Scottish aristocracy proclaimed his son as Charles II, King of Great Britain, France, and Ireland, but also demanded that he accept the Covenant. A Scottish army was later destroyed at Dunbar by Cromwell. It is hardly surprising that Hobbes was impelled to argue in *Leviathan* (1651) for the necessity of an autocrat, or sovereign, to impose peace. The remnant of the Long Parliament, the Rump, refused to dissolve itself, and in 1654 Cromwell entered the Commons and cleared the House. A Nominated Parliament of 140 representatives drew up a written constitution, the Instrument of Government, which declared the Lord Protector (Cromwell) to be the head of the executive.

The lessons from this political experiment were threefold. The first, Hobbesian, lesson was that a powerful veto player (or sovereign) such as Cromwell, was perhaps necessary to prevent factional chaos. Second, this sovereign must be capable of prosecuting necessary wars. In Cromwell's case, these were in Ireland, Scotland, and in Europe against the Dutch and Spain. Third, because the wars were extremely expensive, some method of limiting the sovereign's appetite for war had to be devised. Due to

Cromwell, two further innovations were made which greatly affected the future development of the empire. To counter Dutch trade dominance, the first of the Navigation Acts was passed in October 1651. This forbade the importation of goods into Britain from Asia, Africa, and the Americas, except in British ships. Cromwell also began the development of a powerful navy; forty heavily armored ships were built from 1649 to 1651 (Baugh, 1994).

While Cromwell's innovations proved important, his risk taking and the attendant high taxation exhausted the country. After Cromwell's death in September 1658, his son Richard became Protector, but his inability to command respect made chaos again a possibility. The newly elected Parliament immediately arranged for the restoration of the Stuart line by Charles II in 1660. In a sense, the political game had changed. The lesson of the Civil War was that the King could be defeated by a unified Parliament, together with its allies. On the other hand, the King, together with his Royalist allies and the landed elite could also win. As noted above, such an apex game has a solution involving compromise between the King and Parliament. Notice that the King and his allies do not quite form a collegium, as there is an opposing winning coalition—a united Parliament. Nonetheless, the King's group belongs to almost every winning coalition. I have used the term *semi-collegium* to refer to the power of the King's group.

Part of the resulting "equilibrium" after 1660 involved fixing the King's annual income at 1,200,000 sterling and making arrangements to cover the debts incurred by Charles I. The substantial debts of Cromwell were repudiated. Debts of 500,000 sterling, associated with the navy, were not, however, settled. Charles II made no attempt to offer a threat to Parliament on what I have termed the *labor* axis—religion—and the compromise held until his death in 1685. His brother, James II, was less risk averse, and the Declaration of Indulgence of May 1688, seemingly pro-Catholic, brought the religious threat to bear. Parliament was dissolved by the King in July 1687, and James began building an army of 16,000 in Ireland. The birth of an heir in June 1688, and the suspicion that he would be christened Catholic, was the final straw. Parliament offered the "joint" crown to Mary, James's daughter, and her husband William of Orange. James fled and died in France in 1701.

The new contract underlying this "Glorious Revolution" between the joint sovereigns and Parliament reflected the lessons that had been learned in the previous fifty odd years. In essence, William acted as agent for Parliament, in the prosecution of wars in Ireland and then against France.

As a precaution against autocracy, the Declaration of Rights declared it illegal to maintain a standing army in time of peace. In return, Parliament, in a sense, pledged to provide the resources for the sovereign through the founding of the Bank of England in 1694. Although North and Weingast (1989) suggest this founding was a device to ensure fiscal "credible commitment" it was not unanimously approved. As Clark (1956: 177) noted many years ago, some Whigs feared that the Bank would increase the degree of autocracy of the sovereign. This likelihood was averted by requiring Parliamentary approval before any loans were provided to the crown. Landed Tory interests also opposed it because of the implied obligation that the monied interests would support the revolutionary settlement. Stasavage (2002, 2003) has also commented on the heterogeneous preferences in Parliament and asked why the contract implicit in the settlement and founding of the Bank was binding.

The main point made by Stasavage is that the predominant interests in Parliament were landed. It is therefore not obvious why they would ally with monied interests in a willingness to guarantee the increasing debt. In essence, he suggests that the Tories were landed interests who opposed both taxation and religious tolerance. According to Stasavage, the Whigs, both landed and monied, formed a coalition in support of religious tolerance. Landed Whig interests, by this theory, accepted taxation, which benefited monied interests, as a *quid pro quo* for their support. This implied two dimensionality (capital and religion) is plausible. However, rather than religious tolerance, it would seem more reasonable that war, against France, was the common interest of the Whigs. Approximately 10 percent to 15 percent of the Commons were of the monied interests, creditors essentially holding shares in the Bank of England.[6] For convenience we could describe those creditors as having a "hard money" preference on the capital axis. A commitment to safeguard this debt by eschewing repudiation depended on the willingness of the landed interests to accept taxation. Because the purpose of the debt was war, a bargain could be struck between those of the landed and monied interests who supported Whig prosecution of this war. And because war certainly had a religious connotation, and was regarded generally as involving civil liberty, we can denote preferences in this regard to be on the labor axis.[7]

---

[6] Stasavage cites historical evidence that the "broader mercantile community in Parliament after 1715 was overwhelming Whig" (Stasavage, 2003: 157).

[7] Regarding the third labor axis as religious, Stasavage notes that most dissenters (non–Church of England) voted with the Whigs. However, dissenters would naturally fear

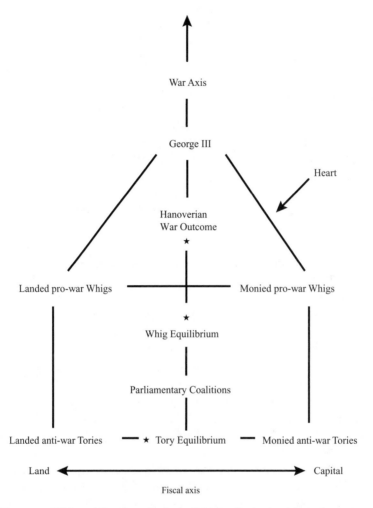

Figure 2.3. Whig and Tory bargains in the British polity in the eighteenth century.

As long as the Whigs held a majority, then there was a natural pro-war equilibrium in this "policy space." I denote this point as the "Whig equilibrium" in Figure 2.3.

By the end of the War of Spanish Succession, in 1713, debt had increased from the 17 million sterling of 1697 to 36 million sterling (Brewer,

the dominance of Catholic France and be more willing to engage in war. In contrast, many Tories (such as Henry St. John, Viscount Bolingbroke, the minister under Queen Anne), had strong Stuart allegiances and might even be Jacobite (favoring James's son, Edward, for monarch after 1714). In general, then, Tories might dislike the possibility of war with France. Such cleavages are reflected in the positioning of the various factions in Figure 2.3.

1988: 30). War weariness brought a Tory majority in the election of October 1710. Stasavage notes that interest rates on long-term government debt jumped from 6 percent to 10 percent after the election, resulting from the increased probability of default.[8] The creation of the South Sea Company in 1711 also reflected an attempt to force an involuntary reorganization of government debt. Queen Anne, during her reign (1702–14), had supported Tory preference for peace. Her ability to affect the composition of cabinets gave her the power to modify the political equilibrium. A probable outcome in such a situation is labeled the "Tory equilibrium" in Figure 2.3. After her death, the Hanoverian dynasty, which was more aggressive against France, led to a period of Whig dominance.

However, the single Whig party eventually broke up into multiple factions. Without the king to act as a semi-collegium (and thus essential to nearly every winning factional coalition) it is probable that the polity would have descended into chaos. British and some American commentators in the eighteenth century followed Montesquieu (1748) in arguing that the combination of King, Lords, and Commons (representing monarchy, aristocracy, and democracy) formed a perfect constitution, combining the best elements of each institution. The "balance" idea came originally from Greek political theory. It is worth noting that eighteenth century commentators might have read the history of Polybius on the Punic Wars between Rome and Carthage 264 BC to 146 BC. Rome's eventual success was attributed to the balance of monarchy (the consuls), aristocracy (the Senate) and democracy (the Popular Assemblies; see Goldsworthy, 2000, for discussion). Commentators would also have been aware of Montesquieu's argument that factionalism was an inherent feature of the Roman polity, but that it was the great increase in Rome's domain that led to Rome's collapse (Montesquieu, 1734; note that Kennedy's imperial argument is not dissimilar from Montesquieu's).

It was this constitutional theory, mentioned by Hamilton, that provided the rationale for the balance of power between President, Senate, and House after the Constitutional ratification in the United States in 1787–8.

In fact, Montesquieu's balance theory owed much to the influence of Viscount Bolingbroke, in exile in France after the Hanoverian, George I, had come to the throne of the United Kingdom. Kramnick (1992 [1968])

---

[8] The land tax, previously 20 percent or 4 shillings in the pound, was cut to 10 percent. As discussed in Brewer (1988), this required an increase in the proportion of government revenue raised by customs and excise.

has used the term "the politics of nostalgia" to describe Bolingbroke's denunciation of the change in the nature of the political economic equilibrium after the death of Anne in 1714. Since Bolingbroke's argument also impressed Thomas Jefferson later in the 1790s (Kramnick, 1990), I offer an interpretation of its logic in terms of Figure 2.3.

As Figure 2.3 suggests, the Tories in Britain in the early eighteenth century were less inclined to prosecute war with France, not just because of "Jacobite" sympathies, but because of the cost and the seeming necessity of the land tax. During the War of Spanish Succession (1702–13), escalating debt and interest payments had led to the creation of a stock company—the South Sea Company. Essentially the company would borrow from commercial interests, lend to the government, and cover interest with earnings from the Asiento concession trade with the Spanish colonies of the Caribbean.

After the Hanoverian succession and the creation of the Whig majority, the South Sea Company absorbed a greater share of government debt. In January, 1720, Sunderland, first lord of the treasury, proposed that the South Sea Company take over 30 million of the 51 million sterling of government debt. The resulting share bubble collapsed in September 1720.

Robert Walpole stabilized confidence in the company by a transfer of South Sea stock to the Bank of England and in April 1721 became both Chancellor of the Exchequer and First Lord of the Treasury—"the first prime minister in fact if not in name" (Williams, 1960: 179).

Walpole remained Chancellor until February 1742. The period of speculation in 1720 was seen by Bolingbroke to herald the end of the noble constitution of England and the beginning of crass commercialism. Indeed Bolingbroke's fulmination against commercialism provided ammunition to Thomas Jefferson when he decried similar speculations in the United States in July 1791 when Hamilton's First Bank of America opened. Bolingbroke was correct to see the creation of the stable political economic equilibrium in 1721 as the foundation of Britain's commercial empire, but he did not understand the reason for its stability. The danger for Walpole in maintaining this equilibrium was that landed interests, whether Whig or Tory, would repudiate the rapidly increasing debt of the government. Walpole dealt with this problem by changing the composition of government revenue and by considerably increasing the amount raised by customs and excise. It is not entirely accurate to call this situation an equilibrium as this suggests immobility. Instead I conceive of it as a balance between differing political interests, stabilized by the preferences of the monarch. The resulting set of outcomes is denoted "Heart" in Figure 2.3.

I contend that this device contributed to the stability of the political heart and had a profound effect on Britain's economic growth. Because Britain's imports were primarily foodstuffs and raw materials which were relatively intensive in the factor of land, the restraint exercised on these imports by the tariff had the effect of increasing the price of land, relative to labor and capital (both of which were relatively abundant). It is compatible with Rogowski's (1989) analysis that landed interests, whether Whig or Tory, would benefit from this contract initiated by Walpole. Moreover, because land became so valuable, it made sense to increase capital investments in agriculture, thereby increasing productivity. This in turn facilitated greater food production and made possible a rapid increase in population. Because of greater intensity of the use of the factors of capital and land in food production, labor might have been used less intensively. Indeed there is some evidence that real agriculture wages declined in this period.[9]

The increased value of the land could thus offset the tax on land, which in turn was needed to ensure the credibility of payment of interest on government debt. Thus the safety of investment by the monied or commercial interests in the government was guaranteed. By this method, Walpole secured the stability of the contact between landed and monied interests. This equilibrium was made even easier to maintain because Walpole was able to sustain peace with France and Spain until October 1739. Obliged by popular sentiment to declare war, Walpole finally resigned in 1742.

To maintain this equilibrium from 1721 to 1739 Walpole constantly bargained with the various factions of the Whig ascendancy (Namier, 1957; Brewer, 1976), bringing "placemen" and "stockjobbers" into the Commons. Belief that these tactics corrupted the constitution was held by many writers in addition to Bolingbroke. Sloan, for example, quotes from Tobias Smollett's *History of England* that

the Whigs ... leaned for support on those who were enemies to the church and monarchy, on the bank, and the monied interest ... and prepared the minds of man for slavery and corruption ... They multiplied places and pensions, to increase the number of their dependents.

(Sloan, 2001: 94)

[9] See Allen (1988) and Crafts (1994). Note also that the "enclosures" of the Commons in the eighteenth century may have been a further consequence. Porter has observed that the "capitalist farm and the common fields ... became parables of industry and idleness respectively" (Porter, 2000: 309).

However, by increasing government revenue though the tariff, and indirectly protecting land, Walpole reduced government debt from about 55 million sterling (with interest of 3.3 million) in 1721 to 47 million (and interest of 2 million) in 1739 (Sloan, 2001: 301).

From the point of view of social choice theory, Walpole acted essentially as a semi-collegium. Even though politics seemed highly factionalized and disordered, the corruption that Bolingbroke and Smollett decried preserved the Whig equilibrium. The war in 1739 suggests that sentiment among the Whigs had moved up the war axis (as represented in Figure 2.3).

From 1739 to 1784 (through three wars against the French, and lastly against the American colonies), British government debt rose to 243 million. This increase was primarily due to military expenditure in the American war, approximately 28 million in 1783 (Brewer, 1988: 30–9). The land tax brought in only 20 percent of revenue, just over 2 million in 1783.

Because the principal source of revenue was customs and excise, this necessitated the creation of an extensive fiscal bureaucracy (approximately 7,500 employees in 1770). Ferguson (2001) comments that this bureaucracy was roughly one person in 1,300. In France and Prussia, generally considered highly centralized states, the comparable ratios were one in 4,100 and one in 38,000, respectively.

After Walpole, the general structure of the Whig equilibrium was maintained, but factionalism became quite pronounced. I suggest that some semblance of coherence was maintained because the Hanoverian monarch, and particularly George III after 1760, came to play the role of semi-collegium. However, because of the degree of heterogeneity in the House of Commons and the House of Lords, actual policy could lie within a larger domain, the set of outcomes denoted the Heart in Figure 2.3.[10]

[10] Suppose that I am correct in assuming the monarch acted as a semi-collegium, so that the Nakamura number of the "constitutional game" in Britain was four. As note 5 asserts, chaos cannot occur if there are at most two dimensions of policy. Although Figure 2.3 presents just two dimensions – a land/labor axis and the war axis – in fact, land and capital represent two distinct dimensions. If there were indeed three dimensions of policy, then there need not be an equilibrium as such. Instead, the particular outcome would depend on bargains between the monarch and powerful political factions. The "Heart" is intended to represent the domain within which these bargains will reside (see Schofield, 1999b for the definition). The policy of the British government toward the Colonies from 1763 to 1776 could indeed be called inconsistent, rather than completely chaotic.

A number of different inferences could be drawn, and were indeed drawn by Hamilton, Madison, and Jefferson, from this British constitutional experience. Hamilton inferred that a strong sovereign, or semi-collegium, was necessary in order to overcome factionalism. Jefferson was also acutely aware of the corruption that had attended the maintenance of the Whig equilibrium and the evolution of Britain's commercial empire. Moreover, he understood that Britain's expanding population required the continual importation of food, primarily from the American colonies. Control of trade, and the agricultural land in North America, was therefore a probable cause of conflict between Britain and its Atlantic colonies. It would have been in Britain's interest to control the price of imported foodstuff, and, indirectly therefore, the price of land in North America. Moreover, the customs and excise taxes levied in Britain were predominantly regressive in nature, effectively taxing the poor rather than the rich. This necessitated a degree of relative disenfranchisement, and possibly accounts for the emphasis on virtual rather than direct representation (Beer, 1993: 6). For these reasons the political economic equilibrium put in place in the United States after Jefferson's election in 1800 was very different from the British one. I contend that this U.S. equilibrium instituted an agrarian empire.

2.7   THE AGRARIAN EMPIRE IN NORTH AMERICA

Chapter 3 makes the argument that the basis of the conflict between Britain and its North American colonies from 1774 to 1783 was land. After gaining Quebec and the entire region east of the Mississippi from France during the Seven Years War (1756–63), Britain had to contend with a fierce Indian revolt, often called "Pontiac's War." This was caused by the flow of settlers into the Ohio Valley. George Washington himself had crossed the Cumberland Gap, had come into violent conflict with French soldiers, and precipitated the war of 1756. Whether to avoid further conflicts, or to defend Indian rights, the British attempted to restrict colonial settlement by the Proclamation Act (1763) and then by the Quebec Act (1774). This apparent act of tyranny infuriated the American elite, most notably Franklin and Washington. In line with Riker's (1964) theory of the link between threat and constitutional change, Franklin negotiated with the French for aid against the British. An argument presented in Chapter 3 suggests that without French aid, revolution would have failed. Promise of aid led to the Declaration of Independence in July 1776. Indeed, French money, together with the role of the French Fleet and an army of 7,000 was crucial in the success of American arms against Cornwallis in 1781 at Yorktown.

The war left the United States highly indebted. Beard (1913) mentions a figure of 50 million dollars (a fairly substantial figure when compared with the debts of Britain and France of 1 billion dollars and 600 million dollars, respectively in 1784). Beard sees the ratification debates of 1787 to 1788 as an argument over how to deal with this debt, with Hamilton, and the Federalists, essentially proposing a hard-money principle on the capital axis. However, the "land" axis was also important. As Riker (1964) noted, the Spanish posed a threat on the Mississippi because of their control of the Louisiana Territory and their declared intention to block American exports through New Orleans. James Madison feared this threat would destroy the fragile confederation of states, and it was this fear that provided the federalist preference for union in 1787. However, the extended domain of the proposed union implied, by Montesquieu's thesis on large republics, that factional[11] collapse would occur. In a brilliant argument, first in "Vices of the Political System of the United States" in April 1787, and later in *Federalist X* (November 22, 1787), Madison reversed Montesquieu's argument. Assuming that factions are generated by common interests, he proposed that "the inconveniences of . . . States contrary to prevailing Theory are in proportion not to the extent, but to the narrowness of their limits" (Rakove, 1999: 79).

The heterogeneity of the extended Republic could then lead to reasoned social choice. Chapter 3 suggests that this argument by Madison is similar in logic to Condorcet's Jury theorem of 1785.

Madison's additional argument in *Federalist LI* was based on the theory of balance of power, as derived from the British constitutional ideas mentioned above. However, because the proposed constitution was federal in nature, bargaining between the central government and the states would be more complicated than in Britain's centralized system. We can, perhaps, modify Figure 2.3 to study social choice in such a federal system. First of all, note that there must be at least two dimensions of policy, land and capital. The "Hamiltonian" Federalists were concerned to put in place a hard-money policy on the capital axis, so as to cope with debt, and prepare the way for economic development. Opening up the West to settlement would, however, be made easier with an easy credit policy.

---

[11] I interpret "factionalism" to mean the complete breakdown of any regularity to government policy making, not the kind of inconsistency just mentioned.

During the constitutional debates of 1787 and the Ratification of 1788, the argument revolved around differing interests of creditors and debtors (as Beard has suggested), but also the necessity of having a centralized authority to deal with foreign threats and with preventing the chaos of factionalism. Madison's argument in *Federalist X* suggests that the differences in the House, Senate and President, together with the system of cross-vetoes, would endow the polity with stability. House Representatives, because of the small size of their constituencies, might be expected to represent local interests. In contrast, the larger domain of interest of the voters in each state would imply, by Madison's heterogeneity argument, that each Senator would encapsulate no particular interest, but rather the concept of the public good appropriate to the state. Finally, the President, chosen by majority rule from the electors of all states, would represent some concept of the public good appropriate for the entire enfranchised electorate. Because Congress could exercise a two-thirds veto against the president, this implied that the President, together with over one-third of both Houses, was collegial in those areas of policy controlled by the Federal Government. Although this constitutional structure was intended to avoid factionalism, it was not originally intended to deal with party conflict.

In fact, the interests of capital and land became extremely divided in the United States, because of Hamilton's attempt to recreate the Whig equilibrium of the 1720s in Britain. To stabilize and fund the debt, Hamilton proposed founding the Bank of the United States, backing it with receipts from customs. However, unlike Britain, America's imports were primarily manufactured goods. In terms of Rogowski's analysis, such a tariff would support the relative price of the scarce factor—capital—more intensively used in the production of these goods. Increasing the relative price of the scarce factor is equivalent to reducing the relative price of the abundant factor—land. Although Jefferson focused on the corruption attending the attempt to create the bank, his other writings make it clear that he was aware of the indirect effects of the tariff (I shall pursue this further in Chapter 4).

In winning the elections of 1800 and 1804, Jefferson effectively constructed a coalition of the land, the Republicans, against the commercial or mercantile interests of the Federalists. Because the Federalists were keenly aware of the advantages of trade with Britain, the two parties came to have distinct preferences on the land/capital axis as well as differing "international interests" in the long Napoleonic War between Britain and France. The United States did, of course, eventually engage in war with Britain from 1812 to 1815, and by necessity had to institute a tariff to finance the considerable government debt that ensued. Nevertheless the landed coalition put in place by Jefferson from 1801 to 1808 proved fairly stable until the 1840s.

The basis for the Jefferson equilibrium was a compromise between landed labor (small farmers in the West) and southern slave-owning landed interests, at the expense, perhaps, of the commercial interests of the Northeast, the Federalists, or the Whigs. The U.S. economy remained focused primarily on raw material and food exports.[12] As long as slave interests did not threaten free labor, then the two parties, Whigs and Democrats, had an intersectional (or north and south) constituency. Part of the logic of the predominantly agrarian Democrat party was the expansion of this agrarian empire by conquest, first of the Floridas and then of Spanish (or Mexican) domains in the West.

As Riker (1982) has discussed, maintenance of the Democratic coalition became more difficult, particularly as free labor and slave interests came in conflict in the West. Moreover, the commercial interests of the Northeast found that the dominance of the Democracy restricted economic growth. Chapter 5 argues that the probable consequences of the Dred Scott decision by the Supreme Court in 1857, and the debates of Stephen Douglas and Abraham Lincoln in 1858, dramatized the threat against free labor.

The compromise over slavery, inherent in the constitutional bargain of 1787, began to collapse, and the third dimension, the labor axis, became increasingly important. Southern slavery interests followed Calhoun in arguing that an anti-slavery permanent (and hence tyrannical) majority had formed. This violated the fundamental logic of *Federalist X* and legitimated secession. In his inaugural speech of March 1861, Lincoln asserted that the primary document of Union was the Declaration of Independence, and this made secession illegitimate. Lincoln also rejected the "Crittenden" compromise, which would have granted all territory south of 36° 30′ to the slave interests. This seemingly made the Civil War inevitable.[13]

---

[12] Britain became heavily dependant on food supplies from the United States (in order to feed its growing population) as well as cotton imports to maintain its textile industry. In a sense, Britain and the United States maintained a symbiotic economic relationship until the aftermath of the Civil War.

[13] The social choice analysis presented above is given in terms of "winning," vetoes, etc., and is not strictly applicable to a situation of war. Nonetheless, the general logic is valid. To maintain peace in the "three-dimensional space" required a compromise

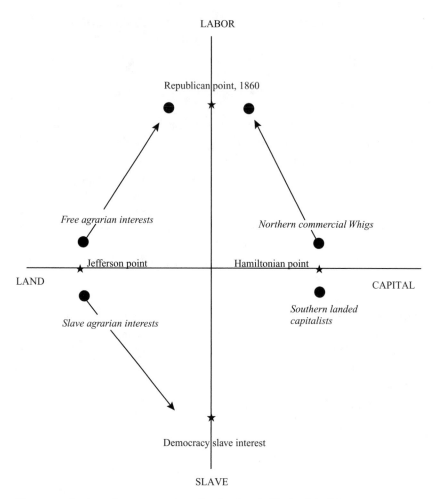

LABOR

Republican point, 1860

Free agrarian interests

Northern commercial Whigs

Jefferson point

Hamiltonian point

LAND

CAPITAL

Slave agrarian interests

*Southern landed
capitalists*

Democracy slave interest

SLAVE

Figure 2.4. A schematic representation of land and capital in the United States, 1800–1860.

Figure 2.4 presents a schematic representation of the transformation from the politics generated on the land/capital axis, circa 1800, to the much more complex situation of 1860. The purpose of the figure is to show how the Republican/Federalist or Democrat/Whig splits were a consequence of the suppression of the labor/slave axis. The threat from the South transformed the underlying policy space, so that the intersection

between North and South. As discussed in Chapter 5, Lincoln himself put a figure of "two thousand million dollars" on the sum required to compensate the South for the emancipation of slaves. Such a bargain was therefore impossible.

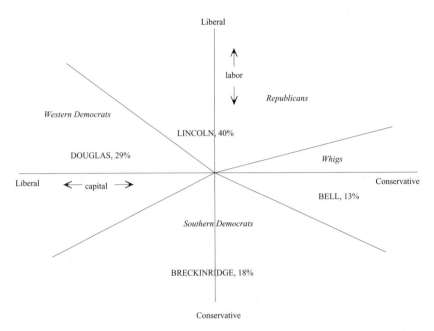

Figure 2.5. A schematic representation of the election of 1860 in a two-dimensional policy space.

compromises collapsed. As Chapter 5 discusses in more detail, the 1860 election involved four presidential competitors—Lincoln, Bell, Breckinridge, and Douglas. The point is made in chapter 5 that Lincoln, an extreme risk taker, resolved the constitutional quandary over slavery. Figure 2.5 provides an illustration of the location of Presidential candidates in the election of 1860.

Chapter 6 argues that, after the Civil War, and the resolution of the slave dilemma, the policy space collapsed. The problem of the balance between capital and land once again became paramount. The growth of capitalism and manufacturing capability in the 1890s contributed to the success of the hard-money Republican, McKinley, against his populist Democrat challenger, William Jennings Bryan. In the 1930s, with the Depression, the labor axis again became relevant. Over the period from Roosevelt in the 1930s until Johnson in the 1960s, Democratic presidential candidates increasingly adopted policy positions that were liberal on both the capital and labor axes. Simultaneously, Republican presidential candidates adopted policy positions that were conservative on both axes.

While it is common to assume that there is a single axis ("left"–"right") in U.S. politics, this assumption seems to be valid only in particular instances in U.S. history. In fact, the more general case may well be that there are three distinct axes—land, capital, and labor. At the present time (December, 2005), land, interpreted in terms of defense of the nation, is clearly a separate issue. Indeed, there are already pronounced conflicts between concerns over civil rights (on the labor axis) and the need to ensure surveillance and defense.

If this argument is correct, then theoretical inferences about political convergence to an electoral center (Hotelling, 1929; Downs, 1957) appear completely invalid. There is an additional point, originally made by Duverger (1954). Plurality rule (unlike proportional representation) forces political parties to construct coalitions of differing interests. This can be seen particularly in the election of 1860, where Lincoln constructed a coalition of western agrarian interests and eastern commercial interests. Because of the plurality rule of the electoral college, only 40 percent of the voting population was sufficient to ensure victory. This suggests that when constitutional quandaries beset the society, they can only be resolved by the acts of political risk takers. In fact, the stronger hypothesis is that plurality rule itself engenders risk taking to face fundamental democratic dilemmas.

2.8 THE END OF EMPIRE IN BRITAIN

The same characteristic may hold true within the British parliamentary system as well. To see this, consider Figure 2.6. I have suggested that the third axis in British politics involved war, at least in the period until the end of the Napoleonic conflict in 1815. Protection of land, via the tariff, was the key element in the maintenance of the Whig equilibrium. However, after 1815, Britain's commercial empire grew apace, and it became increasingly difficult to maintain the tariff against Whig interests. The Irish famine, and the resulting concern of both Robert Peel and the Duke of Wellington (in the Commons and the Lords) over civil unrest led to the repeal of the Corn Laws (in May 1846). However, protection (particularly with regard to wine from France) and high excise duties on alcohol were both maintained. Nye (1991, 1992, 2006) contends that these were calculated to maximize government revenue. After Peel's betrayal of his party, the Tories (or Conservatives) found it difficult to secure a majority against the Whig (or Liberal) free traders. In 1867, the Conservative's master tactician, Benjamin Disraeli, saw that the interest of land could be

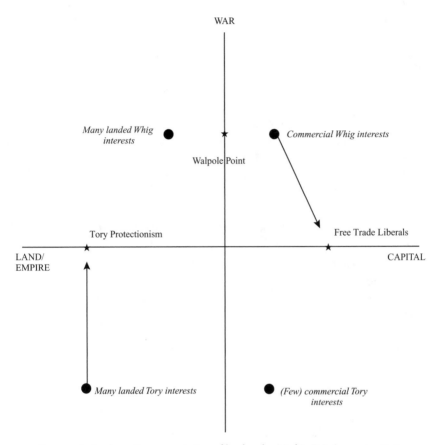

Figure 2.6. A schematic representation of land and capital in Britain, 1720–1846.

interpreted as "Empire," and that this would appeal to a large proportion of the British population. By the Reform Act of 1867, Disraeli completely out-maneuvered the Liberal party leader, Gladstone, and almost doubled the enfranchised population (Woodward, 1962: 187). In the election of 1874, the Conservatives gained 352 seats to the Liberals 242 (McLean, 2002: 92). By this time, the "war" axis of 1720 to 1815 had become transformed into a religious axis. From 1886 there were two Irish factions, one Catholic and the other Liberal Unionist. The alliance of these factions with the Conservative or Liberal parties made coalition politics very difficult until the Anglo-Irish Treaty of 1921 (McLean, 2002, ch. 7).

The rhetoric of empire generally served the Conservative Party well until 1906. In the early 1900's, Joseph Chamberlain tried to integrate the issues of protection and empire, by his strategy of "Tariff

Reform"—"without preferential tariffs you will not keep the Empire" (McLean, 2002: 122). While empire appealed to voters, tariffs did not. The Conservative vote dropped from 50 percent in 1900 to 43 percent in 1906, and the Parliamentary seat share from 60 percent to 23 percent. At the same time, of course, electoral reform and the increasing importance of the labor axis led to the formation of the Labour Party (with 6 percent of the vote and 5 percent of the seats in 1906; McLean, 2002: 88). Over the decades of the twentieth century, the Conservatives kept their pro-empire position, but moved to a pro-capital position, squeezing the Liberal Party against Labour. Again, it is common to assume that British politics is entirely determined by a labor/capital axis, with the Labour Party at one end and the Conservative Party at the other.

However, empire has always been a component of the Conservative Party rhetoric. In fact, the move by the Conservatives to a pro-capital position may have only occurred during the prime ministerial terms of Margaret Thatcher after 1979. Privatization of national industries and the control of trade unions can, after all, be interpreted as pro-capital. Her appeal to nationalism did prove electorally useful. However, after Thatcher, the Conservatives have found that empire or "nationalism," when invoked against the EU, is difficult to use as an electoral tactic. In 1997, the Conservatives took 31.4 percent of the popular vote (and 25 percent of the seats) against Labour's 44.4 percent of the vote (and 63.6 percent of the seats). In 2001, these figures were very little changed. Even in the election of May 2005 (after Blair, by his actions on Iraq, caused some proportion of the electorate to regard him with distrust), the Labour Party vote share was still over 35 percent, while the Conservatives were only able to raise their vote share to about 31 percent.

To show the relevance of the two dimensions (capital and nationalism) in British politics, Figure 2.7 shows voter and party positions in Britain in 1997. Factor analysis of survey responses clearly showed two dimensions, with two dense electoral domains—one pro-Europe, and the other, larger one, fairly anti-Europe. Party positions were obtained from a survey of Members of Parliament. Liberals were centrist economically and very pro-Europe. The single Scottish Nationalist Party (SNP) member was much less pro-Europe. Ulster Unionists (like Liberal Unionists in the past) were more pro-labor than Conservatives, but basically opposed to European union.

The Duverger (1954) hypothesis, that two parties tend to dominate under single member districts and plurality, is clearly not entirely valid in the

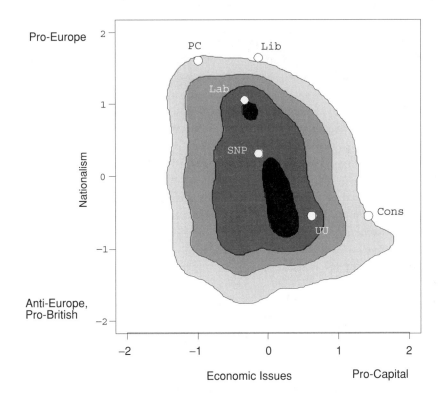

Key: Lab = Labour, Cons = Conservative, Lib = Liberal and Social Democrat, UU = Ulster Unionist, SNP = Scottish Nationalist, PC= Plaid Cymru.

Figure 2.7. Estimated voter distribution and party positions in Britain, 1997.
Source: Adapted from Schofield and Sened, 2006.

British case. There is, however, a more general point to be made on the basis of this thumbnail sketch of British politics. Because there are generally at least two axes of policy, plurality electoral rules force parties to constantly adapt their position in response both to internal quandaries (e.g., reform, the Irish problem) and external ones (e.g., trade competition, war, European union). Downsian convergence does not occur. Instead, politics seem to exhibit a dynamic stability, where major policy shifts are engineered by risk-preferring politicians (e.g., Peel, Disraeli, Chamberlain, Lloyd George, Churchill, Thatcher). Riker (1986) coined the term *heresthetic* for the logic of these policy shifts. My inference from both United States and British political history suggests that it is plurality rule itself, in both presidential and parliamentary systems, that engenders such risk-raking heresthetic. It is possible, in fact, that plurality rule itself creates dynamic stability and leads to "fit" political choices.

The converse hypothesis is that PR systems lead to compromise, and limit heresthetic and risk taking. This cannot, of course, be universally valid, because Hitler rose to power under PR (Riker, 1953: 115; Evans, 2003: 259). However, it is possible to understand this latter phenomenon as a response to extreme social uncertainty in the context of the Depression. This is one of the topics of Chapter 7.

This suggestion about the way democracy functions is, of course, consistent with, but a development of, Condorcet's so-called Jury Theorem (Condorcet, 1785) and is a persistent theme of this book. Democracy, if well constructed, leads neither to chaos nor equilibrium, but to constant transformation, a kind of "structural stability." This very general notion is the topic of Chapter 8.

2.9 CONCLUDING REMARKS

In many respects Madison was the architect of change who propounded the theoretical principles of the U.S. Constitution. These derived from both the Scottish and French Enlightenments as represented by David Hume, Adam Smith, and Condorcet.[14] It is sometimes argued that the two Madisonian principles of heterogeneity (in *Federalist X*) and balance of power (in *"Federalist LI"*) are contradictory (Dahl, 1956, 1998, 2001; McLean, 2003). From a social choice perspective, however, the two principles are complementary. The essence of the Madisonian scheme at the federal level is that it involves three parallel methods of aggregating preference. First, consider presidential elections. Initially, the electoral college was chosen by state legislatures. Today, the electoral college is determined by popular vote, but based on a system of weighting states. Generally, states with low populations are advantaged, and this can lead to anomalous outcomes, as in 2000. In general, however, the plurality nature of

---

[14] Although the influence of the Enlightenment on the ideas of Hamilton, Jefferson and Madison has long been recognized (e.g., Commager, 1977), this book emphasizes the specific influence of Condorcet on Madison and Jefferson. Chapter 4 discusses the connection between the Jury Theorem of Condorcet and Madison's arguments in *Federalist X*, and suggests that the Jury Theorem can give a deep justification of democracy. This theme is pursued with the more formal apparatus presented later in Chapter 8.

the election gives a clear winner. The election of Lincoln in 1860 with 40 percent of the popular vote, and 60 percent of the college, is an illustration. Because the context is winner take all, it is intuitively clear that presidential contests may tend to go to risk takers (e.g., Roosevelt, Kennedy, Johnson). As the early discussion suggests, this may be an advantage in situations where war is possible.

In parallel, House and Senate elections aggregate preferences quite differently. Since Senators are fewer in number, one might expect them to be more risk averse than presidents, but more risk taking than representatives. Finally, there are local elections for House and Senate at the state level. This federal structure requires constant bargaining, and may be time consuming, but it would seem to facilitate the flow of information. The key to the Constitution is the semi-collegial characteristic of the President and the balancing of differing risk postures across political institutions. The tentative interpretation offered here is that the Nakamura number is high. This suggests that the polity can generally deal with complex problems except in exceptional circumstances, such as 1860, when extreme heterogeneity destroys the political economic equilibrium.

The constitutional apparatus of the United States can be compared with that of the EU. Because the electoral systems of the member states of the EU are based on PR, it has seemed natural to rely on a weighted voting system in the Council of Ministers. The Nakamura number of this system can be computed (Schofield, 1995). The larger nations, Germany and France, for example, naturally have greater weight than small countries, like Ireland. However, the system is essentially one of multiple vetoes. This can have the effect of delaying decisions. Moreover, the device of rotating the presidency of the EU means that there is no independent semi-collegium.

It is well known that Condorcet relied on his Jury theorem for his justification of a unicameral legislature, whereas Madison followed the British Constitutional theorists in seeing the need for a parallel system of representatives. As I have suggested here, the semi-collegial structure of the British and U.S. polities in the eighteenth and nineteenth centuries led to the stability of their political economic equilibria. In turn, these contributed to the extension of the commercial British empire and the agrarian U.S. empire. In the U.S. case, the violent conflict of the Civil War seemed necessary to shift the Unites States toward a new equilibrium and the creation of a commercial empire. Since Reconstruction, the U.S. polity appears to have exhibited a degree of dynamic stability.

Although the constitutional scheme of the Founders was designed to escape the dangers of risk avoidance, chaos, and autocracy, one wonders about the future of U.S.–EU relations: how can a "hyperpower" such as the United States with a risk-preferring president, negotiate with a risk-averse confederation such as the EU? One purpose of this book is to attempt to understand how the U.S. hyperpower came into being. This may help us decide whether the United State is indeed an "imperial power."

3

Franklin and the War of Independence

3.1 INTRODUCTION*

One way to understand the logic of the Declaration of Independence is to attempt an estimate of the costs and benefits and plausible subjective probabilities associated with various outcomes that could follow from the Declaration. While it is true that a general belief that "taxation without representation is tyranny" gained ground in the colonies in the period after the end of the Seven Years War in 1763, the studies that have been carried out do not appear to give a realistic account of the motivations of the British and American decision makers. In particular, in declaring independence, the members of the Continental Congress expressed a willingness to accept the great costs of war. To simplify greatly, each member of Congress should rationally compute the expected costs of war after such a declaration (say qC, where q is the subjective probability of war, and C the subjective cost) against the expected costs of the status quo (involving the probability that the British intended tyranny, T being the cost of this tyranny). I give a more precise form of this calculation below. Presented in this fashion, it is evident that unless the magnitude of T is very high, then an "expected utility maximizer" would not choose independence. An alternative way of interpreting this decision problem under risk is to regard the absolute value of T as some prize to be gained by the Colonies through a successful prosecution of a Revolutionary War. I argue that avoidance of taxation is simply inadequate as a sufficient prize. In contrast, I emphasize that the British attempted to close the entire

* This chapter is based on "Evolution of the Constitution," *The British Journal of Political Science* 32 (2002): 1–23, by Norman Schofield, with permission of Cambridge University Press. Professor J. A. Pole, Timothy Groseclose, and Iain McLean kindly made a number of very helpful comments on this earlier version of the chapter.

Ohio Valley to settlement, by passing the Quebec Act in 1774. The Ohio Valley can therefore be seen as the prize to the Colonists. Indeed the Act exemplifies British tyranny. This interpretation of the Quebec Act makes intelligible the British actions. The British were themselves in a constitutional quandary over the appropriate resolution of the conflict between the Indian tribes of the Ohio Valley, and the colonial settlers. This conflict had become obvious during the rebellion of many of the tribes, led by Pontiac, from 1763 to 1765.

Chapter 2 briefly mentioned Riker's (1964) argument that constitutional change is induced by threat. From this viewpoint, the magnitude of the prize of the Ohio Valley was a *necessary* cause or inducement toward the creation of an independent federal republic. That is, if the problem over the Ohio Valley had not been created, then there would have been no declaration. This prize of the Ohio Valley was obviously not a *sufficient* cause because with some subjective probability, p, say, the Colonies would lose a war with the British. I argue that any plausible estimation of the probability of success against the British would be too low for an expected utility maximizer to choose independence. However, I present evidence to indicate that word of the promise of French aid reached the Continental Congress prior to July 1776. This information would have the effect of increasing the estimated probability of success. As a consequence, an overwhelming majority of the Continental Congress came to agree that a declaration of independence was rational. This secondary belief in the rationality of such a choice can also be termed a *core belief* held by members of the Continental Congress. By declaring independence, and thus transmitting a signal to the colonial population, a more general core belief in the justification of war was created.

The two instances of the 1776 Declaration and the 1787 Ratification (discussed in the next chapter) appear to pass through a number of similar phases. As regards the Declaration, it is fairly evident that general dissatisfaction with British actions became manifest, but the actual intentions of the British must have been quite uncertain. It is reasonable to call such a situation a *quandary*. After the passing of the Quebec Act, uncertainty over British intentions diminished because the Act itself made these intentions clear. We might interpret the situation in early 1776 as a *dilemma* because expected costs of accepting the status quo and of declaring independence were both high and comparable. The crucial information about French aid transformed the dilemma into a *choice*, associated with a core belief in the rationality of a declaration of independence.

Of course, it should be noted that this choice depended on the decision by the French king, Louis XIV, to promise aid. As I mention later, had Louis paid attention to his Finance Minister, Turgot, no aid would have been provided. This cause was therefore somewhat contingent. However, Benjamin Franklin had developed close contacts with the French court, and, particularly with the Foreign Minister, Vergennes, and it is not unreasonable, therefore, to regard him, in some sense, as the architect of the decision.[1]

In a similar fashion, after 1784, the uncertainty over Spanish intentions generated a quandary over appropriate actions. Once Spanish intentions were declared through the attempt to close the Mississippi, the decision problem became a dilemma. The costs both of accepting the status quo of the Articles of Confederation, and of moving to a closer Union were high, and again perceived to be comparable. As I suggest in the next chapter, Madison's arguments, about the ability of a republic to defend against factionalism, transformed the dilemma into a choice.

These two transformations in the Constitution occurred rapidly. Chapter 5 suggests that the Civil War may have occurred in a similar fashion through a progression from quandary to dilemma to core belief to choice.

These interpretations of constitutional change, while building to an extent on Riker's work, focus on somewhat different features. It is not so much that Franklin and Madison engaged in heresthetic maneuvers in 1776 and 1787. Both had a clear understanding of the nature of the dilemmas facing the American people and acted through diplomacy and argument to transform the beliefs of the Continental Congress and of the Constitutional Convention.

3.2 THE QUANDARY OF THE DECLARATION OF INDEPENDENCE

The previous section suggested that the framework of fast or slow evolution can be used to re-examine the causes of the War of Independence

---

[1] Franklin was in Paris as Minister Plenipotentiary after 1776, and was very successful in working with Vergennes to persuade Louis XVI that the war with Britain could be won. For this reason we may see Franklin not only as the architect of the Declaration of Independence, but the architect of the success of the War of Independence itself. For the diplomatic background see Dull (1985). For Franklin in France see Hardman (2000) and Schiff (2005).

of 1776–83, as well as the origins of the Constitutional Ratification after 1787. As I have noted above, the "cause" of the War can, of course, be framed in terms of the belief that "taxation without representation is tyranny," and recent analyses have argued for the important role of such "constitutional" ideas (see e.g., Rakove, 1996).

However, if we accept the outline presented above on the cause of a belief cascade, then it is necessary to contrast the costs of this tyranny (T) against the costs of war (C), weighed by the subjective probabilities, q, that the British did intend tyranny; and p, that the Americans would lose the war.

A serious problem for understanding the rational basis for the Declaration is that Britain had shown itself, during the Seven Years War (also called the French and Indian War) of 1756–63, to be an extremely powerful military and fiscal state (Anderson, 2000; Anderson and Clayton, 2005). Any reasonable calculation would give high values to p and C. Even if there is some basis for believing that q was high (close to 1.0), but T was low, then revolution would became irrational. Because there were obvious differences of opinion in the Colonies over the rationality of revolution, it is plausible that subjective estimates of T varied in the colonial population. I contend, however, that many of the colonial elite had good reason to believe T was high. Moreover, I argue that T had almost nothing at all to do with taxation. In 1774, Britain passed the Quebec Act, allocating control of the Ohio Valley to British Quebec. Many historians have commented on this Act in terms of British acceptance of French Catholicism. The real effect for the Colonies was, however, noticed by Thomas Paine:

Should affairs be patched up with Britain, and she remain the governing and sovereign power of America ... we shall deprive ourselves of the very means of sinking the debt we have, or may contract. The value of the backlands which some of the provinces are clandestinely deprived of, by the unjust extension of the limits of Canada, valued only at five pounds sterling per hundred acres, amount to upwards of twenty-five millions, Pennsylvania currency; and the quit-rents ... up to two millions yearly.

(Foner, ed., 1995: 49)

Mark Egnal has also argued that

the revolutionary movement was led by an upper-class faction whose passionate commitment to the rise of the New World was evident well before 1763. The changes in property rights implied by the Quebec Act meant that the expectations of many of the colonial elite (including Washington) of wealth from land speculation were dashed.[2]

As a recent biographer of Washington has put it,

[T]he French Canadian fur traders were rewarded by the extension of the provincial borders [of "French" Canada] to the Ohio River, thus wiping out all the land grants not only of Washington, but of the Franklins and other land-hungry speculators.[3]

It is interesting to note that Jefferson's draft constitution for Virginia, completed on June 13, 1776, makes no direct reference to the Quebec Act but does include, in its list of denunciations of George III of Great Britain, the assertion that the King endeavored "to bring on the inhabitants of our frontiers the merciless Indian savages whose known rule of warfare is an undistinguished destruction" (Peterson, ed., 1984: 337).

In the bill of indictment against George III drawn up by Jefferson in late June 1776, there is a direct reference to the Quebec Act, that the King gave his assent

for abolishing the free system of English Laws in a neighboring province, establishing therein an arbitrary government, and enlarging its' [*sic*] boundaries, so as to render it at once an example and fit instrument for introducing the same absolute rule into these states.

(Peterson, ed., 1984: 21)

This phrase was retained in the Declaration of Independence of July 4.

I contend that this cost of tyranny was enormous, and almost counterbalanced the likely costs of war. However, it was also crucial to the rational calculations of the colonial elite that an ally be found. In fact, Louis XVI of France agreed in March 1776, to help fund the Revolution to the extent of ten million livres (more than $1.6 million). This was against the arguments of the French Finance Minister, Turgot.

---

[2] See Egnal (1988: xi), Baack (1998) and Phillips (1999: 18). Baack argues that the fundamental cause of the Revolution was a mercantilist conflict between Britain and the Colonies over extraction of "rents" from the Ohio Valley. From this perspective, the cost, T, of British tyranny to the Colonies was enormous, but the game between Britain and America was zero-sum, so the gain to Britain of this tyranny was also enormous. I suggest later that the game, from the British side, was more complex.

[3] Randall (1997: 264–5). Washington had, of course, been incensed by the earlier Proclamation of 1763. See his letter to Charles Washington (January 31, 1770) in Rhodehamel, ed. (1997: 134–7).

Section 3.3 outlines a "game" played among the American Colonies, Britain, France, and Spain, which underlay the Declaration. In fact, this game is presented from the perspective of the Colonies. Some attempt is also made to analyze the rationality of the British and French decisions. However, questions can be raised about the British and French choices at this point.

First of all, why did Britain pass the Quebec Act, which I argue is the principal cause of the Revolution? I contend that the intention was not primarily mercantilist, but was an attempt to protect the Indian tribes of the Ohio Valley from the settlers. Pontiac's Rebellion in 1763–5 had made the depredations of the settlers on the Indians very clear to the British. The Proclamation of 1763, closing the West, had little effect, and the British tried to stem the flood by a series of forts. It is possible that the British attempt to defend the Indian tribes was due either to charity or to gratitude for their assistance in the war with France from 1756 to 1763. However, I consider it more plausible that the British perceived themselves to be under a constitutional requirement to maintain the rule of law for all subjects of the King. From this perspective, the Indians were being deprived of their rights. This interpretation suggests that the British were in a constitutional quandary, which they could only solve by threatening force against the recalcitrant Colonies.[4]

This issue of Indian rights is worth pursuing further. During the Indian rebellion under Pontiac all but three of the British forts in the Northwest Territory had been taken prior to June 1763. The Proclamation of 1763 was meant to acknowledge Indian rights and help bring about peace. The Proclamation line essentially defined a huge area between the Appalachians and Mississippi as Indian. The later treaty of 1765 with Pontiac stipulated that, though the Forts were British, the land was not. As a recent commentator has put it: "The . . . Crown . . . wanted to prevent

---

[4] Beer has discussed the differences between the notion of *virtual representation* held in Britain and the notion of actual representation, as it was to be articulated in the Colonies, particularly by Madison. Under virtual representation, a member of the House of Parliament was regarded as speaking on behalf of the whole nation. He should shun "dependence" on the electors and follow his own judgment of the public good. The Colonies' rejection of this notion is part of the explanation for the Revolution. But, of course, the welfare of the Indian tribes should be considered under the public good, if they were perceived as subjects of the King. Thus, the notion of virtual representation was, in a sense, doubly insulting to the Colonies. For these concepts of representation, see Beer (1993: 164–6). For the activities of the British Indian Department from 1763–76, see Colloway (1995). For details on Pontiac's Rebellion, see Anderson (2000: 535–53) and Jennings (1988, 2000).

'unjust Settlement and fraudulent Purchase' of Indian lands.... A question still being argued is whether the Proclamation recognized a pre-existing title or created it" (see Dickason, 1992: 188; see also Stagg, 1981a,b).

As Dickason (1992) notes, the legal questions were still being discussed more than a century later in Canada. Indeed, in 1885 the judgment of the Chancellor of Ontario was that the Indians had become "invested with a legally recognized tenure of defined lands; in which they have a present right as to the exclusive and absolute usufruct, and a potential right of becoming individual owners in fee after enfranchisement" (188).

I shall argue that the Declaration would have been irrational on the part of the members of the Continental Congress had they not known of the promise of French assistance. There is no *direct* evidence that the Congress knew of the promise of French aid prior to July 4, 1776 because there are no existing memoranda of the Committee of Secret Correspondence (which, under Franklin, negotiated with France). However, Benjamin Franklin's papers include a letter, in code, from Charles-Guillaume-Frederic Dumas (in Utrecht) to the Committee, dated April 30, 1776 (Wilcox, ed., 1982: 403–12). Because the company, Roderique Hortalez, set up to supply the Americans from France, was based in Utrecht, it is a plausible inference that Franklin knew of the promise of 10 million livres of French aid prior to July 4, 1776.[5]

Whether it was rational for France to provide this aid is difficult to determine. Turgot tried to dissuade the King because he foresaw the fiscal problems for France that would follow.[6] In fact, economic historians tend to agree that the eventual cost to France for the support it provided the Colonies was in excess of 1 billion livres. The resulting debt precipitated the French bankruptcy of 1788 and, thus, the French Revolution (Norberg, 1994: 252–98).

Initially, of course, Louis XVI must have believed that, by providing aid to the Colonies, he would facilitate Britain's losing the jewel of its empire. However, he was careful to disguise the existence of the aid, and formal treaties of friendship, commerce, and alliance with the Americans were not made until February 1778. These were approved by the U.S. Congress in May 1778, and by June of that year France and Britain were at war.[7] The aid provided in 1776 was, however, known to the British

---

[5] The full story of this secret aid, and the involvement of Pierre-Augustin Caron de Beaumarchais, has yet to be written.

[6] See Roche (1998) for Turgot's reform efforts prior to his dismissal in mid-1776.

[7] Franklin was in Paris as Minister Plenipotentiary and was very successful in working with Vergennes to persuade Louis XVI that the war with Britain could be won.

Cabinet through the efficient British spy network, and it was mutually convenient for both Britain and France to maintain the pretence of peace for two years after 1776. In France's case, it was a question of waiting to see whether the Revolution would succeed. If it did succeed, then the potential gain to France would be the great opportunity, again, to open up the Louisiana Territory. However, the first two years of the Revolution were difficult for the Colonies, and French aid was crucial (McCullough, 2005; Weintraub, 2005). Once the public decision to aid the Colonies was made, then it would be rational to continue the aid in the form of men and matériel, in the hope of eventual success. We can infer that Turgot believed the gamble was too dangerous, because the risk was French bankruptcy.

Once Louis XVI made the decision in 1776 to aid the colonies, reasonable subjective estimates by the members of the Continental Congress of the likely expected costs of war compared with acquiescence to the British led to a majority decision to declare independence. To use the terminology proposed here, a *core belief* was created, within the colonial elite, that war could be justified in terms of expected utility calculations. If a majority of the Continental Congress had not accepted this belief, then independence would not have been declared. Irrespective of the beliefs of the population as a whole, there would have been no War of Independence in 1776.

The interpretation presented here of the American Revolution is that it was triggered by a change in beliefs by (a majority of) the colonial elite. This change was necessary for the Revolution; otherwise there would have been no Declaration of Independence. The change, however, was certainly not sufficient; changes in the beliefs of the colonial population were also required. Historians have suggested various causes based on religion or class for these general responses.[8] In contrast, I have asserted that the reason for this elite belief cascade was the combination of the passing of the Quebec Act and Louis XVI's choice to provide aid. The first of these causes—the passing of the Quebec Act—is intelligible in terms of British Constitutional understanding of virtual representation. The

---

For this reason we may see Franklin not only as the architect of the Declaration of Independence, but the architect of Independence itself. See Stourzh (1954), Hardman (2000) and Schiff (2005).

[8] For example, Phillips (1999) emphasizes the common threat of religious antagonism connecting the British Civil War, the American Revolution, and the American Civil War. See also Draper (1996).

second cause—the decision by Louis XVI—is only weakly acknowl-edged by historians. And the likelihood that Franklin knew of the promise of French aid prior to July 4, 1776 has not been considered important.

An earlier account of Franco-American negotiations by Bemis (1935) noted that a courier was dispatched from France to the Colonies in May 1776, with the news of the promise of aid. However, the ship was sunk, and the information did not reach Philadelphia until December 1, 1776. It is highly implausible that only one courier was dispatched. Because the sea voyage was about two months, it is reasonable to infer that the promise of aid did in fact arrive at the end of June 1776. I suggest that this promise of French aid was pivotal in the sense of making the Declaration rational. Of course, this cause was a highly contigent, unpredictable event.

Although French amity was crucial to the success of the revolution, re-lations between France and the United States deteriorated after the French Revolution. Indeed, during the administration of John Adams (Ferling, 1992; Ellis, 1993; McCullogh, 2001), from 1797 to 1800, France and the United States were almost at war. In August 1800, by a secret treaty, Napolean Bonaparte forced Spain to return Louisiana to France (Adams, 1986 [1889]: 247). Francois Toussaint had led St. Domingue (or Hispan-iola) in revolt against French rule in 1791, and Bonaparte determined to regain the island, and to add Louisiana to his dominion. To this end, he dispatched a fleet and an army of twenty-eight thousand men under his brother-in-law, Leclerc. As Menig (1986) has put it, by 1801 the "recon-quest of St. Domingue, the return of Louisiana, and the recreation of a great French American Empire suddenly became specific and seemingly specific goals." (337). President Jefferson was well aware of this threat, particularly to New Orleans, and wrote to Robert Livingtone, his Min-ister in France, that "[T]he impetuosity of [France's] temper ... render[s] it impossible that France and the United States can continue long friends. From that moment we must marry ourselves to the British fleet and na-tion." (Peterson, 1984: 1105).

By September, 1802, however, almost the entire French army was lost to disease. Adams (1986 [1889]) argued that this defeat was the reason that Napolean sold Louisiana to Jefferson. The purchase was negotiated in New Orleans in December, 1803, and on March, 9 1804, Meriwether Lewis witnessed the signing of the documents in St. Louis, thus capping the "great gamble" that was made, first by Franklin against Britain and then by Jefferson, against France (Cerami, 2003).

3.3 THE DECISION TO DECLARE INDEPENDENCE

One way to deal formally with the Constitutional Congress' decision in July 1776 is to construct a game involving America, Britain, France, and Spain. To do this however, in a technical fashion, requires estimating preferences and Bayesian priors for the combatants. Instead, this section will consider the problem in the context of decision making under risk. That is to say, I consider the problem from the point of view of an "average" member of the Congress, estimating the likely expected costs of choosing to declare independence. Clearly, this estimate will vary among the members of the Congress. However, this problem can be interpreted formally in terms of what we may call a "Condorcet Jury,"and the rational choice of an average "juror" will give insight into the choice of the Congress. To emphasize the point again, it is not so much that the members of this congressional jury do or do not prefer to declare independence. Rather it is a question of whether each one *believes* that it is in the Colonies' best interests to declare independence.

First, consider the military and fiscal capability of Britain prior to 1776. As North and Weingast (1989) have shown, the Glorious Revolution of 1688 induced a constitutional and fiscal revolution that better equipped Britain to borrow and to fight wars. As discussed in Chapter 2, Britain increased its debt to about 120 million sterling during the various wars of the first half of the eighteenth century, and yet was able to fund an increasing proportion of this debt (Brewer, 1988).

During the Seven Years War, Britain demonstrated that it could solve the logistic problem of arranging for a convoy of troop ships, together with their protecting men-of-war, to arrive together and surprise the enemy. By this means, Wolfe captured Quebec City in September 1759, and British forces took Havana, Cuba, and Manila in the Philippines (on August 13 and October 7, 1762, respectively). The Havana force comprised fourteen thousand men, ten thousand of whom became sick or died of tropical disease (Pocock, 1998).

Perhaps in an attempt to bluff the Colonies out of rebellion, a British fleet of more than 130 ships under General William Howe arrived at the port of New York by June 30, 1776 (Bobrick, 1997: 206). By July 12, thirty-two thousand troops were in position to disembark from more than 170 transports, protected by twenty frigates and ten ships of the line. By August, the British naval presence was more than four hundred transports and fifty ships of war. In the battle for New York in August 1776, Washington had fewer than three thousand men. With these facts in mind, consider the decision problem facing the members of the Continental Congress in the month prior to July 4, 1776. Again, the probabilities involved are q (the British will attack if independence is declared) and p (if they attack, the Colonies will lose). The costs involved are T (of tyranny) and C (of war).

Because war is a risky venture, we should incorporate the risk posture of the protagonists. To keep the calculations as simple as possible however, I shall ignore risk posture and deal only with expectations. Let us assume that the purpose of the Declaration of Independence is to avoid the costs of British tyranny. To further simplify, suppose that the prize of freedom is T dollars. We can perform the calculations in Spanish silver dollars, each one of which is worth (at that time) approximately six French livres. A pound sterling was worth about four Spanish dollars. Total French grants and aid in the initial stages of the war totaled 36 million livres, or 6 million dollars. For purposes of illustration, let us assume that the cost of war to the Colonies, if the British attacked, could be estimated at $C = 12$ million dollars (excluding French aid). If the Colonies lose the war, the cost is $C + \Delta$, where Δ is the additional cost of defeat. For example, the members of the Constitutional Congress could expect to be hanged for treason after defeat. Appropriation of property, and so forth, after defeat would suggest an order of magnitude for Δ approximately equal to C.

If the Colonies declare independence, and the British attack (with probability q), the Colonies win the war with probability $(1 - p)$. Thus, the expected utility is

$$q[(1 - p)(T - C) + p(-C - \Delta)]. \tag{3.1}$$

If the British acquiesce, then the prize T is won with probability $(1 - q)$. Independence is a rational choice if and only if

$$q[(1 - p)(T - C) + p(-C - \Delta)] + (1 - q)T > 0. \tag{3.2}$$

Rearranging terms gives the condition

$$(1 - qp)T > q(C + p\Delta). \tag{3.3}$$

For example, suppose beliefs are optimistic in the sense that $p = q = \frac{1}{2}$, and $\Delta = 0$. Then, the condition is $T > \frac{2}{3}C$.

Middlekauff (1982: 150) suggests that the figure for the cost of taxation to the Colonies was 40,000 dollars or $T = 200,000$ dollars, if we take this sum discounted over a decade. Chown (1994: 218) suggests a figure of 16,000 pounds sterling or 64,000 dollars per annum, or perhaps

320,000 dollars discounted over the decade. With $C = 12$ million dollars, the cost (of avoiding taxation) could not possibly make rational the expected costs of war. If the French do offer aid, then the cost of war is divided between the French and the Colonies, so the cost facing the Colonies is reduced to C'. Moreover, French aid can be expected to increase the probability q (that the British attack) to nearly 1. Suppose French aid further affects the probable outcome of war by changing the probability of defeat from $p = \frac{1}{2}$ to $p' = \frac{1}{4}$, say. Then, the requirement is $T > \frac{4}{7}C'$. This is only slightly different from the previous calculation, so again, avoidance of taxation is not a sufficient cause of a declaration.

However, as noted above, Thomas Paine argued that the cost of tyranny was the loss of the Ohio Valley, which he put at a value of 25 million dollars.

For an optimist ($p = q = \frac{1}{2}$), the calculation, assuming no French aid and $C = \Delta = 12$ million dollars, becomes $T > \frac{2}{3}(12 + 6) = 12$ million dollars.

Given a prize of this magnitude, such an optimist would certainly declare independence. A more prudent member of Congress might reason that $p = q = 0.9$, in which case the requirement becomes $T > \frac{0.9}{0.19}$ (22.8) or $T > 108$ million dollars. For such an agent, a declaration (without the promise of French aid) is not justified.

Suppose, however, an offer of French aid has been received, and the prudent calculator reasons that the probability of defeat will, as a consequence, fall from $p = 0.9$ to $p' = 0.5$. With $q = 0.9$, the calculation becomes $T > \frac{0.9}{1-0.45} = 29.45$ million dollars.

Thus, a risk-averse calculator, unwilling to accept high costs such as C and Δ, could reason that the value of the prize is close to the expected costs. As indicated, the calculation depends on the amount of French aid, the effect this will have on the prospect of victory, and on the likely costs, Δ, of defeat.

Some of the members of Congress, and of the population at large, could be highly optimistic and believe in the rationality of a declaration, even without the offer of aid. A more prudent calculator could reason that not only would the costs of war be reduced by French aid, but that probable French military assistance could directly increase the probability of victory.

The implicit argument here is that variation in beliefs and risk postures among the members of Congress would lead to different calculations about the rationality of a declaration of independence. Prior to news of French aid, a majority would not have chosen independence. After the news was received, however, even relatively risk-averse members could choose independence, thus creating a core belief in the rationality of independence.

From the point of view of the French, it would be rational to offer a "pivotal" amount of aid, sufficient to create a majority in Congress in favor of independence. The French offer, by changing beliefs as regards p, and by funding some of the costs of the war, clearly would increase the number in Congress favoring independence. A signal from the French *prior* to July 4, 1776, was, however, crucial for this transformation.

After France entered the War in 1778, and with Spain as its ally to help defend the French empire in the Caribbean, the flow of men and matériel rapidly increased. The crucial battle of the war—Yorktown—was won through French assistance. In fact, a French fleet from Rhode Island and one under Comte de Grasse, from the Caribbean, performed the British trick of a coordinated arrival at the York River in September 1781. A French army of 6,500 helped Washington lay siege to the British forces under Cornwallis at Yorktown, while the French fleet stopped the British ships from relieving the British army.

In mid-1776, it could not be known with certainty that French forces would be supplied in this fashion. However, it was a rational hope that Louis XVI would continue to help, and that this assistance would at least exhaust the will of the British to continue the war.

On the British side, the logic of the problem involves the probability (r) that the Americans will acquiesce if the British attack, and the probability that the British will win (p) if the Americans do not acquiesce.

Using B_1 for "attack" and B_2 for "do not attack," and using u for expected utility we obtain

$$u(B_1) = (1 - r)[p(T - C) - (1 - p)C] + r(T - C'), \qquad (3.4)$$

while $u(B_2) = 0$.

Here, C' is the initial cost of attack, due to placing a fleet in New York in 1776 (say 100,000 dollars). C, as before, is the cost of full-scale war. First of all, let us take $T = T_0$ to be the "benefits" of taxation, or 200,000 dollars. Obviously, if the British do *not* attack (B_2), these benefits are lost through independence. Even with the optimistic value of $p = 0.9$ (for a British victory), the condition requires that r is almost 1.0.

Thus, if the British have no knowledge of French aid to the Colonies, then they should attack only if they expect the Americans to calculate that victory is impossible and to acquiesce to the display of force. This assertion depends on the calculation that British benefits simply had to do with the receipts from taxation, of the order of 40,000 dollars per annum. Chown's (1994) higher figure of 84,000 dollars per annum has to be offset against his estimates of 60,000 dollars in collection costs. Using this estimate, it is totally implausible that the British actions were induced by the benefits obtained from taxation (once collection costs are included). Moreover, it is known that the British were well aware of the French promises to the Colonies.[9] It is reasonable to expect that the British would rationally believe that the Americans would only acquiesce with very low probability. Consequently, under the assumption that the gain to the British was only T_0, they should rationally have acquiesced to American independence. In fact, on March 9, 1778, the British Parliament enacted various Acts to repeal all objectionable Acts involving taxation. By then, it was obvious that r was close to 0. This also suggests that taxation was not the issue.

If we set the prize T to the British for winning the war at 25 million dollars, the costs of carrying out and winning the war at 12 million dollars, and the costs if the war were lost at 15 million dollars, then, assuming $r = 0$, the inequality becomes

$$p(25 - 12) - (1 - p)15 > 0, \text{ or } p > 0.53. \tag{3.5}$$

In contrast to the calculation for the Colonies, I have assumed that the additional cost to the British—3 million dollars, if they lost—is substantially less than for the Colonies. Given the British ability in military affairs, it is plausible that they calculated that the probability of success, p, against both the Colonies and the French, clearly exceeded the value of 0.53.

Although I have assumed that the prize, T, was equal to Paine's estimate of the value of the Ohio Valley, it is obvious that different members of the House of Parliament would have calculated differently. For those who believed that the British had a constitutional obligation to defend the rights of the Indian peoples of the Ohio Valley, T would have higher value. For those, like Burke, who emphasized the value of trade with the colonists, the costs of war would far exceed any possible benefits.[10] It would seem possible that George III and the Cabinet put high value on the Ohio Valley, not because of its intrinsic value, but because of a sense of

---

[9] See, for example, the discussion of the effective British secret agents operating in Paris, in van Doren (1938) and Bemis (1962: 16–39).

[10] See, in particular, the speeches made by Edmund Burke "On American Taxation" on April 19, 1774, and "On Moving His Resolutions for Conciliation with the Colonies," on March 22, 1775, in Canavan (1999: 157–220 and 221–289).

obligation to maintain the rule of law and to satisfy perceived obligations to their Indian subjects.

We may say that the Declaration of Independence was a signal from the Continental Congress that provided information on expected costs and probabilities to a generic member of the population. This signal changed the a priori subjective probabilities, leading to what I have called a *belief cascade* in the Colonies, and inducing at least a good proportion of the population to accept the rationality of the decision.

I argue in Chapter 4 that Madison and Hamilton generated a belief cascade in the country during the Ratification of the Constitution from 1787 to 1789. Chapter 5 further suggests that Lincoln's election in 1860 was the consequence of a belief cascade in the northern electorate. Lincoln's "House Divided" speech in Illinois in June 1858, his debates with Stephen Douglas from August to October 1858, together with his speeches in New York and New Haven in February and March 1860, were focused on the assertion that the Dred Scott decision made by the Supreme Court in 1857, could lead to the extension of slavery to the free states.

In all these cases, a simple expected utility calculation of the kind just performed can give some insight into the basis of the collective calculation.

3.4 APPENDIXES

3.4.1 *The Quebec Act, October 7, 1774*

14 George III, c. 83 (U.K.)

An Act for making more effectual Provision for the Government of the Province of Quebec in North America.

I. WHEREAS, his Majesty, by his Royal Proclamation bearing Date the seventh Day of October, in the third Year of his Reign, thought fit to declare the Provisions which had been made in respect to certain Countries, Territories, and Islands in America, ceded to his Majesty by the definitive Treaty of Peace, concluded at Paris on the tenth day of February, one thousand seven hundred and sixty-three: And whereas, by the Arrangements made by the said Royal Proclamation a very large Extent of Country, within which there were several Colonies and Settlements of the Subjects of France, who claimed to remain therein under the Faith of the said Treaty, was left, without any Provision being made for the Administration of Civil Government therein; and certain Parts of the Territory of Canada, where sedentary Fisheries had been established and carried on by the Subjects of France, Inhabitants of the said Province of Canada under Grants and Concessions from the Government thereof, were annexed to the Government of Newfoundland, and thereby subjected to Regulations inconsistent with the Nature of such Fisheries: May it therefore please your most Excellent Majesty that it may be enacted; and be it enacted by the King's most Excellent Majesty, by and with the Advice and Consent of the Lords Spiritual and Temporal, and Commons, in this present Parliament assembled, and by the Authority of the same. That all the Territories, Islands and Countries in North America, belonging to the Crown of Great Britain, bounded on the South by a Line from the Bay of Chaleurs along the High Lands which divide the Rivers that empty themselves into the River Saint Lawrence from those which fall into the Sea, to a Point in forty-five Degrees of Northern Latitude, on the Eastern Bank of the River Connecticut, keeping the same Latitude directly West, through the Lake Champlain, until, in the same Latitude, it meets the River Saint Lawrence: from thence up the Eastern Bank of the said River to the Lake Ontario; thence through the Lake Ontario, and the River commonly called Niagara and thence along by the Eastern and South-eastern Bank of Lake Erie, following the said Bank, until the same shall be intersected by the Northern Boundary, granted by the Charter of the Province of Pennsylvania, in case the same shall be so intersected: and from thence along the said Northern and Western Boundaries of the said Province, until the said Western Boundary strike the Ohio: But in case the said Bank of the said Lake shall not be found to be so intersected, then following the said Bank until it shall arrive at that Point of the said Bank which shall be nearest to the North-western Angle of the said Province of Pennsylvania, and thence by a right Line, to the said North-western Angle of the said Province; and thence along the Western Boundary of the said Province, until it strike the River Ohio; and along the Bank of the said River, Westward, to the Banks of the Mississippi, and Northward to the Southern Boundary of the Territory granted to the Merchants Adventurers of England, trading to Hudson's Bay; and also all such Territories, Islands, and Countries, which have, since the tenth of February, one thousand seven hundred and sixty-three, been made Part of the Government of Newfoundland, be, and they are hereby, during his Majesty's Pleasure, annexed to, and made Part and Parcel of, the Province of Quebec, as created and established by the said Royal Proclamation of the seventh of October, one thousand seven hundred and sixty-three.

II. Provided always. That nothing herein contained, relative to the Boundary of the Province of Quebec, shall in anywise affect the Boundaries of any other Colony.

III. Provided always, and be it enacted, That nothing in this Act contained shall extend, or be construed to extend, to make void, or to vary or alter any Right, Title, or Possession, derived under any Grant, Conveyance, or otherwise howsoever, of or to any Lands within the said Province, or the Provinces thereto adjoining; but that the same shall remain and be in Force, and have Effect, as if this Act had never been made.

IV. And whereas the Provisions, made by the said Proclamation, in respect to the Civil Government of the said Province of Quebec, and the Powers and Authorities given to the Governor and other Civil Officers of the said Province, by the Grants and Commissions issued in consequence thereof, have been found, upon Experience, to be inapplicable to the State and Circumstances of the said Province, the Inhabitants whereof amounted, at the Conquest, to above sixty-five thousand Persons professing the Religion of the Church of Rome, and enjoying an established Form of Constitution and System of Laws, by which their Persons and Property had been protected, governed, and ordered, for a long Series of Years, from the first Establishment of the said Province of Canada; be it therefore further enacted by the Authority aforesaid. That the said Proclamation, so far as the same relates to the said Province of Quebec, and the Commission under the Authority where of the Government of the said Province is at present administered, and all and every Ordinance and Ordinances made by the Governor and Council of Quebec for the Time being, relative to the Civil Government and Administration of Justice in the said Province, and all Commissions to Judges and other Officers thereof, be, and the same are hereby revoked, annulled, and made void, from and after the first Day of May, one thousand seven hundred and seventy-five.

V. And, for the more perfect Security and Ease of the Minds of the Inhabitants of the said Province, it is hereby declared, That his Majesty's Subjects, professing the Religion of the Church of Rome of and in the said Province of Quebec, may have, hold, and enjoy, the free Exercise of the Religion of the Church of Rome, subject to the King's Supremacy, declared and established by an Act, made in the first Year of the Reign of Queen Elizabeth, over all the Dominions and Countries which then did, or thereafter should belong, to the Imperial Crown of this Realm; and that the Clergy of the said Church may hold, receive, and enjoy, their accustomed Dues and Rights, with respect to such Persons only as shall profess the said Religion.

VI. Provided nevertheless, That it shall be lawful for his Majesty, his Heirs or Successors, to make such Provision out of the rest of the said accustomed Dues and Rights, for the Encouragement of the Protestant Religion, and for the Maintenance and Support of a Protestant Clergy within the said Province, as he or they shall, from Time to Time think necessary and expedient.

VII. Provided always and be it enacted, That no Person professing the Religion of the Church of Rome, and residing in the said Province, shall be obliged to take the Oath required by the said Statute passed in the first Year of the Reign of Queen Elizabeth, or any other Oaths substituted by any other Act in the Place thereof; but that every such Person who, by the said Statute, is required to take the Oath therein mentioned, shall be obliged, and is hereby required, to take and subscribe the following Oath before the Governor, or such other Person in such Court of Record as his Majesty shall appoint, who are hereby authorized to administer the same; *videlicet,*

I A.B. do sincerely promise and swear, That I will be faithful, and bear true Allegiance to his Majesty King George, and him will defend to the utmost of my Power, against all traitorous Conspiracies, and Attempts whatsoever, which shall be made against his Person, Crown, and Dignity; and I will do my utmost Endeavor to disclose and make known to his Majesty, his Heirs and Successors, all Treasons, and traitorous Conspiracies, and Attempts, which I shall know to be against him, or any of them; and all this I do swear without any Equivocation, mental Evasion, or secret Reservation, and renouncing all Pardons and Dispensations from any Power or Person whomsoever to the contrary. So help me GOD.

And every such Person, who shall neglect or refuse to take the said Oath before mentioned, shall incur and be liable to the same Penalties, Forfeitures, Disabilities, and Incapacities, as he would have incurred and been liable to for neglecting or refusing to take the Oath required by the said Statute passed in the first Year of the Reign of Queen Elizabeth.

VIII. And be it further enacted by the Authority aforesaid, That all his Majesty's Canadian Subjects within the Province of Quebec, the religious orders and Communities only excepted, may also hold and enjoy their Property and Possessions, together with all Customs and Usages relative thereto, and all other their Civil Rights, in as large ample, and beneficial Manner, If the said Proclamation, Commissions, Ordinances, and other Acts and Instruments had not been made, and as may consist with their Allegiance to his Majesty, and Subjection to the Crown and Parliament of Great Britain; and that in all Matters of Controversy, relative to Property and Civil Rights, Resort shall be had to the Laws of Canada, as the Rule for the Decision of the same; and all Causes that shall hereafter be instituted in any of the Courts of Justice, to be appointed within and for the said Province by his Majesty, his Heirs and Successors, shall, with respect to such Property and Rights, be determined agreeably to the said Laws and Customs of Canada, until they shall be varied or altered by any Ordinances that shall, from Time to Time, be passed in the said Province by the Governor, Lieutenant Governor, or Commander in Chief, for the Time being, by and with the Advice and Consent of the Legislative Council of the same, to be appointed in Manner herein-after mentioned.

IX. Provided always, That nothing in this Act contained shall extend, or be construed to extend, to any Lands that have been granted by his Majesty, or shall hereafter be granted by his Majesty, his Heirs and Successors, to be holden in free and common Soccage.

X. Provided also, That it shall and may be lawful to and for every Person that is Owner of any Lands, Goods, or Credits, in the said Province, and that has a Right to alienate the said Lands, Goods, or Credits, in his or her Lifetime, by Deed of Sale, Gift, or otherwise, to devise or bequeath the same at his or her Death, by his or her last Will and Testament; any Law, Usage, or Custom, heretofore or now prevailing in the Province, to the contrary hereof in any-wise notwithstanding; such Will being executed either according to the Laws of Canada, or according to the Forms prescribed by the Laws of England.

XI. And whereas the Certainty and Lenity of the Criminal Law of England, and the Benefits and Advantages resulting from the Use of it, have been sensibly felt by the Inhabitants, from an Experience of more than nine Years, during which it has been uniformly administered: be it therefore further enacted by the Authority aforesaid, That the same shall continue to be administered, and shall be observed as Law in the Province of Quebec, as well in the Description and Quality of the Offence as in the Method of Prosecution and Trial; and the Punishments and Forfeitures thereby inflicted to the Exclusion of every other Rule of Criminal Law, or Mode of Proceeding thereon, which did or might prevail in the said Province before the Year of our Lord one thousand seven hundred and seventy-four; any Thing in this Act to the contrary thereof in any respect notwithstanding; subject nevertheless to such Alterations and Amendments as the Governor, Lieutenant-governor, or Commander in Chief for the Time being, by and with the Advice and Consent of the legislative Council of the said Province, hereafter to be appointed, shall, from Time to Time, cause to be made therein, in Manner hereinafter directed.

XII. And whereas it may be necessary to ordain many Regulations for the future Welfare and good Government of the Province of Quebec, the Occasions of which cannot now be foreseen, nor, without much Delay and Inconvenience, be provided for, without intrusting that Authority, for a certain Time, and under proper Restrictions, to Persons resident there, and whereas it is at present inexpedient to call an Assembly; be it therefore enacted by the Authority aforesaid, That it shall and may be lawful for his Majesty, his Heirs and Successors, by Warrant under his or their Signet or Sign Manual, and with the Advice of the Privy Council, to constitute and appoint a Council for the Affairs of the Province of Quebec, to consist of such Persons resident there, not exceeding twenty-three, nor less than seventeen, as his Majesty, his Heirs and Successors, shall be pleased to appoint, and, upon the Death, Removal, or Absence of any of the Members of the said Council, in like Manner to constitute and appoint such and so many other Person or Persons as shall be necessary to supply the Vacancy or Vacancies; which Council, so appointed and nominated, or the major Part thereof; shall have Power and Authority to make Ordinances for the Peace, Welfare, and good Government, of the said Province, with the Consent of his Majesty's Governor, or, in his Absence, of the Lieutenant-governor, or Commander in Chief for the Time being.

[This section was repealed by The Constitutional Act, 1791.]

XIII. Provided always, That nothing in this Act contained shall extend to authorize or impower the said legislative Council to lay any Taxes or Duties within the said Province, such Rates and Taxes only excepted as the Inhabitants of any Town or District within the said Province may be authorized by the said Council to assess, levy, and apply, within the said Town or District, for the Purpose of making Roads, erecting and repairing publick Buildings, or for any other Purpose respecting the local Convenience and Oeconomy of such Town or District.

XIV. Provided also, and be it enacted by the Authority aforesaid, That every Ordinance so to be made, shall, within six Months, be transmitted by the Governor, or, in his Absence, by the Lieutenant-governor, or Commander in Chief for the Time being, and laid before his Majesty for his Royal Approbation; and if his Majesty shall think fit to disallow thereof, the same shall cease and be void from the Time that his Majesty's Order in Council thereupon shall be promulgated at Quebec.

XV. Provided also, That no Ordinance touching Religion, or by which any Punishment may be inflicted greater than Fine or Imprisonment for three Months, shall be of any Force or Effect, until the same shall have received his Majesty's Approbation.

XVI. Provided also, That no Ordinance shall be passed at any Meeting of the Council where less than a Majority of the whole Council is present, or at any Time except between the first Day of January and the first Day of May, unless upon some urgent Occasion, in which Case every Member thereof resident at Quebec, or within fifty Miles thereof, shall be personally summoned by the Governor, or, in his absence, by the Lieutenant-governor, or Commander in Chief for the Time being, to attend the same.

XVII. And be it further enacted by the Authority aforesaid, That nothing herein contained shall extend, or be construed to extend, to prevent or hinder his Majesty, his Heirs and Successors, by his or their Letters Patent under the Great Seal of Great Britain, from erecting, constituting, and appointing, such Courts of Criminal, Civil, and Ecclesiastical Jurisdiction within and for the said Province of Quebec, and appointing, from Time to Time, the Judges and Officers thereof, as his Majesty, his Heirs and Successors, shall think necessary and proper for the Circumstances of the said Province.

XVIII. Provided always, and it is hereby enacted, That nothing in this Act contained shall extend, or be construed to extend, to repeal or make void, within the said Province of Quebec, any Act or Acts of the Parliament of Great Britain heretofore made, for prohibiting, restraining, or regulating, the Trade or Commerce of his Majesty's Colonies and Plantations in America; but that all and every the said Acts, and also all Acts of Parliament heretofore made concerning or respecting the said Colonies and Plantations, shall be, and are hereby declared to be, in Force, within the said Province of Quebec, and every Part thereof.

3.4.2 *Declaration and Resolves of the First Continental Congress, October 14, 1774*

Whereas, since the close of the last war, the British parliament, claiming a power, of right, to bind the people of America by statutes in all cases whatsoever, hath, in some acts, expressly imposed taxes on them, and in others, under various presences, but in fact for the purpose of raising a revenue, hath imposed rates and duties payable in these colonies, established a board of commissioners, with unconstitutional powers, and extended the jurisdiction of courts of admiralty, not only for collecting the said duties, but for the trial of causes merely arising within the body of a county:

And whereas, in consequence of other statutes, judges, who before held only estates at will in their offices, have been made dependant on the crown alone for their salaries, and standing armies kept in times of peace: And whereas it has lately been resolved in parliament, that by force of a statute, made in the thirty-fifth year of the reign of King Henry the Eighth, colonists may be transported to England, and tried there upon accusations for treasons and misprisions, or concealments of treasons committed in the colonies, and by a late statute, such trials have been directed in cases therein mentioned:

And whereas, in the last session of parliament, three statutes were made; one entitled, "An act to discontinue, in such manner and for such time as are therein mentioned, the landing and discharging, lading, or shipping of goods, wares and merchandise, at the town, and within the harbour of Boston, in the province of Massachusetts-Bay in New England;" another entitled, "An act for the better regulating the government of the province of Massachusetts-Bay in New England;" and another entitled, "An act for the impartial administration of justice, in the cases of persons questioned for any act done by them in the execution of the law, or for the suppression of riots and tumults, in the province of the Massachusetts-Bay in New England;" and another statute was then made, "for making more effectual provision for the government of the province of Quebec, etc." All which statutes are impolitic, unjust, and cruel, as well as unconstitutional, and most dangerous and destructive of American rights:

And whereas, assemblies have been frequently dissolved, contrary to the rights of the people, when they attempted to deliberate on grievances; and their dutiful, humble, loyal, and reasonable petitions to the crown for redress, have been repeatedly treated with contempt, by his Majesty's ministers of state:

The good people of the several colonies of New-Hampshire, Massachusetts-Bay, Rhode Island and Providence Plantations, Connecticut, New-York, New-Jersey, Pennsylvania, Newcastle, Kent, and Sussex on Delaware, Maryland, Virginia, North-Carolina and South-Carolina, justly alarmed at these arbitrary proceedings of parliament and administration, have severally elected, constituted, and appointed deputies to meet, and sit in general Congress, in the city of Philadelphia, in order to obtain such establishment, as that their religion, laws, and liberties, may not be subverted: Whereupon the deputies so appointed being now assembled, in a full and free representation of these colonies, taking into their most serious consideration, the best means of attaining the ends aforesaid, do, in the first place, as Englishmen, their ancestors in like cases have usually done, for asserting and vindicating their rights and liberties, DECLARE,

That the inhabitants of the English colonies in North-America, by the immutable laws of nature, the principles of the English constitution, and the several charters or compacts, have the following RIGHTS:

Resolved 1. That they are entitled to life, liberty and property: and they have never ceded to any foreign power whatever, a right to dispose of either without their consent.

Resolved 2. That our ancestors, who first settled these colonies, were at the time of their emigration from the mother country, entitled to all the rights, liberties, and immunities of free and natural-born subjects, within the realm of England.

Resolved 3. That by such emigration they by no means forfeited, surrendered, or lost any of those rights, but that they were, and their descendants now are, entitled to the exercise and enjoyment of all such of them, as their local and other circumstances enable them to exercise and enjoy.

Resolved 4. That the foundation of English liberty, and of all free government, is a right in the people to participate in their legislative council: and as the English colonists are not represented, and from their local and other circumstances, cannot properly be represented in the British parliament, they are entitled to a free and exclusive power of legislation in their several provincial legislatures, where their right of representation can alone be preserved, in all cases of taxation and internal polity, subject only to the negative of their sovereign, in such manner as has been heretofore used and accustomed: But, from the necessity of the case, and a regard to the mutual interest of both countries, we cheerfully consent to the operation of such acts of the British parliament, as are bonafide, restrained to the regulation of our external commerce, for the purpose of securing the commercial advantages of the whole empire to the mother country, and the commercial benefits of its respective members; excluding every idea of taxation internal or external, for raising a revenue on the subjects, in America, without their consent.

Resolved 5. That the respective colonies are entitled to the common law of England, and more especially to the great and inestimable privilege of being tried by their peers of the vicinage, according to the course of that law.

Resolved 6. That they are entitled to the benefit of such of the English statutes, as existed at the time of their colonization; and which they have, by experience, respectively found to be applicable to their several local and other circumstances.

Resolved 7. That these, his Majesty's colonies, are likewise entitled to all the immunities and privileges granted and confirmed to them by royal charters, or secured by their several codes of provincial laws.

Resolved 8. That they have a right peaceably to assemble, consider of their grievances, and petition the king; and that all prosecutions, prohibitory proclamations, and commitments for the same, are illegal.

Resolved 9. That the keeping a standing army in these colonies, in times of peace, without the consent of the legislature of that colony, in which such army is kept, is against law.

Resolved 10. It is indispensably necessary to good government, and rendered essential by the English constitution, that the constituent branches of the legislature be independent of each other; that, therefore, the exercise of legislative power in several colonies, by a council appointed, during pleasure, by the crown, is unconstitutional, dangerous and destructive to the freedom of American legislation.

All and each of which the aforesaid deputies, in behalf of themselves, and their constituents, do claim, demand, and insist on, as their indubitable rights and liberties, which cannot be legally taken from them, altered or abridged by any power whatever, without their own consent, by their representatives in their several provincial legislature.

In the course of our inquiry, we find many infringements and violations of the foregoing rights, which, from an ardent desire, that harmony and mutual intercourse of affection and interest may be restored, we pass over for the present, and proceed to state such acts and measures as have been adopted since the last war, which demonstrate a system formed to enslave America.

Resolved 11. That the following acts of parliament are infringements and violations of the rights of the colonists; and that the repeal of them is essentially necessary, in order to restore harmony between Great Britain and the American colonies, viz.

The several acts of George III which impose duties for the purpose of raising a revenue in America, extend the power of the admiralty courts beyond their ancient limits, deprive the American subject of trial by jury, authorize the judges certificate to indemnify the prosecutor from damages, that he might otherwise be liable to, requiring oppressive security from a claimant of ships and goods seized, before he shall be allowed to defend his property, and are subversive of American rights.

Also George III. ch. 24, entitled, "An act for the better securing his majesty's dockyards, magazines, ships, ammunition, and stores," which declares a new offence in America, and deprives the American subject of a constitutional trial by jury of the vicinage, by authorizing the trial of any person, charged with the committing any offence described in the said act, out of the realm, to be indicted and tried for the same in any shire or county within the realm.

Also the three acts passed in the last session of parliament, for stopping the port and blocking up the harbour of Boston, for altering the charter and government of Massachusetts-Bay, and that which is entitled, "An act for the better administration of justice, etc."

Also the act passed in the same session for establishing the Roman Catholic religion, in the province of Quebec, abolishing the equitable system of English laws, and erecting a tyranny there, to the great danger (from so total a dissimilarity of religion, law and government) of the neighboring British colonies, by the assistance of whose blood and treasure the said country was conquered from France.

Also the act passed in the same session, for the better providing suitable quarters for officers and soldiers in his majesty's service, in North-America.

Also, that the keeping a standing army in several of these colonies, in time of peace, without the consent of the legislature of that colony, in which such army is kept, is against law.

To these grievous acts and measures, Americans cannot submit, but in hopes their fellow subjects in Great Britain will, on a revision of them, restore us to that state, in which both countries found happiness and prosperity, we have for the present, only resolved to pursue the following peaceable measures: 1. To enter into a non-importation, non-consumption, and non-exportation agreement or association. 2. To prepare an address to the people of Great-Britain, and a memorial to the inhabitants of British America: and 3. To prepare a loyal address to his majesty, agreeable to resolutions already entered into.

3.4.3 *Declaration of Independence, July 4, 1776*

The Declaration of Independence of the Thirteen Colonies in CONGRESS.

The unanimous Declaration of the thirteen united States of America,

When in the Course of human events, it becomes necessary for one people to dissolve the political bands which have connected them with another, and to assume among the powers of the earth, the separate and equal station to which the Laws of Nature and of Nature's God entitle them, a decent respect to the opinions of mankind requires that they should declare the causes which impel them to the separation.

We hold these truths to be self-evident, that all men are created equal, that they are endowed by their Creator with certain unalienable Rights, that among these are Life, Liberty and the pursuit of Happiness. – That to secure these rights, Governments are instituted among Men, deriving their just powers from the consent of the governed, – That whenever any Form of Government becomes destructive of these ends, it is the Right of the People to alter or to abolish it, and to institute new Government, laying its foundation on such principles and organizing its powers in such form, as to them shall seem most likely to effect their Safety and Happiness. Prudence, indeed, will dictate that Governments long established should not be changed for light and transient causes; and accordingly all experience hath shewn, that mankind are more disposed to suffer, while evils are sufferable, than to right themselves by abolishing the forms to which they are accustomed. But when a long train of abuses and usurpations, pursuing invariably the same Object evinces a design to reduce them under absolute Despotism, it is their right, it is their duty, to throw off such Government, and to provide new Guards for their future security. Such has been the patient sufferance of these Colonies; and such is now the necessity which constrains them to alter their former Systems of Government. The history of the present King of Great Britain [George III] is a history of repeated injuries and usurpations, all having in direct object the establishment of an absolute Tyranny over these States. To prove this, let Facts be submitted to a candid world.

He has refused his Assent to Laws, the most wholesome and necessary for the public good.

He has forbidden his Governors to pass Laws of immediate and pressing importance, unless suspended in their operation till his Assent should be obtained; and when so suspended, he has utterly neglected to attend to them.

He has refused to pass other Laws for the accommodation of large districts of people, unless those people would relinquish the right of Representation in the Legislature, a right inestimable to them and formidable to tyrants only.

He has called together legislative bodies at places unusual, uncomfortable, and distant from the depository of their public Records, for the sole purpose of fatiguing them into compliance with his measures.

He has dissolved Representative Houses repeatedly, for opposing with manly firmness his invasions on the rights of the people.

He has refused for a long time, after such dissolutions, to cause others to be elected; whereby the Legislative powers, incapable of Annihilation, have returned to the People at large for their exercise; the State remaining in the mean time exposed to all the dangers of invasion from without, and convulsions within.

He has endeavoured to prevent the population of these States; for that purpose obstructing the Laws for Naturalization of Foreigners; refusing to pass others to encourage their migrations hither, and raising the conditions of new Appropriations of Lands.

He has obstructed the Administration of Justice, by refusing his Assent to Laws for establishing Judiciary powers.

He has made Judges dependent on his Will alone, for the tenure of their offices, and the amount and payment of their salaries.

He has erected a multitude of New Offices, and sent hither swarms of Officers to harass our people, and eat out their substance.

He has kept among us, in times of peace, Standing Armies without the consent of our legislatures.

He has affected to render the Military independent of and superior to the Civil power.

He has combined with others to subject us to a jurisdiction foreign to our constitution and unacknowledged by our laws; giving his Assent to their Acts of pretended Legislation:

For Quartering large bodies of armed troops among us:

For protecting them, by a mock Trial, from punishment for any Murders which they should commit on the Inhabitants of these States:

For cutting off our Trade with all parts of the world:

For imposing Taxes on us without our Consent:

For depriving us, in many cases, of the benefits of Trial by Jury:

For transporting us beyond Seas to be tried for pretended offences:

For abolishing the free System of English Laws in a neighboring Province, establishing therein an Arbitrary government, and enlarging its Boundaries so as to render it at once an example and fit instrument for introducing the same absolute rule into these Colonies:

For taking away our Charters, abolishing our most valuable Laws, and altering fundamentally the Forms of our Governments:

For suspending our own Legislatures, and declaring themselves invested with power to legislate for us in all cases whatsoever.

He has abdicated Government here, by declaring us out of his Protection and waging War against us.

He has plundered our seas, ravaged our Coasts, burnt our towns, and destroyed the lives of our people.

He is at this time transporting large Armies of foreign Mercenaries to compleat the works of death, desolation and tyranny, already begun with circumstances of Cruelty and perfidy scarcely paralleled in the most barbarous ages, and totally unworthy the Head of a civilized nation.

He has constrained our fellow Citizens taken Captive on the high Seas to bear Arms against their Country, to become the executioners of their friends and Brethren, or to fall themselves by their Hands.

He has excited domestic insurrections amongst us, and has endeavoured to bring on the inhabitants of our frontiers, the merciless Indian Savages, whose known rule of warfare, is an undistinguished destruction of all ages, sexes and conditions.

In every stage of these Oppressions We have Petitioned for Redress in the most humble terms: Our repeated Petitions have been answered only by repeated injury. A Prince whose character is thus marked by every act which may define a Tyrant, is unfit to be the ruler of a free people.

Nor have We been wanting in attentions to our British brethren. We have warned them from time to time of attempts by their legislature to extend an unwarrantable jurisdiction over us. We have reminded them of the circumstances of our emigration and settlement here. We have appealed to their native justice and magnanimity, and we have conjured them by the ties of our common kindred to disavow these usurpations, which, would inevitably interrupt our connections and correspondence. They too have been deaf to the voice of justice and of consanguinity. We must, therefore, acquiesce in the necessity, which denounces our Separation, and hold them, as we hold the rest of mankind, Enemies in War, in Peace Friends.

We, therefore, the Representatives of the united States of America, in General Congress, Assembled, appealing to the Supreme Judge of the world for the rectitude of our intentions, do, in the Name, and by the Authority of the good People of these Colonies, solemnly publish and declare, That these United Colonies are, and of Right ought to be Free and Independent States; that they are Absolved from all Allegiance to the British Crown, and that all political connection between them and the State of Great Britain, is and ought to be totally dissolved; and that as Free and Independent States, they have full Power to levy War, conclude Peace, contract Alliances, establish Commerce, and to do all other Acts and Things which Independent States may of right do. And for the support of this Declaration, with a firm reliance on the protection of divine Providence, we mutually pledge to each other our Lives, our Fortunes and our sacred Honor.

The signers of the Declaration represented the new states as follows:

New Hampshire: Josiah Bartlett, William Whipple, Matthew Thornton
Massachusetts: John Hancock, Samuel Adams, John Adams, Robert Treat Paine, Elbridge Gerry
Rhode Island: Stephen Hopkins, William Ellery
Connecticut: Roger Sherman, Samuel Huntington, William Williams, Oliver Wolcott
New York: William Floyd, Philip Livingston, Francis Lewis, Lewis Morris
New Jersey: Richard Stockton, John Witherspoon, Francis Hopkinson, John Hart, Abraham Clark
Pennsylvania: Robert Morris, Benjamin Rush, Benjamin Franklin, John Morton, George Clymer, James Smith, George Taylor, James Wilson, George Ross
Delaware: Caesar Rodney, George Read, Thomas McKean
Maryland: Samuel Chase, William Paca, Thomas Stone, Charles Carroll

Virginia: George Wythe, Richard Henry Lee, Thomas Jefferson, Benjamin Harrison, Thomas Nelson, Jr., Francis Lightfoot Lee, Carter Braxton

North Carolina: William Hooper, Joseph Hewes, John Penn

South Carolina: Edward Rutledge, Thomas Heyward, Jr., Thomas Lynch, Jr., Arthur Middleton

Georgia: Button Gwinnett, Lyman Hall, George Walton.

4

Madison, Jefferson, and Condorcet

4.1 THE RATIFICATION OF THE CONSTITUTION*

A constitution is almost a living entity, but it also incorporates institutional features, "the rules of the game in a society, or more formally the humanly devised constraints that shape human interaction" (North, 1990: 3).[1] Much more important than the rules themselves is the conceptual basis for the acceptance of these rules. To use the terminology of game theory, the beliefs that underpin the constitution must themselves generally be in equilibrium.[2] That is, under "normal" circumstances, the rules of the constitution are grounded in what I have called a *core belief.*[3] This is not to assert that the core belief remains unchanged during normal times; if change does occur it will be gradual. In extraordinary times, however, the core belief is fractured in some fashion, typically because of the realization that the society is faced with a deep "quandary." Such a

---

* This chapter uses material from Norman Schofield, "The Probability of a Fit Choice: U.S. Political History and Voting Theory," in *Justice and Democracy*, Keith Dowding, Robert Goodin, and Carole Pateman, [eds]. Cambridge University Press (2004) and from Norman Schofield, "The Founding of the American Agrarian Empire and the Conflict of Land and Capital," *Homo Oeconomicus* 19 (2003): 471–505, by permission of Cambridge University Press and Accedo Publishing.

[1] For the role of Parliamentary institutions see North and Weingast (1989), Weingast (1997a, b), Acemoglu and Robinson (2005) and Acemoglu, Johnson and Robinson (2000, 2005).

[2] Calvert (1995) suggests that an "institution" is in equilibrium of behavior in an underlying game. Implicitly, I am extending this idea by focusing not on behavior but on the *beliefs*, which rationalize the behavior. (See Calvert, 1995: 57–93).

[3] Throughout this book, I use the term *core belief* to indicate an analogy with the notion of a core in a voting game. A *voting core* is an outcome (or set of outcomes), unbeaten under the particular system of rules and preferences of the society. A *core belief* is a belief (or set of beliefs) that is generally accepted in the society. This notion is developed in later chapters.

quandary may be due to an inconsistency, internal to the logical structure of the core beliefs, or to a disjunction between the core belief and some external aspect of social reality. When society faces a deep quandary, then mutually incompatible beliefs may population the society; very often a new equilibrium is attained only in the aftermath of war.[4]

The core belief will generally consist of a number of components, and if one of these is called into question in a profound fashion, then the belief in the relevance of the entire constitution may fail. For example, as Chapter 7 observes, the events of the Depression during the 1930s cast doubt on the belief in the compatibility of the free-market system and democracy. By rejecting a secondary core belief in the validity of "the strong equilibrium hypothesis of economics," John Maynard Keynes was able to cast a new light on this Depression quandary.[5]

The re-creation of the core belief during a period when the quandary is first realized, and then resolved, is a time of great uncertainty. Because the core belief is an equilibrium, the holding of this belief by many agents in the society means that the belief itself can provide a means by which acts are mutually intelligible (Arrow, 1986). That is, the belief itself can provide a basis for "common knowledge." This feature of the belief equilibrium means that each person may have some information about others' preferences, and also know that others have knowledge about the person's own preferences and strategies. Through such common knowledge, "Hobbesian" chaos may be avoided. However, when the core belief is no longer generally tenable, then the common knowledge foundation of cooperation may fail, and the society may also fragment, with each faction engaging in acts that appear incomprehensible, or threatening, to others. It is for this reason that war, or other forms of political violence, may occur at the onset of a quandary. Sometimes, of course, the victor simply imposes a new core belief on the loser (though this is likely to lead to further war). Chapter 7 suggests that the success of post – World War II international economic institutions gives us reason to believe that sometimes the quandary can be resolved by an "architect of change" who

---

[4] Evolutionary game theorists have formally examined the destruction of one equilibrium and the creation of a new one, but the tools they have used have been based on adaptive learning. It seems to me that the more interesting, and difficult, case is when violence rather than learning resolves the quandary. See Young (1998).

[5] See Keynes (1936: 349). The essence of Keynes's argument is that uncertainty may destroy the market equilibrium. Here, I am interested in how uncertainty may give way to consensus. See Chapter 7 for a discussion of Keynes's emphasis on the importance of uncertainty.

is able to transmute, in some fashion, the belief in question so that it is once again tenable, and provides the common knowledge foundation for cooperation.[6] The changes in the constitution, and its institutional apparatus, that accompany such a transmutation tend to occur very rapidly indeed, and in a fashion which at the time appears entirely unpredictable.

This conception of the slow evolution of a constitution in normal times, and rapid change or transformation at the onset of the quandary, is obviously somewhat similar to the notion of a scientific revolution as suggested by Kuhn (1962). A similar idea, that of "punctuated equilibrium," has also been put forward in evolutionary biology.[7] However, my application, in this book, to the evolution of the American Constitution, is essentially an extension of an argument made by William Riker (1982). To explain Riker's point of view, it is necessary to make a brief digression on the results of social choice theory obtained in the late 1970s.

4.2 THE CONFLICT OVER UNION AND CONFEDERATION

The so-called chaos theorem of voting has shown that majority rule equilibria can almost never occur; instead, voting cycles or disequilibria are almost certain.[8] Interpreting these theorems, Riker (1980) argued that "in the long run, nearly anything can happen in politics."

The neo-institutionalists of that time were, however, able to use the device of fixed and stable institutional rules to propose the existence of equilibria of tastes (or preferences), that bypassed the consequences of the chaos theorems (see e.g., Shepsle, 1979).

However, Riker conceived of an institution itself as an equilibrium. As he says,

the losers [in a constitutional system] are likely to want to change the committees and jurisdictions in the hope of winning on another day. In the end, therefore,

---

[6] See Chapter 7 for a brief interpretation of the Marshall Plan and the Bretton Woods Institutions along these lines. In this instance, of course, Truman was the architect of change.

[7] Eldredge and Gould (1972). This notion has been used to account for the very rapid evolution of the genus *Homo*. See Calvin (1991) and Tattersal (1998). It has also been suggested that this rapid evolution was triggered by climatic change induced by chaotic behavior of deep-sea currents in the Atlantic. See Fagan (1999). These connections suggest that, in any evolutionary system, rapid transformation is a consequence of chaotic, or at least, contingent causes.

[8] An outline of these results on voting "chaos" is given by Riker (1982: 185–8), Schofield (1985a), and Austen-Smith and Banks (1999). See the discussion in Chapter 2 and Chapter 8.

institutions are no more than rules and rules are themselves the product of social decisions. Consequently, the rules are also not in equilibrium. One can expect that losers on a series of decisions under a particular set of rules will attempt (often successfully) to change institutions and hence the kind of decisions [made] under them. (Riker, 1980: 444–5)

Riker's concern with the possibility of changing the rules of an institution led him to the notion of heresthetic—the art of constructing choice situations so as to be able to manipulate outcomes (Riker, 1986). The essence of Riker's notion of heresthetic is the claim that, in any political context, the final outcome depends on the way choices are framed, on the precise set of alternatives, or on the details of the rules of political decision making. He used this idea to explain key events in the history of American federalism: the drafting and ratification of the U.S. Constitution and the coming of the American Civil War.[9]

In fact, Riker's work on "historical heresthetics" after 1980 reflected his much earlier interest in the American Constitution, particularly in the nature of the "federal bargain" attained by the Ratification of the U.S. Constitution from 1787 to 1789. His first two books (1953, 1957) had introduced a distinction between the *centralized* federalism of the U.S. after 1789, and the *peripheralized* federalism of the Confederation from 1783 to 1789. His later book on federalism (1964: 13) argued that a necessary cause of the federal bargain was that politicians who accept the bargain perceive that the bargain overcomes an external military or diplomatic threat, or provides access to an obvious military or diplomatic opportunity. By a necessary cause, Riker clearly intimated that, in the absence of a threat or opportunity, a centralized federation would not come into being. While the book made a case for this general inductive hypothesis, Riker also argued that the threat of the British in the Northwest, and of the Spanish in the Southwest, circa 1787, to the Confederated States, together constituted the necessary cause for the federal bargain of the constitution:

Various writings by Jay, Madison, Hamilton, and Washington all suggested the primacy of the military motive in the adoption of centralized federalism. The suggestion is, in fact, so strong that one wonders how Beard ... could ever have believed that the main issues at Philadelphia were domestic matters of the distribution of income.[10]

---

[9] This work includes Riker (1984, 1987, 1993, 1995, 1996).

[10] Riker (1964: 19). Obviously, Riker refers here to Beard (1913).

Much of Riker's later work up until 1980 can be seen as an attempt to develop the foundation of a positive political theory, capable of permitting a study of the possible sufficient cause of dramatic constitutional changes, such as the Ratification. Riker's later focus on the notion of heresthetic is compatible with a perception that sufficient causes of such transformations may be inherently unpredictable, or contingent.[11]

However, in Riker's last book, published after his death, and edited from his collected papers, the emphasis changed from heresthetic to rhetoric. My interpretation of this last piece of work on the Ratification is that it was intended as a detailed study of the way in which participants to the federal bargain became persuaded as to the rationality of the constitutional change.[12] In essence, it was an examination of the sufficient cause of the bargain. The key to Riker's analysis was the assumption of risk aversion on the part of the participants. Arguments on the great costs associated with the failure of confederation to deal with outside threats were indeed credible. For most risk-averse participants these anticipated costs outweighed the costs of the "loss of freedom" of federation. Presented in this fashion, it is clear that Riker's analysis turned on the "beliefs" of the participants to the bargain. As in Chapter 3, I use the term beliefs to mean the "subjective probability estimates" associated with the various anticipated and possibly undesirable consequences of their choices.

To see what I mean, consider an alternative way to model the ratification decision by postulating that the "preferences" of the participants can be embedded in a one-dimensional "policy space." In this space, the status quo (the Articles of Confederation) is at one end of the political dimension, and a strong federal state at the other.[13] Since ratification involved voting, the standard spatial voting model would imply the existence of a political compromise point (a voting "core") located somewhere between the two extremes.[14] However, such an interpretation gives no indication why Hamilton and Madison, for example, were Federalists (strongly in favor of Federation) in 1787, who later diverged in their opinions over

---

[11] For example, Riker traced the cataclysmic event of the Civil War to a heresthetic maneuver by Lincoln in the Lincoln-Douglas debate in Freeport, Illinois, during the Illinois Senate race. See Riker (1986: 1–9). A discussion of this theme in Riker's research is offered in Chapter 5.

[12] Riker (1996). This book built on an earlier article by Riker (1991).

[13] In fact, the ratification decision was indeed studied by Fink and Riker (1989) using this perspective.

[14] See the classic treatment, by Hotelling (1929) and Downs (1957). Obviously, the particular compromise, or core, depends on the institutional voting rule and the distribution of preferred points.

the balance of power between central government and the states. Obviously enough, preferences over a strong or weak state are determined by inferences made about the consequences of each of the possibilities. Since these outcomes cannot be known with certainty, preferences of the kind just postulated are secondary to estimates of probabilities associated with these outcomes. Such an emphasis on probabilities (or beliefs) is compatible with the general model of preference under risk proposed by Leonard Savage (1954).

In this framework, fundamental preferences are the primitive parameters. In choosing between lotteries of outcomes, an individual reveals beliefs (or probability assessments) about states of the world. Given these beliefs, the individual chooses acts that are rational vis-à-vis fundamental preferences. In general, however, the fundamental preferences cannot be deduced from acts, unless the beliefs can also be ascertained. Moreover, because the choices over acts are made in the presence of risk, the risk posture of the individuals must also be determined. It is well known that individual choices under risk can be quite counter to traditional axiomatic choice models (see, e.g., Kahneman and Tversky, 1979).

There is good reason to accept Riker's argument that foreign threat was a necessary cause for accepting Union, a system of centralized federalism, put in place after 1789. We can use the same expected utility calculus as in Chapter 3. To simplify, let us use A_1 to denote a choice for Union and A_2 the choice for the status quo. Under A_2, there was some probability, p, say, that Spain would implement the threat by closing the Mississippi (at a cost T, say). Under A_1, the probability of such a threat would be much reduced, indeed negligible. However, some participants feared that Union would, with high probability q, say, impose a cost F, say, of loss of freedom or autonomy. Comparing expected costs (qF) associated with A_1 and pT with A_2 leads to a choice—an act—for each participant. Riker's earlier argument over the federal bargain was simply that the absence of a threat $(T = 0)$ implies a choice for A_2. However, this analysis does not deal with the possibility that Union would lead to pervasive factional chaos. It is clear from Madison's writings (in *Federalist X* for example) that he considered this a real possibility. If we let r denote the probability of factionalism, and C the cost of chaos, then the choice between A_1 and A_2 turns on the values of $qF + rC$ and pT.

While there was recognition in the period 1784 to 1787 that the expected cost, pT, of the status quo was high, the general understanding of political theory at this time was that factional chaos under Union was very likely. If indeed this theory was correct, then the expected costs for

Union for most participants would necessarily exceed the expected costs of the status quo. This decision problem has many of the elements of a quandary, particularly for those who favor Union. While Union is an obvious solution to the possibility of an outside threat, the likelihood that any federation would be destroyed by factional chaos made such a solution unacceptable. Madison's genius, in his essays on "Vices of the Political System of the United States" (1786) and in *Federalist X* (1787) was to give a theoretical argument why factional chaos need not be feared (see Rakove, ed., 1999: 69–80 and 160–7). The credibility of Madison's argument would have the effect of reducing rC, making A_1 a rational choice. The voting in the Conventions from 1787 to 1789 did result in a majority for ratification, and thus in what I have termed a *core belief* in the rationality of Union. Madison's argument can therefore be seen to be an essential element (in the presence of the outside threat) of a sufficient cause of the federal bargain. Of course, many complex compromises over the nature of the constitutional apparatus were put in place before the final federal bargain was made. Nonetheless, a general acceptance of the necessity of Union seems to have occurred fairly rapidly from 1787 to 1789.[15]

I contend that the resolution of the independence quandary at the end of the war in 1783 led almost immediately to a "security" quandary for the new United States. Because Spain had been ceded the Louisiana territory by France in 1763 (presumably to keep Britain out of the vast area), the Spanish had, by 1783, come to view the entire Mississippi basin as their own. The Spanish flag was planted on the east bank of the Mississippi in November, 1780, and an expedition from Spanish St. Louis later captured a British post in Michigan, and proclaimed the entire Illinois River country as Spanish. By 1784, the Spanish had sought to close the entire Mississippi to American shipping. In a long letter to Thomas Jefferson in Paris (August 20, 1784), James Madison expressed his deep concerns over this Spanish threat (Smith, ed., 1995: 337–42). Negotiations between the Foreign Secretary, John Jay, and the Spanish minister, Gardoquin, dragged on for two more years. As Madison's biographer says:

John Jay proposed that the United States agree for twenty-five years to abandon claims for navigation of the river in exchange for a commercial treaty guaranteeing American fishermen access to the huge Spanish market and favoring American merchants suffering from British discrimination. This,

---

[15] Throughout this book a rapid change in beliefs of this kind is called a *belief cascade*. See Bikhchandani et al. (1992) and Denzau and North (1994).

Jay argued would yield immediate advantages ... Jay's view reflected, ominously, a much keener awareness of the interests of the Eastern, trading portion of the new nation. ... To Southerners and Westerners, of course, the Jay – Gardoquin project was anathema.

(Ketcham, 1971: 177)

Congress chose, by vote of seven to six, not to pursue the negotiations with Gardoquin.[16] That seven states had shown an approval of the treaty led Madison to believe that disagreements between the States could fracture the weak Confederation.

Madison wrote to Jefferson on March 19, 1787, expressing the opinion that "the intended sacrifice [by Jay] of the Mississippi will not be made [but] the consequences of the intention and the attempt are likely to be very serious."[17]

Even Washington expressed the opinion (to John Jay in a letter of May 18, 1786) that the Articles of Confederation needed to be amended. He wrote, "something must be done, or the fabrick [*sic*] must fall! It certainly is tottering" (Rhodehamel, ed., 1997: 600).

Thus, we can say that, by 1786, there was a core belief among the American elite that the Union was threatened by imperial powers, Spain particularly, probably Britain, and possibly France. An obvious solution to this threat would be to devise a stronger Union, a federal apparatus. The quandary that this posed, however, was how to balance the differing interests of the states within this Union.

The essays comprising the *Federalist* (published between October 27, 1787, and May 28, 1788, by John Jay, Alexander Hamilton, and James Madison, in the *New York Independent Journal*) can be seen to first express the security quandary, and then to articulate a theoretical solution to the problem of Union. The essays by Jay and Hamilton (particularly numbers III, IV, V, VIII, and XXIV) all focus on foreign threats and the costs of disunion. In *Federalist X* James Madison presented his famous argument that heterogeneity in a Republic would make it unlikely that factional chaos could occur.[18]

---

[16] Unanimity was required to ratify the treaty.

[17] Smith, ed. (1995: 473). Indeed Rakove quotes from Madison's autobiography that Madison's objective in returning to Congress was to cancel Jay's project. See Rakove (1996: 377).

[18] By a faction, Madison meant "a number of citizens, whether amounting to a majority or a minority of the whole, who are united and activated by some common impulse or passion, or of interests, adverse to the rights of other citizens, or to the permanent and aggregate interests of the community" (Rakove, 1999: 161).

It was generally regarded that democracies would subject to such chaos. As Adam Smith (1981 [1776]) had remarked, the Colonies seemed too small to avoid chaos of this kind:

[A union with Great Britain] would, at least, deliver them from these rancorous and virulent factions which are inseparable from small democracies, and which have so frequently divided the affections of their people, and disturbed the tranquility of their governments ... In the case of total separation from Great Britain ... those factions would be ten times more virulent than ever (945).

However, in *Federalist X*, Madison distinguished between "a pure democracy consisting of a small number of citizens, who assemble and administer the government in person" and a republic where the government is delegated "to a small number of citizens elected by the rest" (Rakove, 1999: 164). He continues in *Federalist XIV*,

Under the confusion of names, it has been an easy task to transfer to a republic, observations applicable to a democracy only ... [for example] that [a republic] can never be established but among a small number of people, living within a small compass of territory.

(Rakove, 1999: 169)

In *Federalist X*, Madison argued that:

[I]t may be concluded that a pure democracy can admit of no cure for the mischiefs of faction ... . Hence it is, that such democracies have ever been spectacles of turbulence and contention; have ever been found incompatible with personal security ... and have in general been as short in their lives as they have been violent in their deaths ... A republic, by which I mean a government in which the scheme of representation takes place, opens a different prospect ...

[I]f the proportion of fit characters be not less in the large than in the small republic, the former will present a greater option, and consequently a greater probability of a fit choice.

(Rakove, 1999: 164–6)

Madison's intuitions on democracy were given formal demonstration in the so-called chaos theorems, almost two hundred years later.[19] But why should a republic differ from a democracy in the fashion proposed by Madison? Beer suggests that: "Representation, which necessitates the big constituencies of the big republic, would presumably restrain passion and enhance reason in the deliberative process of popular government" (Beer, 1993: 280).

---

[19] Arrow (1951) proved that turbulence was possible, while the chaos theorem showed that turbulence could well be expected. See the later discussion in Chapter 8.

As Madison also says in *Federalist X*:

[I]t may well happen that the public voice pronounced by the representatives of the people, will be more consonant to the public good ... . [E]ach representative will be chosen by a greater number of citizens in the large than in the small republic. ... The other point of difference is, the greater number of citizens and extent of territory which may be brought within the compass of republican, than of democratic government; and it is this ... which renders factious combinations less to be dreaded in the former, than in the latter. Extend the sphere, and you take in a greater variety of parties and interests; you make it less probable that a majority of the whole will have a common motive to invade the rights of other citizens. ...

Hence it clearly appears, that the same advantage, which a republic has over a democracy ... is enjoyed by a large over a small Republic—is enjoyed by the union over the states composing it.

(Rakove, 1999: 165–6)

Madison's argument is entirely consistent with the result now known as Condorcet's Jury theorem.[20] Consider a number of individuals choosing between two alternatives under risk. No one knows what is the correct option (but each has some probability of making the correct guess). Assuming that the average of the probabilities exceeds one-half, then a jury, using majority rule, has a better chance of making the correct choice than an average juror. Moreover, as the jury size gets large, the probability of a correct choice approaches 1. The theorem, as presented by Condorcet depends on "independence" of votes.[21] Voter choice is, however, likely to be "pairwise dependent." If the population is heterogeneous, then average dependency may be sufficiently low for the Jury theorem still to be valid.[22] Thus, if a constituency is large, the voter population in the constituency is likely to be heterogeneous. The representative can never appeal to widely differing preferences. In a binary choice involving risk, assuming that representatives do not pursue only the interests of their constituents, and assuming further that on average they have a better than even chance of making a wise choice, then the collective choice of the representatives will be "wise." Condorcet had formally presented his work on the Jury theorem and on factional instability in voting in 1785, in Paris, and we may distinguish between them in terms of a distinction between belief aggregation and preference aggregation.

[20] See Condorcet (1795) and the translated extracts of his work in McLean and Hewitt, eds. (1994).
[21] For versions of the result, see Rae (1969); Taylor (1969); and Schofield (1972a, b) and Chapter 8.
[22] See the discussion in Ladha and Miller (1996).

In many ways these very different results today separate those who consider political choice to be rational or irrational. Whether Madison knew of these results by Condorcet has proved to be controversial.[23] What is clear, however, is that Madison's argument against factionalism in the Republic was novel and credible. In fact, the most compelling argument for its plausibility was the "correctness" of the choice of the Continental Congress in declaring independence in 1776. Clearly, this decision was made in a context of risk. Different members of Congress must have formed different estimates of the probabilities and costs; however, the true state of the world was obscured. The fact that the Revolution succeeded suggests that Congress made, in aggregate, a wise choice. It is true that not everyone would draw the same connection between Madison's argument and the declaration of 1776. Risk-averse decision makers might require additional safeguards against factionalism. Nonetheless, Madison did give a credible argument supporting a belief that it was possible, in principle, to reconstruct the Constitution in such a way as to make the Union stronger against threat, while maintaining the rights of individuals and states. My view of the Ratification process (from the ratifications of Delaware in December 1787 to that of North Carolina in August 1788) is that it was accompanied by the creation of a core belief in the possibility of Union. Using my terminology, Madison was the *architect of change* who principally constructed the theoretical framework that made this belief tenable.

During the Federal Convention in the summer of 1787, and later during their collaboration over the *Federalist*, James Madison and Alexander Hamilton were allies in their support of the Union. By early 1791, Madison had come to view Hamilton's fiscal scheme for the Republic with alarm. As the decade of the 1790s progressed, the two-party system came into being. In essence, the commercial interests cohered into a Federalist party, including Washington, John Adams, and Hamilton, while agrarian interests came together as a Republican party under Thomas Jefferson and Madison.

This early schism among the Federalist supporters of 1787 can be interpreted as an illustration of the notion of "partisan realignment" (Clubb, Flanigan and Zingale, 1980) used by writers such as Sundquist (1983) to characterize political transformations in the late 1890s and mid 1930s.

---

[23] McLean and Hewitt (1994) contend that, although Madison did receive a copy of Condorcet's major work, he either did not read through it or disagreed with it. See McLean and Hewitt (65–69).

I argue that the partisan realignment of the 1790s and the critical election of Jefferson in 1800 created a two-party political equilibrium that persisted until 1852.

Many historians (and economic historians) have discussed the gestation of the two-party system in the 1790s. My purpose in adding to the discussion is to use ideas from modern social choice theory and political economy to throw light on the social beliefs held by Hamilton, on the one hand, and Madison and Jefferson, on the other. Although it is clearly anachronistic to use modern technical theories to interpret the beliefs of agents long dead, I shall argue that the theories that I describe were well understood, though possibly in rudimentary form, by these protagonists.

Although the technical structures of these two theories are well understood today, the applicability of the theories in interpreting modern polities is quite contentious. My purpose is to attempt to show that the developing conflict between the Federalists and the Republicans in the 1790s grew out of differing beliefs over the significance and meaning of these theories for the "design" of the U.S. political economy.

Modern social choice theory has a number of somewhat irreconcilable subthemes. One theme can be interpreted as a version of Montesquieu's constitutional theory. For Montesquieu, monarchy, aristocracy, and democracy all possessed different virtues that could be combined to advantage in a single constitutional system. *Democracy*, while dangerous because of its likely "turbulence," was necessary to prevent the potential tyranny of monarchy. *Aristocracy* was required to temper the arrogance of monarchy with wisdom. As I suggest later, one theme of social choice theory is that democracy is indeed turbulent, but this feature can be controlled by the concentration of power implied by aristocracy or, more generally, *autocracy*. Obviously, the Framers of the Constitution held to a version of this theory, but varied in their emphasis on the dangers of turbulence, and the costs of autocracy. Hamilton's bold version of a powerful U.S. commercial empire inclined him to a preference for autocracy.

In contrast, Madison, in *Federalist X*, offered the entirely different theory of the *extended* republic. Acknowledging that democracies tend to be turbulent, Madison then proposed that a republic, "in which the scheme of representation takes place," provides the cure for turbulence. The "large" republic will "present a . . . greater probability of a fit choice" (Rakove, 1999: 164–5). Present day pluralist democratic theorists interpret Madison's argument to mean that "competing interests cancel one another out" (Williams, 1998: 39).[24] I argue that Madison had an entirely different logic in mind. Although the extended republic argument is usually traced to Hume's "Idea of a Perfect Commonwealth," (Adair, 1943, 2000), there is a deeper connection to Condorcet's *Essai* of 1785. I offer evidence that Madison, in late 1787, had received elements of Condorcet's *Essai* from Jefferson in Paris. Condorcet's *Essai* related to the probability of a jury, or committee, making a "true" choice. If we interpret "true" to mean "valid" or "virtuous," then Madison's argument can be seen as an application or extension of the Condorcet theorem to the election of the chief magistrate.

I contend that this Condorcetian aspect is a key feature of the constitutional thought of both Madison and Jefferson in the 1790s. In his writing up to the *Federalist*, Madison obviously viewed faction, party, and interest as inimical to the stability of the republic and likely to generate mutability or turbulence. Madison's view changed during the 1790s.

In 1790 and 1791, Hamilton, as Secretary of the Treasury, prepared his *Report on the Public Credit*, *Report on the National Bank*, and *A Report on the Subject of Manufactures*. All three reports made it clear that Hamilton had in mind the creation of a commerce-based American empire "able to dictate the terms of connection between the old and the new world" to quote from Hamilton's *Federalist 11* (Freeman, 2001: 208).

As discussed in Chapter 2, it is well known that Hamilton's scheme owed much for its inspiration to the economic and fiscal structures devised in Britain during the period of Whig supremacy under Walpole's leadership from 1720 to 1740. What has been less examined is how, precisely, the Walpole scheme led to the creation of Britain's maritime empire. I argue that Walpole's scheme can be seen to be consistent with a political economic theory relating to the role of the state in balancing the economic factors of land, capital, and labor, and avoiding turbulence. Elements of this theory are present in Hume's *Essay on Commerce* where he comments, with approval, that commercial advancement "augments the power of the state" (Hume, 1985 [1777]: 265).

I argue that Madison and Jefferson were well aware of the probable consequences of the success of Hamilton's scheme. This knowledge presented them (and, in their view, the entire society) with a dilemma.

---

[24] It is unclear precisely what such a phrase means. One possible interpretation is that political competition leads to a "centrist" balance between competing interests (Downs, 1957). This implies that all political parties become identical. The empirical evidence implies that this is a fallacy (Schofield and Sened, 2006).

Although what I call the "Walpole Equilibrium" was crucial for Britain's growth to hegemony, it had deleterious consequences for that century's agricultural laborers. Modern research in economic history has shown how Britain's use of tariffs and excise protected land, drove up the price of land, and stimulated increased agricultural productivity. However, capital substituted for labor, and consequently, real wages for both farm and skilled labor remained flat, or even declined (Allen, 1988; Crafts, 1994). Although the precise economic details of Britain's growth in the eighteenth century may not have been known to Madison and Jefferson, its overall consequences were. For example, as Porter has recently observed, the poem, *The Deserted Village* (1770), by Oliver Goldsmith "damned the depopulating effects of enclosure" (Porter, 2000: 317).

Because of the differing economic structure of Britain and the United States, Hamilton's commercial scheme would necessarily have advantaged capital over both the landed interests and agrarian labor. I argue that Jefferson, during his residence in Paris in the 1780s, had been much influenced by Condorcet's theories of political economy. Condorcet's later *Esquisse* of 1794 summed up these ideas and presented an optimistic view of economic development. This thesis was later contested by Malthus's *Essay on the Principle of Population* in 1798.

One coherent vision of the future development of the United States consistent with Condorcet's view would emphasize the growth of an agrarian empire. By focusing on free trade, and by increasing total agricultural output through expansion, both the landed interest and free agricultural labor would be advantaged. The choice between these two development paths—one commercial and one agrarian—was the point of the election of 1800. To implement this vision held by both Jefferson and Madison, it was necessary to destroy the commercial agrarian coalition that had supported Union in 1787, and to create an agrarian Republican Party. In so doing, I believe, Madison and Jefferson both accepted the underlying logic implicit in Condorcet's *Essai*, and in essence, created a stable two-party system.

What I mean by this requires some elaboration. First, the fact that in 1800 two entirely different development paths were available, one agrarian and one commercial, meant that a compromise between the two was impossible. Contrary to the pluralist notion of democracy, in which various interests cancel one another out, the society in 1800 faced a dilemma over which choice to pursue. From the Condorcetian perspective, only one of the choices could be "true." Of course, in 1800, which one of the choices was "true" was hidden behind the veil of the future. Madison and Jefferson clearly believed that their agrarian vision was superior. The more information available about the consequences of the two choices, the better would be the decision of the society. As a result, the 1790s saw vigorous and intense argument about the policy choices available: about alliance with France or Britain, about the probable growth and structure of the U.S. economy, about government debt, trade protection, and so forth. These debates could not simply be reduced to *interests*, but were based on the *beliefs* of the protagonists.

This distinction between interests and beliefs is implicit in Madison's *Federalist X*, but I shall offer some further clarification, based on modern social choice theory. This theory assumes individual action is based on "rational" preferences of individuals. Such preferences can be derived from "interests," the holding of property or the exercise of "factor" power, such as labor or capital. As the theory suggests, and as Madison feared, such interests can collide to induce instability. Indeed, Madison expressed such fears later in life over the question of slavery and state's rights (McCoy, 1989). If interests dominate among the representatives of the people, then the legislature will itself be turbulent.

However, when the Republic faces a dilemma, as it did in 1800, over the choice between two competing and incompatible visions for society, then these two visions may be represented by two presidential contenders. In such a case, interest plays less of a role than does belief. Because no individual can see the future with certainty, each one can only guess (with some subjective probability) which choice is likely to be the best. While interest may affect such a choice, it does not determine it. However, to create a winning coalition, it is necessary to create faction, mobilize interest, and indeed, bring into existence a party. Madison and Jefferson came to understand this logic during the 1790s. Just as in jury decision making, the selection of a president, and of a choice for the future, depends on persuasion, rhetoric, and contest.

The division of society by 1800 into two parties, one Republican and one Federalist, was, as Beard (1915) has argued, partly based on the opposing interests of land and agrarian labor on the one hand, and capital and industrial labor on the other. However, this division in the United States was very different from the division between Court and Country Parties in Britain in the 1700s. One obvious difference was that the Republican coalition had to dampen the possible conflict between free labor and the slave-owning land interest. The optimistic agrarian vision presented by Madison and Jefferson was important in creating and maintaining this coalition.

What I call the *Madison–Jefferson Equilibrium*, created after the election of 1800, was remarkably stable and dominated U.S. politics until it began to fracture in the 1840s over this issue of slavery. However, it is even more remarkable that the U.S. polity has retained a two-party system throughout two hundred years, even though the coalitions that comprise the parties can be dramatically transformed at a critical election. (This is discussed further in Chapter 5.) At each such critical election, (whether 1860, 1896, 1932, or 1964) the contest between the parties has involved a choice between two competing visions of the future. The resolution of the conflict turns on the creation of a new coalition or partisan alignment among the various interests of land, labor, and capital. The comments made here, on the election of 1800 and on the beliefs of Madison and Jefferson, are offered in the hope of extending social choice theory and political economy in order to understand the phenomenon of long-run dynamic equilibrium.

4.3 SOCIAL CHOICE AND CONSTITUTIONAL THEORY

Figure 4.1 repeats Figure 2.2 from Chapter 2. The first axis describes the degree to which a polity is democratic. As discussed earlier, a *veto group* is a group of individuals, all of whom must agree to any policy choice in some domain of political decision making. A *collegium* is a group that has veto power in every political domain, while an *oligarchy* is a group that not only holds veto power on every domain, but (if they all agree) can also determine policy on any domain. An *autocrat*, or dictator, is a single individual with oligarchic power. A pure democracy obviously cannot have veto groups, collegia, oligarchies, or dictators. The U.S. constitution, as Dahl (2001) has recently argued, is not "democratic" precisely because the balance of power among executive, legislative, and judicial branches allows for veto. (As Chapter 6 discusses, for example, Southern Democrats in the Senate used the filibuster, and the difficulty of creating a countercoalition to effect cloture, in order to block civil rights legislation from the period of Reconstruction until 1964.)

The purest form of democracy is simple majority rule—every enfranchised individual has equal vote, and the coalition of the largest wins. As outlined in Chapter 2, social choice theory suggests that pure democracy can lead to "chaos." In its most general form, chaos means that politics is intrinsically unpredictable. As noted above, "nearly anything can happen in politics" (Riker, 1980: 444).

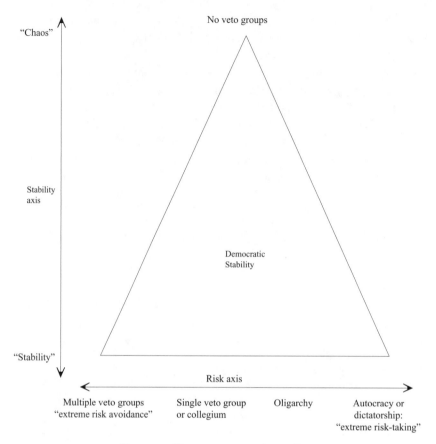

Figure 4.1. Chaos or autocracy in a polity.

Political theorists of the eighteenth century also believed that democracy was fundamentally chaotic. Adam Smith and Madison, in *Federalist X*, expressed the view that democracy was turbulent. Madison also considered that legislatures were chaotic, leading to an incoherence of the law. In *Federalist LXII*, Madison discussed the "mischievous effects of mutable government":

It will be of little avail to the people that the laws are made by men of their own choice, if laws be so ... incoherent that they cannot be understood; if they be repealed or revised before they are promulgated, or undergo such incessant changes that no man who knows what the law is today can guess what it will be tomorrow.

(Rakove, 1999: 343)

The opposite of chaos is equilibrium, or rationality, what Madison called "stability in government" in *Federalist XXXVII*:

Stability in government, is essential to national character, and to ... that repose and confidence in the minds of the people. .... An irregular and mutable legislation is not more an evil in itself, than it is odious to the people.

(Madison, *Papers* Vol 10: 361)

Twentieth century political pluralists have taken Madison's argument about the extended republic from *Federalist X* to mean that factional or "competing interests cancel one another out" (Williams, 1998: 39). This inference, however, is at odds with social choice theory on the operation of democratic rule. I return, later, to Madison's extended republic argument. Before this, however, I comment on two theoretical methods of avoiding chaos. The first is by restricting, in some fashion, the domain of political choice. However, if we follow Madison in acknowledging the heterogeneity of interests in the extended republic, then it would seem impossible to restrict the domain of political choice sufficiently to avoid chaos.

The second method is to concentrate power either in dictatorship, oligarchy collegium, or through some related veto principle. As Figure 4.1 suggests, concentrating power in this fashion can induce stability (Arrow, 1951), but there will be effects on the "risk posture" of the society.

The constitutional theorists of the eighteenth century were well aware that autocracy could induce stability, but at the cost of tyranny. However, tyrants wish to extend their power, and are likely to engage in war. Indeed, the Declaration of Independence, penned by Thomas Jefferson, accused George III of precisely such risk-taking, tyrannical behavior. A common understanding of British political history is that autocracy did indeed lead to risk taking and war. Oliver Cromwell had, in large degree, taken on dictatorial powers precisely in order to prosecute war against France, and in Ireland. As Madison put it, in his "Vices of the Political System of the United States," while a great desideratum of the prince is a sufficient neutrality between the different interests and factions, "In absolute Monarchies, the prince is sufficiently, neutral towards his subjects, but frequently sacrifices their happiness to his ambition" (Rakove, 1999: 79).

Weaker veto power can also induce stability, as in oligarchy or collegium. If we identify collegium with aristocracy, then as Adair observed, there will be an "inveterate and incorrigible" tendency to use the apparatus of government to serve the special interests of the aristocratic few

(Adair, 1974: 173). If the rule in the "aristocratic" Senate permits many veto groups, then the outcome may be the opposite of risk preferring autocracy or monarchy. With many such groups, it will be impossible to make decisions. Such a situation may be termed *risk avoiding*.

Figure 4.1 may be interpreted in terms of Montesquieu's constitutional theory of balance between democracy, aristocracy, and monarchy (Adair, 1974). It was evident in 1787 that Madison and Hamilton differed in how the balance was to be obtained. To judge from Hamilton's essays in the *Federalist*, he clearly had in mind the creation of a commercial empire. As he wrote in *Federalist XI*,

The superiority [Europe] has long maintained, has tempted her to plume herself as the Mistress of the World. . . . It belongs to us . . . to teach that assuming brother moderation. . . . Let the thirteen States, bound together in a strict and indissoluble Union, concur in erecting one great American system, superior to the contoul [*sic*] of all trans-atlantic force or influence, and able to dictate the terms of the connection between the old and the new world!

(Freeman, 2001: 208)

As Adair observed, the constitutional theory of Montesquieu suggested that only monarchy possessed the necessary energy, secrecy, and dispatch to order an empire.

While the Federal Convention would not, of course, accept a monarchy, Hamilton pressed for almost autocratic power for the executive: first, on June 4, 1787, for an absolute veto, and second, on June 18, for appointment for life.

On June 4, Madison had responded that "[t]o give such a prerogative would certainly be obnoxious to the temper of the Country; its present temper at least" (Madison, *Papers Vol. 10*: 24). Later, in developing his balance theory in *Federalist LI*, Madison noted that "[A]n absolute negative, on the legislative appears at first view to be the natural defence with which the executive magistrate should be armed. But perhaps it would be neither altogether safe, nor alone sufficient" (Rakove, 1999: 296).

Although Madison and Hamilton seem from their written and spoken remarks to agree on the political logic inherent in Figure 4.1, they disagreed about how to create the constitutional apparatus of the Republic so as to avoid the costs both of democratic chaos and of risk-accepting autocracy. As I have intimated in the introduction, Britain's experience in the eighteenth century was relevant to this disagreement.

I suggest that the party system that came into being in the 1790s was based on stable factor coalitions of land and agrarian labor against capital and industrial labor. To emphasize the parallel with the Walpole Equilibrium in Britain, based on a coalition of land and capital, I use the aforementioned term *Madison–Jefferson Equilibrium* for the basis of the Republican coalition of land and agrarian labor.

To better understand the nature of this equilibrium, it is useful to elaborate on the background to the conflict between Britain and the colonies, starting in 1756, and on the creation of a land–capital coalition in the United States in the 1770s, during ratification of the Constitution.

4.4 LAND AND CAPITAL IN NORTH AMERICA, 1756–1800

Historians have emphasized many points of conflict between the metropole and the colonies, including religion, hatred of tyranny, taxation, and so forth. My view is that land was the fundamental source of this conflict. Although Chapter 3 discussed this view of the cause of the War of Independence, it is worth adding a few further remarks.

In the 1750s, the American colonies were hemmed in by the French domains of Louisiana and Quebec. Although the Colonies claimed land to the Mississippi, they had no resources to wrest it from the French. Whether by accident or intent, George Washington's expedition into the Ohio Valley and the killing of a young French ensign, Joseph Coulon de Villiers de Jumonville, and some of his troops, set in motion the military machines of Britain and France (Anderson, 2000: 52). During the Seven Years War of 1756 to 1763, Britain took Havana (Cuba), Manilla, Quebec, and Guadalupe in the Caribbean. After France's defeat, Britain kept Cape Breton, Canada, and Louisiana, east of the Mississippi, but returned Guadalupe to France. Possibly to prevent Louisiana, west of the Mississippi falling to Britain, France ceded this domain to Spain, its ally against Britain.

For the landed interest in the Colonies, the close of the Seven Years War gave them hope that the vast region of the Ohio Valley would be available for land speculation and settlement. However, the peace had also brought war with the Native American tribes under Pontiac, a chief of the Ottawa, opposed to colonial settlement. To appease Pontiac, the British government issued a Proclamation closing the Ohio Valley to settlement, but was forced to maintain a series of forts on the line, at a cost of nearly 400,000 pounds sterling. In an attempt to cover some of the costs, the British government passed the Stamp Act and Sugar Act. These, together with the Proclamation, infuriated the agrarian elite. Benjamin

Franklin, in London, in 1764, argued that the Acts were without justification because the conflict with the French and Indians was of no concern to the Colonies. The Quebec Act of 1774 tried to close the Ohio Valley to settlement by including it in the jurisdiction of the Quebec authorities. It was this threat by the British to the expansion of the Colonies that exasperated the agrarian elite. The costs of taxation may have angered the people, but the burden of taxation could not be considered sufficient to induce war. Chown (1994: 218), for example, estimates that the taxes were intended to raise about 16,000 pounds sterling, excluding collection costs. The risk of losing the war against the formidable British naval and military power meant that the Continental Congress delayed declaring independence until there was reasonable cause to believe that France would aid them. Chapter 3 suggested that the Committee of Secret Correspondence, chaired by Franklin, heard news of the promise of aid from Louis XVI in late June 1776. With this aid, combined with the French military and naval assistance, the Colonies were successful, and in the final peace treaty, obtained the entire territory east of the Mississippi.

Spain, however, never recognized the United States, and during the War of Independence laid claim to the northern territory of what is now Michigan, as well as the region bordering the Floridas. It was this threat that John Jay, Secretary of Foreign Affairs, tried to allay by a treaty with Spain's agent, Diego de Gardoquin. Seven of the thirteen states agreed in principle to the proposed treaty, and it was this fact that caused Madison to fear that the weak confederation of states would fragment.[25] Supporters of the Jay–Gardoquin treaty believed that the increased trade offered by Spain would benefit their particular commercial interests. Those opposed tended to be states dominated by the members of the agrarian interest who saw the opportunity of expansion into the Louisiana territory. This threat by Spain, and the resulting disagreement between the states, made it clear that there was a conflict of interest between what Hume called the "landed and trading" parts of the nation (Hume, 1985 [1777]). Although conflict between these interests may indeed have been muted in Britain, this was because of the nature of the Walpole Equilibrium. In the United States, the potential conflict between land and capital was

---

[25] Letters, J. Madison to T. Jefferson, August 20, 1784, in Smith, 1995: 337–42; J. Madison to G. Washington December 7, 1786 in Rakove, 1999: 60; J. Madison to T. Jefferson, March 19, 1787 in Smith, 1995: 472).

temporarily overcome in the period of ratification of the constitution, 1787 to 1788.

In his classic statement, Beard (1913: 17) argued that the supporters of Union in 1787 were adherents of a hard money principle, namely "merchants, money lenders, security holders, manufacturers, shippers, capitalists and financiers." Opponents of Union were those who favored soft money—"non – slave-holding farmers ... and debtors" (Beard 1913: 17).

The threat from Spain, however, was real, and as the essays by Jay and Hamilton in the *Federalist* made clear, Union was the obvious way to overcome this threat (Riker, 1964: 13). For agrarian interests, the choice between Union and the Confederation was determined by whether the subjective costs associated with hard money or the Spanish threat were predominant.

Although the decision was close in many of the states, the new Constitution was eventually ratified. Obviously enough, the constitution involved a complex balance among a number of political objectives. However, it would seem from the above observations that Beard's argument concerning the Federalist coalition of 1787 was not entirely valid. The pro-Union coalition consisted not just of the commercial interest, but of landed interests as well. In general, the landed interest will tend to be opposed to capital, because, as Beard implied, the former tend to be indebted, and therefore, in favor of soft money. The threat from Spain, and the response in creating a federal apparatus, temporarily overcame these conflicts. However, with the threat diminished and the Union completed, the Federalist coalition of commercial and agrarian interests became unstable. Although it was necessary to devise a fiscal apparatus to deal with debt, it became obvious by 1790 that Hamilton's scheme would set the country on a course of commercial, rather than agrarian, expansion. Hamilton's writings suggest that he believed that his scheme would resemble the *Walpole Equilibrium* of Britain in the earlier part of the century, and be compatible with the interests of both land and capital. As I suggest later, economic theory suggests he was incorrect in this inference. His protagonists, Madison and Jefferson, were well aware of the consequences and costs of Hamilton's scheme. Moreover, they had a shared vision of the future of the United States, which, I argue, derived in large part from the constitutional writings of Condorcet. The conflict of the 1790s, and thus the creation of the two-party system, arose out of the incompatibility of these two contrasting theories associated with Hamilton on the one hand, and Madison and Jefferson on the other.

4.5 THE INFLUENCE OF CONDORCET ON MADISON AND JEFFERSON

The intellectual influence of the English and Scottish constitutional theorists on the Founders, and particularly on Madison and Jefferson, has long been studied. Adair (1943: 2000), for example, in his argument against Beard (1913), relied on Hume's assertion that there was no conflict in principle, between the landed and trading parts of the nation. In accepting Hume's logic, Adair asserted that Hamilton's belief about the disequilibrium between democracy and aristocracy was also invalid. However, Hume also contended that the election of the chief magistrate would necessarily be attended by tumult. As Hume says,

The filling of the [position of elective magistrate] is a point of too great and too general interest, not to divide the whole people into factions. Whence a civil war, the greatest of ills, may be apprehended almost with certainty, upon every vacancy.
(Hume, 1985 [1777]: 18)

A similar theme is apparent in the work of Bolingbroke (Kramnick, 1992), and even in Gibbon's *History of the Decline and Fall of the Roman Empire* (Gibbon, 1994 [1781]; see Womersley, 2002). In a later essay, Hume goes on to refer to "the common opinion that no large state, such as FRANCE or GREAT BRITAIN could ever be modelled into a commonwealth, but that such a form of government can only take place in a city or small territory" (Hume, 1985 [1777]: 527).

Hume attempts his refutation of this small republic argument of Montesquieu by proposing that in

a large government, which is modelled with masterly skill, there is compass and room enough to refine the democracy, from the lower people ... to the higher magistrates ... the parts are so distant that it is very difficult ... to hurry them into any measures against the public interest.
(Hume, 1985 [1777]: 528)

Adair is clearly correct to see in Hume's argument the essence of Madison's extended republic thesis. I concur with Adair that Hume's logic was absorbed into Madison's essay, "Vices of the Political System of the United States," written in April 1787 (Rakove, 1999: 69–80). However, there are precise differences between Madison's essay of April 1787, and the clearer thesis of *Federalist X* of November 22, 1787.

As indicated above, I contend that Madison's later logic suggests the influence of the work of the Condorcet (1743–94). Indeed, I argue further that Condorcet's work in constitutional theory, fiscal theory, trade theory, and economic growth were utilized by Madison and Jefferson to provide a coherent logic to what I have called the Madison–Jefferson equilibrium. In this argument, I enlarge on the points made by McLean (2005).

As is well known, Jefferson arrived in Paris as Minister Plenipotentiary in August 1784, to relieve Franklin. As Jefferson's biographer Randall notes, Condorcet, Chastellux, and Lafayette joined Jefferson's intimate circle of friends (Randall, 1993: 431). Condorcet had been appointed the permanent secretary of the Academy of Science, in August 1776 and had close contact with Franklin in that context (Darnton, 1997). His work on social choice theory (surveyed in McLean and Hewitt, 1994) is still relevant today. Condorcet's fame, in social choice theory, rests on his *Essai sur l'application de l'analyse à la probabilitié des voix* (Condorcet, 1785).[26] He is more widely known for his *Esquisse d'un tableau historique* (Condorcet, 1795). This latter work stimulated Malthus to write his famous essay (Malthus, 1970 [1798]).

Condorcet's Jury theorem proposed that each voter, i, say, could be characterized by some probability, $prob_i$, of voting for the truth. The theorem showed that in a binary choice (yea or nay), majority rule maximized the probability $prob_n$, say, that the jury (or committee) selected the truth. Moreover, as the jury size, n, increased without bound, then this probability $prob_n$ approached 1. When Condorcet attempted to extend this result to one with multiple choices, he found an incoherence theorem, similar in kind to what I have termed chaos. Condorcet's results were presented in the French Academy of Science in 1785. Franklin and Condorcet were dinner companions at the Salon of Madame Helvetius, and there they discussed matters of political economy with Turgot, previously Finance Minister to Louis XVI. Brands (2000: 559) mentions that Diderot, d'Alembert, and even Hume, came to call. Claude Anne Lopez (1966, 2000) has described how Franklin entered into the intellectual life of Paris in the 1780s. This has obviously been clearly recognized by historians (Baker, 1975) but what has seemingly not been recognized is that Condorcet's work on *Social Mathematics* would have been discussed. As a member of the French Academy, Franklin must have heard the talks by Condorcet and his protagonist, Borda, in the Academy. Franklin may not have been a mathematician, but he was certainly a scientist, and, in any case, would understand the significance of the result.

[26] Condorcet's work in his *Essai* can be seen as an extension of Hume's idea of "probable belief," set out in Hume's *Treatise* (Hume, 1985 [1752]). Indeed, Condorcet's biographer, Baker (1975: 13), notes the line of thought from Hume through Condorcet to the twentieth century (Keynes, 1921; Popper, 1959). In modern terminology, this theory is called "decision-making under risk." Again, see Chapter 8.

When Franklin returned to the United States in July 1785, he created a *Society for Political Enquiries* in Philadelphia, which Washington certainly attended. Madison visited Philadelphia in early 1787, and presumably discussed the issue of the constitution with Franklin. It is possible that Madison heard more about Condorcet's theorem from Franklin. Moreover, Franklin was interested in the problem of decision making under risk, and discussion in the *Society for Political Enquiries* focused on the various constitutional issues of the times (van Doren, 1938: 771; Campbell, 1999: 209). It is possible that Madison, after sketching the Humean extended Republic argument in his "Vices" paper of April, 1787, discussed the more refined Condorcetian logic with Franklin in Philadelphia and, after reading the *Recherches Historiques sur les Etats-Unis* (by the Italian, Philip Mazzei, in the summer of 1787), adapted it to his purpose in writing *Federalist X* in November 1787.

It has been suggested by McGrath (1983) that Madison was aware of Condorcet's "incoherence" theorem and had it in mind when arguing for the separation of powers implicit in *Federalist LI*. The analyses by Urken (1991) and McLean and Urken (1991, 1992) suggest otherwise. Their arguments turn on Madison's rejection of unicameralism.

It is known that Madison did receive the sketch of Condorcet's work, *Lettres d'une bourgeois de New Haven,* which was included in the book by Mazzei (see McLean and Hewitt, 1994: 64). This was mailed by Jefferson on July 22, 1787. Madison mentions that he had received the package in a letter to Jefferson, dated September 6, 1787 (Smith, 1995: 492). In his contribution, Condorcet asserts that it can be proven rigorously "that increasing the number of legislative bodies could never increase the probability of obtaining true decisions" (McLean and Hewitt, 1994: 325). Obviously, this can be taken as an argument for unicameralism. Because Madison seemingly rejected this principle, in *Federalist LI*, that would seem to be the end of it.

Although Condorcet believed his Jury theorem applied to legislative decision making, Madison evidently did not believe that the theorem was relevant to choice in a House of Representatives. As Madison's remarks on "mutability" imply, a legislative body makes laws, and these may be incoherent. In contrast, when an electorate chooses a representative, or a chief magistrate, it picks a *person*. A person may not be "true" in Condorcet's sense, but can be "pre-eminent for ability and virtue," to use Hamilton's phrase in *Federalist LXVIII* (Freeman, 2001: 364).

Thus, if we interpret Madison's term "a fit choice" to mean a virtuous representative or chief magistrate, then there is a clear similarity between the extended republic argument of *Federalist X* and Condorcet's Jury theorem. As in Condorcet's result, the larger, or more heterogeneous and populous the republic, the greater will be "the probability of a fit choice" (Rakove, 1999: 165). Madison's term "the probability of a fit choice" does not appear in the April 1787 essay, "Vices," but does occur in the *Federalist X* essay of November. Notice that the logic of the theorem only applies formally to binary choice, in situations where there are two candidates, Federalist or Republican, say. Moreover, Condorcet's theorem, and its apparent application by Madison in *Federalist X*, is only valid when the electorate is knowledgeable.

The evidence suggests that Madison, after writing the "Vices" paper in early 1787, discussed the idea with Franklin in Philadelphia and then, (after reading the *Recherches* in the summer of 1787), developed the idea further while writing *Federalist X* in November 1787. This suggestion forms the basis for my argument that this fundamental proposition is important in understanding the actions of Madison and Jefferson in the constitutional disagreement with the Federalists in the 1790s. There also appear to be further influences of Condorcet, both on Madison and Jefferson.

Before Jefferson left France in October 1789, he had witnessed the opening ceremony of the Estates General in Versailles in May, and collaborated with Lafayette and Condorcet on a draft of what was eventually to be the *Declaration of the Rights of Man and the Citizen* in August, 1789 (McLean and Hewitt, 1994: 55). Implicit in Jefferson's thought at this time was, what Randall calls, the "explosive doctrine of perpetual revolution" (Randall, 1993: 486). In Jefferson's letter to Madison of September 6, 1789, he asks, "Whether one generation of men has a right to bind another?" Jefferson answers himself: "no man can by natural right oblige the lands he occupied ... or the persons who succeed him, to the paiment [*sic*] of debts contracted by him." Thus, "the earth belongs in usufruct to the living"(Peterson, 1984: 959).[27]

As Sloan (2001 [1995]: 242) observes, on the same day, Condorcet's letter to Comte de Montmorency mathematically computes the length of time of a generation—about twenty years (in fact, this term is the half-life of a population). Jefferson, using an identical calculation, estimates the half-life at eighteen years, eight months. Then, Jefferson makes the following point: the French debt of ten thousand milliard of livres had

---

[27] Mayer (1994: Ch. 10) discusses the further correspondence between Madison and Jefferson in 1790 over the issue of debt and the possibility of constitutional change.

impoverished the nation. Limiting debt to whatever can be paid within the half-life of a generation would have avoided this unjust imposition on later generations.

This parallel between the calculations of Condorcet and Jefferson merely reflects their mutual engagement and friendship (Sloan records that Condorcet was present at a farewell dinner for Jefferson on September 17, 1789). There are deeper connections. Debt was the prime concern of Anne Robert Turgot, chosen by Louis XVI as Controller General of Finances in 1774 to reorganize France's debt. Turgot's refusal to agree to Vergenne's scheme to aid the American colonies in 1776 led to his dismissal. Indeed, the increase of debt as a result of this decision forced Louis XVI to call the estates general in 1789. Condorcet was Turgot's protégé and wrote Turgot's biography in 1787, as well as editing his work.

Appleby (1992) also indicates that Jefferson accepted the arguments of Turgot and Condorcet on the utility of free trade. Moreover, "Jefferson was an early advocate of the commercial exploitation of American agriculture"(Appleby, 1992).

In a letter to Jefferson on June 19, 1786, Madison assumed that the agricultural surplus of the new lands would increase without bound, and that from the "equal partition of property must result a greater simplicity of manners, consequently, a less consumption of manufactured superfluities, and a less proportion of idle proprietors and domestics" (Smith, 1995: 4224).

McCoy has further argued that Jefferson kept to his "vision of a predominantly agricultural America that would continue to export its bountiful surpluses of food abroad" (McCoy, 1980a: 268).

Indeed, Jefferson later consistently rejected the Malthusian thesis (1970 [1798]) that population would outstrip food production. In 1818, he arranged the translation of an essay, *Treatise of Political Economy*, by Destutt de Tracy to this effect (McCoy, 1980b; Mayer, 1994: 352).[28]

---

[28] Baker (1975: 393) observes that Jefferson seemed to approve of Destutt de Tracy's idea of social science, the notion that society can be understood in scientific terms. There is another intriguing indirect connection between Jefferson, Destutt, and Condorcet. A *Commentaire* by Destutt de Tracy (1798) on Montesquieu's *L'Esprit des Lois* was published in Paris in 1798, and contained an essay by Condorcet on the twenty-ninth book of *L'Esprit*. Since Condorcet died in prison in 1794, Condorcet's essay must have been available earlier to either Destutt de Tracy or, perhaps, Jefferson. The essay seems to deny the relevance of Montesquieu's notions. Mayer (1994: 136) points out that Jefferson himself (after retiring from the presidency) translated Destutt's *Commentaire* and arranged for its publication. The complex intellectual connections between the Scottish Enlightenment thinkers (Smith and Hume),

Jefferson's belief in this regard parallels Condorcet's opinion, as set out in the *Esquisse d'un tableau historique des Progrès de l'ésprit humain.* The *Esquisse* was written while Condorcet was in hiding in 1794 from the Jacobins, and only published after his death by the efforts of his wife Sophie de Grouchy (see the discussion in Gillispie, 2005). Clearly, Condorcet's beliefs about the development of the human spirit could not have been read by Jefferson in the early 1790s; however, there is clear evidence that the optimism that Jefferson and Madison expressed in the late 1790s did owe a considerable debt to Condorcet.[29]

4.6 ORIGINS OF THE TWO-PARTY SYSTEM IN THE 1790S

The conflict between Federalists and Republicans has been described many times (e.g., Weisberger, 2000), so I shall comment only on those features that seem to reflect the coherent political economic philosophies of Madison and Jefferson, on the one hand, and Hamilton on the other.

Madison was defeated in Virginia's Senate election in November, 1788, but elected to the House of Representatives in February 1789. Almost immediately, he moved

> that Congress establish a revenue system to enable the nation to pay its debts .... He proposed high import duties on ... luxuries (rum, liquors, wine, molasses, tea, sugar, spices, coffee and cocoa). ... Madison asserted that though he was a "friend to a very free system of commerce" ... and regarded "commercial shackles as unjust, oppressive, and impolitic," tariffs were nevertheless justifiable in some cases: to protect temporarily new industries ... to discourage luxury spending ... and to retaliate against unfair commercial regulations by other countries.
>
> (Ketcham, 1971: 280)

Madison also argued for discrimination against Britain, to use America's importation of manufactures and export of food as a device to open further trade with Europe so as to oppose Britain's dominance. Madison would return to this theme later, particularly in a number of long speeches in January and February 1794.[30] It is pertinent to the agrarian thesis that, on April 9, 1789, Madison argued in Congress for the encouragement of

> Condorcet, Destutt, and their colleagues in France, and Jefferson and Madison, have not been explored in any great depth.

[29] As Mayer notes, Jefferson wrote in a letter in 1799, that like Condorcet, he believed that the mind of man was "perfectible to a degree of which we cannot as yet form any conception" (Mayer, 1994: 306).

[30] Madison, *Papers Vol.* 15: 167, 180, 182, 205, 206, 247.

the great staple of the United States; I mean agriculture, which may justly be stiled [*sic*] the staple of the United States . . . . If we compare the cheapness of our land with that of other nations, we see so decided an advantage in that cheapness, as to have full confidence of being unrivaled; with respect to the object of manufacture, other countries may and do rival us; but we may be said to have a monopoly in agriculture . . . . If my general principle is a good one commerce ought to be free, and labour and industry left at large to find its object.

(Madison, *Papers vol.* 12: 73)

This speech, together with Madison's earlier letters to Jefferson, make it clear that by 1789, Madison had a well-articulated theory based on free trade and agrarian expansion for the United States. While there was mutual advantage for Britain and the United States to exploit their comparative advantages, nonetheless, the United States had to defend itself against commercial exploitation by Britain.

On January 9, 1790, Hamilton, as Secretary of the Treasury, brought out his *Report on Public Credit* (Freeman, 2001: 531–74). Madison, in Congress, argued against the assumption of debts that had been pressed by Hamilton. The defeat of the proposal by a logroll in Congress may have reinforced Hamilton's belief in the inherent incoherence of the legislature.

The Report on Credit was followed by further long reports, *On a National Bank* (February 23, 1791), and *The Subject of Manufactures* (December 5, 1791).

Madison tried to halt the National Bank by asking, "if the power [to establish] an incorporated bank was among the powers vested by the constitution in the legislature of the United States?" (Rakove: 1999: 481–2).

The bank scheme went ahead. "When subscriptions were opened on July 4, 1791, they were filled within one hour" (Elkins and McKitrick, 1993: 242).

These three reports were indicative of Hamilton's earnest wish to put in place an American analogue of Walpole's British Equilibrium. As I have indicated, since the United States exported land-intensive goods, the only logically feasible path to creating a commercial economy was to sustain manufactures either by tariff or by direct government assistance. It is interesting that Hamilton deals immediately with what I have intimated was an underlying component of the Madison–Jefferson vision—that the future of the U.S. economy lay principally in the cultivation of the land. Indeed, in the Report on Manufactures, Hamilton takes up the argument of Adam Smith (1981 [1776]):

[t]he labour of Artificers being capable of greater subdivision and simplicity of operation than that of Cultivators, it is susceptible, in a proportionably [sic] greater degree, of improvement in its productive powers, whether to be derived from an accession of Skill, or from the application of ingenious machinery.... That with regard to an augmentation of the quantity of useful labour, must depend essentially upon an increase of capital.

(Freeman, 2001: 651)

Hamilton's argument clearly sets out his view of the necessary evolution of the U.S. economy: By the creation of a National Bank to generate capital, by protection of industry and by tariff to cover government debt, the United States would grow rapidly.

On September 9, 1792, Jefferson wrote to George Washington:

That I have utterly disapproved of the system of the Secretary of Treasury, I acknolege [sic] and avow: and this is not merely a speculative difference. This system flowed from principles averse to liberty [and] was calculated to undermine and demolish the republic, by creating an influence of his department over the members of the legislature.

(Peterson, 1984: 994)

By denying that his rejection was speculative, Jefferson meant that he had good reasons (both empirical and theoretical) to believe that the Hamiltonian system would induce corruption and undermine liberty. From Jefferson's own reading of Bolingbroke, he believed that the creation of a capitalist system in the United States would make it possible for a Hamilton, in the guise of Walpole, to bribe and maneuver among the factions of the legislature—to act as autocrat.

In addition to the allegations of corruption, I contend that Madison and Jefferson believed that Hamilton's commercial empire in the United States would generate precisely the same phenomenon of immiseration as in Britain. Were agriculture to be diminished, then agrarian labor would experience a diminution of real income. Indeed, ascendant capital would eventually control land, as in Britain, in the form of great estates.[31] This would necessarily require the further disenfranchisement of labor. Beard (1915) in his analysis of Jeffersonian America quotes from the *Treatise*

---

[31] There is one consequence of the Hamilton scheme that I have not discussed, though it is consistent with the view presented by Madison and Jefferson. If the United States focused on manufacturing development, then it would be dependent on British capital, and thus become a satellite of the metropole. It is possible that the defeat of Hamilton was necessary for the creation of what Jefferson later called the "Empire for Liberty."

of John Taylor, of Caroline County (published in 1814): "The policy of protecting duties to force manufacturing . . . will produce the same consequences as that of enriching . . . a paper interest . . . and the wealth of the majority will continually be diminished" (Beard, 1915: 341).

Indeed, this view of the conflict of land and capital, of the agrarian against the commercial interest, is one that pervades debate in the United States until the Civil War. While Taylor's essay postdates the election of 1800, it is clear that the views expressed by Taylor in 1814 reflected the opinions of Madison and Jefferson in the 1790s.

4.7 CONCLUDING REMARKS

I shall conclude with some brief remarks about the consequences of this conflict. Although I have posed the conflict in terms of an agrarian interest against a commercial interest, I have also suggested that Madison and Jefferson viewed it in terms of how best to organize the economic development of the United States. Consistent with my interpretation of Condorcet's optimism, the two Republicans believed that agricultural expansion could lead to increased economic power for the United States. However, Hamilton appeared correct in his view that only manufacturing was capable of rapid productivity increase. Thus, for the growth of the agrarian empire, it was necessary for the United States to expand its boundaries. This makes Jefferson's appetite for the western territory of Louisiana perfectly intelligible. If this expanded agrarian empire was made available to free labor, then the immiseration of labor would not occur. However, this would depend on maintaining the productivity of free agrarian labor against that of slave labor in the plantation economy.

Second, it is clear from Madison's polemics in Congress in 1794 that he understood that Britain's commercial empire could dominate an agrarian economy, such as the United States, through Britain's control of both capital and trade. The basis for his argument for a trade war against Britain was that Britain's fundamental need for food exceeded America's need for manufactures. In Madison's view, manufactures were superfluities. In actual fact (if I understand nineteenth century British–U.S. trade correctly), Britain maintained a persistent trade deficit with the United States which it covered by a large trade surplus with the rest of the world. Madison appears to have been correct in his long-term view.

For Madison and Jefferson, the issue of reconstructing the political economic configuration in the period leading up to the 1800 election was of paramount importance. From the Condorcetian perspective, such an election involves collective decision making under risk. The more debate and information about possible futures, the more likely would the election lead to the attainment of a superior alternative. I have suggested that Madison considered that a heterogeneous electorate may choose representatives "pre-eminent for ability and virtue." This suggests that the election of Jefferson, and later Madison, justified their particular perspectives on the future.

There is one final point relevant to current political theory. The particular restructuring of political support that occurred between 1787 and 1800 has elements of what is called *partisan realignment*. Current theories suggest that these occur at the onset of critical elections (as in 1896, 1932, 1964). Chapter 6 argues that these critical elections are associated with relatively rapid transformations in the coalition structure among the interests associated with the three factors discussed here—namely, land, labor, and capital. Between such elections there are relatively stable equilibria, based on the competition between two parties. In the presidential election of 1800, while there may have nominally been two parties, there were four candidates: Adams, Pinckney, Burr and Jefferson. We may draw some inferences about how the factional competition of 1798 to 1800 cohered into the relatively stable two-party system that persisted until about 1857.

In September 1798, Jefferson drafted the Kentucky Resolutions. These seemingly denied that the Constitution was a compact among the people: "Whensoever the General government assumes undelegated powers, it's [*sic*] acts are unauthoritative, void, and of no force: that to this compact each state acceded as a state ... each party has an equal right to judge for itself" (Smith, 1995: 1080).

The Virginia Resolutions, drafted by Madison, went further: "[I]n case of a deliberate, palpable and dangerous exercise of other powers not granted by the said compact, the states who are parties thereto have the right, and are in duty bound, to interpose for arresting the progress of the evil" (Rakove, 1999: 589).

The resolutions were passed in their state legislatures on November 16 and December 24, 1798 (McDonald, 2000: 41).

It is obvious enough that, with many factions, derived from very many differing kinds of interests, the creation of a stable, possibly tyrannical, majority would be almost impossible. Indeed the more heterogeneous or the more extensive the society, the less likely is it that such a permanent majority can form. Many readings of *Federalist X* focus on this interpretation. However, this interpretation would hold for a Democracy—the system of direct popular choice. Madison takes pains to argue that Democracy (whether large or small) cannot deal with the problems of faction. It therefore cannot be the tyranny of a majority faction that he fears, but something quite different—namely turbulence.

Federalist X sets out a "ratio" theorem about republics—systems, or schemes, of representation. If the proportion of "fit" characters in the extended republic be at least as large as in the small republic, then the probability of a fit choice in the extended republic will be greater than in the small. The definitions of a "fit character,"and of a "fit choice,"are not clearly set out, however.

Clues about the notion of "fit" are given in the earlier mentioned April 1787 essay, "Vices of the Political System of the U.S."(April 1787). There Madison observes that a great desideratum is a "sufficient neutrality between the different interests and factions":

In absolute Monarchies, the prince is sufficiently neutral, ... but frequently sacrifices their happiness to his ambition or avarice.... . An auxiliary desideratum is a process of elections as will most certainly extract from the mass of Society the purest and noblest characters.

(Rakove, 1999: 79)

Adair is surely correct in pointing to the influence that Hume's "Idea of a Perfect Commonwealth" (Hume 1985 [1777]: 512–29) had on Madison. But Adair does not point out the essential feature of the Republic on which Madison concentrates: Republican elections are for representatives, not outcomes. The term "fit" refers to a *person*, not to an *alternative*.

To see the importance of this distinction, consider political behavior in a House of Representatives. Some of these representatives may well be fit, of pure and noble character. However, as Hume observed, "love, vanity, ambition, resentment" all beget public decision. Factions must dominate, and therefore so must "turbulence." What exactly is this turbulence that follows from faction? I regard it as precisely the same as the social choice notion of "chaos." The chaos theorem shows that if diversity (or dimensionality) is sufficiently high, then sequences of outcomes (associated with particular winning coalitions) can lead anywhere in the set of possible policies. Clearly a permanent, tyrannical majority cannot be expected, unless some cohesive principle—a "party"—is at work. But Madison, in *Federalist X* does not assert that party is a solution to factional turbulence. It follows, therefore, that if the electorate is "numerous extended and diverse in interests" and this diversity is reflected in Congress, "then the development of a majority faction can be limited" (Dahl, 1956: 16). However, this heterogeneity does not imply that "competing interests cancel one another out." In fact, Madison was greatly concerned that factionalism would lead to instability.

The pluralist reading of Madison appears to be only half correct. To limit the effects of turbulence in the House of Representatives requires a different institutional device—that of the presidential veto.

If I am correct in my interpretation of *Federalist X*, then the extended republic argument was irrelevant to the prevention of turbulent instability in the House. In *Federalist LXVIII*, Madison discusses the Senate as an "institution that will blend stability with liberty" (Rakove, 1999: 348). When he uses the argument that "[A]mbition must be made to counteract ambition" in *Federalist LI*, he does not say that ambition *will* counteract ambition (Rakove, 1999: 295). Instead he goes on to comment that, "[a]n absolute negative, on the legislature, appears at first view to be the natural defense with which the executive magistrate should be armed"(Rakove, 1999: 296).

Jefferson, writing from Paris on December 20, 1787, also seemed to be of two minds about the House. He approved that it be chosen by the people directly, principally because of its legislative power to raise taxes, but he also commented that it "will be illy [*sic*] qualified to legislate for the Union" (Smith, 1995: 512).

On the veto by the president he says, "I like the negative given to the Executive with a third of either house, though I should have liked it better had the Judiciary been associated for that purpose, or invested with a similar and separate power" (Smith, 1995: 512).

Rutland and Hobson (1977) comment:

In the debate in the Constitutional Convention on June 4, 1787, Madison had argued against the absolute veto by the executive against Congress, observing that even the King of Great Britain had no such veto power. On September 12, 1787, Madison argued that the relative veto power should be determined by requiring a two-thirds majority of each house to overrule the executive veto. As Madison says, the object of the revisionary power is (1) to defend the Executive Rights, and (2) to prevent popular or factious injustice. (166)

Pulling together these inferences about Madison's thoughts on the relationship between the executive and legislative, we see a common thread. In general, the president will tend to be a "fit," or neutral, choice. When factional interests predominate in the legislature, then the executive veto will overrule the resultant mutability. However, it is possible that the exercise of such power can lead to presidential tyranny. If this occurs, however, it will be obvious to the legislature, and a two-thirds majority should be possible in Congress so as to block such ambition. If this can not be implemented, then the states themselves may threaten veto, or secession.

Madison also saw a need for the exercise of veto, by the Federal government against the states. In a letter to Jefferson (October 24, 1787), Madison observed that the exercise by Congress of a veto against the laws of the states had been rejected by a bare majority: "Without such a check in the whole over the parts, my system involves the evil of imperia in imperio" (Smith, 1995: 498). Indeed he saw such a check as necessary to prevent instability and injustice.

He later comments that "in the extended Republic of the United States, the General Government would hold a pretty even balance between the parties of the particular states" (Smith, 1995: 502).

This observation is consistent with my interpretation. Each State House and Senate, though perhaps not as diverse as the Federal Congress, will nonetheless be turbulent, and this turbulence may induce encroachments on the rights of citizens in the particular state. A veto by the neutral president (or by the Judiciary) is a likely method of prevention of this encroachment.

On the other hand, if the president veers towards autocracy, then the perception of this failure of a "fit choice" will involve judgment in the context of a binary choice, and it can be hoped that the House and Senate would be well equipped to render such a judgment.

4.8 APPENDIX

4.8.1 *Speech by Benjamin Franklin to the Constitutional Convention on September 17, 1787*

Mr. President

I confess that there are several parts of this constitution which I do not at present approve, but I am not sure I shall never approve them: For having lived long, I have experienced many instances of being obliged by better information, or fuller consideration, to change opinions even on important subjects, which I once thought right, but found to be otherwise. It is therefore that the older I grow, the more apt I am to doubt my own judgment, and to pay more respect to the judgment of others. Most men indeed as well as most sects in Religion, think themselves in possession of all truth, and that wherever others differ from them it is so far error. Steele a Protestant in a Dedication tells the Pope, that the only difference between our Churches in their opinions of the certainty of their doctrines is, the Church of Rome is infallible and the Church of England is never in the wrong. But though many private persons think almost as highly of their own infallibility as of that of their sect, few express it so naturally as a certain French lady, who in a dispute with her sister, said "I don't know how it happens, Sister but I meet with no body but myself, that's always in the right-Il n'y a que moi qui a toujours raison."

In these sentiments, Sir, I agree to this Constitution with all its faults, if they are such; because I think a general Government necessary for us, and there is no form of Government but what may be a blessing to the people if well administered, and believe farther that this is likely to be well administered for a course of years, and can only end in Despotism, as other forms have done before it, when the people shall become so corrupted as to need despotic Government, being incapable of any other. I doubt too whether any other Convention we can obtain, may be able to make a better Constitution. For when you assemble a number of men to have the advantage of their joint wisdom, you inevitably assemble with those men, all their prejudices, their passions, their errors of opinion, their local interests, and their selfish views. From such an assembly can a perfect production be expected? It therefore astonishes me, Sir, to find this system approaching so near to perfection as it does; and I think it will astonish our enemies, who are waiting with confidence to hear that our councils are confounded like those of the Builders of Babel; and that our States are on the point of separation, only to meet hereafter for the purpose of cutting one another's throats. Thus I consent, Sir, to this Constitution because I expect no better, and because I am not sure, that it is not the best. The opinions I have had of its errors, I sacrifice to the public good. I have never whispered a syllable of them abroad. Within these walls they were born, and here they shall die. If every one of us in returning to our Constituents were to report the objections he has had to it, and endeavor to gain partizans in support of them, we might prevent its being generally received, and thereby lose all the salutary effects & great advantages resulting naturally in our favor among foreign Nations as well as among ourselves, from our real or apparent unanimity. Much of the strength & efficiency of any Government in procuring and securing happiness to the people, depends, on opinion, on the general opinion of the goodness of the Government, as well as of the wisdom and integrity of its Governors. I hope therefore that for our own sakes as a part of the people, and for the sake of posterity, we shall act heartily and unan-imously in recommending this Constitution (if approved by Congress & confirmed by the Conventions) wherever our influence may extend, and turn our future thoughts & endeavors to the means of having it well administered.

On the whole, Sir, I can not help expressing a wish that every member of the Convention who may still have objections to it, would with me, on this occasion doubt a little of his own infallibility, and to make manifest our unanimity, put his name to this instrument.

5

Lincoln and the Civil War

5.1   INTRODUCTION*

This chapter pursues the key theoretical idea of this book: An institutional equilibrium can be destroyed or transformed by rapid belief changes in the population. The changes in electoral beliefs in the period prior to the election of Lincoln in 1860 and the commencement of the Civil War are examined in an attempt to understand the political transformation that occurred at that time, as well as its ramifications to the present day.

As observed in Chapter 2, Riker (1980) in his book, *Liberalism against Populism*, argued that Lincoln's success in the 1860 election was the culmination of a long progression of strategic attempts by the Whig coalition of commercial interests to defeat the "Jeffersonian–Jacksonian" Democratic coalition of agrarian populism. Riker adduced Lincoln's success to his "heresthetic" maneuver to force his competitor, Douglas, in the 1858 Illinois Senate race, to appear anti-slavery, thus splitting the Democratic Party in 1860. Riker also suggested that electoral preferences in 1860 exhibited an underlying "chaotic" preference cycle.

However, these accounts do not explain why the slavery question became paramount from 1858 to 1860. I suggest in this chapter that U.S.

---

* Chapter 5 uses material from "Quandaries of War and Union: 1763–1861," *Politics and Society* 30 (2002): 5–49, and from "Constitutional Quandaries and Critical Elections," *Politics, Philosophy and Economics* 2 (2003): 5–36, both by Norman Schofield. This material is reprinted by permission of Sage Publications Ltd. The discussion of the Dred Scott decision is based on Kim Dixon and Norman Schofield, "The Election of Lincoln in 1860," *Homo Oeconomicus* 17 (2001): 391–425 and Norman Schofield, "The Amistad and Dred Scott Affairs: Heresthetics and Beliefs in Antebellum America, 1837–1860," *Homo Oeconomicus* 16 (1999): 49–67, and "Quandaries of Slavery and Civil War in the US," *Homo Oeconomicus* 21 (2004): 315–354.

politics, from 1800 to the 1840s, can be interpreted in terms of a single land—capital axis that sustained the preeminence of an agrarian coalition, first created by Jefferson, of both slave interests and free labor. Lincoln's strategy from 1858 to 1860 was to persuade free labor in the northern and western states that they were threatened by the consequences of the Dred Scott decision by the Supreme Court in 1857. Lincoln argued that although the decision applied to the Territories, it was indicative of the intention of the South to extend slavery to the free states. Lincoln's speeches from 1858 to 1860 made this threat credible to the North, and initiated a belief cascade among the electorate. For southern voters, the North consequently appeared to be a "tyrannical" majority, whose creation violated the constitutional logic of Union, and legitimated secession. I argue that this second "civil rights" dimension, created in the election of 1860, is necessary for understanding critical elections that have occurred at irregular intervals in U.S. political history.

I argue that the electoral choice of Lincoln in 1860 was an illustration of the design of the U.S. Constitution and facilitated the election of a risk-taking president at a time of social quandary.

5.2 THE INTERSECTIONAL PARTY BALANCE

Although standard models of elections based on the work of Downs (1957) assume a single dimension of *economic* policy making, more recent empirical electoral analyses in various postwar polities have demonstrated the relevance of a second *social* dimension. The claim made here is that a second dimension involving civil rights has been a fundamental feature of U.S. politics since 1860. How this social/civil rights dimension is construed may well change over time, just as the economic dimension will involve varying specific issues at different times. However, it remains qualitatively the same in affecting the beliefs of voters.

Chapter 4 has already made the argument, originally due to Beard (1913) that, from the inception of the United States at the Founding in 1787, the principal dimension relevant to political choice could be identified with the capital/land axis. Indeed the conflict between the Federalists, most notably Alexander Hamilton, and the Republicans, led by Thomas Jefferson, was interpreted as the result of a successful coalition move to combine the agrarian interests of the country, whether slave-holding or free, against the commercial interests of the northeast. It is worth mentioning that Jefferson's success in 1800 was due to the constitutional rule that a slave was counted as three–fifths of a person in calculating each state's electoral college strength (Wills, 2003a,b).

Obviously, though, for this coalition to survive, any conflict of interest between slave-owners and free labor had to be suppressed, or dealt with through a stable compromise. In essence, this compromise was first established by the Northwest Ordinance of July 1787, which specified that slavery could not exist in the Territory northwest of the River Ohio (North and Rutten, 1984). On the other hand, when the remnant of Louisiana was renamed the Missouri Territory in 1812, no mention was made of the Northwest Ordinance or its anti-slavery article.

Given the stability of the compromise from 1800 on, the Jeffersonian Republican Party was pre-eminent over the Federalists, or Whigs, until 1824. In that election, John Quincy Adams of Massachusetts was able to win that with a plurality of just 32 percent of the electoral college vote against Jackson, Crawford, and Clay, but lost to the Democrat, Andrew Jackson in 1828. Jackson re-established the dominance of the agrarian party, the Democracy, and he was followed by his vice president, the New York Democrat, Martin Van Buren after the election of 1836. The issue of slavery did become important, briefly, in 1840 over the Amistad affair. Probably as a consequence of this affair, Van Buren was denied the Democratic nomination in 1844 through the imposition of the two-thirds rule by the South in the Democratic convention. Polk, for the Democrats, beat Henry Clay in the presidential election, only because he won New York (by 5000 votes). After that election, the efforts by John Quincy Adams to break the gag-rule against discussion of slavery in the House was successful because the intersectional Democratic Party almost split up, as Northern Democrats and Northern Whigs in the House voted (with John Quincy Adams) to rescind the rule (Miller, 1995).

Prior to 1840, the two intersectional parties, Whig and Democrat, were roughly comparable, with neither party clearly associated with either the North or the South. Political conflicts between Whigs and Democrats until this time had concentrated on economic concerns (Riker, 1982; Weingast, 1998). The Whig industrial and commercial interests of the East focused on protection and trade regulation, whereas Democrats, concentrated in the South and West, were concerned with issues of land and agriculture. Rogowski's model of factor endowments can be used to sketch the basis for these differing preferences (Rogowski, 1989). Because the United States could be assumed to be relatively poor in capital (in contrast to Britain) and poor also in the supply of labor (in contrast to Europe generally), a natural protectionist coalition of capital and labor could form.

Such an electoral coalition formed the basis for the Federalist Party, later called the Whigs. However, land was relatively abundant, so agricultural interests (whether based on slave or free labor) would favor increased trade and decreased tariffs. This common interest was the basis of the Jeffersonian Republican Party, or Democratic Party. Moreover, landed interests are generally capital poor, and so favor a soft-money principle, and, in particular, low interest rates. The Whig and Democratic Parties cohered around quite different policy positions on a single axis, putting capital and land in opposition. Both northern and southern regions depended on agriculture, so the two electoral coalitions would necessarily be "intersectional." Table 5.1 gives the distribution of electoral college votes in the elections from 1836 to 1860, and clearly indicates this intersectional feature.

By 1852, however, the Whig popular presidential vote had fallen to 44 percent. The plurality mechanism of the electoral college meant the Whig candidate, Scott, took only 42 seats (out of 296, or 14 percent). It was obvious that the great expansion of available western land resulting from the war with Mexico and the Treaty of Guadalupe Hidalgo (1848) essentially guaranteed that the Democratic coalition, if it held together, would become dominant. However, this coalition depended on a compromise between western farmers and landed slave interests. As long as slavery did not threaten free labor, this coalition was stable.

From an economic point of view, the rapid development of a new northern trade route through the Erie Canal had led to a dramatic fall in transport costs. This created the potential for an export-oriented coalition of eastern capital and labor-intensive western farmers (Fogel, 1994).

Riker (1982: Ch. 9) has suggested that the Whigs were unwilling or unable to exploit the issue of slavery, whereas Frémont, the first Republican presidential candidate in 1856, tried to construct this new coalition against the Democratic Party. To do so, however, required using the slavery dimension to split the agrarian coalition into "pro-slave" and "free" components. His moderate success (33 percent of the popular vote) suggested it was possible. Nonetheless, Fillmore, essentially a Whig candidate, took 22 percent, while the Democrat, Buchanan, won 45 percent of the popular vote, and 174 seats (or 59 percent) of the electoral college. Stephen Douglas, a Democrat, was well-positioned, in 1856, to maintain the Democrat agrarian coalition and gain the presidency in 1860. For Douglas to win in 1860, however, he had to preserve a coincidence of interests, based essentially on an ideology of expansion, by overcoming an

Table 5.1. *U.S. Presidential Elections: 1836–1860*

Year	Candidate	Party	Popular Vote %	North	West	Border	South	Total
1836	Van Buren	Democrat	51	101	8	4	57	170
	Harrison	Whig	37	15	30	28	0	73
	White	Whig	10	0	0	0	26	26
	Webster	Whig	2	14	0	0	0	14
Total								294
1840	Harrison	Whig	53	123	33	28	50	234
	Van Buren	Democrat	47	7	5	4	44	60
	Birney	Liberty	.3	–	–	–	–	–
Total								294
1844	Polk	Democrat	49.5	77	36	7	60	170
	Clay	Whig	48	35	23	23	24	105
	Birney	Liberty	2.5	–	–	–	–	–
Total								275
1848	Taylor	Whig	47	97	0	23	43	163
	Cass	Democrat	43	15	57	7	48	127
	Van Buren	Free Soil	10	–	–	–	–	–
Total								290
1852	Pierce	Democrat	51	92	66	20	76	254
	Scott	Whig	44	18	0	12	12	42
	Hale	Free Soil	5	0	0	0	0	0
Total								296
1856	Buchanan	Democrat	45	34	28	24	88	174
	Fremont	Republican	33	76	38	0	0	114
	Fillmore	"Whig"	22	0	0	8	0	8
Total								296
1860	Lincoln	Republican	40	107	73	0	0	180
	Douglas	N. Democrat	29	3	0	9	0	12
	Bell	"Whig"	13	0	0	12	27	39
	Breckinridge	S. Democrat	18	0	0	11	61	72
Total								303

Source: Ransom (1989: 103, 156), with permission of Cambridge University Press.

implicit potential conflict of interest between free labor and slave owners over whether the west was to be free or slave.

For those southern interests that depended on slave labor, the maintenance of this particular institution was paramount. For free labor, whether in the south or north, the institution would only impinge on their factor reward if the products of the two kinds of labor were competitive. However, as long as labor was relatively scarce, there was little economic effect on free labor. The westward expansion of slave labor could change this "equilibrium." Moreover, any dramatic change in the economic and constitutional equilibrium on the labor axis, particularly over the use of slave labor in the North, would clearly affect free labor.

For Douglas, it was critical to separate the issue of land and labor, and it was for this reason that he proposed the notion of "popular sovereignty." By leaving the decision over slavery to the electorate of each territory (once it became populous enough for statehood), he hoped to placate southern interests.

However, on March 6, 1857, the Supreme Court, under Chief Justice Taney, made its decision on *Dred Scott v. Sanford*, effectively asserting that blacks had no rights as citizens. In essence, the decision declared that the federal authority had no right to deny slavery in the Territories. This destroyed what had been a long-standing compromise over slavery on the labor axis, and seemingly legitimized the expansion of slave interests into all western territories. While the factor of land was relevant, it was so only because of the implicit conflict between free and slave labor in the West.

Riker (1986) argued that Lincoln's victory in the presidential election of 1860 stemmed from an "heresthetic" move by Lincoln in 1858 against Stephen Douglas, at Freeport, Illinois, during their contest for the Illinois Senate seat. By posing a question that forced Douglas to appear anti-slavery to the Illinois voters, Lincoln effectively gave the election to Douglas. According to Riker, Douglas's reply to Lincoln's question induced southern pro-slavery voters, in the later presidential race of 1860, to reject Douglas. Riker contended that the resulting split in the Democratic Party, between Breckinridge and Douglas, gave Lincoln the presidency. I argue for a different interpretation of these events. First of all, the South was deeply hostile to Douglas even prior to the Freeport debate. For example, an editorial in *The Mobile Register* (August 20, 1858) argued that to reject the Douglas compromise would mean permanent destruction of the Democratic Party. To accept the compromise would mean "demoralization as well as disaster."

The South clearly understood that accepting Douglas could give them a victory, but one which would leave their particular institution undefended. This intransigence became quite apparent at the Democratic convention in Charleston in April 1860.

Before nominating their presidential candidate, the convention decided to adopt the platform for the party. The Southern platform, supported by the delegates of fifteen slave states (together with Oregon and California) asserted that Congress had no power to abolish slavery in the Territories, and that the national government had the duty to defend the right of property in slaves everywhere. The opposing Douglas platform included as its second plank the declaration that decisions over slavery should be left to the Supreme Court. Realizing that passing this plank would force the dissolution of the convention, many of Douglas's supporters voted against it. At the same time, southern delegates saw that their "slave-code" platform would not pass and the delegates of eight slave states retired from the convention. It was then decided that no man be nominated without a two-thirds vote of the original 304 delegates. Douglas took 145.5 in the first ballot (the 0.5 being a split vote), against five other contenders, and eventually reached 152.5 (more than a simple majority). However, it was impossible, even after sixty-five ballots, to obtain the required supra-majority, of 203, of the delegate votes. By 148 to 100 the convention agreed to adjourn (Nevins, 1950). As *The New York Times* (May 3, 1860) editorial remarked, "[T]he South believes sincerely that the North seeks power in order to 'crush slavery' but it must instead make up its mind to lose the sway it has exercised so long."

In essence, the South forced the split between the two wings of the Democratic Party, because it believed, correctly, that Douglas would not give it what it wanted, namely the spread of slavery throughout the Republic. Jefferson Davis, soon to be President of the Confederacy, expressed a typical Southern attitude to Douglas's party when he called it "the spurious and decayed offshoot of democracy" (Cooper, 2000).

Had the split between Douglas and the Southern Democrat candidate, Breckinridge, not occurred, a combined Douglas–Breckinridge platform in 1860, even with 59.2 percent of the popular vote, could only have increased the total Democratic electoral college vote from 84 to 91. (Table 5.2 gives the popular and electoral college votes by state in 1860, and makes it clear that only in Oregon and California did the combination of Douglas and Breckinridge give them a majority against Lincoln.) Lincoln would still have had a majority of 173 of the electoral college out of 303.

Table 5.2. *The Election of 1860*

State	Percentage of Vote				Electoral College Votes			
	LN	BR	BL	DG	LN	BR	BL	DG
Vermont	78.99	0.51	4.60	15.90	5	–	–	–
Maine	63.97	6.49	2.08	27.46	8	–	–	–
Minnesota	63.42	2.15	0.18	34.25	4	–	–	–
Mass.	62.97	3.51	13.20	20.32	13	–	–	–
Rhode Island	61.37	0.00	0.00	38.63	4	–	–	–
Michigan	57.18	0.52	0.26	42.04	6	–	–	–
New Hamp.	56.89	3.20	0.67	39.24	5	–	–	–
Connecticut	56.69	18.9	4.26	20.09	6	–	–	–
Wisconsin	56.58	0.58	0.11	42.73	5	–	–	–
Pennsylvania	56.26	37.5	2.68	3.52	27	–	–	–
Iowa	54.87	0.82	1.37	42.94	4	–	–	–
New York	53.71	0.00	0.00	46.29	35	–	–	–
Ohio	52.35	2.58	2.76	42.32	23	–	–	–
Indiana	51.09	4.52	1.95	42.44	13	–	–	–
Illinois	50.68	0.71	1.45	47.16	11	–	–	–
New Jersey	48.15	0.00	0.00	51.85	4	–	–	3
Oregon	36.57	34.7	1.27	27.42	3	–	–	–
California	32.96	28.8	5.74	32.41	4	–	–	–
Delaware	23.75	45.7	24.09	6.38	–	3	–	–
Missouri	10.29	18.9	35.27	35.53	–	–	–	9
Maryland	2.48	45.9	45.14	6.45	–	8	–	–
Virginia	1.15	44.4	44.66	9.74	–	–	15	–
Kentucky	0.93	36.3	45.18	17.54	–	–	12	–
Tennessee	0.00	44.5	47.67	7.81	–	–	12	–
N. Carolina	0.00	50.4	46.75	2.81	–	10	–	–
Georgia	0.00	48.7	40.32	10.90	–	10	–	–
Louisiana	0.00	44.0	40.00	15.10	–	6	–	–
Florida	0.00	59.5	37.9	2.56	–	3	–	–
Arkansas	0.00	53.1	37.17	9.67	–	4	–	–
Mississippi	0.00	59.0	36.23	4.75	–	7	–	–
Alabama	0.00	54.0	30.85	15.11	–	9	–	–
Texas	0.00	75.4	24.51	0.00	–	4	–	–
S. Carolina[a]	0.00	0.00	0.00	0.00	–	8	–	–
Totals	39.8	18.2	12.6	29.4	180	72	39	12

Source: [a]Electoral College vote allocated by the state legislature.
BR= Breckinridge; BL = Bell; DG = Douglas; LN = Lincoln.

Rather than engage in "heresthetic" maneuvers, Lincoln's strategy, from as early as June 26, 1857, was to examine the logic and possible consequences of the Dred Scott decision in order to assess the future intentions of the South over slavery. At the Freeport debate in 1858, the most important question Lincoln asked Douglas was whether Douglas would acquiesce to a Supreme Court decision, if it were made, that decreed "that states cannot exclude slavery from their limits" (Fehrenbacher, 1989a: 542).

In later speeches in 1860, Lincoln implied that the eventual consequence of the Dred Scott decision could be the legal use of slave labor in Northern free states.

Just as in the analysis of the Ratification choice, examined in Chapter 4, we can put Lincoln's logic in terms of an expected utility calculation. The status quo, A_2, will be associated with a high probability, p, that the South did intend to implement such a threat against the North. The cost, T, of this threat to free labor would clearly be very high indeed. The machinations of southern delegates at the April Democratic Convention, and their refusal to accept Douglas as a compromise candidate, must have had the effect of increasing the subjective estimate of p. A vote for Lincoln would, in all likelihood lead to a change from A_2 to a new constitutional equilibrium, A_1, possibly necessitating war. We may let F denote the cost of factionalism resulting from some kind of compromise with the South, and q be the probability of this outcome under a Lincoln presidency. However, there would be some real probability, r, of "chaos" or war, under Lincoln, at cost C. A reason for a voter to choose Lincoln would be the credible belief that the eventual cost of the status quo, pT, exceeded the outcome $qF + rC$. (Needless to say, I am not attempting a very formal analysis of what was necessarily a complicated subjective estimation.)

Approximately 1.3 million voters had chosen Frémont, the Republican candidate in 1856. At that point, any expectation of a real threat, or of war, would have been low. After 1856, however, many Republicans were uncompromising in their rejection of slavery. William Seward, who was to be one of the contenders for the Republican presidential nomination in 1860, asserted that slavery was a "blight," a "pestilence," an "element of national debility and decline"(Foner, 1970: 44). A "prophet of chaos" like Seward only increased the depth of the quandary facing the northern electorate. In his speeches between 1857 and 1860, Lincoln focused on the threat facing the North, making it real and credible. At the same time, he asserted that his intention was to contain Southern slavery, not destroy it. This held out the promise of a constitutional compromise between North

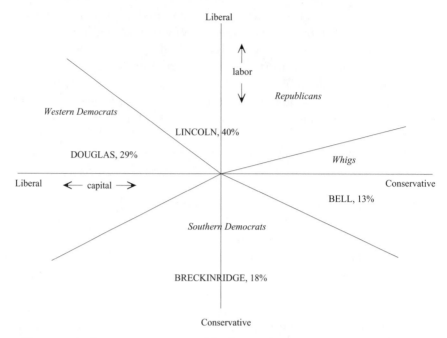

Figure 5.1. A schematic representation of the election of 1860 in a two-dimensional policy space.

and South that might at least remove the threat implied by Dred Scott and avoid war. It is for this reason that the Republican delegates chose Lincoln as their presidential candidate. In the election, the Republican vote increased by 520,000 (over the 1856 figure).[1] All fifteen states north of a line from New York to Illinois, gave Lincoln an outright majority of the electoral college (see Table 5.2).

By clarifying the nature of the southern threat, Lincoln may well have created a dilemma for members of the northern electorate, since neither the status quo nor the possibility of war could have been deemed attractive. As in the earlier "electoral" decision over the ratification of the Constitution, the degree of risk, associated with the election and the probable consequences, was very high. The fact that a clear majority of the northern electorate chose Lincoln (and this choice was reflected in a majority of the electoral college) means that a *core belief* was created in the electorate over the necessity of a constitutional transformation. Lincoln was the architect of this transformation. Figure 5.1 reproduces

---

[1] It is true that the total number of voters increased by about 600,000 between 1856 and 1860, but about 240,000 of these were in the border and southern states.

Figure 2.5, and is intended to indicate that Lincoln's success in 1860 depended on the transformation of northern electoral beliefs, through the acknowledgment of the relevance of the second labor (or slave) axis in addition to the primary land/capital axis that had governed U.S. politics until then.

Riker (1980) reasoned, on the basis of the chaos theorems, that the existence of a "social preference cycle" in the electorate meant that the outcome could be manipulated in an "heresthetical" fashion and it was the existence of such a cycle that allowed for the success of Lincoln's move against Douglas in 1858. Whether there was indeed a "social preference cycle" in 1860 is impossible to tell. In contrast, Mackie (2001) has argued that the 1860 election can be interpreted in terms of a single dimension, where "latitude is attitude." That is, the "Upper North" voted for Lincoln, the "Lower North" for Douglas, the "Upper South" for Bell, and the "Lower South" for Breckinridge. While there is some evidence for this view in Table 5.2, a formal explanation can be given in terms of the electoral model of Chapter 1. An individual, in the North, who accepts Lincoln's argument that the expected cost, pT, is very high would choose Lincoln and the state A_1, at cost $qF + rC$. Another way of expressing this is that, for such a voter, Lincoln's valence, λ_{Lin}, would be much higher than any other candidate's, and this would induce a vote for Lincoln.

The southern view, in contrast, was that the election destroyed the "Madisonian" logic of the federal bargain of 1787. A tyrannical majority, the North, had come into being through the institutional device of the electoral college. This gave the South the constitutional authority to secede. After the election, an attempt was made in the form of the Crittenden Resolution of January 16, 1861, to allocate all land south of the Missouri Compromise line of $36°30'$ to slave interests. This would have given the South less than the Dred Scott decision implied, but almost all that could have been desired by the slave-owning elite. Lincoln's veto of the compromise confirmed to the South that the North did, indeed, threaten the institution of slavery. South Carolina was the first state to secede on December 29, 1860. As more southern states seceded, the costs for the remaining states, such as Virginia, of remaining in the Union, obviously increased. Although institutional rules over the secession vote varied from state to state, the "belief cascade" so generated in the south led eventually to secession by eleven states. Gary's work on the secession decision in the southern states (Gary 2004) suggests that the belief in the necessity of secession was not necessarily supported by a majority in the seceding states. Nonetheless, I refer to this belief as a "core" or equilibrium belief in the South, because it was indeed held by those who had the power to institute the choice.

Lincoln, in his inaugural address of March 4, 1861, asserted that the fundamental document of the Union was the Declaration of Independence. Moreover, the compact implied by the Declaration made secession unconstitutional. For the Confederacy, the constitutional compact of 1787 was broken because of the tyrannical threat of the North. Because these beliefs were incompatible, war became inevitable.

Once the issue of slavery had become relevant in the minds of the voters, then electoral choice in the resulting two-dimensional space became very different from voting in a single-dimensional policy space. The constitutional transformation that occurred before and after the Civil War was the consequence of the creation of two incompatible beliefs that depended on differing interpretations of the constitutional changes of 1776 and 1787. I argue here that the election of 1860 can only be made intelligible in such a two-dimensional space. Moreover, once embedded in the polity, these two dimensions have persisted, although their interpretation may have varied over time. In the sections that follow, I present an argument that the slavery dimension became profoundly relevant to the electorate as a direct consequence of Lincoln's interpretation of the Dred Scott decision in the Supreme Court in 1857. In a sense, the Dred Scott decision and Lincoln's interpretation of it were necessary causes of the Civil War.[2] In concluding remarks, I also present some hypotheses about the nature of critical elections, and electoral realignments, that have occurred in U.S. politics over the very long run.

5.3   DRED SCOTT AND THE SUPREME COURT, 1857

Dred Scott was born into slavery about 1800 in Virginia, and in 1830 resided, as property of the Blow family, in St. Louis. After the deaths in the early 1830s of Elizabeth and Peter Blow, Scott was sold to Dr. John Emerson. Following his appointment as assistant surgeon in the Army of the United States, Emerson took Scott to the State of Illinois in 1833, and

---

[2] An event A is a necessary cause of an outcome B if the absence of A implies the absence of B. As I interpret Lincoln's argument, the Dred Scott decision gave an indication of the South's intentions. Notice that I do not argue that the Dred Scott decision, by itself, was a sufficient cause.

then to Fort Snelling in Wisconsin Territory. In 1836, Dred Scott married Harriet Robinson at Fort Snelling, in a civil ceremony. Slave states did not recognize slave marriages, because slaves were not deemed to have the right to make contracts. Emerson left the Scotts in Fort Snelling while he worked in Fort Jesup, Louisiana, where he married Eliza Sanford in 1838. Emerson died in Davenport, Iowa, in 1843, leaving Mrs. Emerson in St. Louis in full control of his property. The Scotts, who had returned to St. Louis about 1840, attempted to buy their freedom in 1846. When Mrs. Emerson refused, the Scotts sued for their freedom. The basis for the suit was that they had lived in the "free" state of Illinois, and in the Wisconsin Territory. More precisely, the State of Illinois had been admitted to the Union in 1818, with a constitution that prohibited slavery. That constitution was still in effect when Dred Scott lived there from 1833 to 1836. Moreover, Fort Snelling was on the west bank of the Mississippi River, north of the line 36°31′. As part of the Missouri Compromise of 1820, slavery was forever prohibited in that part of the Louisiana cession lying north of the line.

The case of *Dred Scott v. Irene Emerson* began on April 6, 1846 when petitions were filed in the Missouri Circuit Court in St. Louis. As Fehrenbacher (1981) notes,

> the central question raised in the suit—whether extended residence on free soil liberated a slave—was not an issue in American politics and had already been tested many times in the Missouri courts with consistent results (129).

The point here was that because slavery was banned in any territory covered by the Northwest Ordinance of 1787, then residence by a slave in such territory implied freedom. Transit by a slave, with the slave's master, did not however guarantee freedom.[3] However, on the technicality that Scott's attorney, Samuel Bay, had not proved that it was Mrs. Emerson who held Scott in slavery, the jury found for Mrs. Emerson. Bay moved for a new trial, and Mrs. Emerson relinquished ownership of the Scotts, leaving them in the custody of the sheriff of St. Louis County.

---

[3] The Northwest Ordinance of July 1787 applied to the territory of the United States northwest of the River Ohio. In its sixth article, it specified: "There shall be neither slavery nor involuntary servitude in the said territory." The Constitutional Convention, later in 1787, stated, "The legislature shall have power to dispose of and make all needful rules and regulations respecting the territory or other property belonging to the United States." It followed that this expansion of congressional power included the Northwest Territory.

The case was called in January 1850, and eventually the judge ordered that Dred Scott recover his freedom. Mrs. Emerson's attorneys then filed a bill of exceptions, setting in motion the appeal procedure to the Missouri Supreme Court. In the new brief presented to the Court, the question of the applicability of the Northwest Ordinance and the Missouri Compromise was now raised for the first time. The background to the case was the appeal in May 1849 by Thomas Hart Benton, one of the U.S. Senators for Missouri, to the people of the state to stand by him against the Missouri legislature. The legislature had passed the "Jackson resolutions," supporting Calhoun's pro-slavery resolutions in the U.S. Senate, and instructing Benton to conform to them. Two of the three Missouri Supreme Court justices were Benton's political and personal enemies.

The Missouri Supreme Court declared that the judgment of the lower court be reversed. The circuit court in St. Louis took up the case of *Dred Scott v. John F.A. Sanford* in April 1854.[4] In his plea of abatement, Sanford argued that Scott was neither a citizen of Missouri nor even of the United States, but a slave. The Court held, however, that every person born in the United States, and capable of holding property, was a citizen having the right to sue in U.S. courts. If Scott was free, he had the right to sue. Thus the trial had to go forward to determine if Scott was indeed free. Scott's lawyer requested the court to instruct the jury that Scott was free by virtue of the Ordinance of 1787 and the Missouri Compromise. The judge refused, and explained to the jury that removal to Illinois only suspended slavery temporarily. The jury found in favor of Sanford.

That month, President Franklin Pierce, a Democrat, signed into law the Kansas-Nebraska Act, repealing the slavery prohibition of the Missouri Compromise.

Montgomery Blair, attorney for Scott, filed a brief in December 1854 to the U.S. Supreme Court, arguing the jurisdictional question that Scott was indeed a citizen of the United States. For the first time the constitutionality of the Missouri Compromise was considered. Sanford's attorneys argued that Congress did not have the authority to proscribe slavery in the territories, and thus Scott had never been free (Ehrlich, 1979: 129). The court unanimously ordered the case to be reargued, and considered the case again in December 1856. In the meantime, the Democrat, James Buchanan, won the presidential election of November 1856. In his last State of the Union address in December 1856, the outgoing Democrat President, Pierce, asserted that Congress did not possess the constitutional

---

[4] It is still unclear why Mrs. Emerson's brother, John Sanford, became involved.

power to impose restrictions upon any present or future state of the Union. Pierce referred here to restrictions on slavery such as those implied by the Missouri Compromise.

Blair's brief for Scott, filed in December 1856, argued for the constitutionality of the Missouri Compromise, citing thirteen acts of Congress legislating over slavery in the territories, and fourteen judicial decisions which recognized this right of Congress. If the argument offered by Sanford's attorneys were accepted, then state authority would supersede federal authority, subjecting Congress to state legislatures.

Ehrlich (1979) suggests that after the arguments, the five justices from the slave states decided that the Court could peacefully settle the slavery issue by declaring the Missouri Compromise unconstitutional. Buchanan, in his inaugural address, noted that

a difference of opinion had arisen in regard to the point of time when the people of a Territory shall decide this question [of slavery] for themselves. This is a judicial question, which legitimately belongs to the Supreme Court of the United States, before whom it is now pending. (Ehrlich, 1979: 129)

The Opinion of the Court of March 6, 1857 was that people of Scott's race were not intended to be granted rights and benefits in the Constitution. Thus Scott was not a citizen of Missouri and not entitled to sue in federal court. Even so, the Court evaluated the case on its merits, and concluded that Congress could neither prohibit slavery nor pass any law depriving a citizen of property. Consequently, despite Scott's residence in Illinois and the Wisconsin Territory, he had never been free.[5]

5.4 THE ILLINOIS ELECTION OF 1858

The opinion of the Court, written by Chief Justice Taney, was based on the conclusion that Dred Scott, as a black, had

no rights under the Constitution and hence no standing to sue in federal court. The decision about this issue, the most racist and also the longest part of Taney's opinion, had virtually no support in either legal precedent or history ... And the conclusion was devastating to free blacks, since it deprived them of all federal rights, including access to federal court. (Drobak, 1993: 239)

---

[5] Nonetheless, Taylor Blow, the son of Scott's original master, obtained ownership of the Scott family and they were emancipated in late 1857. Dred Scott died a year later in St. Louis.

As Jaffa (2000) comments, "Taney took dead aim at the heart of the anti-slavery argument when he denied that Negroes were comprehended in the proposition of human equality in the Declaration" (290).

In a speech as early as June 26, 1857, at the Illinois State House in Springfield, Lincoln argued that

[T]he Dred Scott decision is erroneous.

If this important decision had been made by the unanimous concurrence of the judges, and without any apparent partisan bias and had been in no part based on assumed historical facts which are not really true ... it then might be, perhaps would be, factious, nay, even revolutionary, to not acquiesce in it as a precedent.

If [the decision] shall be forced upon the country as a political issue, it will become a distinct and naked issue between the friends and enemies of the constitution—the friends and enemies of the supremacy of the laws.

[T]he Dred Scott decision was, in part, based on assumed historical facts which were not really true ... Chief Justice Taney, in delivering the opinion of the majority of the Court, insists at great length that negroes were no part of the people who made, or for whom was made, the Declaration of Independence, or the Constitution of the United States ... [But] Judge Curtis, in his dissenting opinion, shows that in five of the then thirteen states ... free negroes were voters ... and had the same part in making the Constitution.

(Fehrenbacher, 1989a: 393–5)

For these reasons, Lincoln asserted that the Dred Scott decision was erroneous and he would do what he could to overrule it.

On June 16, 1858, Lincoln was nominated Republican candidate for Senator from Illinois, and in his famous acceptance speech predicted that

A house divided against itself cannot stand.

I believe this government cannot endure, permanently, half *slave* and half *free*. ... I do not expect the Union to be dissolved—I do not expect the house to *fall*—but I *do* expect it will cease to be divided. It will become *all* one thing, or *all* the other. Either the *opponents* of slavery, will arrest the further spread of it, and place it where the public mind shall rest in the belief that it is in [the] course of ultimate extinction; or its *advocates* will push it forward, till it shall become alike lawful in *all* the States, *old* as well as *new*—*North* as well as *South*.

(Fehrenbacher, 1989a: 426)

Stephen Douglas, the incumbent Democrat candidate for the Senate position, retaliated on July 9, 1858, by denouncing Lincoln's "crusade" against the Supreme Court. In the debates between the two protagonists, between August 21 and October 15, 1858, Douglas attempted to defend his "position of popular sovereignty" against Lincoln's precise attack on the implications of the Taney Opinion. (The speeches of Douglas and

Lincoln, together with their questions and answers are collected in Holzer, 1993). For Lincoln, this Opinion by the Supreme Court only made sense if the South intended to extend slavery throughout the Territories, as far as the Pacific. This violated the compromise implicit in the Ratification, that slavery be accepted, but only in those states that had, by tradition, been slave states. In Lincoln's later speeches on the East Coast in 1860, he seemingly argued that the intention of the South was to extend slavery throughout the entire Union. I contend that the credibility of Lincoln's argument dramatically changed the beliefs, and thus the preferences, of the Northern electorate.

In the debates at Ottawa and Freeport Illinois, on August 21 and 27, 1858, Lincoln had attacked Douglas for his support of the Taney Opinion, arguing that the Opinion would lead, and was intended to lead, to the extension of slavery to all states. In referring to the Nebraska bill, Lincoln said, "[I]f another Dred Scott decision shall come, holding that they cannot exclude it [slavery] from a *State*, then we shall discover [why the particular wording of Territory or *State* were used in the Nebraska Bill]" (Fehrenbacher, 1989a: 520).

At the second debate, Lincoln asked Douglas if he would acquiesce in such a decision by the Supreme Court [asserting that slavery could not be excluded from a state]. Douglas had earlier declared that the Supreme Court decisions were binding, and therefore could make no reply compatible with the concept of "popular sovereignty." Lincoln's second question to Douglas, at Freeport, was, "Can the people of a United States Territory, in any lawful way, against the wishes of any citizen of the United States, exclude slavery from its limits prior to the formation of a State Constitution?" (Fehrenbacher, 1989a: 542).

Were Douglas to answer "no" to this, "then he would appear to capitulate entirely to the southern wing of the party and alienate free-soil Illinois Democrats" (Riker, 1986: 5).

By answering "yes," Douglas improved his chances in the Illinois Senate election, but, by angering southerners, he decreased the likelihood of winning the 1860 presidential election.

In fact, Douglas answered an emphatic "yes," even though this logic appeared counter to the Taney Opinion. His argument, that local regulations would allow the people to make their own choice in this matter, obviously contradicted federal guarantees of private property (in this case, of slaves).

At the fifth debate at Galesburg on October 7, 1858, Lincoln pursued the attack. By the Taney Opinion,

"[T]he right of property in a slave is distinctly and expressly affirmed in the Constitution!"... Nothing in the Constitution or laws of any State can destroy a right distinctly and expressly affirmed in the Constitution of the United States. Therefore, nothing in the Constitution or laws of any State can destroy the right of property in a slave.

(Fehrenbacher, 1989a: 714)

As Fehrenbacher remarks (2001), this "new Court doctrine ... could produce a ruling protecting slavery within the northern states as well as in the western territories" (Fehrenbacher, 2001: 287).

The *Chicago Daily Press and Tribune* was quick to point out that the answer that Douglas gave to this question, and his apparent complete acceptance of the Supreme Court decision on Dred Scott, contradicted one another. The *Tribune* argued that the Court's decision implied that slavery could not be excluded from the Territories.[6] Douglas tried to overcome this obvious contradiction in his answer by asserting that

slavery cannot exist a day or an hour anywhere, unless it is supported by local police regulations. ... Hence, no matter what the decision of the Supreme Court may be on the abstract question, still the right of the people to make a slave territory or a free territory is perfect and complete under the Nebraska bill.

(Fehrenbacher, 1989a: 552)

However, the *Tribune* (August 30, 1858) quoted the Supreme Court's assertion that

no tribunal acting under the authority of the United States, whether Legislative, Executive or Judicial, has a right to deny the benefits of the provisions or guarantees which have been provided for the protection of private property against the encroachments of the government. ... Since slaves are property, the local legislature has not the right to deny the provisions and is required to furnish the necessary police regulations to maintain slavery.

In fact, this attempt by Douglas to effect a "compromise" by appealing to southern interests with his acceptance of Dred Scott, and to use "popular sovereignty" to appeal to Illinois voters, had already failed. As I noted above, the editorial of *Mobile Register*, an influential southern journal, had declared, on August 20, 1858, that Douglas was

---

[6] *Chicago Daily Press and Tribune*, August 30, 1858. The point here was that for these territories, not states, covered by the Northwest Ordinance of 1787, slavery was not permitted by federal ruling (North and Rutten, 1984). Once the territory became a state, then its voters could, of course, choose for or against slavery.

in a position to offer the Democrat party the alternative of a probable success in the next presidential campaign if [the South] accepted the modified platform he has prepared for them or of certain defeat and permanent destruction as a party if they do not. There is ruin to them as a national party in either horn of the dilemma ... but there is demoralization as well as disaster in one.

If we read this as a denunciation by the South of Douglas's attempt at compromise, then it is clear that he had no alternative but to pursue the popular sovereignty argument in his attempt to win Illinois.

In the November election, Douglas was returned as a U.S. Senator by a joint vote of the Illinois House (comprising 40 Democrats and 35 Republicans) and Senate (14 Democrats and 11 Republicans). There was no popular vote for U.S. Senator; the closest to such a vote was for the State Treasurer. Using this, the tallies were approximately 125,400 (Lincoln, Republican), 121,600 (Douglas, Democrat), and 5,000 (Buchanan, Democrat).[7] The pro-Lincoln *Chicago Tribune* declared that Lincoln should have won the race, but was cheated by out-of-date districting. There was some truth to this allegation of gerrymandering. The Republicans took 49.9 percent of the popular vote for House representatives but their 35 House seats gave them only 46.6 percent of the total, while the Democrats, with 48.5 percent, took 53.3 percent of the total. In the Senate, thirteen members were holdovers from the previous election and split (8, 5) for Democrat, Republican, respectively, while the new members split (6, 6) for the two parties. Even had the House apportionment been exact, the Republicans would have been in a slight minority 49 to 51 (see also Donald, 1995: 228).

What is clear from the election result is that close to half the voters (principally from southern Illinois) accepted Douglas' compromise over popular sovereignty. It seems unlikely, however, that Lincoln's second question was merely a ploy to split the Democrat coalition in the future presidential election.

Lincoln's biographer, Donald (1995), observes that Lincoln was bitterly disappointed, but not surprised by the election result, and quotes him as saying,

I am glad I made the last race. It gave me a hearing on the great and desirable questions of the age, which I could have had in no other way; and though I now sink out of view, and shall be forgotten, I believe I have made some marks which will tell for the cause of liberty long after I am gone. (220)

---

[7] Holzer (1993: 373). In percentage terms, these are 49.7 percent, 48.2 percent, and 2.1 percent, respectively.

Although Donald and Riker both emphasize the importance of Lincoln's second question at Freeport (because it related directly to the Dred Scott decision), it was Lincoln's third question to Douglas that raised the question of the threat posed by the South to the free states of the North and West: "If the Supreme Court of the United States shall decree that STATES cannot exclude slavery from their limits, are you in favor of acquiescing in adopting, and following such decision as a rule of political action?"[8]

In the fifth debate at Galesburg, Illinois, on October 7, 1858, Lincoln had spoken after Douglas, observing that Douglas had essentially ignored this question, in making the assertion that the Supreme Court could never make such a decision. Lincoln went on to say, "I did not propound [this question] without some reflection, and I wish now to address some remarks upon it." He then quoted from the Constitution that it "shall be the supreme law of the land, that the Judges of every State shall be bound by it, any law or Constitution of any State to the contrary notwithstanding" (Fehrenbacher, 1989a: 714). As I have noted above, Lincoln had declared that the Dred Scott decision rested on the proposition that "the right of property in a slave is distinctly and expressly affirmed in the Constitution!" From this syllogism, Lincoln had deduced that "nothing in the Constitution or laws of any State can destroy the right of property in a slave."

But, argued Lincoln, this is false.

I believe the entire records of the world, from the date of the Declaration of Independence up to within three years ago, may be searched in vain for one single affirmation from one single man, that the negro was not included in the Declaration of Independence.

(Fehrenbacher, 1989a: 702)

The contradiction lay in the falsehood of the premise concerning slavery.[9] As Lincoln said, "I believe that the right of property in a slave is not distinctly and expressly affirmed in the Constitution, and Judge Douglas thinks it is" (Fehrenbacher, 1989a: 714). Lincoln was to return to this

---

[8] Here I quote the transcript of the speech from the *Chicago Daily Press and Tribune*, August 30, 1858. This differs from the version in Fehrenbacher (1989a: 542) in that STATES is capitalized. I emphasize this point, since Lincoln does not refer here to the Territories, the subject of the Dred Scott decision but to the constituent States of the Union.

[9] See Fehrenbacher (2001: 287) for further discussion of the implications of this deduction from the Dred Scott decision.

moral contradiction in his speeches in 1860, just before the presidential election.

In 1859, there was, of course, no guarantee that Lincoln would be nominated presidential candidate by the Republican party. The obvious candidate was, in fact, the abolitionist William H. Seward, originally of Massachusetts. The strategic choice for the party would depend on whether Douglas was nominated by a unified Democratic Party. However, the Douglas-Lincoln debates had aroused strong interest in the country, and Lincoln responded to the resulting controversy by contributing autobiographical information (December 1859) to a journalist (J. W. Fell), who was interested in writing about Lincoln's life. Lincoln also prepared a version of the debates for publication. Moreover, he replied quickly to an invitation to lecture at the Cooper Institute, New York, in February 1860. Donald suggests that Lincoln's two-week visit to the East Coast in early 1860 was necessary if he was to gain support from potential Republicans who would otherwise vote for Seward (Donald, 1995: Ch. 9).

Lincoln gave two speeches, "The Address at Copper Institute," February 27, 1860 (Fehrenbacher, 1989b: 111–30 and Holzer, 2004: 249–284) and "Speech at New Haven, Connecticut," March 6, 1869, (Fehrenbacher, 1989b: 132–50). In these speeches Lincoln addressed two issues: the first was the relevance of the Constitution for how slavery was to be judged; the second was the significance of the Dred Scott decision for free labor.

The first aspect of the constitutional issue was the proposition that the Constitution forbade the federal government from controlling slavery. Lincoln asserted that Douglas agreed with this proposition (because of the principle of "popular sovereignty").

In the Address at Cooper Institite, Lincoln examined the voting of Congress in 1784, 1787, and 1789 over the Northwest Territory, and inferred that seventeen of the original thirty-nine Founding Fathers (the signers of the 1787 Constitution) judged this first proposition false. Moreover, in Acts of 1798 (Mississippi) and 1804 (Louisiana), Congress forbade the importation of slaves from foreign ports into the Territories, and insisted that no slave at all be imported, except by the owner for his own use as settler. In all, Lincoln judged that at least twenty-three of the thirty-nine Founders approved of control of slavery in some way (Fehrenbacher, 1989b: 115).

Lincoln then went on to argue that the Supreme Court based its Dred Scott decision on the fifth amendment (that "no person shall ... be deprived of life, liberty, or property, without due process of law") while Douglas' "popular sovereignty" was based on the tenth amendment ("powers not delegated to the United States by the Constitution ... are reserved to the States respectively or to the people"). The two amendments could not be in logical contradiction to the legal control of slavery by the federal government because they were debated and approved by Congress (and ratified by the states) within the same period (1789–92) that Congress did indeed pass legislation to control slavery.

The second aspect of the constitutional issue was the understanding of the Founding Fathers as to the essential nature of slavery. Was it to be seen as a permanent feature of the society, or as a temporary compromise between economic interests? In the speech at New Haven, Lincoln said, "When men are framing a supreme law and chart of government, ... they use language as short and direct and plain as can be found ... But the Constitution alludes to Slavery three times without mentioning it once!"

First,

The Migration or Importation of such Persons as any of the States now existing shall think proper to admit, shall not be prohibited by the Congress prior to the year 1808, but a Tax or duty may be imposed on such Importation, not exceeding ten dollars for each Person.

(Article I, Section 9)

As Lincoln observed, "They speak of the "immigration of persons," and mean the importation of slaves, but do not say so."

Second,

Representatives and direct Taxes shall be apportioned among the several States ... according to their respective Numbers, which shall be determined by adding to the whole Number of free Persons, including those bound to Service for a Term of Years, and excluding Indians not taxed, three fifths of all other persons.

(Article I, Section 2)

Lincoln pointed out that they say "all other persons,"... "when they mean to say slaves" (Fehrenbacher, 1989b: 142).

Third,

No Person held to Service or Labour in one State, under the laws thereof, escaping into another, shall, in Consequence of any Law or Regulation therein, be discharged from such Service or Labour, but shall be delivered up on Claim of the Party to whom such Service or Labour may be due.

(Article IV, Section 2)

From these ambiguities in the Constitution, Lincoln inferred that

Only one reason is possible, and that is supplied us by one of the framers of the Constitution ... they expected and desired that the system would come to an end, and meant that when it did, the Constitution should not show that there ever had been a slave in this good free country of ours!

(Fehrenbacher, 1989b: 142)

Thus,

In forming the Constitution they found the slave trade existing; capital invested in it; fields depending upon it for labor; and the whole system resting upon the importation of slave-labor. They therefore did not prohibit the slave trade at once, but they gave the power to prohibit it after twenty years.

Moreover, "they prohibited the spread of Slavery into the Territories ... they considered that the thing was wrong." (Fehrenbacher, 1989b: 141).

By his interpretation of the meaning of the Constitution as reflected in the action and words of the Founders, Lincoln could justifiably demand that slavery be marked, just as the Founding Fathers marked it, as an evil. "We think that species of labor an injury to free white men-in short We think Slavery a great moral, social and political evil, tolerable only because ... its actual existence makes it necessary to tolerate it" (Fehrenbacher, 1989b: 135).

Its "necessity" lay solely in the "magnitude of [the] subject! One sixth of our population ... two thousand million dollars" (Fehrenbacher, 1989b: 134).

The intent of the Dred Scott decision clearly was to extend slavery to the entire United States. Lincoln does not fully spell out the consequences of the decision. However, in concluding his speech at New Haven he says: "I am glad to see that a system of labor prevails in New England under which laborers CAN strike when they want to. ... One of the reasons why I am opposed to Slavery is just here."[10]

---

[10] Fehrenbacher (1989b: 144). Capitals in the original published version.

It would seem obvious that, by this remark, Lincoln implied that, under the Dred Scott decision, slaves could be legitimately imported into northern free states to work in industrial manufacturing.[11] I contend that Lincoln, in these two speeches, initiated a "belief cascade" in the North. Slavery was an evil that violated the fundamental beliefs of the Founders as these were embodied in the Constitution. Moreover, the economic interest of the South, in extending slavery (via the mechanism of the Dred Scott decision), threatened the way of life of free labor in the North.

5.6 THE PRESIDENTIAL ELECTION OF 1860

As I have observed, the Republican choice for presidential candidate in 1860 depended in large degree on the Democrats' choice. If the Democratic coalition persisted, and chose Stephen Douglas, then the strategic choice for the Republicans would be a candidate equally popular in the West. Lincoln, of Illinois, would be a likely contender. If the Democrats chose a southerner, such as John Breckinridge of Kentucky (the incumbent Vice President), then an eastern abolitionist like Seward (Senator, and former governor of New York) would be a strategic choice. In his speeches in the East, Lincoln was careful to appear in a somewhat moderate position, not abolitionist, but demanding that the status quo, as implicit in the Constitution, be retained, and that the southern pro-slavery advances be halted. One of Lincoln's letters in 1860 suggests that he did not agree with Seward's "higher-law" view of slavery. Lincoln felt clearly that Seward's intransigence frightened moderate Republicans.

The Democratic National Convention, meeting in April 1860, had been unable to choose between Douglas and Breckinridge, and adjourned. The uncertainty over its choice, when the Democracy was to reconvene in separate conventions in June, meant that neither Lincoln nor Seward were advantaged. On May 10, the National Union Party (the rump of the Whigs) nominated John Bell (of Tennessee), with Edward Everett (of Massachusetts) as the vice-presidential candidate. Because this combination would do well against Seward, many delegates to the Republican convention in Chicago in late May hoped for a candidate who (unlike Seward) would be popular in the West (particularly Illinois, Ohio, and Indiana).

Before moving to nomination, the Republican Party Convention adopted a platform of seventeen "planks." The second plank argued

---

[11] See Jaffa (2000) for further discussion of Lincoln's arguments on the significance of Dred Scott for free labor.

for the maintenance of the Union, as bound by the principles of the Declaration of Independence and the Federal Constitution. The eighth denied "the authority of Congress, or a Territorial Legislature—to give legal existence to slavery in any territory of the United States." The twelfth argued for an increase in the tariff "to encourage the development of the industrial interests of the whole country" and to secure "to the working man, to mechanics and manufacturers an adequate reward for their skilled labor and enterprise." Two further planks demanded "the passage by Congress of the complete and satisfactory Homestead measure" and a "railroad to the Pacific Ocean" (*The New York Times*, May 18, 1860). The policy position of the party was quite precisely located at a compromise position on the capital and land axes, moderately protectionist but expansionist in outlook. On the labor axis, the platform was obviously anti-slavery. The policy proposals were designed to appeal to voters of the Northeast who might have voted Whig, as well as to voters of western states (Iowa, Ohio, and Indiana, for example) who saw a coincidence between their own "expansionist" interests and those of Douglas. The choice of presidential nominee was crucial for the Republicans. As Donald (1995: 243) has noted, had a unified Democratic Party chosen Breckinridge then the anti-abolitionist Seward would have been a plausible choice. However, as an easterner, Seward would probably do poorly in western states, especially if he had to compete against Douglas. Had Douglas been chosen as the single Democrat candidate, then Lincoln, with his support in Illinois, would have been the obvious choice.

Because of the uncertainty due to the breakup of the Democratic Convention, Seward gained 173.5 (about 37 percent) of the total delegates, compared to Lincoln's 102, in the first ballot at the Republican Convention. Cameron (of Pennsylvania) took 50.5, while Chase (Governor of Ohio) took 49, and Bates (a Whig from Missouri) took 48 (Donald, 1995: 250). The other votes were scattered among candidates such as Fremont (the defeated Republican candidate of 1856). Because Seward had not obtained the required majority of 233, a second ballot was held giving Seward 184.5 and Lincoln 181. On the third ballot, Lincoln took 231.5 which increased to 235.5 when some Ohio delegates switched. The delegates moved to the bandwagon, first giving Lincoln 364 out of 466, and then nominating him unanimously. To balance the ticket, Hannibal Hamlin of Maine (a former Democrat) was selected as vice-presidential nominee.

The Democratic Party division in June, between Douglas and Breckinridge, meant that the Lincoln-Hamlin combination would do well in the North. Indeed, the October state election victories of the Republican Party in Pennsylvania, Ohio, and Indiana suggested that Lincoln had a good chance of winning the presidential election in November.

As I have noted, Riker (1982: 230) saw Lincoln's success in the election in November, 1860, as the culmination of a long progression of strategic attempts by the Whig coalition of commercial interests to defeat the larger "Jeffersonian-Jacksonian" Democratic coalition of agrarian populism. While there is some validity in this perspective, I believe it puts too much weight on the preferences of the political actors in this drama. In contrast, I suggest that the crucial feature of the election was the way in which Lincoln triggered changes in the beliefs of a large portion of the electorate about the meaning of the U.S. Constitution, and in their beliefs about the significance of the Dred Scott decision for free labor.

Lincoln had first to gain the nomination of his party by defeating Seward. While Seward had political support in the Northeast, he had argued that there was "an irrepressible conflict between opposing and enduring forces," going on to say that "the United States must and will, sooner or later, become either entirely a slave-holding nation, or entirely a free-labor nation" (Foner, 1970: 69). These remarks led some Republican delegates to view Seward with alarm.

In the run-up to the presidential election, Lincoln's analysis of the Constitution and of the Dred Scott decision must have been in the minds of many northern voters. Such swing voters would have cause to reject the Democrats, and Douglas's popular sovereignty position, for two reasons. First, they would be persuaded by Lincoln's arguments that popular sovereignty entailed an extension of slavery that was constitutionally illegitimate. Second, this extension threatened the livelihood of free labor. However, Lincoln had been careful to distinguish himself from Seward, and to not imply that conflict was inevitable. In the New York speech he had said:

It is exceedingly desirable that all parts of this great Confederacy shall be at peace, and in harmony, one with another. ... Even though the southern people will not so much as listen to us, let us calmly consider their demands, and yield to them, if, in our deliberate view of our duty, we possibly can. (Fehrenbacher, 1089b: 128)

I interpret Lincoln's speeches to have been designed to persuade the northern electorate that the threat of the South (at expected cost, pT) was real. Under Lincoln this threat would be faced, either by some compromise measure (at cost qC) or, if the South refused conciliation, possibly through war (at cost rF).

In November, 1860, there were four presidential candidates: Lincoln, Douglas, Breckinridge, and Bell. As Table 5.2 has shown, Douglas took about a third of the popular vote in twelve of the thirty-three states, all in the Northeast and West. Bell's policy of the status quo gave him the electoral college votes of Virginia, Kentucky, and Tennessee, while Breckinridge won all nine states of the deep South. (South Carolina allocated its electoral college vote by a session of the legislature.) Lincoln won a majority (over 50 percent) in fifteen states, and pluralities in Oregon and California. Only in the last two states did Douglas and Breckinridge gain between them a majority. New Jersey was equally divided between Douglas and Lincoln, and split its college vote. With almost 40 percent of the popular vote, Lincoln won 180 (out of 305) votes in the electoral college.

Even after the presidential election, but before the counting of the electoral college votes (to take place in February 1861), Lincoln was careful over possible misinterpretation of his intentions. For a speech drafted for Lyman Trumbull, given in Springfield, Illinois, on November 20, 1860, Lincoln wrote:

> I have labored in, and for, the Republican organization with entire confidence that whenever it shall be in power, each and all of the States will be left in as complete control of their own affairs respectively, and at as perfect liberty to choose, and employ, their own means of protecting property ... as they have ever been under any administration.
>
> (Fehrenbacher, 1989b: 186)

Donald suggests that Lincoln may have viewed southern "secessionist" responses to his election as a bluff. However, the South Carolina Legislature unanimously decided on November 10, 1860, to authorize a state convention to consider future relations between that state and the Union. Perhaps in response, Lincoln concluded the speech for Lyman Trumbull on November 20 with the sentence, "I am rather glad of this military preparation in the South. It will enable the people the more easily to suppress any uprising there, which their misrepresentation of purposes may have encouraged" (Fehrenbacher, 1989b: 187).

Between November 1860 and Lincoln's inaugural speech of March 4, 1861, the Union fragmented, with secession by South Carolina on December 20, 1860, followed by Florida, Mississippi, Alabama, Georgia, and Louisiana. Congress had proposed the Crittenden Resolutions, on January 16, 1861, and Lincoln rejected this attempt at compromise. In a letter to Seward on February 1, 1861, he wrote, "I am for no compromise which assists or permits the extension of the institution [of slavery] on soil owned by the nation" (Fehrenbacher, 1989b: 197).

In his various speeches before the inauguration, Lincoln's words were calm and measured, referring to his devotion to the Union, the Constitution and the liberties of the people.

In his inaugural address on March 4, 1861, Lincoln spelled out his view of the contract on which the Republic was based:

The Union is much older than the Constitution. It was formed, in fact, by the Articles of Association in 1774. It was matured and continued by the Declaration of Independence in 1776. It was further matured and the faith of all the then thirteen States expressly plighted and engaged that it should be perpetual, by the articles of Confederation in 1778. And finally, in 1787, one of the declared objects for ordaining and establishing the Constitution, was "to form *a more perfect union.*"...

It follows from these views that no State, upon its own mere motion, can lawfully get out of the Union,—that *resolves* and *ordinances* to that effect are legally void; and that acts of violence, within any State or States, against the authority of the United States, are insurrectionary or revolutionary, according to the circumstances ...

A majority, held in restraint by constitutional checks, and limitations, and always changing easily, with deliberate changes of popular opinions and sentiments, is the only true sovereign of a free people. Whoever rejects it, does, of necessity, fly to anarchy or to despotism. Unanimity is impossible; the rule of a minority, as a permanent arrangement is wholly inadmissable; so that rejecting the majority principle, anarchy or despotism in some form, is all that is left ...

This country, with its institutions, belongs to the people who inhabit it. Whenever they shall grow weary of the existing government, they can exercise their *constitutional* right of amending it, or their *revolutionary* right to dismember, or overthrow it.

I therefore consider that, in view of the Constitution and the laws, the Union is unbroken.

In *your* hands, my dissatisfied fellow countrymen, and not in mine, is the momentous issue of civil war ... *You* have no oath registered in Heaven to destroy the government while *I* shall have the most solemn one to "preserve, protect and defend" it.[12]

---

[12] See Fehrenbacher (1989b: 215–24) for the text. Also see Wills (1999: 184) and Fletcher (2001: 2) for further discussion.

For the elite in the southern states, secession was legitimate because the Constitution itself was regarded as the founding compact between states. Lincoln's election had destroyed the heterogeneity of the republic, creating a tyrannical majority- the North- that directly threatened the South. This violated Madison's logic in *Federalist X*. Moreover, Madison had expressed the opinion, in *Federalist XLIII* that "a breach committed by either of the parties [to a compact between independent sovereigns or states] absolves the other; and authorizes them, if they please, to pronounce the compact violated and void" (Rakove, 1999: 251).

The share of the popular vote in 1860 for Bell (and his policy of the status quo) had been significant in Virginia, Tennessee, Arkansas, and North Carolina. This suggests that a majority, possibly, of the electorate in these states, saw no reason to secede. Gary (2004) contends that delegate elections and the secession conventions in 1861 were manipulated by the slave-owning elite to force the secessions that did occur between February and June 1861. It is, in any case, difficult to understand the logic of secession. Lincoln had made it clear that their institution would be preserved, but would not be allowed to envelop other states. It is consistent with the logic of risk discussed here that Lincoln was perceived as a threat to the expansion of slave-owning elite interests toward the Pacific. To prevent this, secession, and the very considerable risk of war (implied by Lincoln's inaugural speech), appeared worth accepting. For this calculation to be rational it must have been believed that Lincoln would acquiesce to some compromise that would have given the western territories to slave interests. For Lincoln, however, the expansion of slavery would have destroyed the Empire of Liberty crafted by Jefferson. His argument was accepted by the majority of the northern electorate. However, it required the terrible cost of Civil War to prove that this belief was a *core belief*, in the sense that it was held by a winning subset of the population. It is compatible with my interpretation of the intent of the Founders, in constructing the constitutional apparatus in 1787, that Lincoln thus proved to be the decisive risk taker who saved the Union.

5.7   CONCLUDING REMARKS

Prior to 1857, the position of Stephen Douglas, and his principle of popular sovereignty, would have made perfect sense. However, the issue of

populism, or "state rights," had become confused because of the interpretation that state rights permitted southern states to maintain their
peculiar institution. It was the nature of the distinctiveness of the "slave"
and "economic" ideologies that led to the incoherence of the Supreme
Court decision over Dred Scott. As I have attempted to show in this
chapter, Lincoln could exploit this incoherence to expose Douglas' position, and make credible the Southern threat to the North. The election of
1860 thus brought the second ideological dimension of civil rights into
focus.

The fact that there have been two distinct ideological cleavages in U.S.
politics can be used to clarify the relative positions of the two principal
parties since that time.

Following the Civil War, it was natural for the Republican Party to
move to a pro-capital position on the right of the economic ideological
axis (Bordo and Rockoff, 1996). The Democratic Party, under William
Jennings Bryan, moved simultaneously to a more populist position on the
left of this axis in 1896. However, it was not until 1928 through 1932
that the Democratic Party could include both populist agrarian interests
and urban social liberals.[13]

The move by L. B. Johnson in the 1960s to create the Great Society in
turn made it possible for the Republican Party to begin to attract social
conservatives, who had, in the past, traditionally chosen the Democratic
Party. The positions of both Democrat and Republican presidential candidates by 1992 had become almost identical on the economic ideology
dimension. Populism, in the form of soft money, was no longer a political
issue. As in 1860, the political positions of the two parties in the 1990s
were more clearly differentiated on the civil rights axis.

From this perspective, the elections of 1896, 1932, 1964, and possibly
1980 were all "critical," because they involved movements by the parties
in response to social and economic quandaries.

In this chapter I have presented the view that the election of 1860 was
the result of a transformation of beliefs in the electorate. This transformation led eventually to war, and to a transformation in the Constitution,

---

[13] What I have called the dimension of slavery ideology had of course been transformed
by that time into one involving civil and individual rights. The winning Democratic
coalition of F. D. Roosevelt included southern, socially conservative Democrats as
well as voters both socially and economically liberal. These topics are discussed in
Chapter 6.

the institutional apparatus adopted by the society. If I am correct in my view of the elections of 1896, 1932, and 1964, they too were preceded by transformations in electoral beliefs, following on from generally perceived social quandaries. If voter choice is, in some sense, "stochastic," then it is plausible that rapid changes in electoral beliefs are part of a process during which individual changes in opinion are no longer "independent," but are highly correlated. Chapter 6 suggests how models of voting may be constructed to reflect this possibility.

6

Johnson and the Critical Realignment of 1964

6.1 INTRODUCTION*

It is commonly assumed that politics is inherently one dimensional. In such a world, theory suggests that political candidates would be drawn into the electoral center in order to maximize votes. Against such a tendency would be the motivation of ideological political activists to pull their preferred candidate away from the center. The balance of electoral incentives and activist pull creates the "political equilibrium" at any election.

But is politics inherently one dimensional? This chapter continues with the argument that politics is fundamentally two dimensional. Politics may appear to be characterized by a single cleavage, but this is because the two parties themselves "organize" politics along the dimension that separates them. Party disagreement on one dimension of politics makes that dimension more salient, while the other dimension is obscured by tacit party agreement.

The existence of a submerged or passive dimension of politics transforms the calculus of activist support and electoral preferences. Activists who are most concerned about the dimension of politics on which parties passively agree constitute a pool of disaffected voters who see no perceptible difference between the two main parties on the issues that matter most to them. These disaffected activists often offer a temptation to vote-maximizing candidates who may see them as the potential margin

* Chapter 6 reprints material from Gary Miller and Norman Schofield, "Activists and Partisan Realignment," *American Political Science Review* 97 (2003): 245–60, with permission of Cambridge University Press. The figures in the chapter are reprinted from Norman Schofield, Gary Miller and Andrew Martin, "Critical Elections and Political Realignment in the U.S.A.: 1860–2000," *Political Studies* 51 (2003): 217–40, with permission of Blackwell Publishing.

of victory in a close election. Such a development would be resented and resisted by party activists who are most concerned about the active dimension that differentiates the two parties, and would rather see their party go down to defeat than re-orient itself to a new set of policy issues and a new agenda.

Party realignments have long fascinated scholars of American politics, but no simple model has apparently been sufficient to capture the phenomena. These transformations have been conceived as due to exogenous change in the economic or international environment. I view such transformations as the direct consequence of the unrecognized two-dimensionality of the political space. The premise of this chapter is that "partisan realignment" cannot be understood without understanding the tension existing between vote-maximizing candidates and policy-specialized party activists, operating in a two-dimensional strategy space. Although each election outcome may be the result of an equilibrium in the context of the contemporary party alignment, over a longer time span there is a kind of "dynamic stability." Each temporary political balance results from candidates' efforts to re-form the optimal coalition of party activists. These forces destroy the old equilibrium and create a new one.

Taking the long view, American politics can be seen as a prolonged, slow manifestation of the inherent instability of multi-dimensional politics long posited by rational choice theory. For example, the period in American politics between 1896 and 2000 can be visualized as manifesting two full re-orientations of party politics along distinct ideological dimensions.

6.2   PARTISAN REALIGNMENTS FROM 1896 TO 2000

Knowing whether a state went for Kennedy or Nixon in 1960 does not allow one to predict whether that state's electoral votes went to Bush or Gore in 2000. Party voting in 1960 was still primarily driven by the economic cleavage of the New Deal. Income and class variables were strong predictors of individual voting behavior, with middle-class and professional homeowners voting Republican, and working class union members voting Democratic. Democratic candidates since the New Deal had tried to suppress racial voting in order to appeal simultaneously to northern liberals and southern segregationists; as a result, the Republican Party while lukewarm on civil rights, was still arguably more liberal than the Democratic Party.

By 2000, however, the New Deal party alignment no longer captured patterns of partisan voting. In the intervening forty years, the Civil Rights and Voting Rights Acts had triggered an increasingly race-driven distinction between the parties. Carmines and Stimson (1989) argue that racial issues had become the dominant cleavage in American politics. Huckfeldt and Kohfeld (1989) claim that race-based voting had driven out class-based voting. Racial polarities had come to subsume a variety of other social issues as well, including abortion, women's rights, and prayer in schools. Among whites, church attendance was a primary predictor of Republican voting (Smith, 2002).

As a result, it is no surprise that a state that went for Kennedy in 1960 was not particularly likely to vote for Gore in 2000. In fact, virtually half of the states (Nevada and ten southern states) that had voted for Kennedy voted for Bush in 2000. Similarly, eight New England and upper Midwest states went from the Republican column in 1960 to the Democrats in 2000. A redefinition of party cleavages had happened in the intervening forty years.

Similarly, it is not possible to predict which states went for Nixon in 1960 based on the state's choice between Bryan and McKinley in 1896. Once again, the basis of party voting had changed too much. The Republican Party's view of the parties was still largely a relic of the Civil War trauma. The Democrats were a rural, conservative party, whose candidate was a product of rural, Protestant America with no affinity for the growing population of urban immigrants in the cities of the Northeast. The New Deal coalition of southern, agrarian states with Northern liberal states was not even a remote possibility in 1896. As a result, only 10 of the 22 states that voted for McKinley in 1896 voted for Nixon in 1960.

Despite the fact that the partisan status of the states in 1896 does not predict their partisan status in 1960, and that partisan status in 1960 does not predict that in 2000, the partisan status of the states in 1896 does predict the electoral behavior of the states in 2000 remarkably well. If one were to predict that a Republican state in 1896 would be Democratic in 2000, and vice-versa, one would get all but 6 states correct. Between 1896 and 1960, eleven Republican upper-Atlantic and upper Midwest states joined the Democratic coalition, while twelve primarily plains and border states left the Democratic coalition and joined the Republicans. Beginning in 1964, California, Oregon and most of the rest of the Northeast have become reliably Democratic, while the South has become

reliably Republican.[1] The composition of these two unpredictable transformations is a nearly perfect reversal of the partisan alignment of 1896.
Urban, cosmopolitan states supported the Republican McKinley in 1896,
and the Democrat Gore in 2000. Virtually all of the rural and southern
states that supported Bryan's brand of traditional (not to mention funda-
mentalist) values in 1896 supported Bush in 2000.

Furthermore, a state that was more strongly Democratic in 1896 is pre-
dictably more strongly Republican in 2000. Miller and Schofield (2003)
showed that a simple regression of percent Democratic vote in 2000 on
percent Democratic vote in 1896 gives a strongly significant negative coefficient. Indeed, one can get a more accurate prediction with this negative
relationship ($r^2 = .37$) than by predicting the 2000 election outcome from
the much more recent 1960 election ($r^2 = .23$).

This fact does not make sense from the perspective of the traditional
literature on realignment. In that literature, new "shocks" to the political
system occasionally come along, and sometimes such a shock results in a
partisan realignment. If this were an accurate model, then each new partisan realignment should result in cumulatively "noisy" transformations
of the partisan alignment. There is no reason to believe that a series of
such realignments would result in the parties effectively "trading places"
(Smith, 2002).

This chapter has several purposes. The first is to argue that the striking
"mirror image" of the 1896 election in 2000 is understandable through
a two-dimensional spatial model. The two underlying dimensions have
remained remarkably similar for a century and a half, even while the
maneuverings of party leaders (candidates and activists) have resulted in
quite different party positions in that underlying two-dimensional space.

The second purpose is to produce a formal argument that explains
the spatial positions of the parties through time as a result of both
activists and candidates. The literature on the internal organization of
parties (Schlesinger, 1994) emphasizes the differences in goals of party
candidates and party activists—but the traditional spatial modelling literature regards parties as monolithic rational actors, with a single coherent
goal of winning elections. I argue that this spatial modelling literature

---

[1] Examining the 1964 election, Burnham (1968: 6) noted that the pendulum had begun
to swing back toward the 1896 cleavage. Indeed he noted both a sharp shift from
the 1960 and preceding elections, and a similarity with such sectionally polarized
elections as the Bryan–McKinley contest of 1896.

cannot account for the peculiar pattern by which parties have transformed themselves in their search for electoral victory.

Party candidates are motivated primarily to win elections, but use activist contributions to increase vote shares. Such candidates will on occasion engage in "flanking" moves so as to enlist coalitions of disaffected voters, at the risk of alienating some of their traditional activist supporters. A result of such "flanking" moves, in the early part of this century, was a shift in emphasis from an underlying social dimension to the economic dimension. In the last four decades, elections have seen salience shift from economics to social policy. The net result of a series of such flanking moves, over more than a century, has been to reproduce the partisan alignment of the end of the nineteenth century, but with the parties in reversed positions in two-dimensional space.

A third purpose of the chapter is to use the distinction between activists and candidates to introduce a concept of "dynamic equilibrium." This means that, in a given election, candidates seek to win elections against a constraint given by the location of the current cadre of party activists and their preferences; this may or may not involve an attempt to relocate the center of party gravity by building a coalition with disaffected activists. Between elections, current and potential party activists reconsider the impact of party leaders in the recent election on their own decisions to join or leave the party activists. The net result of those decisions is, quite possibly, a new configuration of party activists constraining the next party candidates. These "flanking" maneuvers over short-term horizons give rise, over the long run, to the historically documented partisan realignments of the late nineteenth and twentieth centuries.

6.3 PARTY COMPETITION IN TWO DIMENSIONS

The model assumes that American voters have preferences that can be represented in a policy space of as few as two dimensions. The two dimensions underlying partisan competition since the Civil War may be thought of as an *economic* and a *social* dimension (see Figure 6.1). The *economic* dimension is one in which the left side represents a pro-redistribution position articulated by rural, populist, consumerist, and environmentalist interests. The right side represents a policy position in opposition to the use of the state to support redistributional policies from the rich to the poor. This ideological stance is associated with large businesses and professionals who oppose redistributional taxes, strict regulation of business, and large expenditures on welfare and other social policies in aid of

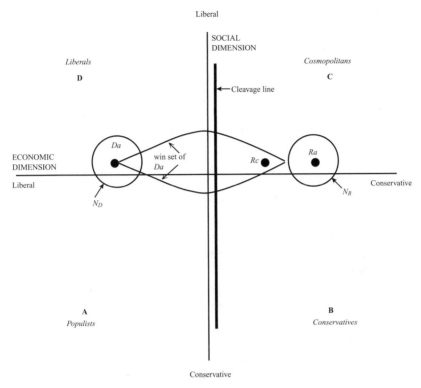

Figure 6.1. Illustration of Republican and Democrat economic policy positions in a two-dimensional policy space.

low-income groups. Throughout the era since the Civil War, this axis has distinguished pro- and anti-business segments of the population.

As assumed in Chapter 5, the vertical dimension is a *social* dimension. The issue most consistently loading on this dimension has been racial, where "liberalism" has been identified with policies favorable to blacks and other minorities. "Social" conservatives oppose the use of government, especially the national government, to provide additional benefits or opportunities to Afro-American minorities, for example. This distinction between racial liberals and conservatives has had much the same content since Reconstruction. The debate has involved those who consistently oppose greater political, economic, or legal concessions for racial minorities, as advocated by the other side (although, of course, the status quo has changed over this time). This social policy dimension has also been correlated with other policy issues; racial conservatives from Bryan through Wallace have been associated with Protestant fundamentalism and traditional family values. At different times, the issues of women's rights, crime, abortion, prayer in schools, the military draft, and anti-communism have been indicators of this underlying social preference dimension.

While many policy dimensions are correlated with one ideological dimension or the other, the two dimensions are relatively independent. There are leaders and voters who are both economically and socially conservative (Region B); these include figures from Grover Cleveland, through the Taft family, up to and including Robert Dole. There are also politicians who are both economically and socially liberal (Region D). These include Bob LaFollette, Hubert Humphrey, George McGovern, and Ralph Nader.

There are also a large number of voters who mix one form of conservatism with another form of liberalism. The group in Region A can be called "populists"—social conservatives with a marked antipathy for big business, who favor policies that benefit "the little guy." These include notable Southern populists from Huey Long and Wright Patman to George Wallace. Outside of the South, there are other socially conservative blue-collar workers who are opposed to big government (Jarvis of the tax revolt) or hostile both to affirmative action and to big business (the northern blue-collar followers of Patrick Buchanan). Aside from their antipathy to big business, however, this group shares a conservative position on race, religion, and patriotism issues.

The mirror image of the populists is the group that may be thought of as "cosmopolitans"—a term that is meant to imply a linkage with national economic interests and an appreciation of social diversity. These have included Nelson Rockefeller, William Weld of Massachusetts, and Pete Wilson of California, but also many other urban professional and business interests who are likely to be in favor of abortion rights, opposed to prayer in schools, and supportive of some form of affirmative action for minorities. Most recently, these include moderate Republicans who have identified with James Jeffords' exit from the Republican Party.

In a European style proportional representation system, such a two-dimensional diversity of opinion would no doubt be represented by a diversity of parties (Laver and Schofield, 1998[1990]). As suggested by Duverger's (1954) work, however, the American system of first-past-the-post, single-member legislative districts, along with the presidential system, is generally prohibitive of a multi-party system. The pressures to negotiate majority coalitions out of minority positions are strong. While third parties may play an important role in realignment, they do not do so by winning a significant number of seats in Congress, but by serving as catalysts for change in the main parties' coalitional structures. (Third parties are discussed more fully below.)

Because the U.S. system is essentially a two-party system in two dimensions, American political parties have to encompass a broad diversity of policy opinion in order to win a presidential election. A winning electoral coalition will have to combine voters who have quite different preferences on at least one dimension. In Figure 6.1, the traditional position of the Democratic and Republican Parties during the New Deal alignment is approximated. The parties are sharply differentiated on the economic policy dimension, but largely undifferentiated on social policy. As Carmines and Stimson (1989) note, the Republican Party was, if anything, slightly more liberal on racial policy up until 1964. Members of the Democratic Party, in particular, while sharing many elements of an economic ideology, held sharply different positions on race.

In other words, successful American parties must be coalitions of enemies. A party gets to be a majority party by forming fragile ties across wide and deep differences in one dimension or the other. Maintaining such diverse majority coalitions is necessarily an enormous struggle against strong centrifugal forces. Consequently, there will always be an electoral incentive for the losing party to split the majority party by means of the suppressed policy dimension, and then woo away some pivotal voters from the winning party. A partisan realignment, I argue, takes place when shifting public perceptions of the partisan positions of the two parties lead some subset of the population to switch voting patterns, creating a new winning partisan coalition.

When two parties differentiate themselves on the basis of one given dimension, I call that an *active* dimension. The very fact that the New Deal parties differed on economic policy guaranteed that legislative debate, electoral conflict, and media attention were focused on that dimension.[2] At the same time, the New Deal coalition required strict suppression of

---

[2] At any time, politics will appear largely one-dimensional because the existing party activist equilibrium will define party differences along the dimension that distinguishes them. Uni-dimensional models will successfully predict most of the variation in legislative voting patterns (Koford, 1989). Over time, shifts in the composition of the party activist coalition will change the policy "meaning" of the partisan cleavage (Karol, 1999). An attempt to estimate the two dimensions underlying party cleavages over time is found in Schofield, Miller, and Martin (2003) and Schofield and Sened (2006).

racial policy, because Southern Democrats and Northern liberals were so opposed on that dimension. Franklin Roosevelt's famous explanation for why he could not openly support a federal anti-lynching bill (it would alienate key Southern Democrats in Congress) is a striking example of the threat that activation of the social policy posed to the fragile Democratic coalition. Race was a potential fault line within the Democratic Party, which the Republican opposition tried to exploit. Every party alignment must create for the minority party a similar opportunity to divide the majority coalition.

This chapter argues that the reversal of party positions between 1896 and 2000 can only be understood if there are at least two such ideological dimensions. At times (e.g., the New Deal), the party cleavage line has divided economic liberals from economic conservatives. At other times (e.g., the Reconstruction and the 2000 election), the party cleavage line has more consistently divided social liberals from social conservatives. A party candidate, especially a candidate in a party that has lost recent elections, may try to emphasize a previously suppressed policy dimension. This may have the effect of both splitting the opposing party's coalition, and bringing disaffected voters who have intense preferences about that suppressed policy into their own party. Success by activating a previously suppressed dimension of policy may result in pivoting of the party cleavage line between the two parties. Two 90° movements (over whatever time period) of a party cleavage line result in a complete reversal of the ideological positions of the two parties. This chapter provides both a model of how this may occur, and an historical interpretation of the two such movements that have occurred between 1896 and 2000. The model will take as an illustration the transformation of the New Deal alignment by means of the activation of the social policy dimension since 1960.

6.4 EQUILIBRIUM IN CANDIDATE COMPETITION

The literature on party realignment often represents party alignments as lines of cleavage in a two-dimensional space such as in Figure 6.1. See Sundquist (1983) for example. This is consistent with the rational choice literature on spatial modelling, where cleavage lines can be derived from a "deterministic" model of rational choice by voters. Chapter 2 has emphasized that the most important theoretical result from the spatial modeling literature is that no party may take a position which cannot be beaten by a challenging party taking some other policy position in the space. Given any party position such as *Da* in Figure 6.1, there will in general exist a set of alternatives, called the "win set," each of which can defeat *Da*. The opposition party, by taking position *Rc* in the win set of *Da* should be able to shift its coalition of support to defeat an incumbent.

Candidates, according to the literature on political parties, are interested in winning elections (Schlesinger, 1994). An unconstrained challenging candidate trying to defeat an incumbent identified at location *Da* would move the party position from *Ra* to location *Rc*. The standard spatial modelling assumption is that the party's position is unilaterally chosen by the candidate. That assumption, together with the assumption that the candidate always wants to win elections, leads to the conclusion that two-party competition should be a chaotic series of ever-shifting party coalitions.

Although the recent literature on realignment (Brady, 1988; Carmines and Stimson, 1989; Huckfeldt and Kohfeld, 1989) acknowledges the possibility of shifting party positions, it has not considered the likelihood of permanently chaotic party configurations. This chapter regards party realignments as being a rather controlled manifestation of underlying two-dimensional electoral instability. The "instability theorem" previously alluded to assumes that voters choose "deterministically" (by, for example, voting for the candidate nearest the voter "ideal" point). An alternative theory "smooths" voter preferences by assuming that each voter is "stochastic." That is, each voter is described by a probability vector; the nearer the candidate is to the voter, the higher the probability that the voter will choose that candidate. Under the assumption that candidates choose positions to maximize expected vote shares, and accepting a number of reasonable conditions, it can be shown that candidates converge to the mean of the distribution of the voter ideal points.[3] However, neither

---

[3] The existence of such pure strategy Nash equilibria (PSNE) in these "stochastic models is discussed in Enelow and Hinich (1984), Coughlin (1992), Lin, Enelow and Dorussen (1999), Banks and Duggan (2005), and Schofield and Sened (2006). This convergence parallels the equilibrium result of Downs (1957) in one dimension. A third, non-stochastic model assumes deterministic voters (with "Euclidean" preferences, for example) and candidate "mixed strategy Nash equilibria" in a two- candidate symmetric voting game. An earlier result by McKelvey (1986), demonstrated more formally in Banks, Duggan, and Le Breton (2002), shows that the support of the mixed strategy Nash equilibria lies within the so-called uncovered set. However, with a large electorate this set will be small and centrally located. Consequently, those results also effectively imply that candidates will "converge" to the center (typically, the multidimensional median) of the voter ideal points.

the "instability" nor the convergence results of these classes of models is supported by empirical evidence (Merrill and Grofman, 1999; Schofield and Sened, 2006).

In contrast to the assumption of these models that candidates are unconstrained, it is evident that candidates in U.S. presidential elections are, to some degree, constrained by the necessity of winning primaries, raising funds, and mobilizing volunteers. These constraints are associated with party activists, who have different goals from candidates. The next section describes the Aldrich model, in which party "location" in policy space is determined by the decisions of party activists.

6.5 PARTY ACTIVIST EQUILIBRIUM

As noted by Schlesinger (1994) and Aldrich (1983a, 1983b, 1995), activists are less concerned with winning elections than with maintaining the ideological stance of the party. "The political role [of party activists] is to attempt to constrain the actual leaders of the party, its ambitious office seekers, as they try to become the party-in-government by appealing to the electorate" (Aldrich, 1995: 183).

Aldrich argues that party activists, not candidates, play the primary role in creating the public's perception of the "location" of the party in ideological space. Voters take the location of the "average" Democratic and Republican activists as their cues; those voters who find that the location of one party's activists is much closer to their own preferences than that of the other party may decide to become activists themselves. For example, if a voter finds that the average Democratic activist has policy preferences very like her own, she is more likely to enlist as an activist. In doing so, she may "move" the location of the average Democratic activist slightly in the direction of her ideal point—which may include a strong pro-choice position, for example. In that way, a pro-life activist may find himself at too much of a distance from the gradually moving typical Democratic activist position, and resign. Both the enlistment of the pro-choice activist and the deactivation of the pro-life activist have the effect of moving the public's identification of the Democratic Party. At the same time, as the Democratic Party becomes more pro-choice, the strongly pro-life voter may decide to become a Republican activist, initiating a similar adjustment of the Republican party.

Aldrich's contribution is to show that the aggregation of such decisions to join or exit the cadre of party activists may constitute a stable, activist equilibrium in which parties maintain a certain distance in the ideological space, as illustrated in Figure 6.1 by Da and Ra. Activists preserve their ideological distance, and at the same time, create stability in partisan alignments.

In Figure 6.1, the domains N_R and N_D are used to denote the support of ideal points of those voters who choose, in Aldrich's model, to become activists for the Republicans and Democrats, respectively. Note that the radii of N_R and N_D are determined by parameters of the model, and in particular by the cost, c, that each activist chooses to pay in support of the chosen party. In Aldrich's model, Da and Ra are, respectively, the average policy positions taken over the preferred (or ideal) points of Democratic and Republican activists. Aldrich's model has the great theoretical virtue of predicting neither chaos nor convergent equilibrium.

The constraint implicit in this model can be illustrated in Figure 6.1. While a move from Ra to Rc might be favored by the challenging candidate as a winning move, it is one that would be viewed by economic conservatives as "selling out." The economic conservatives will inevitably play a key role in a party alignment (such as the New Deal alignment), in which parties are differentiated primarily on economic policy. They will feel that a great deal is at stake in the difference between the parties, and will be most likely to vote in primaries, donate money, and engage in canvassing. During the 1940s and 1950s, for instance, Republican activists were professional and small business entrepreneurs who were activated by the classic party conflicts over unionization, nationalized medicine, and taxation. Democratic activists in that period were much more likely to be active union members and farmers, with an equal stake in an economically liberal stance by their party.

What control do party activists have over the public perception of the party? First of all, they will play a major role in selecting the party candidate. Time and again since 1964, we have seen a majority of party activists throw their support for more extreme over more centrist candidates in primary elections. In 1964, it was Barry Goldwater who defeated William Scranton of Pennsylvania. In 1972, George McGovern won the nomination in the primaries with a liberal position that proved disastrous at the polls. In 2000, centrist John McCain's popularity with Independents and moderate Republicans proved insufficient to defeat George W. Bush when traditional conservatives rallied to the latter's side. Furthermore, candidates, once selected, must act to keep party activists happy enough to continue to make contributions of money, time, and effort.

It appears that there is a great deal of evidence for Aldrich's argument. First of all, there is the empirical observation that in the United States (and other political systems), parties do not converge to the center (Poole and Rosenthal, 1984, 1997, or Adams and Merrill, 1999). Furthermore, party activists in the United States tend to be more ideologically extreme than the average Democratic or Republican voter. Finally, political parties do not constantly shift and re-align as would be predicted by a model of candidate vote maximization in two-dimensional space. In fact, the "disciplining" force of party activists can be seen in virtually every election.

However, while Aldrich's model rationalizes non-convergent activist equilibrium, it fails to do two things. First of all, it does not contain party candidates—who do want to win elections first and foremost. Second, it does not explain how party activist equilibria are themselves disrupted. For it is clear that occasionally party positions do change, in ways that often dismay traditional party activists and disrupt existing party activist equilibria. In 1964, traditional Republican activists were upset by the nomination of Goldwater; in 1972, many traditional Democratic activists dropped from the rolls of party activists rather than support a more socially liberal Democratic candidate. Evidently, there are destabilizing forces that occasionally disrupt party activist equilibria as described by Aldrich. The purpose of the next section is to provide a formal model, building on Aldrich (1983a, b) and Aldrich and McGinnis (1989), in order to examine the forces that party candidates may exploit to try to win elections.

6.6 A JOINT MODEL OF ACTIVISTS AND CANDIDATES

Aldrich showed, essentially, that these conditions could be satisfied, such that Ra was given by the mean of the bliss points of the set N_R, while Da was the mean of the set N_D. It is obvious that for such an activist equilibrium to exist, it is necessary that λ_j, the effect on the popularity of candidate j is concave (or has diminishing returns) in contributions to candidate j. Because candidates can transform activist contributions into nonpolicy-related votes, they cannot be indifferent to the policy preferences of those who are motivated to be activists in a given existing activist equilibrium. On the other hand, as vote maximizers, they may be willing to trade off current activist support for the support of other potential activists—hence the much-documented tension between party activists and candidates. How might candidates (who are passive in the Aldrich model) go about finding a policy position that induces an optimal

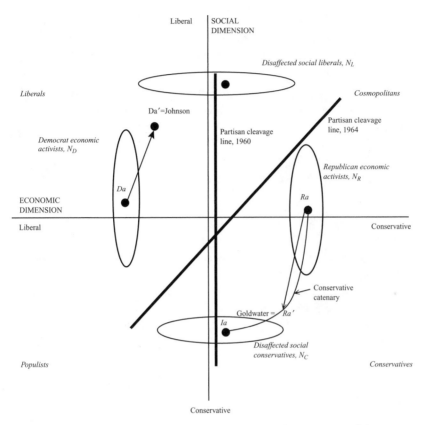

Figure 6.2. Illustration of flanking moves by Republican and Democrat candidates circa 1964 in a two-dimensional policy space.

corps of activists? As Figure 6.2 indicates, a typical socially conservative voter would regard Democratic and Republican candidates during the New Deal as equally unattractive, and tend to be indifferent. Civil rights supporters, for example, were frustrated by FDR's refusal to support an anti-lynching law, and occasionally threatened to "sit out" elections. Similarly, Dixiecrats walked out of the only New Deal-era Democratic convention (1948) that took a strong pro-civil rights position.

Suppose now that such a socially conservative voter, g, has an ideal point (s_g, t_g) say, near the position Ia, with utility function

$$u_g(x, y) = \lambda_R(z_R) - \left(\frac{(x - s_g)^2}{e^2} + \frac{(y - t_g)^2}{f^2} \right). \qquad (6.1)$$

The term $\lambda_R(z_R)$ is some measure of the nonpolicy evaluation of the competence or "valence" of the Republican candidate, R. (Chapter 8 gives more detail about the formal voting model.)

Let N_C be the set of such "disaffected" social conservatives who would be willing to contribute to a candidate as long as this candidate adopted a policy position (x_k, y_k) close to (s_g, t_g). Such a social conservative would regard social policy to be of greater significance and so $e > f$ in equation (6.1). Similarly, let the utility function of an economically conservative voter be

$$u_i(x, y) = \lambda_R(z_R) - \left(\frac{(x - s_i)^2}{a^2} + \frac{(y - t_i)^2}{b^2} \right), \qquad (6.2)$$

where this voter's ideal point is (s_i, t_i), close to Ra. Because this voter is more concerned about economic policy rather than social policy, it is natural to assume that $a < b$. Now, let N_R be the set of such traditional Republican activists.

Unlike Aldrich, suppose further that the Republican candidate adopts a position, not at the mean Ra, but at some compromise position Ra' between Ra and Ia. It is easy to demonstrate that the "contact curve" between the point (s_i, t_i) and the point (s_g, t_g) is given by the equation

$$\frac{(y - t_i)}{(x - s_i)} = S \frac{(y - t_g)}{(x - s_g)}, \qquad (6.3)$$

where

$$S = \frac{b^2}{a^2} \cdot \frac{e^2}{f^2}. \qquad (6.4)$$

I shall use the term *catenary* to describe this curve.

If the Republican candidate moves on this locus, then the resulting Republican activists will be a subset of N_C and N_R. Because of the asymmetry involved, the total number of activists may increase, thus increasing overall contributions to the Republican candidate. Clearly, there are plausible conditions under which $\lambda_R(z_R)$ increases as a result of such a move by a Republican candidate, thus increasing the effective vote share of this candidate. Thus the Republican candidate's desire to win elections may well transform the existing party activist equilibrium.

Determination of the existence of a candidate pure strategy Nash equilibrium (PSNE) depends on continuity and quasi-concavity (or concavity) of the candidate utility functions $\{U_j\}$. While each U_j will be a function of z, the vector of candidate positions, its dependence on positions will be more complex than the simple relationship implicit in the standard spatial model. It is important to note that this proposed model involves differing voter utility functions. To preserve continuity of voter response, it is necessary that the coefficients of voter policy loss vary continuously with the voter-preferred policy. This means that the salience parameters change continuously with the bliss point of the voter.

With these assumptions, candidate vote share functions $\{V_j\}$ will be continuous in (the vector of) candidate strategies. Candidate utility functions are generally derived from the vote share functions, and so quasi-concavity or concavity of the candidate utility functions and thus existence of political equilibria can then be shown (see Schofield and Sened, 2006, for the technical argument). It is worth emphasizing that the greater the relative saliences (b/a and e/f), the greater will be S, and thus, the more significant will be the attraction of building a coalition with dissident activist groups to enhance electoral support.

The mixed activist-voter model suggests why a transformation in activist-generated equilibria can occur. In contrast to Aldrich, the policy positions of the two parties are chosen by "expected" vote-maximizing candidates. The voter model itself is of the standard probabilistic variety (Enelow and Hinich, 1984; Lin, Enelow, and Dorussen, 1999). However, the novel feature is that the voter calculus involves a nonpolicy, valence variable, associated with each candidate. This nonpolicy variable is a monotone increasing, concave function of the respective party activist to-tal contributions. It is an immediate and obvious feature of this model that candidates do not converge in Downsian fashion to the center of the electoral distribution. Instead, a "rational" candidate will choose a policy position so as to "balance" activist contributions and voter responses. In this variant, potential activists who place high valuation on policy shifts can offer significant contributions, and thus *affect* rather than *control* candidate locations.

Note, also, that if one of the presidential candidates initiates a flanking move of the kind described, then the opponent should move even further round the opposing catenary. We can illustrate existence of the pure strat-egy Nash equilibria (or PSNE) using Figure 6.2 as a guide. Let Ra' and Da' be the positions of the Republican and Democratic candidates which maximize their total contributions from activists. These positions will be on the respective catenaries and will be independent of each other (because activist contributions will be determined solely by the respective candi-date positions). At these positions, the "valence" effects, now labeled λ_R

and λ_D, will be maximized. Draw the arc between the positions Ra' and Da'. If the Republican candidate moves on this arc, toward the origin, λ_R will fall, but the overall policy or spatial component of the voteshare may rise. Concavity of the vote-share function means that there will be a unique point on the arc where the Republican candidate's vote share is maximized. Indeed, by the implicit assumptions of continuity and concavity, the Republican candidate will have a continuous best response to the Democratic candidate's position. Mutual best response defines the PSNE. This PSNE can also be characterized by the partisan cleavage line, which separates those voters with a higher probability of voting Republican than Democrat. Note that if liberal social activists attract the Democratic candidate to move toward them on the liberal catenary, then the best response of the Republican will be to move further toward the conservative social activists. (More details of existence of PSNE can be found in Schofield and Sened, 2006.)

The catenary or contract curve (and thus the best response position) depends on the ratio of the intensities of relative preferences on the two axes associated with the activist groups. For example, if economic activists care relatively very strongly about the economy, and social activists care greatly about social policy, then the optimum position will be extreme on both axes. In a very intuitive fashion, the model allows for response to the relative numbers of the activist groups, their intensity of preferences, and their "willingness" to contribute. A party's candidate should be more willing to seek to move farther down the catenary in an attempt to enlist the social activists when the social activists are larger in numbers, and when the intensity of their preferences induces a greater willingness to contribute.

6.7 THIRD PARTIES

Third parties play a particularly interesting role in this model. They represent voters who are particularly concerned about issue dimensions that are suppressed by the existing party alignment. For example, in 1968, Wallace represented those who were alienated from the Democratic Party by its sponsorship of the 1964 Civil Rights Act and the 1965 Voting Rights Act. In 1935, Franklin Roosevelt was moved to consolidate the economic liberal position of the New Deal in order to avert a third-party threat from the economic Left. In 1980, Anderson ran a campaign appealing to upper-income, college-educated liberal Republicans on the coasts who

were upset about the socially conservative course that Reagan was setting for the GOP. In 2000, Ralph Nader insisted that both major parties
were in thrall to corporate elites, and that he alone represented economic
liberals who felt that the "culture wars" competition between Democrats
and Republicans had left New Deal liberalism behind.

Once organized, such third parties demonstrate to party elites the electoral advantage of the "flanking maneuver" described in the model above.
In the run-up to 1972, the attraction of the millions of socially conservative Wallace voters rationalized Nixon's "Southern Strategy," and exerted
a powerful tug on Nixon toward the point *Ia* in Figure 6.2. Anderson's
third-party run in 1980 offered the prospect of disaffected socially liberal Republicans whose votes were up for grabs; many of these became
Clinton Democrats in the nineties.

The Wallace candidacy of 1968 and the Anderson candidacy of 1980
represented two groups of activists who had quite distinct perspectives
about a re-orientation of the Republican Party. The Wallace candidacy
illustrated what I call a *leading* third party for the Republicans in the
seventies, since it served to attract Nixon and other Republican elites
toward a new party position that emphasized conservative social policy
rather than the historic economic conservatism. By contrast, the Anderson candidacy represented traditional New Deal Republicans who were
dismayed to see the Republican Party moving away from their position;
consequently, I call the Anderson candidacy a *dragging* third party. More
recently, the Nader candidacy was quite consciously a dragging third party
for the Democrats, as Nader objected that the Democratic Party had in
the nineties abandoned the traditional economic liberalism of the New
Deal. In the opinion of Nader and his supporters, the Democratic Party
was indistinguishable from the Republican party in its support of big
business.

6.8 SUMMARY OF THE MODEL

The elements of the model are as follows:

Some voters are motivated by the policy proximity of one set of party
activists (and the distance from the other party activists) to join the cadre
of activists. Each decision to exit or enter the cadre of activists changes
the mean location of the activist core, and thus the public perception of
the locations of the parties. Stable divergence in the parties' public image
is the result of what Aldrich calls an activist equilibrium.

Candidates, unlike party activists, are primarily interested in winning elections; consequently, each candidate has an incentive to try to move the public's perception of his or her party to a position that maximizes expected vote share.

At any point in time, a candidate is likely to find that current party activists are intensely concerned with one dimension, while a "disaffected" group is more intensely concerned with a different dimension of ideology. Consequently, the candidate may reasonably hope to make a "flanking" move that appeals to one group of disaffected voters without losing too many party activists. When successful, this initiates a shift in partisan activists, and therefore a redefinition of the public's image of the "relocation" of the parties.

For any given party alignment, "disaffecteds" may try to hasten a realignment by means of a leading third-party attempt. The success of a leading third party is often the excuse that a vote-maximizing party candidate is looking for to destabilize the current party activist equilibrium. Party activists who are disgruntled with the existing activist equilibrium may form the core of a dragging third-party attempt.

From this perspective, the partisan realignments of the past century have been fundamentally linked to the multi-dimensionality of the potential policy space. They have been initiated by "flanking movements" rather than by frontal assaults. Rather than fighting toe-to-toe for the moderates in the exact center of the space, candidates have tried to appeal to disaffected voters in the dimension that has recently not distinguished the two parties.

Of course, an outward thrust on a party's left flank leaves its own right flank exposed and vulnerable, at least in the long run. If this is the case, then each attempt to build a new majority party sows the seeds of the next party realignment.

It is important to note that the model suggests that there exists a voter-activist equilibrium at each election, conditional on the various parameters of the model. However, this does not necessarily imply that the sequence of equilibria will vary smoothly over time. Each equilibrium is determined by candidate calculations over the relative "value" of "activist" and "disaffected" coalitions (and thus by the configurations of the utility functions of such actors). These parameters may shift dramatically as the result of exogenous social and economic shocks.

In the rest of this chapter, the implications of this model will be used to provide an interpretation of the past century of partisan shifts in ideology.

6.9 PARTISAN STRATEGIES

The purpose of this section is to demonstrate how the dynamics implied by the model in the first half of this chapter can explain the switching of party positions in the United States between 1896 and 2000. Between 1960 and 2000, party differences along the economic cleavage line were replaced by a social cleavage between the two parties. And between 1896 and 1960, the Reconstruction social cleavage was ultimately replaced by the New Deal economic cleavage. The net result of both transformations was the flipping of party positions described in the introduction.

The Decline of Race and the Rise of Class: 1896–1960

While the period of 1960 to 2000 saw the undoing of the New Deal partisan cleavage, the period from 1896 to 1960 saw the creation of that economic cleavage from a system that had been primarily divided over the issue of race, civil war, and reconstruction. After the Civil War, the Republicans were most clearly associated with the successful emancipation of slaves, and the less successful Reconstruction of the South on an integrated basis. The Republican coalition was united on a social policy dimension. Some Republicans, like Lincoln, were already pro-business advocates, but some Republicans were emancipationists who had joined the party for social liberal reasons only. After the Civil War, the Republican Party continued to include liberal supporters of Reconstruction, new black voters, and what historian Eric Goldman calls "patrician dissidents," who were also known as "goo-goos" and "mugwumps," who resisted the increasing influence of industrialists in the Republican Party (Goldman 1956: 16).

The two wings of the Republican Party had no strong differences of opinion on social policy; they did, however, have markedly different positions on economic policy. They were kept in alliance by frequent electoral "wavings of the bloody flag"—references to the losses of the Civil War that served to reaffirm the Civil War party alignment. As a result, the Reconstruction Republican position was socially liberal, but relatively neutral on the economic dimension.

The Democrats had to bear the burden of the Civil War legacy; they also took the racially conservative position that allowed the gradual reimposition of white supremacy in the South. They represented largely rural interests and opposed the tariff, but Democrats, like Republicans, included both pro-business and anti-business forces. Cleveland was a Democrat who gave aid and comfort to business forces. He supported the gold standard, kept tax burdens low for corporations, and fought to keep the government out of economic life, especially where it might benefit low-income groups. He used federal troops to help the Pullman Company put down its desperate workers during their famous strike, which made fellow Democrat William Jennings Bryan charge, "Cleveland might be honest, but so were the mothers who threw their children in the Ganges" (Goldman 1956, 33). Because each party combined economic liberals and conservatives, the cleavage line between the parties was best thought of as a horizontal line separating the party of Reconstruction from its socially conservative opponent.

Who were the "disaffected" voters in the Reconstruction Era? Both economic liberals and economic conservatives had reason to feel inadequately represented in the Reconstruction party alignment. Economic liberals had necessarily agrarian interests, who formed various agrarian interest groups, culminating in the Populist Party, to fight what they saw as the stranglehold of eastern banks and railroads on the pocketbook of the small farmers.

The creation of the Republican majority after 1896 carried with it a long-term opportunity for the Democratic Party. After 1896, Republicans were increasingly identified with a pro-business economic position, and associated with a hard money principle (Bordo and Rockoff, 1996), as represented in Figure 6.3.

As that issue became more salient, the Bull Moose Progressives under Theodore Roosevelt were in an increasingly disaffected position. Because the Republicans had made the pro-business position their defining position, the Progressives' advocacy of economic regulation and socially liberal positions (social welfare agencies, public health, pure food and drugs) made them the obvious target for Democratic cooptation.

Up until the 1920s, the Democrats had been primarily a rural party, and therefore an unacceptable alternative for the largely urban Progressives. But during the twenties, Al Smith began to push the Democratic Party to take positions that appealed to Catholics, Jews, immigrants, and the new urban working class. Al Smith, and in particular, FDR, were more persuasive wooers of urban liberal Republicans than Bryan had ever been. The 1928 Democratic convention marked the beginning of a new Democratic coalition that combined the Bryan populists (Region A) with urban liberals (Region D).

Although Roosevelt was elected in 1932 as a moderate, and tried for two years to maintain a centrist position, the potential for third-party candidates drove him to finish the economic radicalization of the Democratic

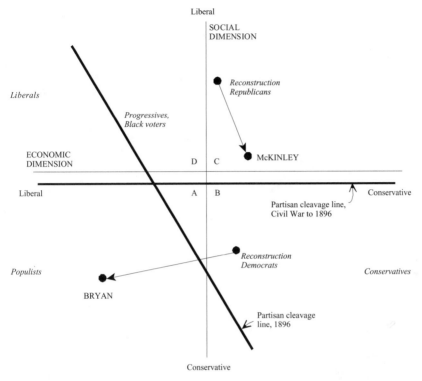

Figure 6.3. Policy shifts by the Republicans and Democrats, 1860–1896.

Party after 1934. Roosevelt viewed the principal threat to his re-election as being a leftist candidate such as Huey Long. In the Second New Deal, in the two years before his re-election in 1936, Roosevelt moved decisively leftward to forestall such a third-party attempt. In the process, he consolidated the economic orientation of the New Deal coalition, bringing the liberals from region D into alliance with the rural southern Populists of Bryan. The New Deal pulled such old Bull Moosers as Harold Ickes out of the Republican Party and into the administration (Fine, 1976: 392), where they were perfectly comfortable. In addition, they pulled black voters, urban ethnic minorities and other Republican constituencies, making the Democrats the majority party for the middle third of the twentieth century.

The cleavage line between the two parties became, for the first time since before the Civil War, a vertical, class-defined boundary (as in Figure 6.4). Huckfeldt and Kohfeld (1989) document that during the New Deal, class was a good predictor of partisan voting in a way that it was not

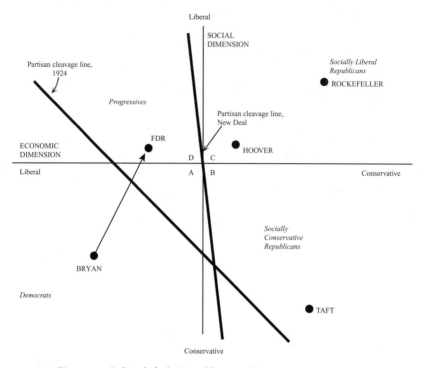

Figure 6.4. Policy shifts by Republicans and Democrats, 1896–1932.

before or after the New Deal. The difference between the proportion of working class whites voting Democratic and Republican peaked in 1948 at about forty-four percentage points. By maintaining the New Deal coalition, Democrats were able to win every presidential race from 1932 to 1964, with the exception of those won by Eisenhower, the World War II hero.

However, the price of being a majority coalition in a two-dimensional world is having to deal with the huge policy differences within different elements of the party. Just as the Republicans of 1912 had faced a split between the Progressive Republicans and the conservatives, the class solidarity of the Democrats did not eliminate the social policy differences between Southern segregationists and Northern liberals. The contradictions were already apparent in 1948 when Hubert Humphrey's riveting call for racial justice divided the Democratic Party. These contradictions presented the inevitable opportunity for Republicans to put together a counter-coalition by further pivoting the cleavage line between the parties.

The Decline of Class and the Rise of Race: 1960 to 2000

The New Deal coalition put together by Franklin Roosevelt necessitated the suppression of the social policy differences between the racial conservatives in the solid South and the racial liberals of the North. This coalition had faltered in 1948, when the Democratic Party split over a civil rights plank and the Dixiecrats ran as a third party. But in 1960, the coalition had been patched up, and the parties were still primarily differentiated by economic ideology and class-based voting. As late as 1962, most of the public (55.9 percent) saw no difference between the two parties on civil rights, and the rest were evenly split (Petrocik, 1981: 135–8). In April, 1963, it was still only 4 percent of the population that felt that civil rights was the most important issue (Gallup, 1972). It is no wonder that Kennedy felt he might be re-elected the next year by the old New Deal coalition, including the solid South.

However, after 1962, civil rights leaders succeeded in their policy of destabilization—breaking up the New Deal coalition by forcing the Kennedy administration to choose the side of federal law or state segregation in schools, inter-state travel, and voter registration. After the success of the Birmingham protest in May, 1963, Kennedy became the first Democratic president to ask Congress for a strong civil rights bill. By October of the same year, after the Birmingham bombings, Wallace standing in the doorway at Tuscaloosa, and the March on Washington, the Gallup Poll revealed that 52 percent of the public felt that civil rights was the most important issue facing the country (Gallup, 1972). Lyndon Johnson was convinced that he had to have a civil rights success in order to lead the Democrats to victory in 1964 (Kotz, 2005). By his actions in 1964 and 1965, he reached out to civil rights activists and brought them definitively into the Democratic Party. The New Deal coalition was shattered.

In Figure 6.2, the move from *Da* to *Da'* is not a move toward the center, and can be taken to represent the change of Democrat position implemented by Johnson. Notice the logic of this flanking move. A move toward the center would have alienated the traditional New Deal Democratic activists—the economic liberals of labor and the consumer movement. However, an upward move gave no sign of alienating the party activists most concerned about economic policy. The Democrats' labor allies were solidly behind the Civil Rights Act. The upward move consequently succeeded in keeping economic liberals who were inclined toward social liberalism. At the same time, an upward shift earned the loyalty of the previously disaffected civil rights workers, who were to become a principal component of the post-1964 Democratic activist cadre, in a new, post-realigment activist equilibrium. In terms of the model, Johnson was able to earn the valence benefits of both economic and social liberal activists.

The shift in the public's perception of the Democratic Party created a huge landslide in 1964. Not only did Johnson win the White House by a margin of 16 million votes, but the Democrats added 2 seats to their majority in the Senate and 48 seats in the House. No member of the House who had voted for the 1964 Civil Rights Act was defeated in either party. Half the Northern members who had voted against the bill were defeated (Branch, 1998: 522). Civil rights activists had succeeded in their goal of forcing the Democratic Party off of its New Deal equilibrium. Table A6.1 (of the Appendix to this chapter) shows that Johnson took over 60 percent of the popular vote, against his socially conservative opponent, Barry Goldwater. Goldwater only won 52 electoral college seats (from six states).

The success of the civil rights activists in forcing the Democratic Party to take a stronger civil rights position had the kind of disequilibrating effect that Aldrich (1995) hypothesized, on the New Deal party activist equilibrium. For as more civil rights activists became involved in politics, it encouraged more social liberals to become activists, and drove social conservatives out of the Democratic Party. It moved the center of gravity of the Democratic activists upward. These social activists had other social concerns as well as civil rights, which became an agenda for the Democratic Party: women's rights, civil liberties, consumerism, environmentalism.

As Aldrich hypothesized, this also had implications for Republican activists. Let us consider the kind of person who had been a New Deal-era Republican activist. Presumably, the activist's ideal point is near *Ra* (in Figure 6.2). In addition, however, she is probably more intensely concerned with economic policy than with social policy, because for decades it had been only the economic dimension that differentiated the two parties. The party differential on social policy had been zero. This is indicated in Figure 6.2 by the ellipsoidal indifference curve for the Republican activists.

From Goldwater through Reagan, the strategy of Republican candidates was to build a coalition along the contract curve between economic and social conservatives. Barry Goldwater in 1964 clearly served to destabilize the party activist equilibrium. In July, 1964, Goldwater was one of only eight non-southern Senators to vote against the Civil Rights Act. A few weeks later, the Republican National Convention refused to seat the traditionally black southern delegates to the Republican convention and nominated Goldwater to be the Republican candidate. It was a disruptive shock to the GOP and to the public's perception of what the GOP stood for (Carmines and Stimson, 1989; Branch, 1998: 403).

As just noted, Goldwater won the electoral votes of five states of the Deep South in 1964, four of them states that had voted Democratic for 84 years (Califano, 1991: 55). He forged a new identification of the Republican Party with racial conservatism, reversing a century-long association of the GOP with racial liberalism. This in turn opened the door for Nixon's "Southern strategy" and the Reagan victories of the 1980s.

The effects are shown in Tables A6.2 and A6.3 (in the Appendix to this chapter). These give the state-by-state presidential results for the Nixon, Humphrey, Wallace election of 1968 and the Nixon, McGovern election of 1972.

A small initial success with social conservatives could lead to a positive response by some social conservative activists; their arrival in the party could alienate some of the social liberals within the Republican Party, who would become less active; this in turn would lead to a closer identification with social conservativism, which would encourage still more social conservatives to become involved (Aldrich, 1995: 184–5). At the same time, social liberals might be increasingly tempted to become activists for the Democratic Party. As Carmines and Stimson (1989) argue, the "Goldwater gamble" worked for the Republican party because "it did break the tie of southern whites to the Democratic party" (188).

The success of Goldwater in 1964 induced Wallace to run as an Independent in 1968. Wallace attempted to mobilize voters on the newly salient social policy dimension. Wallace's campaign earned votes not only from southern whites but northern social conservatives who were concerned about riots, court-ordered busing, the sexual freedom of the sixties, protests against the Vietnam War, and the breakdown of traditional values. Many of the same Milwaukee Polish Catholics who had voted for Kennedy over Humphrey in the 1960 Wisconsin primary voted for Wallace over Humphrey in the 1968 presidential election.

In a biography of George Wallace, Carter (1995) argues that Wallace and the voters he represented were a continuing obsession with Nixon during his first term (1969–1972). During this time, Nixon engineered various rapprochements with Wallace individually while appealing to potential Wallace voters with a strong "law and order" position, and especially an anti-bussing policy stance. The result was a smashing triumph of Nixon and the "Southern Strategy" over McGovern in 1972. As Tables A6.2 and A6.3 show, Nixon took 56 percent of the popular vote in 1968 and 61 percent in 1972. Although Wallace only took six states in 1968, his vote was substantial in many southern states (Texas, Kentucky, Tennessee, Virginia, North and South Carolina, Louisiana, Florida, Arkansas). This result paved the way for Nixon's overwhelming win in 1972.

By the decade of the 1970s, class had been largely displaced as the organizing principle of two-party competition in the United States:

Race conflict [was] the major new element in the party-system agenda. The most visible difference between the party coalitions that entered the turbulent 1960s and those that exited in the middle 1970s is to be found in their new-found distinctiveness on race-related policy issues.

(Petrocik, 1981: 148–9)

While Reagan was successful in keeping the coalition of economic and social conservative activists in the Republican camp, the tensions between the two were increasingly apparent during the eighties. Hostility between southern populists and eastern business interests are an ancient tradition in the United States. In a GOP that attempted to keep these two warring camps in the same party coalition, economic issues are as divisive as racial issues were for the New Deal Democrats. The old Rockefeller Republicans, especially the social liberals, felt increasingly alienated within their own party. Fortune magazine, the vehicle for big business, ran a front cover suggesting what they heard as the message from the Republican party: "GOP to Business: Drop Dead?" Inside, the article went on: "In a political arena dominated by small-business populists, anti-government conservatives, and the religious right, corporate America's the odd man out—mistrusted, resented, impotent" (Kirkland, 1995: 50).

In this article, big business announced that they increasingly felt themselves the "disaffected" voter in a party alignment based more and more on social policy.

It was this fault line in the Republican Party that Clinton was able to take advantage of in the 1990s. Many cosmopolitans, while historically loyal to the Republican Party, were frightened of a GOP that was hostile to affirmative action and abortion rights, and aggressively pushed traditional social values over economic conservatism. Clinton's actions in the

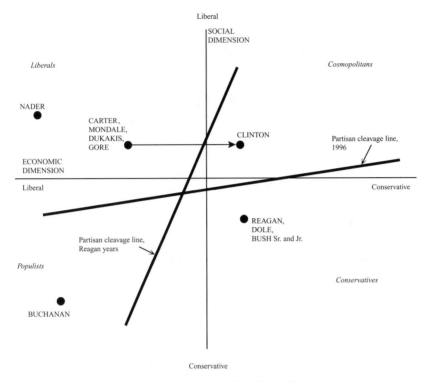

Figure 6.5. Estimated positions of presidential candidates, 1976–2000.

mid-nineties—especially welfare reform, a major crime bill, support for NAFTA, a balanced budget—upset many of his liberal supporters, but made many upper-income social liberals comfortable voting for him in 1996. Clinton was acknowledged to have moved right on the economic dimension, while preserving the Democrat's position of social liberalism (see Figure 6.5). Clinton made it legitimate for a professional suburban homeowner with a six-figure income, concerned about taxes, crime, and welfare fraud, to vote Democratic.

The special prosecutor's investigations into the Clinton sex scandals had the perverse (for the Republicans) effect of further helping to drive group C cosmopolitans into the Democratic fold. While much of the new Republican Party was convinced that the public would be as outraged as they were by the Clinton scandal, it became apparent that the Moral Majority was in fact a minority. Social liberal Republicans and Independents did not want to be a part of Starr's sexual inquisition. The impeachment issue became a defining moment for the Republican Party in much the same way that the Civil Rights Act of 1964 was a defining moment for the Democrats: It identified clearly which voters were now vulnerable to the opposition party.

The extent of the realignment is shown by the shift in voting behavior on the part of cosmopolitans and populists. Cosmopolitans voting for Democratic congressional candidates rose from 46 percent in the seventies to 65 percent in the decade of the nineties. The percentage of low-income moral traditionalists, whom we would identify as populists, voting for Democratic congressional candidates dropped from 63 percent in the 1970s to 29 percent in the 1990s. The fact that this statistic is for congressional voting rather than presidential voting, and over five elections in each decade, suggests that the trend is broader, deeper, and more lasting than simply a feeling based on Clinton or other particular presidential candidates. Low-income social conservatives have left the New Deal coalition for the Republican Party, and high-income social liberals are increasingly comfortable voting for the Democratic Party (Smith, 2002).

A number of political scientists have documented how partisan voting has evolved since 1960. According to Huckfeldt and Kohfeld (1989), party voting has been characterized since the New Deal by "the decline of class and the rise of race" (2). They point out that the difference between the proportion of blacks and whites voting Democratic rose sharply from less than 25 percent in 1960 to more than 50 percent in 1968 (3). This trend has continued: Democratic presidential candidates have never won more than 47 percent of the white vote, or less than 83 percent of the black vote, since 1976 (Connelly, 2000: 4). Even a winning candidate like Clinton in 1996 won only 43 percent of the white vote, but 84 percent of the black vote. Social liberals are now the core of any winning Democratic coalition, and in 2000, social conservatives were the core of the winning Republican coalition.

6.10 CHOICES, CREDIBLE COMMITMENT, AND PATH DEPENDENCE

Figure 6.2 causes one to wonder whether a Republican candidate has a choice about appealing to disaffected social activists of either the liberal or the conservative persuasion. Could Nixon, for example, have appealed to civil rights activists rather than to Wallace supporters in 1972? Was there an equally viable "Northern Strategy" that would have substituted for his "Southern Strategy" in that year? After all, in 1957, Nixon had hoped to earn support from black voters by positioning the Republican Party as a backer of a civil rights bill (Mann, 1996).

Candidates are, however, constrained by recent historical events and these introduce an asymmetry into the calculations of party candidates. In 1972, for example, Nixon could not credibly make a claim for pro–civil rights activists. That option had already been ruled out by the public's awareness of the early changes in the cadre of Republican activists in the 1964 national convention, and their selection of Goldwater as the candidate in that year. As recently as 1962, the public felt that Republicans were equally as likely to see that African Americans got fair treatment in jobs and housing (21.3 percent for Republicans, 22.7 percent for Democrats, 55.9 seeing no difference in the two parties). But by late 1964, the Democrats had already earned the civil rights advocacy reputation by 56 percent to 7 percent, with 37 percent seeing no difference (Petrocik, 1981: 135–8). A determined Republican could at best have neutralized the civil rights issue, without constructing a coalition. But by 1972, Nixon was able to show the way for two decades of Republican victories by giving the civil rights advocacy honors to the Democrats, while earning the support of social conservative activists.

Similarly, in the mid-nineties, Clinton was under a great deal of pressure from liberals in his party to restore the Democratic Party to the economic liberalism of the New Deal. However, in the mid-nineties, the Democratic Party had irrevocably lost a vital component of the successful New Deal coalition: the South. As a result, Clinton had only one choice; he could keep the Democratic Party as a minority party, isolated in the upper-left hand quadrant of Figure 6.5, or he could reach out to the cosmopolitans of the upper-right hand corner. Appealing to southern and other social conservatives was no longer credible for the party that had supported civil rights and affirmative action for thirty years—but reaching out to cosmopolitans via a more moderate economic policy was viable. Figure 6.5 makes a guess about Clinton's policy position in the elections of 1992 and 1996, together with the likely positions of some of the presidential candidates over the last twenty-five years.

6.11 CONCLUDING REMARKS

The "positions" of the parties in the minds of voters are largely influenced by the policy preferences of party activists, who are not vote maximizers but policy driven. Party activists can, as Aldrich has argued, achieve equilibrium positions vis-à-vis each other, and from that position act as a significant constraint on the ability of candidates to locate themselves in winning positions (Aldrich, 1983a,b, 1995; Aldrich and McGinnis, 1989).

Nevertheless, candidates sometimes seize on forces outside their activist cadres to enhance their short-term prospects for winning elections. Disaffecteds, especially disaffecteds organized in leading third parties, are destabilizing features that give party candidates the opportunity to disrupt activist equilibria, as they maneuver to win against the opposing party's position. Striving to put together a coalition that adds a group of mobilized disaffecteds to the cadre of current party activists, candidates create what appears in two-dimensional ideological space as a "flanking" move. Roosevelt's consolidation of an economically liberal New Deal coalition, Nixon's southern strategy to woo social conservatives, and Clinton's move to the center in economic policy while appealing to social liberals, all constitute such flanking coalition building efforts.

The net effect of these periodic flanking movements, over the course of a century and a half, has been to move from primarily a social, to an economic, to once again a social cleavage between the two parties. By 2000, however, the positions of the two parties are reversed from where they were in 1860. The Democratic Party of 2000, like the post-Reconstruction Republicans, was a party advocating racial equality and urban tolerance, and the greater use of the national government to protect those ends. The Republican Party of 2000, like the post-Reconstruction Democrats, advocated states' rights, allied with traditional Protestant values.

In order to understand the pace and mechanisms of party realignment, it is important to recognize that parties are not unitary actors—they are coalitions of party activists and candidates, with differing goals. Party activists are a force for stability; they have chosen to be party activists because of the existing party alignment, and they discourage by the possibility of their exit any substantial changes in party ideology. The desire of candidates to construct winning coalitions is, on the other hand, a dynamic force. When disaffected activists have enough to offer, party candidates may seek to establish coalitions on the contract curve between existing and disaffected voters.

This implies a kind of "structurally stable" dynamic in which, in a given election, candidates are partially (but not wholly) constrained by the preferences of existing party activists. They may seek to reposition themselves so as to bring in disaffected voters and activists; this causes a reconfiguration of the party activist equilibrium in response to the strategic coalition formation of both parties.

Table A6.1 *The Election of 1964*

State	Percentage of Vote			Electoral College		
	LBJ	Goldwater	Other	LBJ	Goldwater	Other
D.C.	85.50	14.50	–	3	–	–
Massachusetts	76.19	23.44	.37	14	–	–
Hawaii	78.76	21.24	–	4	–	–
Maine	68.84	31.16	–	4	–	–
Minnesota	63.76	36.00	.24	10	–	–
New York	68.56	31.31	.13	43	–	–
W. Virginia	67.94	32.06	–	7	–	–
Connecticut	67.81	32.09	.11	8	–	–
Michigan	66.70	33.10	.20	21	–	–
Pennsylvania	64.92	34.70	.38	29	–	–
Washington	61.97	37.37	.66	9	–	–
California	59.11	40.79	.09	40	–	–
Wisconsin	62.09	37.74	.17	12	–	–
Illinois	59.47	40.53	–	26	–	–
New Jersey	65.61	33.86	.54	17	–	–
New Hamp.	63.89	36.11	–	4	–	–
Oregon	63.72	35.96	.32	6	–	–
Missouri	64.05	35.95	–	12	–	–
Vermont	66.30	33.69	.01	3	–	–
Ohio	62.94	37.06	–	26	–	–
Alaska	65.91	34.09	–	3	–	–
S. Dakota	55.61	44.39	–	4	–	–
Maryland	65.47	34.53	–	10	–	–
Delaware	60.95	38.78	.27	3	–	–
Montana	58.95	40.57	.48	4	–	–
Colorado	61.27	38.19	.54	6	–	–
Iowa	61.88	37.92	.20	9	–	–
Texas	63.32	36.49	.19	25	–	–
N. Mexico	59.03	40.42	.54	4	–	–
Nevada	58.58	41.42	–	3	–	–
N. Dakota	57.97	41.88	.15	4	–	–
Indiana	55.98	43.56	.47	13	–	–
Kentucky	64.01	35.65	.33	9	–	–
Utah	54.71	45.29	–	4	–	–
Wyoming	56.56	43.44	–	3	–	–
Arizona	49.45	50.45	.10	–	5	–
Kansas	54.09	45.06	.85	7	–	–
Tennessee	55.50	44.49	–	11	–	–
Virginia	53.54	46.18	.28	12	–	–
S. Carolina	41.11	58.89	–	–	8	–
Oklahoma	55.75	44.25	–	8	–	–
Nebraska	52.61	47.39	–	5	–	–
Rhode Island	80.87	19.13	–	4	–	–
Florida	51.15	48.85	–	14	–	–
Idaho	50.92	49.08	–	4	–	–
Arkansas	56.06	43.41	.53	6	–	–
N. Carolina	56.15	43.85	–	13	–	–
Louisiana	43.19	56.81	–	–	10	–
Georgia	45.87	54.12	.02	–	12	–
Mississippi	12.86	87.14	–	–	7	–
Alabama	–	69.45	30.55	–	10	–
Total	61.05	38.47	.48	486	52	–

Table A6.2 *The Election of 1968*

State	Percentage of Vote				Electoral College			
	Humphrey	Nixon	Wallace	Other	Humphrey	Nixon	Wallace	Other
D.C.	81.82	18.18	–	–	3	–	–	–
Mass.	63.01	32.89	3.73	.37	14	–	–	–
Hawaii	59.83	38.70	1.47	–	4	–	–	–
Maine	55.30	43.07	1.62	–	4	–	–	–
Minnesota	54.00	41.46	4.34	.20	10	–	–	–
New York	49.74	44.29	5.28	.68	43	–	–	–
W. Virginia	49.60	40.78	9.62	–	7	–	–	–
Connecticut	49.48	44.32	6.10	.10	8	–	–	–
Michigan	48.18	41.46	10.04	.32	21	–	–	–
Pennsylvania	47.59	44.02	7.97	.42	29	–	–	–
Washington	47.23	45.12	7.44	.21	9	–	–	–
California	44.74	47.82	6.72	.72	–	40	–	–
Wisconsin	44.27	47.89	7.56	.29	–	12	–	–
Illinois	44.15	47.08	8.46	.31	–	26	–	–
New Jersey	43.97	46.10	9.12	.82	–	17	–	–
New Hamp.	43.93	52.10	3.76	.21	–	4	–	–
Oregon	43.78	49.83	6.06	.32	–	6	–	–
Missouri	43.74	44.87	11.39	–	–	12	–	–
Vermont	43.53	52.75	3.16	.56	–	3	–	–
Ohio	42.95	45.23	11.81	.02	–	26	–	–
Alaska	45.28	42.65	12.07	–	–	3	–	–
S. Dakota	41.96	53.27	4.76	–	–	4	–	–
Maryland	41.94	43.59	14.47	–	–	10	–	–
Delaware	41.61	45.12	13.28	–	–	3	–	–
Montana	41.59	50.60	7.29	.52	–	4	–	–
Colorado	41.32	50.46	7.50	.72	–	6	–	–
Iowa	40.82	53.01	5.69	.49	–	9	–	–
Texas	39.88	41.14	18.97	.01	–	25	–	–
N. Mexico	39.74	51.84	7.86	.56	–	4	–	–
Nevada	39.29	47.46	13.25	–	–	3	–	–
N. Dakota	38.23	55.94	5.75	.08	–	4	–	–
Indiana	37.99	50.29	11.45	.28	–	13	–	–
Kentucky	37.65	43.79	18.29	.27	–	9	–	–
Utah	37.07	56.49	6.73	.06	–	4	–	–
Wyoming	35.51	55.76	8.73	–	–	3	–	–
Arizona	35.02	54.78	9.56	.64	–	5	–	–
Kansas	34.72	54.84	10.19	.25	–	7	–	–
Tennessee	34.02	37.85	28.13	–	–	11	–	–
Virginia	32.49	43.36	23.64	.51	–	12	–	–
S. Carolina	32.30	38.09	29.61	–	–	8	–	–
Oklahoma	31.99	47.68	20.33	–	–	8	–	–
Nebraska	31.81	59.82	8.36	–	–	5	–	–
Rhode Island	31.78	64.03	4.07	.12	–	4	–	–
Florida	30.93	40.53	28.53	–	–	14	–	–
Idaho	30.66	56.79	12.55	–	–	4	–	–
Arkansas	30.36	30.77	38.87	–	–	–	6	–
N. Carolina	29.24	39.51	31.26	–	–	12	1	–
Louisiana	28.21	23.47	48.32	–	–	–	10	–
Georgia	26.75	30.40	42.83	.01	–	–	12	–
Mississippi	23.02	13.52	63.46	–	–	–	7	–
Alabama	18.72	13.99	65.86	1.42	–	–	10	–
Total	35.50	55.90	8.60	–	191	301	46	–

Table A6.3 *The Election of 1972*

State	Percentage of Vote			Electoral College		
	McGovern	Nixon	Other	McGovern	Nixon	Other
D.C.	78.10	21.56	.34	3	–	–
Massachusetts	54.20	45.23	.57	14	–	–
Hawaii	37.52	62.48	–	–	4	–
Maine	38.51	61.49	–	–	4	–
Minnesota	46.07	51.58	2.35	–	10	–
New York	41.18	58.51	.31	–	41	–
W. Virginia	36.39	63.61	–	–	6	–
Connecticut	40.13	58.57	1.31	–	8	–
Michigan	41.81	56.20	1.98	–	21	–
Pennsylvania	39.13	59.11	1.76	–	27	–
Washington	38.64	56.92	4.44	–	9	–
California	41.54	55.00	3.47	–	45	–
Wisconsin	43.72	53.40	2.87	–	11	–
Illinois	40.51	59.03	.46	–	26	–
New Jersey	36.77	61.57	1.66	–	17	–
New Hamp.	34.86	63.98	1.16	–	4	–
Oregon	42.33	52.45	5.23	–	6	–
Missouri	37.61	62.13	.26	–	12	–
Vermont	36.47	62.66	.87	–	3	–
Ohio	38.07	59.63	2.30	–	25	–
Alaska	34.62	58.13	7.25	–	3	–
S. Dakota	45.52	54.15	.32	–	4	–
Maryland	37.36	61.26	1.38	–	10	–
Delaware	39.18	59.60	1.22	–	3	–
Montana	37.85	57.93	4.23	–	4	–
Colorado	34.59	62.61	2.80	–	7	–
Iowa	40.48	57.61	1.92	–	8	–
Texas	33.25	66.23	.52	–	26	–
N. Mexico	36.53	61.00	2.47	–	4	–
Nevada	36.32	63.68	–	–	3	–
N. Dakota	35.79	62.07	2.14	–	3	–
Indiana	33.34	66.11	.55	–	13	–
Kentucky	34.77	63.37	1.86	–	9	–
Utah	26.39	67.64	5.97	–	4	–
Wyoming	30.47	69.01	.51	–	3	–
Arizona	30.38	61.64	7.99	–	6	–
Kansas	29.50	67.66	2.84	–	7	–
Tennessee	29.75	67.70	2.56	–	10	–
Virginia	30.12	67.84	2.03	–	11	1
S. Carolina	27.72	70.78	1.49	–	8	–
Oklahoma	24.00	73.70	2.30	–	8	–
Nebraska	29.50	70.50	–	–	5	–
Rhode Island	46.81	53.00	.19	–	4	–
Florida	27.80	71.91	.29	–	17	–
Idaho	26.04	64.24	9.72	–	4	–
Arkansas	30.69	68.87	.44	–	6	–
N. Carolina	28.89	69.46	1.65	–	13	–
Louisiana	28.35	65.32	5.32	–	10	–
Georgia	24.65	75.04	.32	–	12	–
Mississippi	19.63	78.20	2.18	–	7	–
Alabama	25.54	72.43	2.04	–	9	–
Total	37.53	60.69	1.76	17	520	1

7

Keynes and the Atlantic Constitution

7.1 INTRODUCTION*

A constitution is a system of rules and beliefs that governs the behavior of a society or family of societies. The heart of a constitution incorporates the fundamental core belief, or a set of beliefs essential to the constitution. The "Atlantic Constitution" is the family of constitutions (both written and implicit) of the member states of the "Atlantic Coalition" together with those rules and understandings that govern interstate behavior. A *quandary* for a constitution is a situation where the core belief is destroyed, either because of an empirical disjunction or because of a philosophical or theoretical inconsistency. The key episodes in British and U.S. history (circa 1668, 1776, 1787, 1860 and 1964) discussed in this book can be seen as quandaries for their respective constitutions.

I contend that the periods leading up to 1944 and 1982 were also associated with constitutional quandaries. The quandary of 1944 was generated by the incompatibility of the economic equilibrium theorem and the events of the Depression. I suggest that the key insight of Keynes' *The General Theory of Employment, Interest and Money* (1936) was his denial of the relevance of the equilibrium theorem for asset markets. This insight allowed Keynes to conceive of a new core belief, involving a reconfiguration of both citizen rights and economic efficiency.

The post-1944 "Keynesian synthesis" may have perverted Keynes' insight. This macroeconomic synthesis led to a retreat to an economic equilibrium perspective that proved, by the 1970s, to be invalid. The resulting quandary was solved, in a sense, in the early 1980s by the creation of

---

* This chapter is based on Norman Schofield, "The Heart of the Atlantic Constitution: International Economic Stability, 1919–1998," *Politics and Society* 27 (1999): 173–215, by permission of Sage Publications Ltd.

a new core belief associated with the de-coupling of politics from the operation of the international market.

Recent events in this market suggest that the Atlantic Constitution faces a new quandary over whether or not it is necessary to regulate the international flow of capital. The duration of the previous two quandaries (1929–1944 and 1968–1982) suggests that serious attention needs to be devoted to the possibility of a global market "cascade." The avoidance of such a cascade would seem to require an adaptation of the current heart of the Atlantic Constitution.

Chapter 8 indicates why recent results in game theory suggest that a version of the *chaos hypothesis* is valid. The chapter also attempts to give a clearer idea of *core beliefs* and the *heart*, using notions from both cooperative game theory and the philosophy of science.

7.2 ORDERING THE POLITICAL ECONOMY

For before constitution of Sovereign Power ... all men had right to all things; which necessarily causeth Warre. (Hobbes, 1960 [1651]: 234)

We all live out our lives within some system of social rules. For those of us in the developed political economies, many of these rules are founded in a constitution, whether formally written down, as in the United States, or implicit, and based on precedent and practice, as in Britain. Just as with citizens, so with corporations and countries. Corporate economic entities carry out their activities in an environment that also has explicit and implicit rules. Even countries engaged in economic or military war acknowledge implicit rules that provide the context for negotiation over cooperation, conflict, and surrender.

The very general system of implicit and explicit rules holding for citizens within states, for corporations in the global economy, and for countries in the world polity, I shall term a *constitution*. I shall use the phrase "The Atlantic Constitution" to refer to the family of constitutions of the developed economies, principally within the OECD, together with the overall system of rules that govern economic and political behavior within this group.

It is my contention that this Atlantic Constitution has evolved over many centuries, and that crucial elements of it have been constructed by "design." The purpose of a constitution is to mitigate the consequences of anarchy, by Hobbes called "Warre," within which "the life of man [is] solitary, poore, nasty, brutish and short" (Hobbes, 1960: 186).

Many of the "contractarian" philosophers of this century have too readily assumed that Hobbes' solution, the great Leviathan, *is* the state, with its ability to regulate, tax, and enforce the contract between citizens and the state. They have concentrated on the ability of a "predatory" state to violate this contract, and on the capacity of the citizens to punish such a violator. Other "anarchic" philosophers have pursued the suggestions of Michael Polanyi (1958) and Friedrich von Hayek (1973), contra Hobbes, that "spontaneous order," in the absence of a state, is possible, indeed generic.[1] The more technical arguments of the "anarchists" have been framed in the context of game theoretic equilibria arising out of the framework of the "prisoner's dilemma" interpretation of Hobbesian chaos.

I agree with the philosophers that Hobbes' calculus of war and co-operation is a profound insight into the basis of the Constitution. I shall argue, however, that while the Atlantic Constitution is indeed a Hobbesian Leviathan, it is not restricted simply to the contractarian basis of relations between citizen and state. Nor is it solely a consequence of a "spontaneous evolution" of a system of law and habits of behavior. Fundamental components of it have been constructed "by Art" (to use Hobbes' phrase)— that is, by architects of change. These architects have added or adjusted components of the constitution in response to problems or dilemmas that have arisen in the world. Indeed these problems have often been perceived and displayed in terms of Hobbesian "Warre" by philosophically-inclined Cassandras. I call these *prophets of chaos*.

A *quandary* for a constitution is a situation in which *prophets of chaos* have cast doubt on one of the *core beliefs* of the constitution. Recent events in the international economic system suggest that we currently face a quandary over the degree to which it is necessary to regulate the international flow of capital. Professional economists, politicians, fund managers, and the like, were deeply concerned about the contagion of monetary instability that become apparent in developing markets, particularly in Asia, in Russia, and in Latin America in the late 1990s.

However, a powerful core belief, which I term the *economic equilibrium hypothesis*, is still almost universally accepted among international policy makers. This core belief came into being in a strong form in the early

---

[1] See, for example, Gray (1984: 4) where he suggests that von Hayek synthesized the philosophies of Mach, Popper, Wittgenstein, and Michael Polanyi into a coherent system.

1980s as a consequence of a partial resolution of the obvious quandary of that time. This earlier quandary of the late 1970s was brought into focus by various prophets of chaos, including Beer, Brittan, and Olson.[2] These authors, using the tools of Public Choice Theory, led us to view politicians as potentially predatory, in need of regulation. It was argued that the framework of Keynesian macroeconomics allowed such predatory politicians to engage in strategies which, while rational in terms of electoral support, were economically irrational in the long run.

In response, the *architects of change* of the early 1980s based their solution to this quandary on the argument that it was impossible to induce "unnatural" growth by political intervention.[3] In particular, the policy initiatives of that time, initiated by the United States and Great Britain, were based on the hypothesis that markets left to themselves will tend to an "optimal" equilibrium. Those countries that chose to weaken market rigidities would benefit from greater productive efficiency, and the resulting lower obstacles to trade would enhance economic growth.

It is evident that the acceptance of this core equilibrium belief has had remarkable consequences. Trade and growth have, until recently, been sustained, and the United States and Britain, especially, have obtained results that are quite at odds with the pessimistic predictions made in the 1970s and 1980s.[4]

The success of these policies during the last decade or so has meant that policy makers are unwilling to consider "global" economic changes that are not consistent with the equilibrium hypothesis. Moreover, because of

---

[2] See Beer (1982); Brittan (1977); and Olson (1982a,b). In a sense, these prophets of political chaos derived their arguments from the fundamental impossibility theorem of social choice. See also Arrow (1951).

[3] See, for example, Friedman (1968). The argument fundamentally depends on the economic equilibrium theorems (Arrow and Debreu, 1956; Arrow and Hahn, 1971).

[4] In July 1999, annual GDP growth rates in the United States and Britain were 4.0 percent and 0.6 percent, respectively, compared with the Euro area of 2.4 percent. (The Euro area comprises the member states of the European Union who committed to currency union in January 2002.) Unemployment rates were 4.3 percent (U.S.), 6.2 percent (Britain), and 11.6 percent (Euro area). Currently, the GDP growth rates are 3.6 percent (U.S.), 1.7 percent (Britain), and 1.2 percent (Euro area) and the unemployment rates are 5.0 percent (U.S.), 4.8 percent (Britain), and 8.7 percent (Euro area). The continuing high unemployment rates in Italy (7.8 percent), Germany (11.6 percent), and France (10.0 percent) suggests the EU countries face a structural rather than temporary problem. These data are taken from the website http://www.oecd.org/linklist. See also Chapter 2, Tables 2.2 and 2.3.

the way in which the quandary of the late 1970s was understood, the arguments of the prophets of chaos, with regard to political instability, are also accepted. Thus collapse, a few years ago, in Russia, Indonesia, Malaysia, and foreseen for Mexico, and other Latin American countries, is generally regarded as a consequence of political "imperfections." However, the difficulty that Japanese leaders face, in attempting to create the conditions for economic growth, does pose more serious problems of explanation.[5] There may indeed be something peculiar about the connections between Japanese politicians and corporate actors, effectively forbidding resolution of what appears to be an economic crisis. Nonetheless, it is inconceivable that the cause of these disparate economic crises, in so many parts of the world, is fundamentally political.[6]

This chapter argues that the strong form of the economic equilibrium hypothesis is generally invalid. This strong hypothesis asserts that both commodities and asset markets will, in fact, typically be in equilibrium, and will result in outcomes that are Pareto optimal.[7] I use the term *commodities market* for what Keynes referred to as a market governed by prospective yield, or risk. This is the typical market studied in general equilibrium theory. The individuals in such a market are characterized by utility or preference; each individual can readily rank bundles of such commodities by subjective worth.[8]

As discussed at greater length in Section 7.6, Keynes took pains to distinguish the behavior of such commodities markets from what I term *asset markets*, namely those governed by speculation. Keynes believed that asset markets were characterized by uncertainty, rather than risk. The term *uncertainty* is used for those situations where it is intrinsically impossible

---

[5] During the crisis in late 1998, GDP "growth" rates were strongly negative: Japan (-3.6 percent), Indonesia (-17.4 percent), Malaysia (-8.6 percent), South Korea (-6.8 percent), and Russia (-9.9 percent), and Hong Kong (-5.2 percent). By August 2005, these economies had generally recovered: Indonesia (6.4 percent), Malaysia (5.7 percent), South Korea (3.3 percent), and Russia (5.2 percent). Japan still has a growth rate of only 1.3 percent. Again, the unemployment for Japan is 4.2 percent, suggesting that the problem for Japan is structural. (These data are taken from the website http://www.oecd.org/linklist.)

[6] The great differences in political regimes among the affected countries clearly suggests that economics rather than politics is the essential cause. Political inefficiencies could, of course, exacerbate economic instabilities.

[7] As usual, the outcome, x, is Pareto optimal if and only if there is no other feasible state y that all economic agents weakly prefer to x.

[8] It may be necessary to date these commodities by time; equilibrium then requires complete future markets. Recent extension of the standard theory then can be used to demonstrate existence of equilibrium, as long as there are complete future markets.

for any individual to assign probabilities to various eventualities, in any coherent form.

To illustrate the notion of uncertainty, consider Russia's choice to renege on its interest payments due on its public debt in August 1998. The event surprised even such an experienced international financier as George Soros.[9] The effects of the Russian decision induced uncertainty into the international economy because the effects were due not simply to the economic ramifications, but to the interpretation of this event by other actors in the global economy. An immediate consequence was a considerable decline in the U.S. stock market as fund managers fled to "safer" havens.[10] Although the stock market recovered, it started to fall from the high in May 2000. After the election of Bush, and the uncertainty associated with the events in the Middle East, the market fell further. At the time of writing (December, 2005), there is considerable uncertainty over the effects of global economic and political change, not just in the Middle East, but also in Latin America.

The scale of international asset markets has increased markedly in recent years, and technological developments have dramatically reduced transaction costs (and, of course, time of transaction). The consequence is that the "virtual," or speculative component, of world markets has become increasingly important in comparison with the "real" components of labor and of flows of traded goods and services. I concur with Keynes' argument that markets in commodities, especially traded goods, are likely to be governed by what we regard as the law of supply and demand. Such commodities markets may well exhibit equilibrium. What concerned Keynes was the degree to which instability or chaos in asset markets

---

[9] See the interview with Soros in the *New York Review of Books* (January 14, 1999). Soros is reputed to have gained over 1 billion pounds sterling by betting 10 billion pounds sterling that the British pound would be forced to devalue in 1992. This 1992 situation was one of risk only, since it was fairly clear that the overvaluation of the pound could not be sustained.

[10] Hamish McRae (in an article in *The World Press Review* in January, 1999) noted the irony that the 1997 Nobelists in economics, Myron Scholes and Robert Merton, were involved in long-term capital management (LCM). The theoretic work of Scholes and Merton was predicated on risk analysis and proved entirely useless at preventing the loss of at least a billion dollars by LCM. McRae applauded the Nobel Committee for recognizing, in 1998, Amartya Sen for his work in welfare economics and social choice theory (Sen, 1970). It is obvious that the LCM debacle occurred because market-based risk analyses proved utterly incompetent to deal with situations of uncertainty. In contrast, much of Sen's work has to do with the degree to which political institutions may either mitigate, or possibly exacerbate, economic uncertainty.

could undermine the stability of commodities markets. Given the events that had occurred in Keynes' lifetime, his preoccupation was with effects of this kind not only in the labor market (where the result is persistent unemployment), but also in the international polity (and the attendant competitive devaluations).

Keynes accepted this weak version of the equilibrium hypothesis (only for commodities markets), because he saw a terrible danger to the Atlantic Constitution. Consider for a moment a world in which it is generally believed that all markets, both asset and commodity, are chaotic. In such a world, the returns to capitalists and the wages of labor have no legitimate basis. To escape this chaos, the citizens of a nation would be rational in giving up their freedom to the agents of the state. Bound by such a Hobbesian contract, the citizens could at least hope for some certainty in their lives. It is true that the political economists of the 1930s, who studied a socialist state of this kind, generally came to the conclusion that the "calculation problem" made it impossible for the state to set prices in such a way as to ensure economic efficiency (see, e.g., von Mises, 1935: 87–130). Keynes was keenly aware that authoritarian state systems could solve the problem of unemployment by paying the price of efficiency while necessarily depriving their citizens of their freedom. It seemed all too probable in the 1930s that citizens would be willing to pay the double price of inefficiency and loss of freedom to avoid the great and apparent risk of unemployment.

The solution that Keynes sought to the quandary of the 1930s was based on the logical distinction between the two kinds of markets. He proposed limited government intervention only in the potentially unstable asset market in order to create stability in the commodity market and the return of full employment.

Lest we feel that Keynes' concerns are of little interest in a world of relatively low unemployment (at least in the developed nations), consider again the rational calculus of citizens of Russia, or of the countries of Southeast Asia, Latin America, or the Middle East. In Russia, in partic-ular, although the so-called market was introduced with great fanfare it has only led to mafia domination, currency collapse, government enfee-blement, barter exchange, and varieties of unemployment and underem-ployment. It would be no surprise at all if the majority of the Russian people was to choose an authoritarian regime, under the plausible belief that they were paying for release from chaos with their freedom.

As I discuss in later sections of this chapter, the success of the developed countries of the OECD in solving the quandaries they faced at the end of World War II and in the 1970s, has helped persuade the citizens of other parts of the world that capitalism can work. More important, many countries in Latin America and Asia have been willing to experiment with democratic reforms. The uncertainty generated by recent events could induce the leaders of such countries to renounce both free market notions and democratic freedom.

To preserve the vitality of the Atlantic Constitution, it makes sense therefore to probe, in some detail, the validity and relevance of the equilibrium hypothesis in the more general context of global political economy. To do this, the next two sections of the chapter describes in greater detail what is meant by a constitution. In particular, the notion of a core belief is outlined, using, where appropriate, recent concepts from game theory. To pursue the manner in which the core economic equilibrium belief has evolved during this century, in Section 7.5 I consider the collapse of U.S. hegemony in the 1970s. I then follow the notion back in time by considering, in Sections 7.6 and 7.7, the quandaries that were apparent in the 1930s and in 1944, over how to structure the post-war international economy. Section 7.8 examines the debates in the U.S. and the final policy decisions that led to a solution of this quandary. Section 7.9 attempts to give some conclusions that are relevant for today.

7.3   PROPHETS OF CHAOS

For by Art is created that great Leviathan called a Common-Wealth, or State ... which is but an Artificiall Man.

(Hobbes, 1960 [1651]: 81)

Those of us in the developed economies are all fortunate to have lived in a post-1945 world within which no global wars have occurred and economic growth has gathered apace. We sometimes forget that the economic basis for the international component of the Atlantic Constitution was laid down in a system of institutions, rules, and understandings devised at the Bretton Woods Conference (of July 1944). The Bretton Woods System was an "institution" in the sense used by Douglass North. Such an institution can be understood in terms of "the rules of the game in a society, or more formally the humanly devised constraints that shape human interaction ... [that] structure incentives in human exchange, whether political, social or economic" (North, 1990: 3).

The Smithsonian Agreement of December 1971 is usually taken to signal the collapse of the Bretton Woods System. It would be more correct to say that the institution of Bretton Woods had been found inadequate to deal with the complicated Hobbesian problem of maintaining cooperation and rapid growth in an evolving global economy. During the 1970s, the voices of the prophets of chaos were loud and generally heeded. Problems of equilibrating the monetary system, and of the apparent incompatibility of democracy and economic competitiveness, were increasingly perceived. To a considerable extent, the solutions were sought in the arguments of what I call the *anarchic philosophers*. The strategy of regulating the domestic and international economy was increasingly seen as impossible, indeed irrelevant. Instead of attempting to control exchange rates, the flow of capital, and so forth, the developed polities "distanced" themselves, to a degree, from managing the global economy. The occasional interference (as in Britain's later attempt to maintain an over-valued exchange rate for sterling in 1992–3) made it apparent that the costs of so doing, by a single polity, could be enormous, and the effort self-defeating.

These changes in the institutional arrangements implied modifications in the Atlantic Constitution, in the implicit rules that governed economic behavior at the international level. These were conditioned by changes in beliefs, particularly about the behavior of markets. The notion of a natural equilibrium in an international system of exchange economies was generally accepted, and the possibility of economic chaos was seen as less credible. This change in belief was entirely rational (indeed "Bayesian"). From an empirical standpoint, a lessening of the degree of intervention by government in the macroeconomy, after 1982 or so, certainly appeared to produce a drop in overall inflation. The arguments that had been made during the 1970s by political economists seemed to be borne out. By changing the rules of political action, by credibly committing politicians to a less interventionist role, it was possible to reduce inflation to negligible levels. In essence, these changes in the "rules" were induced by changes in beliefs over the validity of the Keynesian framework. It is important to note, however, that these changes in beliefs were not just based on empirical analysis. They were substantiated by plausible models, both of the economy and of the polity. Indeed these models became part of the accepted language of discourse.

This suggests that what I have called the "Atlantic Constitution" is not just a set of rules of behavior, nor is it simply a set of "rules of the game," as North suggests. It is rooted in *beliefs*, and these beliefs have both empirical and theoretical bases. When the "rules of the game" of the constitution produce effects that are intolerable, then the philosophers, the prophets of chaos, become engaged to seek both the reasons and cures. The beliefs that underpin the constitution necessarily evolve, in a way that might be termed "Popperian" (Popper, 1957). In fact, Popper (1972) has asked the question: "How [can] such non-physical things, as purposes, deliberations, plans, decisions, theories, intentions, and values ... play a part in bringing about physical changes in the physical world?"

That such non-physical things are part of the constitution suggests that the constitution has embedded within it a formal language of discourse. Some of the anarchic philosophers follow Hume in regarding language simply as a system of conventions. As Sugden (1980) says, "We all wish to speak and write in a form that is comprehensible to the people with whom we wish to communicate, and so there is a self-reinforcing tendency for communities to evolve common languages."

From this point of view, a language as convention is a particular equilibrium solution to a coordination game. But a language is clearly more than this. It has a grammatical structure that is internally consistent, to some degree.

In my view, the constitution does provide a language through which citizens, corporations, and countries can communicate. But there is a further element of this constitutional language which should be emphasized. As I wrote a number of years ago,

[T]he fundamental theoretical problem underlying the question of cooperation is the manner by which individuals attain knowledge of each others' preferences and likely behavior. Moreover, the problem is one of common knowledge, since each individual, i, is required not only to have information about others' preferences, but also to know that the others have knowledge about i's own preferences and strategies.

(Schofield, 1985b)

This constitutional language aims not only at internal consistency, and empirical relevance, but also provides the framework within which the acts of agents (whether citizens, corporations, or countries) are mutually intelligible. That is, it makes it possible, at least potentially, for us to understand what it is we, and others, are doing.

These remarks lead us to a conception of the constitution that is much more general than that of an institution. Clearly, the "rules of the game," since they must be regarded as humanly devised constraints, are open to human choice. Because the rules can be socially chosen, the internal consistency and stability of the constitution depends on the degree to which it is in equilibrium with respect to the beliefs of its citizens. At certain times in the evolution of the constitution, there exists one, or a number of core beliefs that are stable or persist in the population. These provide the basis for the consistency or coherence of the constitutional "language."

However, the game theorists, who have studied the prisoners' dilemma model of cooperation and war, have realized that the evolution of such Hobbesian societies depends almost entirely on the way beliefs are created and destroyed.[11] In contrast to the earlier work of the "neo-institutional" political economists, who tended to see political or social equilibrium resulting directly from institutional constraints,[12] the more recent perspective has emphasized the way in which equilibria may be destroyed or recreated by a belief cascade.

Denzau and North (1994) mention two different modes of belief cascades that have been discussed in entirely different contexts. First there is the situation studied by Bikhchandani, Hirschleifer, and Welch (1992) where a small group of decision makers "change their minds" on the basis of their private information, inducing the rest of the population to "free ride" by following suit. Second, there is the notion of a scientific revolution destroying an existing paradigm (Kuhn, 1962).

Chapter 8 presents a more detailed examination of versions of these two modes of belief cascades. To illustrate the first type, suppose individuals hold two hypotheses, say "the market is a bull" as against "the market is a bear," but assign a higher probability to the former. Obviously enough, this is a self-fulfilling social belief. If, however, in a domain of uncertainty, market leaders act in a way that is consistent with their increasing belief in the latter hypothesis, then a belief cascade may ensue. Whether or not it will depends on the common knowledge foundation of the collective beliefs: Is it the case that the acts of the market leaders are clearly intelligible to the market followers? Recent results in game theory suggest that the common knowledge foundation, the basis of intelligibility, may, in fact, collapse near the onset of the cascade. Another way of expressing this is by the observation that the outcome, as well as the onset, of the belief cascade may very well be unknowable in principle. It is this argument which sustains the claim that asset markets are potentially chaotic.[13]

---

[11] There is enormous literature on this topic. For a very useful survey, see Denzau and North (1994).

[12] For a discussion of these perspectives, see Calvert (1995).

[13] The argument on unintelligibility is based on a Gödel-Turning paradox, that each agent, i, in interpreting the market must assume that the other agents in the market are different in kind from i. When this realization hits, as it must in general, then the basis for rational choice by i is destroyed. The onset of this "irrationality" by

Chapter 8 also considers an important example of a Kuhnian paradigm shift, namely the transformations in physics that occurred after 1905, when Einstein "banished" the core scientific belief in the absolute existence of time and space. This led to the shattering of the subdisciplines of physics, and the creation of entirely new disciplines, including quantum mechanics, among others. Indeed, physics during this century has thrown up numerous profound quandaries, not the least of which is the problem of the integration of gravitation with quantum theory. The point about the belief in absolute space and time was that it created barriers to thought that hindered the development of our understanding of the world.

I suggest that the economic equilibrium hypothesis has been a *core belief* of the Atlantic Constitution in much the same way that the belief in absolute space and time was at the core of nineteenth century physics. Keynes himself found it extremely difficult to overcome the barrier presented by the "Marshallian orthodoxy" of a belief in the strong equilibrium hypothesis.

A total rejection of the validity of the equilibrium thesis, for both commodity as well as asset markets, calls into question the fundamental political beliefs that underpin the Atlantic Constitution. For this reason, policy makers have retained this belief in one form or another. This does not mean to say that the belief has remained unchanged throughout the entire period. Section 7.7 suggests that, in attempting to solve the constitutional quandary of 1944, the architects of change of that time adopted some of Keynes' insights, particularly with regard to the problem of cooperation in the international economic arena. A complex belief about the compatibility of the Bretton Woods international institution and a Keynesian macroeconomic equilibrium thesis became generally accepted during the 1950s and 1960s. In turn, the events of the 1970s persuaded first the prophets of chaos of that time, and then the international policy makers, that the only resolution to their particular quandary was a return to the economic belief based on the strong form of the equilibrium hypothesis.[14]

---

market leaders cannot be determined beforehand. When it does occur, it may well trigger a belief cascade into market instability. It is apparent that Keynes' intuition on the collapse of market bubbles was similar, though not, of course, framed in precisely these game theoretic terms. Chapter 8 discusses this further.

[14] This chapter only sketches the nature of the constitutional quandaries of 1944 and of the 1970s. A point to note is that the solution of the 1944 quandary was still rooted in an equilibrium thesis but also involved certain beliefs about the nature of a bipolar world split between communism and capitalism.

The theoretical arguments just made suggest that the form of the resolution of these two quandaries could not, in principle, be determined beforehand, precisely because belief cascades were involved in both cases. The same holds for the current quandary. However, examination of such quandaries does permit a clearer focus on the underlying core beliefs preceding the onset of the cascade.

It should be remarked that the use of the word *core* in *core belief* is meant to designate a generally accepted principle. When a quandary is universally perceived, then there is no consensus in belief,[15] and the common knowledge foundation of choice and action dissipates. Even so, what beliefs there are in the collectivity will still induce barriers to thought and to behavior. As the core beliefs fragment, it is not implausible that acts become mutually unintelligible, indeed "irrational." This phenomenon can be observed in some of the laboratory experiments based on the prisoners' dilemma (Richards, 1990). Indeed the "resource wars" and aggressive currency devaluations of the 1970s may have had a similar basis.

Social choice theory indicates that the absence of a core belief may induce cyclical or apparently random behavior. The set of all such behavior is termed *the heart*. Thus the *heart* of the Atlantic Constitution, at any time, is the set of collective actions that may be "rationally" entertained by the citizens or organizations within the community. The social choice framework underpinning this book suggests that as core beliefs fragment at the onset of a quandary, then the heart of the constitution expands to include behavior that was previously inconceivable.[16] The next section briefly discusses the extent to which the Atlantic Constitution does truly face a quandary at present, and offers some observations as to possible consequences if core beliefs do not adapt to the situation before us.

7.4 POLITICAL AND ECONOMIC BELIEFS IN THE CONSTITUTION

This is the biggest financial challenge facing the world in half a century, and the United States has an absolutely inescapable obligation to lead and lead in a way that's consistent with our values[.]

---

[15] Throughout this book, the use of the word core in core belief is adapted from social choice usage. When there is no consensus, then the core is empty, and the core belief is void.

[16] To speculate, it is possible that the irrationality of World War II had at its source the collapse of the core beliefs during the 1920s and 1930s.

We know that our future prosperity depends on whether we can, with others, restore confidence [and] stabilize the financial system. We will urge the major industrial economies to stand ready to use the $15 billion I.M.F. emergency funds to help stop the financial contagion from spreading to Latin America and elsewhere. . . .

Today I have asked Secretary Rubin and Federal Reserve Board Chairman Greenspan to convene a major meeting of their counterparts within the next 30 days to recommend ways to adapt the international financial architecture to the 21st Century.

(President Bill Clinton, address to the Council on Foreign Relations, New York, September 15, 1998)

As I have already suggested, the transformations in the Atlantic Constitution after the late 1970s had shifted our understanding of the balance between politics and economics. Prior to about 1970, a Keynesian understanding of the necessity for intervention in the economy was compatible with a general view of politicians as social welfare maximizers. One could say that polities were "simple" and economies "complex." By the 1980s, theory and reality had suggested that politicians were complicated agents, potentially predatory and requiring constant vigilance. Models of politics necessarily become increasingly complex. In contrast, the general acceptance of the belief in an equilibrium tendency of economies meant that the science of economics became simpler.

As noted in the previous section, there is a theoretical problem with the economic equilibrium belief. The theorem on which the belief is grounded deals with commodities whose value for each individual is well defined. The very success of the transformed constitution since 1982 has led to a vastly increased international flow of monetary assets, and to enormously enhanced activity on the world's stock exchanges. These flows are derived not from the intrinsic value (utility) of assets, but from beliefs of agents about the future value of the assets. To fully understand such asset markets, it is necessary to model the behavior of the agents involved in the exchange, and this means understanding their beliefs. As Arrow (1986) has noted, this means solving an infinitely complex common knowledge problem.[17] In the fashion described above, belief cascades can destroy economic equilibrium within such markets. In practical terms, a cascade from one equilibrium to another could involve a collapse first of the Mexican peso, then the Southeast Asian currencies and stock markets, then the Japanese economy, and then the Russian. There is no theoretical reason at all to suppose that such events are impossible. In fact, formal analyses

---

[17] Another way of seeing the problem is in terms of the incompleteness of future markets.

of such belief cascades have suggested that it is impossible to know how, or by what, the cascade is triggered. It is for this reason that such cascades have been called "chaotic."[18]

The current predisposition to view polities as complex, and economies as simple has guided commentators on the current chaotic events to focus on "politics." It is easy to point to nepotism in Indonesia, to senility in the Liberal Democratic Party in Japan, and to autocrats and the mafia in Russia. It is difficult, however, to see why such political incapacity has only now made itself felt.

The monetary institutions of the Atlantic Constitution have deployed their resources of many tens of billions of dollars in the last few years to assist the floundering economies of Russia and Southeast Asia. It is possible that the Latin American economies will follow the earlier collapse in Mexico and that the resources of the World Bank and IMF will be completely overwhelmed.

The point to be made, of course, is that these cascades have occurred despite the strongly held belief, implicit within the current Atlantic Constitution, that the global economy can generally be left to fend for itself. I consider this belief to be unfounded for the reasons already mentioned. At the same time, the belief (held strongly prior to 1965) that the international monetary institutions can control the global economy appears just as unfounded.[19]

If this quandary is not solved, certain consequences for the structure of the Atlantic Constitution appear inevitable. The pronounced triumphalism of the last decade will surely disappear, if events play out the way suggested. Pessimism will again rule. The earlier pessimisms of the interwar era and of the decade of the oil crisis had given way, by 1989, to

[18] It is not so much that such belief cascades are sensitive to initial conditions (the usual definition of chaos). Rather, the resulting behavior can "go anywhere."

[19] Attempts to regulate any market by controlling price fluctuations necessarily requires a reserve fund of a scale that is related to (1) the volume of the potential speculative assets flow, (2) the degree of correlation between the individual commodity markets, and (3) the inverse of the chosen price band. Although there may well be welfare benefits from reducing risk through such restriction of volatility, these should be set against the cost of maintaining the reserve fund. For a discussion of the theory as applied to commodity markets, see Newberry and Stiglitz (1981). As section 7.5 mentions, attempts to regulate the international monetary system and the world commodity markets (under the auspices of the UNCTAD integrated commodities program) both failed in the decade after the Smithsonian Agreement. The reasons fairly obviously were to do with the scale of speculative flows and the extent of the correlation. This does not mean to say that it is impossible to regulate, but only in a much weaker sense than these earlier experiments.

the optimistic view that liberal democracy may constitute the "endpoint of mankind's ideological evolution and the final form of human government" (Fukuyama, 1992).

This "triumphalism" was based on the fading away both of communism in Russia and Eastern Europe and of autocratic regimes in Latin America and Asia. The reason for their decline and disappearance clearly seems to have been the effect that the success of the Atlantic Constitution had on the beliefs of populations in these countries. On the one hand, if the Atlantic Coalition is manifestly unable to solve its economic dilemmas, then a citizen of a predatory regime will be willing to accept the depredations of that regime. On the other hand, if the risk of economic collapse under the Atlantic Constitution falls relative to the obvious benefits of citizen and property rights, then the depredations become unbearable. Cascades of citizen unrest can then overthrow the autocracies. But liberal democracies can also fall. If beliefs in the likelihood of chaos increases, then politicians, in their pursuit of power, will rationally rise up to institute predatory autocracies, and citizens may well fear the relative cost of rebellion.[20]

The events in Russia in late 1998 give us all cause to fear that this fall into autocracy could be unbelievably swift. An even greater fear is that the expected amelioration of the regime in China may very well be reversed.

In the developed countries of the Atlantic Coalition, the belief in the legitimacy of the market could be eroded equally rapidly. It is not surprising that those countries, particularly Britain and the United States, where the economic equilibrium belief has been most readily accepted, are also those at present experiencing low unemployment, and, perhaps, an increasing degree of wealth inequality. When this equilibrium belief was less potent, both Britain, most obviously, but also the United States, to some degree, were beset by labor unrest.

In many of the countries of the European Union, the consequences of the economic equilibrium hypothesis have met with substantial political resistance. It seems reasonable to suppose that the effect has been to weaken the desire or will to impose restrictions on government intervention in the economy.[21]

---

[20] It is clear how to model this formalism. I need only assume that citizens and politicians are rational, but with different motivations. The essence of the model is given in Weingast (1997a, b). I have simply added the idea of risk to the cost calculation of the citizen.

[21] I have argued elsewhere that the interrelationship between beliefs and constraints on government is mediated by the electoral system. Thus, in electoral systems based on

Obviously, beliefs about the appropriate relationship between politics and economics do indeed differ, as I have suggested, among the United States, Britain, and the European polities. This is entirely consistent with the notion of an Atlantic Constitution, since I assume only that the broad pattern of the beliefs will still be compatible. However, my understanding of the constitution as based on a coherent language suggests that if the fundamental beliefs start to diverge, then policy coordination between the countries will become increasingly difficult.

Suppose the degree of perceived risk in the global economy increases, while attempts to solve the quandary fail. It is obviously impossible to read the future, but it would seem all too plausible that the European Union, in implementing monetary union, the Euro, between twelve of its members, will also become increasingly protectionist. I have no proof of this assertion, but my colleague, Andrew Sobel, has kindly brought to my attention the comments of the French Prime Minister, Edouard Ballader, in 1993:

Can we [West Europeans] take it for granted that we will remain sufficient leaders in sufficient numbers of sectors to survive in the face of countries with populations infinitely larger than ours and with levels of social protection infinitely smaller? I say we should leave this to the market, but only up to a certain point. What is the market? It is the law of the jungle, the law of nature. And what is civilization? It is the struggle against nature.[22]

If the coherence of the core political and economic beliefs is called into question to such a degree that countries fall into autocracy or protectionism, then the consequences would be profoundly unpleasant. It seems to me that this is not simply an empirical policy matter. It is not just a question of juggling the flows from the monetary institutions to the countries at risk to enable them to overcome a temporary economic difficulty. It is a question of probing the core beliefs of the constitution more vigorously than we have chosen to do since the onset of the last quandary in the late 1970s.

As I have noted, the earlier crisis originated in the fall of the Bretton Woods system. The later sections of this chapter use the notion of the Atlantic Constitution in an attempt to gain a better understanding of the proper balance between politics and economics. To do this I detail my

proportional representation, parties involved in coalition government are unwilling, as it were, to increase the risk their voters face if labor markets are made more competitive. Majoritarian systems, such as Britain, appear to have been more risk preferring since 1980. See Chapter 2.

[22] Quoted in Sobel (1998).

view of the nature of the problem, as perceived by the architects of change circa 1944 and circa 1980. Their beliefs were conditioned by the empirical reality that they had already experienced, and by the theoretical apparatus that they had at their disposal. I see these architects as concerned actors of political and economic reason, fully aware of the dangers to the Atlantic Constitution, and determined to protect it and the pattern of citizen rights and responsibilities that had been created over many centuries.

Whereas Popper recommends piece-meal engineering over utopian visions, it is obvious that, at times, the stakes can be so high that vigorous social "experimentation" is rational. By focusing on the quandaries as perceived in 1944 and in 1980 and the solutions that were devised, we may better understand the recent evolution of the Atlantic Constitution.[23]

To do so, we must first recreate the fears, as presented by the prophets of chaos, in terms of the theoretical and empirical framework within which they were expressed. Second, I discuss, in each case, how the framework was reinterpreted by architects of change, so that a solution could be constructed, through transformations in the fundamental core beliefs underlying the Atlantic Constitution.[24]

7.5 THE COLLAPSE OF HEGEMONY IN THE 1970S

Hegemon (from ηγεμιν, Greek) *leader; hegemony, preponderance, especially of one state of a confederacy or union, over others.* (O.E.D.)

As far as I am aware, Kindleberger (1973) gave the first interpretation of the international economic system of states as a "Hobbesian" prisoners' dilemma, which could be solved by a leader, or "hegemon."

A symmetric system with rules for counterbalancing, such as the gold standard is supposed to provide, may give way to a system with each participant seeking to maximize its short-term gain. ... But a world of a few actors (countries) is not like [the competitive system envisaged by Adam Smith]. ... In advancing its own economic good by a tariff, currency depreciation, or foreign exchange control, a country may worsen the welfare of its partners by more than its gain.

---

[23] Implicit in my understanding is that the Atlantic Constitution evolves through "punctuated equilibria." See Eldredge and Gould (1972). For a general argument to this effect, see Chapter 8.

[24] This kind of analytical narrative, focusing on deadly quandaries within the Atlantic Constitution, has been discussed in the earlier chapters. See also Rakove, Rutten, and Weingast (1999) for the period of 1760–1776, prior to the American Revolution, and the essays in *Analytical Narratives* (1998) by Robert Bates, Avner Greif, Margaret Levi, Jean-Laurent Rosenthal, and Barry Weingast.

Beggar-thy-neighbor tactics may lead to retaliation so that each century ends up in a worse position from having pursued its own gain. ...

This is a typical non-zero sum game, in which any player undertaking to adopt a long range solution by itself will find other countries taking advantage of it. ...

In these circumstances, the international economic and monetary system needs leadership, a country that is prepared, consciously or unconsciously, under some system of rules that it has internalized, to set standards of conduct for other countries and to seek to get others to follow them. ... Britain performed this role in the century to 1913; the United States in the period after the Second World War until, say ... 1963. ... [P]art of the reason for the length of ... the world depression was the inability of the British to continue their role of underwriter ... and the reluctance of the U.S. to take it on until 1936.[25]

In the 1970s, Robert Keohane and Joseph Nye (1977) rejected "realist" theory in international politics, and made use of the idea of a hegemonic power in a context of "complex interdependence" of the kind envisaged by Kindleberger. Although they did not refer to the formalism of the prisoners' dilemma, it would appear that this notion does capture elements of complex interdependence. To some extent, their concept of a hegemon is taken from realist theory rather than deriving from the game-theoretic formalism.

However, it is very easy to adapt the notion of a symmetric prisoners' dilemma, so as to clarify the concept of a hegemon. A non-symmetric n-agent prisoners' dilemma (nPD) can be constructed as follows. Let $d_i \in [0, 1]$ be the strategy of the ith country ($d_i = 0$ means defect, $d_i = 1$ means cooperate). Each country was a weight (proportional to its GDP), a_i say. The total collective good of the system, N, of states is

$$B(N) = \sum_{i=1}^{n} a_i d_i. \qquad (7.1)$$

The payoff u_i to state i, when it adopts strategy d_i is

$$u_i(d_i) = \frac{r}{n} \sum_{i=1}^{n} B(N) - d_i. \qquad (7.2)$$

For a prisoners' dilemma, $1 < r < n$. The term in d_i is

$$\frac{r}{n}(a_i d_i) - d_i. \qquad (7.3)$$

---

[25] Kindleberger, 1973: 11. In the next section, I discuss earlier remarks in this vein by Keynes in 1936.

Clearly if

$$\frac{r}{n}(a_i) < 1, \tag{7.4}$$

then u_i is maximized at $d_i = 0$. If

$$\frac{r}{n}(a_i) > 1, \tag{7.5}$$

then u_i is maximized at $d_i = 1$.

In the symmetric game, $a_i = 1$ for all i, so the "rational" strategy for each country is to defect, by choosing $d_i = 0$. If

$$a_i > \frac{n}{r}, \tag{7.6}$$

then this country, i, rationally must cooperate, irrespective of the strategies of other countries. To keep things simple, suppose $a_j = 1$ for all j other than this hegemon, i. In this very trivial formulation, some things are obvious. If more states join the game (so n increases), it becomes more "difficult" for a_i to be large enough for cooperation. The coefficient r is the "rate of return on cooperation." As r falls it becomes more difficult again for i to remain the cooperative hegemon. In this formulation the term *hegemon* is something of a misnomer, since i is simply a rational cooperator. However, if coalitions are permitted and a hegemonic power leads a coalition M of states, dictating policy to these states, then the optimality condition for the joint cooperation of the states in the coalition M is

$$\sum_{i \in M} a_i > \frac{n}{r}. \tag{7.7}$$

The collective benefits of the coalition M can then be redistributed by the hegemon in some way, to keep the coalition intact.

A number of years ago, I analyzed a prisoners' dilemma model of this kind and observed that it could be used to understand international economic cooperation. The conclusion was pessimistic.

In the postwar years we have seen the development of a dominant cooperative coalition: the Atlantic Community. At the core of this cooperative coalition was the United States; through its size it was able to generate collective goods for this community, first of all through the Marshall Plan and then in the context of the Defense Alliance. ... Since the sterling devaluation of 1967 we have seen intermittent stop-go or inflation-deflation strategies by many of the developed economies.

To simplify, we may regard such strategies as bargaining strategies of the type considered here. These strategies necessitated coalitional readjustments or agreements over distribution, such as the Smithsonian Agreement of 1971. ... In a sense the United States has found it costly to be the dominant core of the coalition ... the Atlantic coalition may be in the process of fragmentation, with its individual members oriented to individually rational, or "beggar-my-neighbor" strategies.[26]

Obviously these comments were made at a time when the size of the U.S. economy had declined relative to the overall GDP of the OECD. Following the logic of the prisoners' dilemma, it was apparent that cooperation within the Atlantic Community would become more difficult. Throughout the late 1960s, economic behavior had indeed become increasingly chaotic. The problem had, of course, been noted early on by Triffin (1960), who asked how stability could be maintained by a constant flow of dollar assets out from the United States. The round of devaluations, including the sterling devaluation of November 1976 and of the French franc in August 1969, made it clear that the Bretton Woods system could not be retained. The monetary instability of that period may also have created the context for the "political business cycle." Coincident elections in many of the OECD countries induced incumbent governments to simultaneous reflation. Average inflation moved up from about 4 percent to nearly 8 percent in two years in the early 1970s (McCracken, 1977); the rest of the decade of the 1970s was taken up with the two oil crises, with the arguments in the context of UNCTAD over changing the relationship between developed and less developed countries, and (by the early 1980s) with the third world debt crisis.[27] Although the earlier analysis was based on the one-shot n-person prisoners' dilemma (nPD), it is possible to pursue the Hobbesian metaphor in the context of an iterated nPD. Analyses of such games suggest that they are chaotic, that anything can, in principle, occur.[28] In other words, while the one-shot nPD will tend to fall into Hobbesian war when there is no hegemon, in the iterated version cooperative coalitions may rise and fall in an indeterminate fashion.

The formal problem presented by the iterated nPD (with n agents) is that the strategy space is extremely complex. Although the results of

---

[26] Schofield (1975). Dynamic aspects of such a game were considered in Schofield (1977a, b).

[27] These crises have been discussed by many authors. An overall view of their interactions is given in Schofield (1984b).

[28] This is my interpretation of the so-called folk theorem for infinitely repeated games. See Fudenberg and Tirole (1992).

Axelrod (1984) are generally seen as providing an avenue of escape from defection into cooperation, via tit-for-tat strategies, his work was only concerned with two agent models. With many countries participating, strategies may well involve complicated history-dependant punishments against other countries, or groups of countries. Keohane (1984), in his more recent work, has attempted to provide an explanation for international cooperation in the post-hegemonic world of the 1980s. In essence, his argument is that a new regime came into being, based on new expectations and mutual assumptions. A formal interpretation of his argument is that a convention—a self-reinforcing "Nash" equilibrium in the iterated nPD—was created. But what exactly was this new regime, this equilibrium convention?

As I have intimated previously, an international economic regime is more than a convention. It is a system of rules and modes of meaning, a language, embedded in a framework—a constitution—that is intelligible to the participants. Most importantly, it must provide the common-knowledge background so the agents know the game and can interpret the actions of others. I have argued in the previous sections that the shift in the constitution circa 1980 involved an acceptance of the economic equilibrium thesis.

By the end of the 1970s, it had become obvious to all that global capital was capable of swamping the resources of any individual country, even the United States. Already by 1973, the Long Report[29] had estimated that private Eurodollar assets were of the order of 270 billion dollars (in current terms over 1 trillion dollars). By 1983, the capital requirements of the developing nations were being met principally by private capital sources. It is true that this had precipitated the so-called debt crisis.[30] However, by the end of the 1980s this crisis had been accommodated to some degree.

Given that no individual country could immunize itself against international capital, it made sense to accept the fact and consider strategies that were consistent with the logic of the market. As I observed earlier, this is not to say that all countries adopted identical strategies. Differences in electoral and political patterns in the developed countries resulted in varied microeconomic strategies in labor markets, and capital markets

---

[29] The U.S. Government Printing Office: *The Long Report to the U.S. Senate* (1973).
[30] For example, by 1983 it was estimated that the Latin American countries owed approximately 300 billion dollars. Debt service at that time exceeded earnings in many of these countries.

responded in obvious ways. For third world countries in particular, political chaos or internal strategies of excessive manipulation led to increases in perceived risk, and their capital flow declined (Sobel, 1999). Acceptance of the logic of the market thus imposed a degree of discipline on both developed and less developed nations.

The strategic domain available to countries contracted. While the game still probably retained the fundamental characteristics of the *nPD*, the "externalities" (the effect of the strategy of one country or another) diminished. Although the U.S. trade deficit remained a problem, it was no longer seen as a fundamental disequilibrating feature of the global economy, but as a topic to be tackled by bilateral negotiation, usually with Japan, and later with China.

This modification to the Atlantic Constitution was put in place, principally by Reagan and Thatcher, in the early 1980s. These changed beliefs were accepted by decision makers in the international economy, since they made both logical and empirical sense.[31] The arguments of those prophets of chaos, who had asserted the fundamental incompatibility of democracy and economic rationality, appeared unfounded. As I have indicated, there were beneficial unanticipated consequences, including the democratization of regimes in Latin America and in the old Soviet Union.

Even more surprisingly, the Cassandras who had foreseen the increasingly rapid decline of hegemonic U.S. power, and the recurrence of economic "Warre"[32] were confounded by the obvious economic vitality both of the United States and Britain. However, the coherence of the core belief that was created after 1982 or so depended crucially for its validity on the economic equilibrium thesis. Although I have argued that there are theoretical reasons to reject the strong equilibrium hypothesis, there could, nonetheless, be reasons to accept its empirical validity. To see whether the thesis has universal validity, it makes sense to look again at the events of the interwar period. In the following two sections of the chapter, I interpret these events in terms of Keynes' understanding of the quandary implicit within the Atlantic Constitution in the period before and during World War II.

---

[31] I have not found a complete account of this belief cascade, but Yergin and Stanislaw (1998) do provide a readable account. Although the book was written before the "crisis" of 1998, they do mention in their conclusion the consequences of any disruption of the international financial system.

[32] See Kennedy (1987) as well as Thurow (1992, 1996) and Chapter 2.

7.6   KEYNES AND THE QUANDARY OF THE 1930S

Chaos, (from χαοσ, Greek), *void, confusion.*

The Treaty of Versailles was signed on June 28, 1919. Keynes had been involved in the negotiations and was appalled by the reparations required of Germany by the Allies. He calculated that at best Germany could pay 1500 million pounds sterling over thirty years. As he wrote, in his *Economic Consequences of the Peace* (1919), "The fact that we have no adequate knowledge of Germany's capacity to pay over a long period of years is no justification ... for the statement that she can pay ten thousand million pounds."[33]

Keynes also outlined his plan for a peace treaty involving "limited reparations as well as cancellation of inter-ally debts; creation of a European free trade area; ... an international loan to stabilize the exchanges; and encouragement of Germany's natural organizing role in Eastern Europe" (Skidelsky, 1983: 391).

Without these remedies,

Nothing can then delay for long that final civil war between the forces of reaction and the despairing convulsions of revolutions, before which the horrors of the late German war will fade into nothing, and which will destroy, whoever is victor, the civilization and progress of our generation.[34]

There was a distinct Malthusian tone to much of Keynes' book.

The feeding of the peoples of Central Europe is the fundamental problem in front of us. ... Some of the catastrophes of past history, which have thrown back human progress for centuries, have been due to the reactions following on the sudden termination of temporarily favourable conditions which have permitted the growth of populations beyond what could be provided for.[35]

Kindleberger (1973) suggests that reparations "may not have been directly responsible for the depression, but together with war debts they complicated and corrupted the international economy at every stage of the 1920s and during the depression through to 1933" (23).

Just to indicate the amounts involved, France and Britain owed the United States 8.7 billion dollars (which should be scaled up by a factor of more than 30 to convert into current dollars). Interallied debt (including

---

[33] Quoted in Skidelsky (1983: 391) from Keynes (1919: 128).
[34] Ibid., 391, quoting from Keynes (1919: 170).
[35] Ibid., 387, quoting from Keynes (1919: 146).

Russia's) was approximately 900 billion dollars in current terms, with German "reparations" of the order of 300 billion current dollars.

The story of the run-up to the Great Depression is well known. An important decision, in terms both of the global economy and Keynes' interpretation of it, was the British decision to return to the gold standard, at a parity for sterling of 4.86, on May 14, 1925. There is reason to believe that the Chancellor of the Exchequer, Winston Churchill, was against this decision. However, the return to the gold standard was seen by nearly everyone as a necessary move to stabilize the international monetary system. Perhaps the Japanese were less sanguine: It was not until 1929 that attempts were made to return the yen to par. A boom did follow, but the flow of capital in to the U.S. stock market reduced overseas lending by the United States to the extent of 2 billion dollars (60 billion dollars current; Kindleberger, 1973: 59). Economists disagree about this effect, of course, but Kindleberger's analysis seems justified. Kindleberger (1973: 76–7) notes that from 1925 to 1931 there was a worldwide deflation in commodities. For example, rubber prices fell from 340 cents per lb. in 1925 to 75 cents per lb. in 1931. From early 1929, speculative pressure on sterling and other currencies rapidly increased (Kindleberger, 1973: 101).[36]

As I argued earlier, speculative asset markets are potentially chaotic: The particular event that triggers the cascade, the collapse of the bubble, is impossible to determine. On September 3, 1929, the Dow-Jones Industrial Average reached 381 (over twice the average 1926 value); it started to slip on October 3, and to fall seriously on October 24. On October 29, 16.4 million shares were traded, and the Dow fell to 198. It continued to fall until mid-1932.

It would seem incontestable that the Wall Street crash was the result of a belief cascade that in turn led to a further belief cascade that had profound, real, rather than virtual, economic effects. It is still debated whether the Depression could have been avoided. Whatever the case in theory, the core beliefs that were still in place at the time made it almost impossible for the United States to act in any vigorous fashion to stabilize the international monetary system (certainly while staying on the gold standard). The logic of the prisoners' dilemma aspect of international

---

[36] International pressures, and the fears over monetary instability because of the inadequacy of the Young Plan of April–May 1929 led to a further flow of gold into the United States. Sterling's gold par came under speculative pressure, and the Bank of England's gold stock fell 640 million dollars in four months.

trade became apparent with the signing of the Smoot-Hawley Tariff Act on June 17, 1930. Kindleberger describes the retaliatory responses first of Canada, then France, Australia, and so on. World trade continued to contract (from about 3 billion dollars in January 1929 to much less than one-third this value in March 1933). The obvious economic consequences made it not at all surprising that the incumbent, Hoover lost the U.S. presidential election to Roosevelt in 1932. Almost the first acts by Roosevelt were to accept the Thomas amendment on April 18, 1933, to issue 3 billion greenbacks (not backed by gold or silver), and more generally to announce an abandonment of the gold dollar, during the World Economic Conference in June, 1933. Kindleberger (1973) asserted that "[t]he Democratic administration had little interest in or knowledge of the world economy. ... It would be three years before the administration [in 1936] felt a responsibility for the operation of the international monetary system" (229).

An immediate consequence of Roosevelt's unilateral move was that the member countries of the British Empire met formally to create the sterling area. With regard to domestic U.S. policy to restore prosperity, Brinkley (1998) says, "in truth, the New Dealers [in the U.S.] had no idea how to end the Depression because they had only the vaguest idea of what caused it" (18).

Two solutions to the quandary of the Depression were implicit in Keynes' *The General Theory* (Keynes, 1936). They derive not just from empirical induction, but from a profound theoretical assertion. I have alluded to this previously. For convenience let us now call it *the Hypothesis of Chaotic Asset Markets*. Obviously, this is an anachronistic phrase, since the term *chaos* has a formal mathematical meaning that dates from 1975.[37] However, chaos has a meaning in common language that is close to the technical interpretation. It is of some interest to speculate on the origins in Keynes' thought on this hypothesis. To do so, we can be guided by Skidelsky's biography of Keynes (Skidelsky, 1983, 1992, 2000).

Keynes went up to King's College, Cambridge, in 1902, and took the Tripos in 1905, coming twelfth wrangler. As Skidelsky observes, his exams involved algebra, optics, elliptic functions, integral calculus, and so forth. After the exam, Keynes started work on Marshall's *Principles of Economics* (1890). But more than economics, it was G. E. Moore's

---

[37] As noted in Chapter 1, the term chaos was first used by Li and Yorke (1975), and then adopted in order to describe indeterminate social choice processes in Schofield (1979).

Principia Ethica (1903) that influenced Keynes. Moore had based his argument for the necessity of general rules of conduct ("conventions") on the lack of rational grounds for asserting that one of two propositions is even probably right. In a paper Keynes delivered to the Apostles in 1903, he argued that saying A is more probable than B implicitly judges the relevance of available evidence on the relation. This interpretation became the key notion in a dissertation that Keynes submitted in December 1907 for a prize fellowship at King's. The final version, after much intense effort, was not published until 1921.[38] In the Michaelmas term of 1905, Keynes had returned to Cambridge to study economics under Marshall, reading Jevons, Cournot, Edgeworth, and the like. By December 1905, he had decided to study instead for the civil service exam in August 1906, reading psychology, the Greeks, history, mathematics, and logic. He came in second. Skidelsky notes that Keynes' worst mark was in economics.

Almost 30 years later, the most important book of the century in economics, and possibly in social philosophy, was published. *The General Theory* appeared on February 4, 1936. In my judgment, the profound inference from Keynes' arguments was that the strong economic equilibrium thesis had to be modified in order to understand a sophisticated capitalist economy. In coming to this conclusion, Keynes depended both on the theoretical "wrestling," fifteen years previously, that he had devoted to the task of finishing the *Treatise on Probability*, and on his effort at induction, his attempt to make sense of the post-1929 world of the Depression. To reconceptualize economics, he had to deny the fundamental framework of Marshallian equilibrium theory.[39]

Skidelsky intimates, and I concur, that Moore's *Principia Ethica* forced Keynes to think in a new way about rationality. Interestingly, Keynes' denial of the equilibrium thesis was not put in the form of a theorem, but rather in common sense, but metaphorical, language:

If I may be allowed to appropriate the term speculation for the activity of forecasting the psychology of the market, and the term enterprise for the activity of

---

[38] Keynes (1921: 341). Keynes takes issue with a consequentialist argument by Moore that utter ignorance of the far future forbids us from making choices for the greater good. Keynes argues that it may be possible to make "probabilistic" judgments, that is, in the presence of risk. Clearly, however, Moore's argument has validity if interpreted in terms of uncertainty, and it was this insight that Keynes pursued in *The General Theory*.

[39] From my viewpoint (and seemingly from Keynes' as well), equilibrium theory, as represented by the formalism of Marshallian economics, was a barrier to understanding the economic world. On conceptual barriers, see Margolis (1993).

forecasting the prospective yield of assets over their whole life, it is by no means always the case that speculation predominates over enterprise. As the organization of investment markets improves, the risk of the predominance of speculation does, however, increase. ...

Speculators may do no harm as bubbles on a steady stream of enterprise. But the position is serious when enterprise becomes the bubble on a whirlpool of speculation.

(Keynes, 1936: 158–9)

As Skidelsky (1983: 611) notes, "the mathematization of *The General Theory* started immediately" in work by Viner and Hicks.[40] In his analysis of Keynes' contribution, Minsky (1975) argues that Keynes' key insight was that uncertainty is not identical to risk. Moreover, uncertainty vitiated the formal economic models of Keynes' "teachers and colleagues Marshall, Edgeworth, and Pigou" (Minsky, 1975: 66). These classic authors had held that

At any given time facts and expectations were assumed to be given in a definite and calculable form; and risks ... were supposed to be capable of an exact actuarial computation. The calculus of probability was supposed to be capable of reducing uncertainty to the same calculable status as that of certainty itself. ... By "uncertain" knowledge, let me explain, I do not mean merely to distinguish what is known for certain from what is only probable. ... Even the weather is only moderately uncertain. The sense in which I am using the term is that in which the prospect of a European war is uncertain, or the price of copper and the rate of interest twenty years hence. ...

(Keynes, 1937)

From uncertainty comes the possibility of speculative booms and crashes, of "real" effects in the economy, including persistent unemployment (the obvious specter of the time). Minsky faults Keynes, in a sense, for not pursuing the full ramifications of his insight, and for retaining much of the equilibrium Marshallian apparatus in determining the likely consequences of the conjecture for the operation of the macroeconomy. Keynes himself was well aware of the difficulty of working outside the "Marshallian orthodoxy." In the preface he notes that "The composition of this book has been for the author a long struggle of escape ... from habitual modes of thought and expression" (Keynes, 1936: xviii).

Hicks' geometrization of Keynes' theory and the neoclassical synthesis that followed, put equilibrium theory back in center stage. As Skidelsky (1983) observes, "The determinate system in which the 'authority' could act on the multiplier either by monetary or by fiscal policy also gave economists a potentially key position at the centre of government" (349).

[40] See Viner (1936) and Hicks (1937).

One of Keynes' colleagues, Richard Kahn (1984), later wrote:

Keynes' insistence on the overwhelming importance of expectations, highly subject to risk and uncertainty, was one of his biggest contributions. This completely undermines the prevalent idea—for which Keynes' attempt at simplification is responsible—that his schedules can be regarded as stable relationships handed down from heaven.

In fact, Keynes seems to have lost interest in the ensuing debate. Skidelsky observes that it took Keynes six months to reply to Hicks, and then diffidently, after receiving the first draft of Hicks' paper. Indeed, both Minsky and Skidelsky suggest that Keynes wrote *The General Theory* to expose the pathology of capitalism, not to suggest a cure through a modification of classical equilibrium theory. With hindsight, the events of the 1970s obviously suggest that Keynes was correct in dismissing the "equilibrating" capability of the eventual "Keynesian" synthesis.

The conclusions that Keynes drew from his own theory have generally been ignored (although not by Minsky). Of particular interest is his insight into the prisoners' dilemma aspect of the economic game, even when there is a supposed equilibrating mechanism—the gold standard—in place.

After a surprising discussion of the theoretical and practical consistency of mercantilism, Keynes (1936) commented

We may criticize them for the apparent indifference with which they accepted this inevitable consequence [the tendency to promote war] of an international monetary system. But intellectually their realism is much preferable to the confused thinking of contemporary advocates of an international fixed gold standard and laissez-faire in international lending who believe that it is precisely these policies which will best promote peace.

[In this gold standard, laissez-faire system] there is no orthodox means open to the authorities for countering unemployment at home except by struggling for an export surplus and an import of the monetary metal at the expense of their neighbours. Never in history was there a method devised of such efficacy for setting each country's advantage at variance with its neighbours' as the international gold ... standard. (349)

In his concluding chapter, Keynes (1936) observed that "authoritarian state systems ... seem to solve the problem of unemployment at the expense of efficiency and of freedom"(381). Against socialism he argued that "it is not the ownership of the instruments of production which it is important for the State to assume" (378). Instead he proposed "a somewhat comprehensive socialization of investment will prove the only means of securing an approximation to full employment" (378).

There were two entirely different solutions to the capitalist quandary as perceived by Keynes in 1936. One was in the direction of "national Self-Sufficiency" as discussed in his paper (Keynes, 1933). The other was toward an "international socialization of investment." These two possibilities must have been on Keynes' mind prior to his participation in the reconfiguration of the post-war Atlantic Constitution at Bretton Woods in 1944.

7.7 THE CONSTITUTIONAL QUANDARY OF 1944

Quandary, a state of extreme perplexity or uncertainty.

Before discussing the attempt to resolve the Depression quandary by the architects of change of 1944, it will be useful to give a more precise view of Keynes' significance for the Atlantic Constitution.

As I have argued in the earlier sections of this chapter, a fully-developed constitution must necessarily relate political and economic rights in the context of a credible theoretical and empirical framework. We might indeed use the term *paradigm* for this framework (Kuhn, 1962). The equilibrium thesis had been of fundamental importance for the constitution since at least the time of Adam Smith. Once the thesis is accepted, then it is credible that political liberty is compatible both with economic liberty and efficiency. If there are strong empirical reasons to deny the equilibrium thesis, then the step to autocracy is fairly easy. Keynes clearly believed that efficiency in exchange could only be maintained in a decentralized economy.[41] From this perspective, autocracy trades efficiency against the risk of the monetary collapse that capitalism seemed to engender. Since a constitution is maintained by credible beliefs, the apparent irrelevance of the equilibrium thesis during the Depression meant that the entire Constitution could fail.[42] However, the equilibrium thesis was deeply embedded in what Keynes termed "habitual modes of thought" and the thesis had proved impossible for policy makers to deny in a fundamental way. As a consequence they could not proceed to attack the problem of unemployment.

---

[41] There was an extensive literature in the 1930s on this proposition, with Oskar Lange (1938) and Michael Kalecki pitted against Ludwig von Mises (1935) and Friedrich von Hayek.

[42] Note that a constitution involves an equilibrium in beliefs, what I call the *core belief*. Just as with asset markets, such a belief equilibrium may crash. I discuss this possibility further in Chapter 8.

It seems fairly clear, on reading the record, that Keynes welcomed Roosevelt's pragmatic attempts to relieve unemployment by various means from 1933 to 1936. It was not obvious in 1936, though it became clear the next year from the U.S. downturn of 1937, that such pragmatic efforts were not guaranteed success. To attack the unemployment quandary, Keynes had to overcome the "barrier" of the conceptual power of the equilibrium thesis. This he did in a sense, by distinguishing commodities markets from "speculative" asset markets. While accepting the relevance of the equilibrium theorem for the former, he denied that it was appropriate for the latter.[43] If the potentially chaotic, speculative characteristic of asset markets could be overcome, say, by "socialization of investment" then both the efficiency of the decentralized commodity market and political freedom could be retained. Thus a modified version of the Atlantic Constitution could be preserved.

My discussion, following Minsky, of the Keynesian interpretations made by Viner and Hicks, suggests how powerful was the Marshallian equilibrium thesis. It appears obvious that the later "Keynesian orthodoxy" was dependent on a version or interpretation of the equilibrium proposition that governments could reimpose full employment equilibrium by appropriate monetary and fiscal strategies.[44]

The vision held out by Keynes differed significantly from the one which derived from the later Keynesian orthodoxy. However, Keynes' conclusions seem not so much to expose the capitalist "pathology" as to suggest that, if the investment quandary could be solved, then capitalism would fade away, and a more equitable economic system evolve. More significantly "there would be no important economic forces calculated to set the interest of one country against that of its neighbors. ... International trade would cease to be what it is ... but [instead become] a willing and unimpeded exchange of goods and services in conditions of mutual advantage" (Keynes, 1936: 382).

---

[43] I have argued in the earlier sections of this chapter that Keynes was correct in this separation. Although a generally applicable equilibrium theorem for commodity markets would not be available until 1956, a weaker version (but one more general than that of Marshallian economic theory) was known in the 1930s. See von Neumann (1945) for the translation of his original paper of 1932 (written in German).

[44] It seems to me that the step by Keynes away from Marshallian equilibrium, followed by the half step back by Viner (1936) and Hicks (1937) resembles the move by Copernicus away from the Ptolemaic planetary orthodoxy toward the heliocentric system. This move was followed by a half a step back by Tycho Brahe (to an incoherent system, where planets orbit the sun, which orbits the earth). See Margolis (1993).

At the cost of "the enlargement of the functions of government [to involve] the task of adjusting to one another, the propensity to consume, and the inducement to invest" (Keynes, 1936: 380), the liberty and efficiency derived from the Atlantic Constitution could not only be preserved but enhanced. The prisoners' dilemma-like characteristics of international economics could be made to disappear. As I have observed previously, our understanding of the international economic system, during the period from 1960 to the end of the 1970s, is that it was indeed an nPD. Because most of the OECD countries during that period utilized principles of neo-Keynesian demand management, either Keynes' vision was wrong, or the theoretical principles underlying the neo-Keynesian synthesis were invalid. The combined evidence from the period suggests the latter hypothesis. This does not, of course, require us to suppose that Keynes was right. It does, however, make it plausible that the Keynesian orthodoxy of the 1950s and 1960s had very little to do with Keynes' vision.

Given that the Atlantic Alliance had been beset by autocratic regimes, which rejected the foundation of the constitution, it was entirely credible in 1944 that general belief in the constitution could indeed "collapse." My reading of the final chapter of *The General Theory* is that Keynes saw the quandary in terms not just of solving the problem of unemployment, but of saving what I call the Atlantic Constitution. For this reason, I use the term the *Constitutional Quandary of 1944* to refer to the problem faced by the architects of change in their attempt to reconstruct the global political economy after World War II.

As we have seen, in the last two chapters of *The General Theory*, Keynes contrasted two differing beliefs about the nature of the international system. The "mercantilist" belief was of a zero-sum world. In pursuing national advantage and relative strength, mercantilists acknowledged the tendency to promote war. In contrast, Marshallian equilibrium theory rejected the relevance of mercantilist belief. Keynes (1936) comments ironically, that "we were brought up to believe that [mercantilism] was little better than nonsense, so absolutely overwhelming and complete has been the domination of the classical school" (335).

Marshallian principles asserted that the rule of the gold standard induced a cooperative characteristic to trade, under which laissez-faire would benefit all nations. Keynes' analysis, and what I have called his chaos hypothesis, led him to the quite different conclusion that trade was not, in fact, a cooperative game, but involved mixed motives. As we have seen above, this game can be considered to be an nPD. The possibility that a hegemon could induce cooperation seems not to have been considered a possibility by Keynes in 1936. By 1944, however, Keynes had developed the idea of an International Clearing Union.[45] If we accept the notion of an *nPD*, then such a union would appear able "to protect national economies from deflationary pressures by providing free access to an international pool of credit" (Block, 1977). We may call this solution "International Keynesianism."

There are two other possibilities that derive from Keynes' thinking, both associated with the notion of "national self-sufficiency." In 1933, Keynes made this famous observation:

Ideas, knowledge, science, hospitality, travel—these are the things which should of their nature be international. But let goods be homespun whenever it is reasonably conveniently possible, and, above all, let finance be primarily national. (758)

Such a recommendation assumes, to some degree, a mercantilist structure to the world. To speculate somewhat, the Sterling Area, and its system of Imperial preference set up in the British Empire after 1933, is compatible with this view. Such a mercantilist world would, in all probability, evolve into blocs, potentially antagonistic. Keynes had also argued in *The General Theory* that if the investment quandary could be solved within each nation, then the mutual advantages of trade could be realized. Such a world need not be mercantilist. These two possibilities for the future I, somewhat clumsily, call "National Mercantilism" and "National Keynesianism."

A fourth non-Keynesian possibility for the future focused on "Hegemonic Internationalism." It was obvious to any observer of world events in 1944 that the interwar era was different from the "golden age" of 1816 to 1910. Although financial crises had occurred with some regularity,[46] the gold system of the nineteenth century had generally seemed to function well. Indeed this fact probably endowed the Marshallian equilibrium thesis with credibility. The one obvious difference between the golden age and 1918 to 1939 was the dominance of Great Britain in the earlier period, and the lack of such a dominant, hegemonic power in the latter (Ferguson, 2001, 2002, 2003). An empirically credible hypothesis, as of 1944, was that the United States could act as hegemonic leader.

---

[45] See the discussion in Harrod (1971).

[46] Kindelberger (1973) mentions nine (in 1816, 1825, 1836, 1847, 1857, 1866, 1873, 1890, and 1907).

A brief digression on the nature of a hegemon is appropriate. The prophets of chaos, who had interpreted the events of the 1970s in terms of an *nPD*, tended to focus on the cooperative benefits of trade. From this point of view, the earlier British hegemony in the nineteenth century was coupled with free trade policy, even though it was a costly exercise, in some respects.

Nye (1991) has reviewed the recent literature from economic history on Britain's role in the nineteenth century and argued, "To the extent that Britain maximized, it was out of the imperatives of narrowly individual economic well-being and without any considerations for ... shaping the international system" (209).

Here he directs his comments to the theorists who seem to suggest that the hegemon guides the international system to cooperation by accepting costs resulting from increasingly open trade. My view of the *nPD* differs from these theorists. I assume that the hegemonic power has a reasonably clear understanding of the game, and realizes that by "cooperating" either in trade, or money, it will realize both short- and medium-term benefits. The medium-term benefits result from the inducements that the hegemon can offer to potential allies. These side-payments are intended to offset the selfish benefits of beggar-thy-neighbor strategies and are paid for out of the hegemon's own gains. A danger for the hegemon is that its potential allies will demand too much. In such a situation, it is not inconceivable that the hegemon can resort to punishment of some kind. By ensuring cooperation from its allies and thus facilitating their economic growth, international trade increases, and all benefit. The long-term problem for the hegemon is the probable decline of its relative power. Whether it is rational in the long-run for the hegemon to pursue this "cooperative" strategy depends both on its beliefs and on its discount rate.

As we know, a version of hegemonic internationalism was, in fact, adopted after World War II, and functioned fairly successfully until about 1965. In the next section I examine why this solution was chosen, and how it meshed with a set of core beliefs that came into being in the immediate post–1944 period in the United States.

7.8   ARCHITECTS OF CHANGE, 1944–1948

Core, possibly from old French, *cors*, body or Italian, *cuore*; French, *coeur*, and Latin, *cor*, the heart.

The story of the post-war decision has been told many times. I depend in large degree on the account by Block (1977) for the period from 1944 to 1948, starting with the disagreement between Secretary of the Treasury, Henry Mongenthau, and Secretary of State, Cordell Hunt, over how to structure the international economy.[47]

Morgenthau's assistant, Henry Dexter White, had, by 1942, already drafted a proposal for an international bank, with capital stock of 10 billion dollars, and a stabilization fund with 5 billion dollars. (In current terms, these amounts are approximately 200 billion and 100 billion dollars, respectively.) The first institution would become the International Bank for Reconstruction and Development (IBRD) and the latter the International Monetary Fund (IMF).

In the negotiations between the United States and Britain, Keynes essentially kept two options open: International Keynesianism as opposed to a form of national mercantilism, involving the maintenance of the system of imperial preference in the sterling area. For the former, he proposed a total of 26 billion dollars, or 520 billion dollars in current terms, for the clearing union, with quotas of the order of 5 billion dollars for Britain, 3 billion dollars for Germany, and 2 billion dollars for France. Members would be entitled to draw a quarter of their quota per year for five years. The Articles of Agreement were drawn up in July 1944 at Bretton Woods. The non-interventionist aspect of the Agreement induced many members of Congress to oppose approval of the fund because of the likelihood that countries could escape monetary discipline. Nonetheless, the Bank started operations in June 1946, with an authorized capital stock of 10 billion dollars.

Before the Bank even started, Franklin D. Roosevelt died (April 1945). President Truman immediately replaced Morgenthau with Fred Vinson. White's influence, and the acceptability of the Treasury's "Keynesian Internationalism," both faded. The State Department wanted to force Britain to open up the sterling bloc to U.S. interests, and, in particular, to oblige sterling to become, once again, fully convertible.

The problem with this aim was the 14 billion dollars of sterling balances held by the member states within the British Empire. The termination of lend/lease and the flow of U.S. capital to Britain obliged the new Labour government (as of June 1945) to deal with a serious balance of payments problem. Keynes, as principal negotiator for Britain, requested 6 billion dollars, but the United States scaled this down to 3.75 billion dollars, and required commitments that the British would open the sterling area.

---

[47] My discussion of the founding of the World Bank and of the Marshall Plan is drawn, with permission, from unpublished work by Imke Kohler (1998).

Legislation would probably have failed in the House of Parliament in December 1945, had not Keynes spoken up for the plan in the Lords. The loan agreement almost failed in the U.S. House of Representatives as well, but passed partly because of the recognition of Britain as an ally against possible Soviet threats in Europe. The French also requested a 4 billion dollar trade credit, which was reduced to 650 million dollars.

At the founding meeting of the IMF in Savannah, Georgia, in March 1946, Keynes had expected that White would be appointed managing director and the fund located in New York. The Americans vetoed White, arguing that both the IMF and the Bank should be guided by people considered to be cautious by the financial community. Eugene Meyer was appointed the first President of the Bank, and Camille Gutt, a former Belgian Finance Minister, was chosen as the Fund's first Managing Director. U.S. voting power in the Bank was particularly pronounced. The United States with a subscription of 41.4 percent had 37 percent of the voting weight, while the second strongest was Britain with about 17 percent of the subscription and 15.3 percent of the voting weight.[48] The Bank's president, Meyer, resigned in December 1946 and a Wall Street lawyer, John McCloy, took over somewhat later in March 1947.

On July 15, 1947, Britain started to move toward convertibility. Some of the U.S. loan had already been used by this time; conversion of sterling to dollars immediately drained the remaining dollars from the British account. The experiment finished on August 21, 1947.

Keynes had died a few weeks after the Savannah meeting in 1946. The third volume of Skidelsky's biography (Skidelsky, 2000) suggests that by 1945 Keynes realized that some form of International Keynesianism could not be brought into existence. On the other hand, it seems that he did believe that protection of British interests, within a framework of National Keynesianism, was viable. The high costs of the British experiment with convertibility would have suggested, however, that international cooperation would have to depend on U.S. capital flows.

The immediate problem facing the European nations was, of course, the terrible destruction of the war. The UNRRA (U.N. Relief and Rehabilitation Administration, set up in November 1943, prior to the founding of the United Nations) had channeled 2.6 billion dollars of U.S. funds, principally to Europe. This institution closed, however, in March 1947. Partly as a result of this aid flow, the U.S. export surplus for 1946 was of

---

[48] The voting weight was computed as follows: Each country had 250 votes (out of 86,000) plus an additional one for each 100,000 dollars invested in the Bank.

the order of 38 billion dollars. This surplus would obviously decline unless some form of capital flow could be organized.[49] Incidents in 1946 in Europe reinforced the views of prominent U.S. policy makers that it would be irrational to provide money to an institution such as the UNRRA.[50] On the other hand, there was much enthusiasm for the recently established United Nations and support for the principle that aid should be channeled through a multilateral agency. Indeed, George Kennan (who moved to the State Department to set up the Policy Planning Staff, in May 1947) has made this point in his memoirs (1976: 338). An offer of aid by the United States, to be channeled through the Economic and Social Council of the United States, was considered in June 1947 by the Foreign Ministers of Britain, France, and the USSR. Russia's Foreign Minister, Molotov, rejected the plan. This implied that aid flow would be directed at Western Europe, (possibly through the OEEC, the Organization of European Economic Cooperation).

The Bank was an obvious, potential channel for the aid flow. This would obviously be more attractive to members of Congress than the UNRRA. However, McCloy, the Bank's president, had declared in early 1947 that if "European recovery required massive new loans, then the American taxpayer [will] have to finance a bilateral program" (Bird, 1992: 292).

In 1947, the Bank did provide a number of loans and credits: 250 million dollars to France in May, 195 million dollars to the Netherlands, in August, and 52 million dollars to Denmark and Luxembourg. An offer in the region of 3.1 billion dollars to the Bank by the United States was turned down by McCloy. In addressing the Bank's Board of Governors, he observed that accepting the loan would have gone against the Bank's

---

[49] Between the second quarter of 1946 and the fourth, overall U.S. aid dropped from 6.5 billion dollars to 4.2 billion dollars. During the same period, the U.S. export surplus in goods and services dropped from 9.9 billion dollars to 7.7 billion dollars. By the third quarter of 1947, when aid had increased to 7.8 billion dollars, the surplus had increased to 10.3 billion dollars. It could be fairly easily deduced that there was almost a linear relationship between aid and surplus. Thus, the initial flow of aid that seemed to be required under a strategy of hegemonic internationalism can be deemed to be rational for the United States in terms of immediate trade consequences.

[50] According to Secretary of State James Byrnes, Czech delegates had applauded a denunciation of the United States by a Soviet official just after the United States had approved a 50 million dollar credit. In his view, there was no point in an institution that the United States funded and yet held only one vote in seventeen. See Byrnes (1947: 143).

international standing, and essentially turned it into a U.S. organization (Kapur, Lewis, and Webb, 1977: 292).

Concerns about the stability of Greece and Turkey in early 1947 contributed to the formulation of the so-called Truman doctrine of March 1947. As President Truman said, "It must be the policy of the United States to support free peoples who are resisting attempted subjugation by armed minorities or by outside pressures."[51]

In conjunction with the Truman proposals, directed against the Soviet Union, it was seen as important to provide substantial aid for reconstruction to Western Europe, as a buttress against communism.[52] However, McCloy, in a speech in New York in April 1947, said that the Bank "can't and won't grant loans in order to accomplish political objectives."

The Bank became a specialized agency of the U.N. on November 15, 1947,[53] and in January 1948, McCloy again declared that the Bank could not be used as a vehicle for massive aid flow, through the ERP (the European Recovery Program) of the Marshall Plan:

[We] would give consideration to [any loan tied to the ERP]. We might, however, not have enough money to meet all of the good hard loans that may be needed, because of my dependence on the market. ... I want to keep emphasizing the fact that we have 46 nations with which to deal, not 16.[54]

The process of approving the ERP speeded up after Czechoslovakia was taken over by the Soviet Union in February 1948. After Marshall's speech in 1947, the Europeans had put in a proposal for 40 billion dollars in aid, which had been reduced to 20 billion dollars (about 360 billion dollars current). The plan was approved on April 3, 1948, and commenced on July 1, 1948. The actual overall aid flow to Europe was, in fact, of the order of 13 billion dollars.

Of the ERP capital flow, from then until 1952, 80 percent was in the form of grants, and the interest rate on loans was about 2.5 percent. In contrast, the Bank depended almost entirely on the market for its capital.

---

[51] President Harry Truman, address delivered before a joint session of Congress, Eightieth Congress, March 12, 1947.

[52] The outlines of the proposed flow of aid to Western Europe were given in a speech by Secretary of State George Marshall at Harvard on June 5, 1947. The whole program became known as the Marshall Plan. For the formulation of this plan by the U.S. architects of change, see Jones (1955).

[53] However, the Bank insisted that it was required "to function as an independent organization." See Mason and Asher (1973).

[54] John McCloy, hearings before the Committee on Foreign Relations (concerning the European Recovery Program), Eightieth Congress, January 16, 1948.

Although the "authorized" capital stock was 10 billion dollars, 80 percent of this was "on call." Of the other 20 percent (2 billion dollars), 1.8 billion dollars was paid in the respective currency of the member country, and 200 million dollars paid in dollars or gold. Since only dollars were convertible, the loanable assets were about 740 billion dollars. In July 1947, the Bank, under McCloy, had issued bonds in the U.S. stock market of 100 million dollars (at an interest rate of 2.25 percent over ten years) and 150 million dollars (3 percent over twenty-five years). These brought total loanable assets to just under 1 billion dollars. Any loans that the Bank could make during the operation of the ERP would clearly be less attractive than Marshall aid or loans. In fact, the Bank loaned only 28 million dollars from 1948–1949 (to Belgium and the Netherlands) although it had earlier made a major loan to France of 250 million dollars.

Although McCloy had supported the ERP during the Congressional Hearings in 1948, he believed by 1949 that the United States should cede the loan component of the Marshall Plan to the Bank. His letter to Truman, making such a case, received no reply from the president.[55] By 1949, McCloy's attempt to preserve something of Keynesian Internationalism had clearly failed. Hegemonic Internationalism, as represented initially by the Marshall Plan, was firmly in place, and was to persist in a strong form through the 1950s. Although the early phase of the strategy required a substantial aid flow to Europe, the significant benefit to the United States, in the form of a large export surplus, is consistent with the analysis of hegemonic behavior in the international economy. A further key element in U.S. strategy was to push for convertibility of currencies. To facilitate this, trade cooperation within the little Europe of the EEC was emphasized. To attempt to stabilize currencies, a dollar–gold standard was adopted, involving devices such as the "snake in the tunnel" (Solomon, 1977: 276).[56]

The strategy of hegemonic internationalism was, in a sense, based on two economic beliefs. First, assuming that convertibility could be attained, then a dollar–gold standard would support economic equilibrium. Second, this equilibrium could be maintained even when member countries utilized internal macroeconomic neo-Keynesian strategies to attain

---

[55] Bird (1992: 299). See also McCloy (1949). In fact, Truman's proposal shortly afterwards, to initiate a U.S. loan program for non-European countries, suggests that McCloy's argument was completely rejected.

[56] The "snake" was the 2.5 percent bound within which the European currencies were allowed to fluctuate, while the "tunnel" was the 5 percent bound restricting fluctuations against the dollar.

full employment. As has been well documented, it became increasingly difficult in the 1960s to maintain this international equilibrium, and by 1971 it was obvious to everyone that the attempt had failed. Keynes' intuitions about the propensity to engage in "beggar-thy-neighbor" strategies were eventually seen to be justified.

For the next ten years, fairly erratic attempts were made to find a new core belief, a theoretical foundation for the stabilization of the international system. As we have seen, such a foundation was eventually put in place in the early 1980s.

It was not inevitable, however, that "hegemonic internationalism" would be the strategy adopted from 1944 to 1948. It is clear from McCloy's argument, both to the Bank's Board and to Truman, that he believed that the Bank could have played a much more important role in restructuring the world economy after 1948. Indeed, McCloy obviously felt that it was important that the Bank remain a multilateral institution, rather than an instrument of U.S. policy. A difficulty for McCloy, of course, was that the resources on which the Bank could draw never exceeded 1 billion dollars, while Marshall aid was of the order of 13 billion dollars. The U.S. policy makers were not inclined to let the ERP resources go to a "multilateral" agency, such as the Bank. However, it is inconceivable that the larger resources of an enhanced IBRD could ever have been used directly against U.S. interests in the way these policy makers feared. There is also no reason to suppose that channeling the aid flow through the Bank would have slowed down the process toward a liberal economic order.

Given McCloy's respectability and familiarity with Wall Street, it is clear that the Bank, under his leadership, could have been the instrument by which private capital was channeled to Europe. Combing both private capital and U.S. aid, under the aegis of the Bank, could have led to a very different international regime. In any case, McCloy did not play a role in the future development of hegemonic internationalism.[57]

It is, of course, impossible to do full justice to the political complexities of the period 1944 to 1948 in a few pages. But one general point is worth making. I have emphasized the two related economic equilibrium hypotheses that underpinned the Bretton Woods system. However, the Marshall aid flow, which was so crucial to the stabilization of the European economies, was acceptable to U.S. policy makers precisely because of

---

[57] McCloy resigned from the presidency of the Bank in 1949 to become high commissioner for Germany (until 1952). He came back from private life (in finance) in 1961 to be Kennedy's advisor.

a political belief in the necessity for "containment" of the Soviet Union. While the Truman doctrine to this effect was first proposed in March 1947, it would appear from George Kennan's memoirs (1976) that his own paper of 1947, "The Sources of Soviet Conduct," had a significant impact on the U.S. interpretation of Soviet intentions (354–67). As I understand Kennan's observations, made in 1967, he regretted that the belief cascade that occurred in 1947 among U.S. policy makers did not allow for the nuanced responses to Soviet actions recommended in his article.

Obviously enough, the strategy of hegemonic internationalism was one solution consistent with both the economic core beliefs, and the containment belief. It is unclear whether a strategy of some kind of Keynesian internationalism would have been possible in the presence of a strongly held belief in "containment." In any case, given the present absence of any obvious threat from an aggressive nuclear power, a vigorous multilateral strategy based on some of Keynes' insights could be relevant in framing a solution to the current international quandary.

7.9 CONCLUDING REMARKS

In the current situation, it is entirely possible that very large volumes of capital will be required in the near future to stabilize the "emerging markets" of the world. One can only guess at the necessary volumes, but a first estimate would be the scale of the initial proposal for Marshall aid flow (about 20 billion dollars in 1948 terms, or about 320 billion dollars currently). Such an amount is easily within the scope of private financial markets. It is evident today that private capital is abundant, but in need of a relatively risk-free haven. The currency turmoil in Southeast Asia and Russia in the late 1990s dramatically increased global financial risk. As a consequence, capital flowed into the U.S. bond, money, and stock markets in the period December 1998 to May 2000. Although the U.S. stock market fell from May 2000 to the re-election of George Bush in November, 2004, because of uncertainty about events in the Middle East, it has risen during 2005. However, the vast, and rapidly growing Federal Budget Deficit and U.S. trade deficit have begun to seem unsustainable at the time of writing (December, 2005).

It seems obvious that a bond market, based on the IBRD, could be established, with a risk-premium of the order of a few percent over and above the U.S. bond rate, in order to stabilize the capital outflows from the "emerging" economies. Risky financial institutions, in Russia, for example, are currently unable to attract capital even at very high interest rates, because potential investors are afraid of potential economic and political chaos there. Thus, there is a pronounced mismatch between the beliefs of holders of capital, even those called *enterprise* by Keynes, and the needs of developing markets. A reconfiguration of the Articles of the World Bank would help resolve this disequilibrium. This is not, of course, to suggest that speculative flows would be completely damped, though the effects could be mitigated.

One of the triggers for the current disequilibrium is the scale of losses in Japanese financial and property markets. This is at least of the order of a trillion dollars. Unfortunately, the Japanese polity is "sclerotic" (for reasons that are obvious from the viewpoint of public choice theory). To free up the Japanese market appears impossible because of the debts and obligations that link corporate and banking entities to the polity. It is probable that these markets will eventually crash completely, bringing down the Japanese political system with them. Such a prospect reminds us of the 1930s. It would be more prudent, perhaps, to bring increasing pressure to bear on the Japanese polity to free itself from these obligations to the corporate world.

A possible solution to the quandary that appears before us could involve a combination of the Keynesian Internationalism based on a Clearing Union, as in the original Bretton Woods scheme, together with the discipline of the market.[58] On the one hand, this resolution might avoid the specter, feared by Keynes, of a global speculative crash. On the other hand, it would be different from the distorted form of the Bretton Woods

---

[58] See Block (1996) for suggestions on how the international economic system might be "weakly regulated" in this fashion. Note that the difficulty on regulation depends on scale, correlation, and the degree of acceptable volatility. Because the dangers at present lie in emerging economies and Japan, it would be prudent to set up an institution of whistle-blowers to provide advance warning of economic or political shocks in such countries. None of the international economic institutions provide such information at present. Moreover, Sobel (1999) suggests that the market itself does not interpret such information efficiently. With greater resources than at present, the clearing union would be able to mitigate the effect of capital flight, when it did occur, more successfully. Because much of the problem of capital flight is due to short-term investment, this could also be mitigated through the use of long-term investment under the aegis of the International Bank for Reconstruction and Development. The purpose of such local strategies would, obviously, be to reduce the degree of contagion, or correlation of economic instability, among a large number of economies. Block estimates that the daily trading volume on international exchange markets is about 1.2 trillion dollars and that 90 percent of this is speculative. Clearly, no reserve fund of plausible size could hope to regulate such a flow. The mechanisms suggested above are intended as devices to decrease the possibility that speculative cascades might occur.

system, namely Hegemonic Internationalism, that Keynes obviously believed would be inadequate to the task of maintaining mutual cooperation in the long run, both within the Atlantic Alliance, and between the developed and less developed economies.

At a more abstract level, the rejection of the strong equilibrium thesis could result in the overthrow of the hegemony of economic theory, and open the way to a more "disordered" family of social, political, and economic subdisciplines that could, paradoxically enough, give a better understanding of, and basis for, the Atlantic Constitution.

8

Preferences and Beliefs

8.1 INTRODUCTION*

The great theorems of social mathematics discovered during the twentieth century can be separated into those that emphasize equilibrium and those that hint at chaos, inconsistency, or irrationality.[1]

The equilibrium results all stem from Brouwer's Fixed Point theorem (Brouwer, 1910): A continuous function from the ball to itself has a fixed point. The theorem has been extended to cover correspondences (Kakutani, 1941) and infinite-dimensional spaces (Fan, 1961) and has proved the fundamental tool in showing the existence of equilibria in games (von Neumann, 1928; Nash, 1950, 1951), in competitive economies (von Neumann, 1945; Arrow and Debreu, 1954; McKenzie, 1959; Arrow and Hahn, 1971), and in coalition polities (Greenberg, 1979; Nakamura, 1979).[2]

The first of the inconsistency results is the Gödel-Turing theorem on the *decidability-halting problem* in logic (Gödel, 1931; Turing, 1937): Any formal logic system (able to encompass arithmetic) will contain propositions whose validity (or truth value) cannot be determined within the

* This chapter is adapted from Norman Schofield, "Equilibrium or Chaos in Preference and Belief Aggregation," in *Competition and Cooperation*, J. Alt, M. Levi, E. Ostrom, [eds]. (Russell Sage Foundation: New York 1999): 32–50, with permission of the Russell Sage Foundation.

[1] The term "social mathematics" was first used by Marie-Jean-Nicolas, Marquis de Condorcet, in 1785 (see MacLean and Hewitt, 1994).
[2] All of these equilibrium results depend on the intuition that a dynamical system (or "vector field") on certain types of spaces (like balls or tori or even-dimensional spheres) must have singularities ("equilibria"). This intuition allows one to develop the mathematics using the qualitative theory of global analysis (Smale, 1973; Mas-Colell, 1985; Schofield, 2003d).

system. Recently this theorem has been used by Penrose (1989, 1994) to argue against Dennett (1991, 1995) that the behavior of the mind cannot be modelled by an algorithmic computing device. A version of the Turing theorem has been used more recently to show that learning and optimization are incompatible features of games (Nachbar, 1997, 2001, 2005). There is still controversy over the meaning of the Gödel theorems, but one interpretation is that mathematical truths may be apprehended even when no formal proof is available (Yourgrau, 1999; Goldstein, 2005).

The second fundamental inconsistency result is Arrow's Impossibility theorem (Arrow, 1950a, 1950b, 1951), which shows that apparently innocuous properties of a social welfare function are sufficient to ensure that it is dictatorial. My reading of these works by Arrow suggests to me that Arrow was concerned not simply with the possibility of voting cycles, nor with the intransitivity of domination in voting games (von Neumann and Morgenstern, 1944). Rather, he was interested in the larger issue of the interaction between the political and economic realms, the topic that concerned the political economists and philosophers such as Schumpeter (1942), von Hayek (1944, 1948), and Popper (1945), in the period around World War II. If I am correct in my inference, in order to understand Arrow's theorem it is necessary to set out the fundamental problem of political economy, namely, the nature and evolution of the social relationship between human beings. To do this, I comment on my perception of the main themes of this debate since the time of Hobbes.

Because I understand this debate to focus on the possibility of equilibrium in contrast to disequilibrium (or disorder), I shall also mention what I judge to be the third significant anti-equilibrium discovery of this century: *chaos*.

Smale (1966) is responsible for the key mathematical result that relates to chaos: Structurally stable dynamic systems are not generic when the underlying space has three or more dimensions.[3] To illustrate, astronomers since the time of Laplace (1798) have believed that the solar system is structurally stable: It was supposed that small perturbations in each planetary orbit (induced by other planets) cannot dramatically change the nature of the orbit. Although Newton was aware of the problem of perturbations (Newton, 1995[1687]), even Poincaré in his treatise of 1890 could not solve the differential equations.[4] However, Poincaré's work in

---

[3] A *structurally stable system* is one that, when perturbed slightly, has identical qualitative properties. *Generic* means "almost all."

[4] See discussion on theories of the solar system in Peterson (1993) and Saari (2005).

celestial mechanics (Poincare, 1993[1892–1899]) led to the beginning of differential topology and the work of Morse, Milnor, and Smale in this century. If the solar system were structurally unstable, or indeed chaotic, then it would be impossible to predict its evolution. It seems indeed that the system is not chaotic, although subsystems (such as asteroids) are.[5] As a result of popular books (Gleick, 1987), we can conceive of natural phenomena (hurricanes) or even large-scale dynamic systems (such as climate) as potentially chaotic (Lorenz, 1993). Although still a young science, human evolutionary theory suggests that chaotic transformations in weather may have had a profound effect on the human diaspora out of Africa (Calvin, 1991; Stanley, 1996; Boaz, 1997). Equilibrium-focused evolutionary theory may also need a revision (Eldredge and Gould, 1972; Gould, 2002).

Many scholars of human society believe that society's evolutionary progress is intelligible, in the sense that predictions, of at least a qualitative form, can be made. This, I presume, is the understanding of economists when they base their reasoning on the fact of equilibrium. Even North (1990, 1994, 2005), in his discussion of economic development, suggests that an understanding of institutions allows us to infer something about the social "laws of motion." Contrary to North's suggestion that institutions are the "rules of the game," it appears to me that institutions are equilibria. If these equilibria are in constant flux, then the dynamic that describes this motion (if indeed there is one) is just as likely to be chaotic as to be structurally stable.

It is, of course, possible that this belief, in the structural stability of society, is sustained by the apparent stability of the "world out there." Indeed, the bipolar world from the late 1940s until about 1990 did appear stable. Since then, the collapse of the Soviet Union, the disintegration of the Warsaw Pact, tumult in the Balkans, genocide and starvation in Africa, the troubles in Israel, all suggest that qualitative change is a permanent characteristic of the world.

To tie the three instability theorems together in a kind of hierarchy, we may start with Penrose's argument that the Gödel-Turing theorem suggests that, at the fine level of analysis, individuals can display surprising, or apparently incomprehensible, behavior. Indeed, it is obvious that cognitive psychology can give only a very coarse-grained account of human motivation. One possible coarse-grained account is that each individual

---

[5] Chaotic phenomena can, of course, have profound consequences. A chaotic event, an asteroid collision, may have led to the extinction of the dinosaurs.

is "approximately" characterized by a preference correspondence (satisfying the usual properties assumed in microeconomics). However, game theory has made it obvious that the *beliefs* of agents are as important as (or even more important than) their *preferences*. Preferences are relatively easy to model, but beliefs are much more complicated. (In fact, they lie in function spaces.) Thus, while it is a standard formal procedure to use a Brouwer Fixed Point theorem to show the existence of optima in preferences, it is much more difficult to postulate conditions under which stable beliefs (a "belief equilibrium") can occur.

Arrow's theorem suggests that, even when individuals can be described by their preferences, only under particular circumstances can these preferences be aggregated to induce a "social vector field" that is "well behaved" in an appropriate sense. This is not to say that the social vector field can never exist; rather, there may be circumstances under which this field is badly behaved (or ill defined) in some sense. Obviously, I am transposing Arrow's theorem from the discrete world where it was located to the continuous world of political economy. By a *social vector field* I mean a method of defining a direction of change compatible with the Pareto unanimity condition. If such a vector field could be defined, then in the usual political economy world (which is compact and convex), Brouwer fixed point arguments would give a singularity (a "social equilibrium"). The field could be badly behaved, for example, if it were not defined in some zone outside the Pareto set. Consequently, following the field would not lead into Pareto preferred outcomes. Arrow's theorem suggests that the only way to avoid such bad behavior is for one individual to be dictator.[6]

Suppose now that Arrow's theorem is avoided by some device. For example, consider a world where everyone has strictly economic preferences and no public goods exist. In such a world, a competitive price equilibrium does exist. However, to attain it, we must imagine a price adjustment process (a vector field) based on excess demand. As an example by Scarf (1960) suggests, this vector field can be cyclic. Indeed, later results by Mantel (1974), Sonnenschein (1972), and Debreu (1974) show that it can be anything at all. As Saari (1991) has emphasized, this economic field could be chaotic.

---

[6] To illustrate, voting mechanisms without vetoers (or collegia) can be badly behaved in the sense that voting trajectories ("following" the social vector field) may lead away from the Pareto set. The social choice chaos theorem basically suggests that this is a generic property when choice is based on preferences alone and the voting rule is non-collegial. See the discussion in Chapters 1 and 2.

This, of course, does not imply that the world is indeed chaotic. Some aspects of the political economic world may be chaotic without implying that the entire human universe is. To use the metaphor of the solar system, perhaps the overall process of human society is structurally stable, but contains locally chaotic subsystems.

To illustrate the idea of chaos, it may be worth a detour to mention von Neumann again, since his work touches on many aspects of social mathematics (as well as other fundamental areas of quantum mechanics, group theory, and so on).

Even before his game theory paper of 1928 and the work on general economic equilibrium (1945), von Neumann had published results on completing Hilbert's program for proving the consistency of classical mathematics by finitary means. A recent biography of Gödel (Dawson, 1997) notes that Gödel presented his inconsistency theorem at Köningsburg in 1930 to an audience that (aside from von Neumann) failed to grasp its significance. As far as I know, von Neumann ceased to work in formal logic after 1930.

Von Neumann met Turing in Cambridge in 1935, and later during Turing's visit to Princeton from 1936 to 1937 (Hodges, 1983), but appears to have paid little attention to Turing's results on the halting problem. However, von Neumann does appear to have made use of Turing's later work on computation during the Second World War, as well as Turing's essay on artificial intelligence (Turing, 1950). Beginning in 1943, von Neumann was involved in approximate numeric solutions using some form of computing device. Turing's notion of a universal machine seems to have been indispensable to the design of British and American decoding devices during the war and to the construction of the computation machines (Edvac, Eniac, Maniac) necessary for the solution of nonlinear dynamical problems associated with the design of the hydrogen bomb (see Ulam and von Neumann, 1947). Von Neumann took Turing's idea of a universal computing device and extended it to a model of the brain (von Neumann, 1958) and of life (self-reproducing automata) in work later edited by Burks (von Neumann, 1966).

What is interesting about this research is that Ulam, von Neumann's collaborator, had found chaos in a stochastic, or Monte Carlo, simulation of a relatively simple dynamical system (Fermi, Pasta, and Ulam, 1955). As far as I know, this is the first example of a computational model generating chaos. (It predates Lorenz's meteorology simulation by seven years.) Monte Carlo simulation by von Neumann and his associates in numerical weather prediction and in their work on the bomb does not appear to have observed chaos (Galison, 1997).

In von Neumann's book with Morgenstern (1944) on cooperative game theory, the focus (as I understand it) is on trying to "equilibriate" the obvious cyclicity inherent in constant-sum voting games, using such devices as the von Neumann-Morgenstern solution. Later work in cooperative game theory also attempted to introduce equilibrium ideas (such as the bargaining set; see Aumann and Maschler, 1964). These attempts seem unsatisfactory, and this may be why cooperative game theory is currently less influential than noncooperative game theory (and the powerful notion of Nash equilibrium).

These observations about chaos bring us back to the argument by Penrose (1989) that the indeterminacy of the quantum world implies that the mind is non-algorithmic (see also Popper, 1972, and Popper and Eccles, 1977). The connection between the quantum world and the world of the mind may be somewhat tenuous: Nevertheless, Penrose's argument that the mind is not like a computer is very powerful. More important, the recent extension of Gödel's argument by Nachbar (1997, 2005) suggests that to play a "game" successfully each agent must already know an impossible amount about every other agent playing the game. In particular, "algorithmic" agents cannot learn enough about the other agents as the game progresses.

This is not to deny that computers can play games; but I do deny that people play games like computers (see also Searle, 1999, for a similar argument). More generally, I would say that the kinds of games people play are like poker rather than chess. Predicting how people will play the game of life is well nigh impossible. Although each of us can gain some insight into the minds of other people, and may thus believe we understand something of the social world around us, we can never fully understand the acts of our fellows. As Arrow (1973: 262) wrote (though in a somewhat different context than considered here):

> To the extent that individuals really are individual, each an autonomous end in himself, to that extent they must be somewhat mysterious and inaccessible to one another, there cannot be any rule that is completely acceptable to all. There must be, or so it seems to me, the possibility of inadjudicable conflict.

However, to live in society, we do have to understand one another. The next few sections will attempt to see how we can model this interaction.

8.2 HOBBESIAN AND LOCKEAN VIEWS OF SOCIETY

Hobbes returned to the England of the Protectorate in December 1652, ten years after his departure, three years after the execution of Charles I, and a few months after the publication of *Leviathan*. Hobbes's biographer, Rogow (1986), quotes sources suggesting that during Hobbes's meeting with Galileo in Florence from 1635 to 1636, "Galileo gave Hobbes ... the first idea that the doctrine of ethics ... can be brought to a mathematical certainty by applying the principles of geometry" (109).

As MacPherson (1968) says in his introduction to *Leviathan*:

The resolutive part of Galileo's method was an exercise in imagination. What simple motions or forces could be imagined which, when logically compounded, would provide a causal explanation of the complex phenomenon which was to be explained? ... The resolutive stage ... consisted in resolving political society into the motion of its parts—individual human beings. (26)

Although it is the appetites and aversions that move men, the effect is a "generall inclination of mankind, a perpetuall and restless desire of Power after power, that ceaseth only in Death. ... It is manifest, that during the time men live without a common Power to keep them all in awe, they are in that condition which is called Warre. ... And the life of man [is] solitary, poore, nasty, brutish and short" (Hobbes, 1968: 185).

Hobbes goes on to discuss the nature of contract or "Covenant":

If a Covenant be made ... in the condition of meer Nature ... it is Voyd; But if there be a common Power set over them both, ... it is not Voyd. ... But when a Covenant is made, then to break it is Unjust. ... A multitude of men, are made One person, when they are by one man, or one Person, Represented ... And if the Representative consist of many men, the voyce of the greatest number, must be considered as the voyce of them all. (220)

On the form of the commonwealth, whether monarchy, democracy, or aristocracy, Hobbes suggests that the difference is not in power, but in "Convenience, or Aptitude to produce the Peace, and Security of the People" (241).

In chapter 18, Hobbes compares the benefits of life in the commonwealth with "the miseries, and horrible calamities, that accompany a Civill Warre" (238).

In chapter 24, he discusses the economy of the commonwealth—the distribution of land, the nature of taxes, and, most important, the role of money, the Sanguinification of the Commonwealth. In this chapter, Hobbes refers again to his somewhat shocking metaphor: "For by Art is created that great Leviathan called a Common-wealth, or State ... which is but an Artificiall Man" (81).

Many political theorists of the recent past (Taylor, 1976, 1982; Sugden, 1980; Axelrod, 1984) have interpreted Hobbes's argument for Leviathan in terms of the prisoners' dilemma. That is, the state of nature, of "Warre," is the Nash equilibrium (indeed, the joint dominant strategy in the game). All players prefer the state of cooperation, of peace, but it is unattainable without a covenant. The arguments have often proceeded to suggest that the "game form" is that of an n-person-iterated prisoners' dilemma. In such a game, cooperative equilibria may be possible if they are sustained by appropriate beliefs on the part of the agents. Much of the work of these theorists can be seen as an extension of Nozick's famous book *Anarchy, State, and Utopia* (1974) to argue, *contra* Hobbes, that the state (Leviathan) is unnecessary for security. For example, Sugden argues that "conventions" (such as language, or driving on one side of the road) arise spontaneously as solutions to games of coordination and cooperation. But if we think of language as a convention, then it is obvious enough that it evolves quite rapidly. In Papua New Guinea, where human settlements are geographically separate, the evolving languages became extraordinarily diverse. (In fact, it has been estimated that there are about one thousand distinct languages, clustered in thirty phyla, among a population of about four million.) Although there may be some validity in Taylor's (1982) argument that "community" can indeed sustain cooperation in the absence of a Hobbesian Leviathan, or state, the argument works only for small communities. Arrovian disorder between such communities would appear to be generic.[7] Moreover, the evolution of the "equilibria" of these cooperative conventions would seem to be as indeterminate as the formal models of n-person-iterated prisoners' dilemmas (Kreps et al., 1982). I return to this later when discussing "belief equilibria."

Locke's *Two Treatises of Government* was published anonymously in 1690. This work is often taken as a response to both the Glorious Revolution of 1688 and Hobbes's *Leviathan*. However, Laslett (1988), in his introduction to the *Treatises*, suggests that they were written approximately

---

[7] Just to give an example, Greif (1997) has analyzed the pattern of behavior in twelfth- and thirteenth-century Genoa. In the absence of an outside threat (the Holy Roman Emperor), Genoa collapsed into a thirty-year civil war. By "chance" the city adopted the idea of a *podesta*, a paid pivotal "Leviathan," with whom the Genoese families made a covenant. From 1190 to 1300, Genoa was able to engage extensively in trade with the countries of the western Mediterranean.

ten years earlier in response to Filmer's essays, *The Natural Power of Kings Defended against the Unnatural Liberty of the People* (1632) and *Observations Concerning the Origins of Government* (1652). In the second treatise, Locke (1988 [1690]) develops further the notion of a contract but seems to remove the almost metaphysical Hobbesian conception of Leviathan.

And Thus every Man, by consenting with others to make one Body Politik under one Government, puts himself under an Obligation to every one of that Society, to submit to the determination of the majority ... For if the consent of the majority shall not in reason, be received, as the act of the whole ... nothing but the consent of every individual can make anything to be the act of the whole: But such a consent is next to impossible to be had. (97)

Locke's version of the compact has obviously strongly influenced the twentieth-century contractarian visions of Rawls (1972), Gauthier (1986) and particularly Nozick (1974). For Nozick, property (and especially labor) is a fundamental feature of Lockean liberty. Nozick constructs what has been called a *meta-utopian framework* (Gray, 1984), within which free individuals migrate to preferred communities, agree on public provision, and live in peace. The formal underpinning of this framework is that of the "core," the set of allocations that are coalitionally rational. But the conditions sufficient for the existence of a core (balancedness, "private" preferences, and so on) are likely to occur only in pure private goods economies. If power is a feature of the Nozickean political economy then the appropriate formal model is not the exchange economy but the constant-sum game. In such a world, the core is generically empty, and cycles or Arrovian intransitivities are pervasive. Nozick's anarchic utopia is thus void.

Gray goes on to describe von Hayek's (1944, 1948, 1973, 1978) meta-utopian framework in terms of the idea of "a spontaneous order, of self-organizing and self-replicating structures [that] arise without design or even the possibility of design."

This framework is based on the inference that

unhampered markets display a tendency to equilibrium ... (In a world of constantly changing beliefs and preferences, of course, equilibrium is never achieved, but is to be viewed as a[n] ... asymptote). ... We find the spontaneous formation of self-regulating structures in the growth of language, [in] the development of law and in the emergence of moral norms.

(Gray, 1984: 31)

Although Gray sees Hayek's ideas as Humean, *contra* Hobbes's "constructivist rationalism," it seems to me that the Hayekian vision of how social order comes into being is very similar to that of the Hobbesian Leviathan. Although the order is not based on a covenant and may not be intelligible to human analysis, it would seem to have an "artificiall life."

Somehow the beliefs of the members of society are "aggregated" in such a way as to generate the motion of this Leviathan. In an attempt to determine whether Hayek's view of order has theoretical justification, the next section extends the Arrovian notion of preference aggregation to that of "aggregation of beliefs."

8.3 CONDORCET AND SOCIAL TRUTH

As I intimated earlier, the Galilean logic of motion was developed by Newton to formally relate matter, motion and space, first in his article "Light and Colours" (Newton, 1984 [1672], then in *Principia* (1687) and finally in *Opticks* (1704). Voltaire's volume *Newton's Philosophy* (1738) helped transmit Newton's underlying philosophy of science throughout Europe. Part of Newton's argument was against the "light of Reason" of Descartes' *Discourse on Method* (1637) and for the "light of Nature"— that is, to follow the injunction to reason from the world, to find its underlying principles. It is hardly surprising that Newton's awesome achievement in natural science sparked attempts by scholars, particularly in Britain and France, to construct a calculus of the moral or human sciences.[8]

Although Adam Smith was probably influenced by the French scholars Mandeville, Condillac, Cantillon, and Anne-Robert-Jacques Turgot, it is Smith's work in moral philosophy and political economy that is par-

---

[8] For a discussion of the influence of Newton's philosophy in Europe, and Voltaire's contribution to this influence see Feingold (2004).

The work in the moral and human sciences could include the following:

Mandeville, *Fable of the Bees; or Private Vices, Publick Benefits* (1924 [1714]).

Cantillon, *Essay on the Nature of Commerce in General* (1755).

Hume, *Essays Moral, Political, and Literary* (1985 [1742, revised edition 1748]).

Condillac, *Essay on the Origin of Human Knowledge* (1746).

Jean-Jacques Rousseau, *The Social Contract* (1762).

Anne-Robert-Jacques Turgot, *Reflections on the Formation and Distribution of Wealth* (1766).

Adam Smith, *Theory of Moral Sentiments* (1758) and *Wealth of Nations* (1776).

See the discussion in Rothbard (1995), Israel (2001), and Buchan (2003).

A recent study by Rothschild (2001) has examined the ideas of and connection between Adam Smith and Condorcet.

ticularly remembered. However, I wish to focus not on Smith but on Condorcet (born 1743). As far as I know, Condorcet was viewed (and is generally still regarded) as a utopian theorist of little interest other than as providing provocation for Thomas Malthus' *Essay on the Principle of Population* (1798).

Condorcet, a protégé and friend of Turgot, was certainly influenced by him and by Adam Smith, whom he met in Paris in 1766. The debt to Smith is most evident in Condorcet's *Esquisse d'un tableau historique des progrès de l'ésprit humain* (edited by Condorcet's widow, Sophie, and published posthumously in 1795). The influence of this work and of the Jury theorem (Condorcet, 1994 [1785]) on Madison and Jefferson, has already been discussed in Chapter 4. This theorem was part of Condorcet's attempt to construct a grand theory of human behavior, based on collective choice by a society in the presence of risk. Assuming that there is an external truth (a best choice out of the two alternatives), and supposing that each individual chooses the truth with probability at least one-half, then majority rule will be correct more often than the average juror. Moreover, as the jury increases in size, the probability that it will attain the truth approaches unity. The theorem assumes that voters are (pairwise) independent in their choices. As might be expected, however, if the average pairwise correlation between voter choices is low, then the theorem still holds (Ladha, 1992, 1993; Ladha and Miller, 1996). Moreover, it is not necessary to assume that each voter is described by a probability greater than one-half; a sufficient condition for the theorem is that the average probability exceeds one-half (Boland, 1989).

As Condorcet's biographers (Baker, 1975; McLean and Hewitt, 1994) have observed, Condorcet believed not in the notion of the "general will" (as had Rousseau), but in the possibility of the exercise of reason. In particular, he believed that political representatives would exercise their judgments (or beliefs) and be less swayed by the passions (or preferences) than would a mass of voters. In the years following the calling of the Estates-General (1789), he was active as president of the French Legislative Assembly, as a member of the National Convention (1792), and as the architect of the "Girondin Constitution" of 1793. Prior to the trial of the King, Louis XVI, Condorcet had struggled to institute a constitutional monarchy, and during the trial (in January 1793), he spoke at length against capital punishment. Chapter 4 has already observed that, with the expulsion of the Girondins in the Jacobin Terror in 1794, Condorcet was pursued to his death.

Although historians of the period typically emphasize the Lockean ideals implicit in the beliefs of Jefferson,[9] the evidence presented in Chapter 4 suggests that the influence of Condorcet on the Constitution of the United States was profound. The argument presented there is that Madison's "theorem" in *Federalist X* rests on the postulate that belief heterogeneity is likely to result in choices that are for the public good. Of course, Condorcet's Jury theorem is only valid for voting in binary decisions. He was unable to extend the theorem to three or more choices, and indeed, in attempting to so extend the theorem, he discovered the possibility of voting cycles. If we consider voting in terms of aggregation of preference, then not only will an equilibrium generally fail to exist (Black, 1958; Plott, 1967), but the resulting cycles may fill the entire "policy space." As suggested above, this voting indeterminacy may reasonably be considered to be chaotic. Although these spatial voting theorems and Arrow's Impossibility theorem are formally distinct, they do suggest that the greater the degree of preference heterogeneity, the more likely that the method of preference aggregation will be chaotic. In contrast, if political and economic decision making should properly be viewed as *belief* aggregation, rather than as *preference* aggregation, and if the Madisonian postulate is justified, then we may infer instead that these processes will be well behaved in some sense.

There have been attempts to develop models of "belief aggregation" in economics (Aumann, 1976; Geanakoplos and Polemarchakis, 1982; McKelvey and Page, 1986), and Arrow (1986) has recently commented on these in the context of market behavior. These models are conceptually related to Condorcet's Jury theorem, and can be seen as attempts to determine those conditions under which belief convergence occurs. The basic construction is one in which individuals, each with his or her own prior and private information, together generate a statistic (essentially a price vector). If the model that each individual employs is common knowledge, then every individual can compute a posterior belief on the basis of reasonable inferences about the nature of the other individuals' private information. After a few rounds, these posterior beliefs (or subjective probabilities) converge.

---

[9] The terms used by Jefferson in, for example, *The Draft Constitution for Virginia* (June 1776) to describe George III and his "detestable and insupportable tyranny" (Peterson, 1984: 336) are similar to expressions used by Locke in his *Two Treatises* of 1690.

As Arrow (1986) has observed, however, this result does depend on seemingly very strong common knowledge assumptions. To illustrate, consider agents in a typical market trading assets of some kind. Unlike the standard picture of an exchange economy, the agents cannot really be said to have preferences for the assets. Whether one wishes to buy or sell an asset depends not so much on current prices as on expectations (beliefs) about the probable behavior of the prices. But these beliefs, of course, are determined by the agents' interpretation of the other agents' beliefs. In other words, unlike the Aumann problem, (which deals essentially with nature), this market is a game between rational actors. Formally analyzing such a game requires us to model the mental processes and strategic behavior of each agent. Nachbar's theorem (1997, 2005) implies that each agent (in a symmetric game) will adopt strategies that the agent believes cannot be adopted by the other players.

Of course, this interpretation of the game may be denied. That is, it could be argued that this market should be viewed as a decision-theoretic problem, in which each agent plays against nature and attempts to guess (statistically) how this nature behaves. This argument is based on the assumption that the world is Gaussian, with stochastic events obeying a law of large numbers, derived from the normal distribution. This may be an invalid assumption (Mandelbrot and Hudson, 2004). Indeed, Arrow (1986) suggests that the presumed advantage of markets (that they are effective decentralized methods of aggregating beliefs and preferences) rests on an unreasonable assumption: For the market to work, each agent must have (at least approximately) a model of every other agent's thought processes and a general economic equilibrium calculator to integrate everything.

If we suppose instead that each individual responds, in a "game-theoretic" fashion, to the overall behavior of the market, then it seems plausible that the aggregate behavior of the market could be indeterminate. Analyses of much simpler models of collective behavior (Bikhchandani, Hirschleifer, and Welch 1992; Huberman and Glance, 1995) have found complex bifurcations and cascades.

In his recent comments on the research carried out on complex systems at the Santa Fe Institute, Arrow (1988) has observed that markets appear to have both homeostatic and chaotic features.

Equilibrium Theory would tend to suggest that as technology spreads throughout the world, the per capita national incomes would tend to converge, but any such tendency is very weak indeed. ... Instead of stochastic steady states, we observe that volatility tends to vary greatly over time, quiescent eras with little

Figure 8.1. A hierarchy of models.

period-by-period fluctuations alternating with eras of rapid fluctuations. ... These empirical results have given greater impetus to the closer study of dynamic models and the emphasis on application of new results on non-linear dynamic models. They have also given rise to criticism of the models themselves, and this goes far back; it suffices to mention the alternative theories of J. M. Keynes. (278)

Some of the work being carried out under the auspices of the Santa Fe Institute (Holland, 1988; Kauffman, 1993, 1995) emphasizes the notion of complexity, of chaos generating order. These concepts are perhaps influenced by the work of Prigogine (1980) in the physical sciences; and before him by the ideas of von Neumann (1966). As I suggested earlier, there appears to be a connection between the ideas of "order out of chaos" and the non-mathematical, neo-Hobbesian views of Hayek. These recent ideas about complexity are of very general applicability, and in a later section of this chapter I discuss them in the context of some of the abstract models of the world that we have been considering.

8.4   SCIENTIFIC TRUTH

Paradigm, from the Greek, $\pi\alpha\rho\alpha\delta\varepsilon\acute{\iota}\gamma\mu\alpha$, "pattern"

Figure 8.1 suggests how to relate the models of the world that we have been discussing. Newton's laws framed the first formal, mathematical model of "the world of the large"—the interaction of matter in space. The development of mathematics to deal with this world led to the new insights in differential geometry and topology of Poincaré, Smale, and others that we have discussed. This in turn led to the Brouwer Fixed Point theorem and the various applications in economic theory. For convenience, we can view this general class of game-theoretic models of "the social world" as belonging to the von Neumann research program. The focus of this program is to describe the interaction of individuals who are fundamentally described by "preferences," "utilities," and so on.

Game theory has been influenced by, and in turn has influenced, research in the Darwinian or evolutionary research program focused on "the biological world." The idea of "fitness" in the Darwinian research program is much like that of utility or preference, and the notion of the game-theoretic equilibrium has been modified to that of the "evolutionary stable strategy."

One might view Popper's work in the philosophy of science as being concerned with evolutionary models of knowledge or beliefs. As Popper (1972) has written: "[T]he growth of our knowledge is the result of a process closely resembling what Darwin called 'natural selection'; that is the natural selection of hypotheses" (261). In other words, Popper was concerned about how individuals form beliefs about the world, how they test these hypotheses, and how these beliefs "compete" with one another through their ability to describe the world. The more recent and related work of Aumann and others suggests that this process "converges to the truth."

Figure 8.1 distinguishes between the Popperian and Condorcetian research programs because I judge there to be an important difference between the two. Condorcet was interested in collective choice in an uncertain world: Once individuals have formed their judgments, how could these differing beliefs be aggregated in a "rational" fashion?

It seems clear that Arrow, in his *Social Choice and Individual Values* (1951) and his two earlier papers (Arrow 1950a, 1950b), was also interested in the collective aggregation of values rather than simply tastes or preferences. However, the formal structure that he imposed on values was that of transitivity—a property natural to preferences.[10] I thus distinguish between the Condorcetian and Arrovian research programs. As I have argued above, the importance of Arrow's Impossibility theorem is that it suggests that disorder of some kind is a real possibility. In this, it is very different from the orientation of the three other research programs in Figure 8.1 (von Neumann, Popper, and Condorcet), which also attempt to structure the social world. It seems to me that Arrow gave the first formal

---

[10] One way to demonstrate Arrow's theorem (Kirman and Sondermann, 1972) is to show that "order" requires that the family of all decisive coalitions of agents be an "ultrafilter" (namely, a family with a single dictator in common).

demonstration of the possibility of social disorder of the kind hinted at earlier in the work of Keynes (1936) and Schumpeter (1942).

To grapple with these themes of order and disorder, it may be worth-while to consider the context within which Keynes, Schumpeter, Hayek, and Popper formulated their key ideas. Clearly the terrible political and economic events of the 1930s must have influenced their work. Chapter 7 interpreted Keynes's argument (Keynes, 1936) to mean that, under certain conditions, a belief equilibrium can come into being that (contrary to the general equilibrium economic model) sustains high levels of unemployment and low levels of economic activity. Only the state, acting as Leviathan, can change the belief equilibrium to the advantage of all members of the society. Schumpeter (1942) wrote about the waves of technological innovations and business cycles that can engulf the economy. With reason, we may interpret these cycles of economic activity as chaotic belief cascades.

In contrast, Popper (1945) saw democracy as an "optimal" institution that was compatible with open competition in ideas and beliefs. In the same way, he suggested that scientific development follows a process of natural selection that is "truth seeking." Von Hayek (1948), in a somewhat similar way, saw markets as "truth seeking" in their ability to generate and aggregate information efficiently. Out of competition in the market and polity come stable institutions. As the discussion in Chapter 7 emphasized, Keynes had first to overcome a "core belief" in the existence of general economic equilibrium.

This notion of a "core belief" has been raised a number of times in this book. To try to express what I mean by this, it is worth illustrating the concept by way of a consideration of Einstein's "annus mirabilis" of 1905.

Einstein's Annus Mirabilis

In 1905, Einstein published three papers entitled "On the Electrodynamics of Moving Bodies," "On a Heuristic Viewpoint Concerning the Production and Transformation of Light," "Does the Inertia of a Body Depend on its Energy Content?" as well as a fourth, "On the Motion of Small Particles," on Brownian motion, all in *Annalen der Physik* (French, 1979; Calaprice, 2005). These papers are seen by philosophers of science as truly constituting a scientific revolution. To write them, indeed to conceive of the ideas that they express, Einstein had to deny the profound conceptual assumption that time and space are absolute (in fact that there is an "aether" in which light takes its wave-like form). It is well known that Einstein was able to do this by thought experiments that were unique to his imagination. It is also possible that the pathway to the insight came from Einstein's realization that Maxwell's field equations were not invariant under transformation of a certain kind. The insight led both to special relativity and the quantum theory. Feyerabend (1970, 1975) has provided a very interesting discussion of the state of affairs before 1905, which I contrast with post-1905, in order to articulate some notions about belief cascades.

According to Feyerabend, there were three different and mutually incompatible "paradigms" in the nineteenth century physics: mechanics, electrodynamics, and heat. Let us refer to these as schools, or research programs, rather than as paradigms. Each of these schools had its own well-developed theoretical framework (of beliefs), and, as Feyerabend emphasizes, they interacted in an essentially "anarchic" fashion. Indeed, Feyerabend has asserted, "Science is an essentially anarchic enterprise." To see what this may mean, we may conceive of the "scientific heart" of a set of research programs as the combination of all conceivable activity spanned by the dominant beliefs in the three schools. Activity can be disordered ("anarchic") within this set. We may think of voting as a metaphor for the interaction of the schools. In this case it is not true that "anything can happen," though it will be true that certain features of one program will be unintelligible to other programs. But certain beliefs common to all schools will generate boundaries to what is conceivable, and these boundaries will condition behavior. The heart then is the set of activities, together with the supporting beliefs, generated by the boundaries. In sum, anything *inside* the heart is possible.

There was a "core belief" within nineteenth century science, that comprised the agreed-on commonalities held by all of the three schools: the belief in absolute time and space. This "core belief," of course, made sense within each of the separate "paradigms" of the three schools.

Prior to 1905, however, both Lorentz and Poincare had suspected the existence of a "quandary," in a scientific sense, on the relationship between mechanics and electrodynamics. By overcoming the barrier of the assumption of absolute time and space, Einstein created a full-fledged quandary.[11] Eventually, it was realized that the rejection of this core

---

[11] It is also worth mentioning that many years later, Einstein and Gödel became close friends at the Institute for Advanced Study at Princeton and continued discussing solutions of the model of general relativity "without time." See Yourgrau (1999, 2005).

belief transformed the configuration, or "heart," of nineteenth century physics.

In our own time, there have been numerous attempts to create a new core belief, by integrating quantized forces with electromagnetism, and more recently with gravitation. The search for "a theory of everything" can be seen to be motivated by a non-scientific, aesthetic *belief* that there is indeed some conceptual resolution, some core belief, underlying the various schools within physics. The cascade initiated in 1905 is still underway. Local core beliefs, such as those derived from the integration of the weak nuclear force and electrodynamics, have been constructed, but at present the "general scientific core" is empty. The "scientific heart" is the evolving configuration of scientific activities generated by the family of local core beliefs.

8.5 CORE BELIEFS AND THE HEART

As discussed in Chapter 7, there is good reason to accept the validity of the Arrow-Debreu theorem on existence and Pareto optimality of economic equilibrium, but only for markets involving commodities, factors, and well-specified preferences. Since the theorem has been extended to economies that may be infinite-dimensional, it can incorporate time-denominated preferences (Zame, 1987). Beliefs, however, are not preferences. As Keynes noted, if agents in the market engage in enterprise, then they value assets in terms of "real" economic data. They are characterized by preferences (possibly even in an infinite dimensional space) and we may trust in existence of an equilibrium. However, a speculator forms beliefs about the preferences, and choices, of others. Implicitly the speculator assumes that "he" is different from (almost all) other agents in the market. As Keynes argued, with a preponderance of enterprise, speculators cause no severe problems for the existence of equilibrium. Suppose, however, that there is a preponderance of speculators: Each one must predict the others' actions, and act in a way different from them. Consider the situation when a speculator fears that the market may fall; he wants to escape before the others, so his belief is that he is different in kind from the others. But all speculators are identical in this regard. The speculator must reason that his state of mind cannot be a part of belief equilibrium, since it is not credible that he is indeed different from other speculators, assuming private information is of no help. Keynes saw this intuitively, but gave no formal proof. A proof, at least of a version of the hypothesis, is given in the theorem, mentioned above due to Nachbar (1997, 2005).

To see the problem, consider a game, such as "scissors, paper, stone," involving two players. With equally valued wins and losses, the Nash equilibrium is for each player to randomize with probability one-third to each strategy. An enterprising agent may play thus and gain zero in expectation. In the iterated version, a speculator attempts to win by forecasting, by learning his opponents' strategy. If his opponent bases his calculations on "enterprise," to use Keynes's term, there is little the speculator can do but to randomize. With two speculators, the game changes. Player A attempts to learn whatever Player B is doing, and realizes Player B is probably trying to learn what Player A is doing. The infinite regress does not close. Although the theorem was suspected earlier, Nachbar's result appears to be relevant for a very large class of games.

Two empirical questions are obvious. What ratio of speculators to enterprisers, in a particular situation, is compatible with equilibrium? In a complex international asset market, can the "socialization of investment" at some level available to government, or an international institution, induce stability?

There is clearly an even more general question. My notion of the "heart of a constitution" incorporates an implicit set of "core beliefs." If we accept Keynes' chaos hypothesis for asset markets, why not accept it for a constitution? While it is true that the world of a constitution is generally not composed entirely of "speculators,"it is also evident, however, that very different beliefs may "populate" a constitution.

Throughout this book I have used the term *core belief* to refer to whatever belief is in equilibrium, or is collectively agreed upon (in some appropriate social choice sense) by the members of the community. If there is a clear discord between the essential beliefs of the constitution, and some empirical aspect of reality, then some of the members of the society may be forced to change their beliefs. If others observe the effects of a small number switching beliefs, then (acting as rational Bayesians) their propensity to change beliefs will increase. Thus, what I have termed a *cascade* can be generated. The conditions under which the cascade can destroy the previous core belief are unclear and may indeed be unknowable.

To gain some inkling into the stability of a core belief of a constitution, consider again the notion of a competitive equilibrium in a market. This is simply a state of the world that cannot be changed to anyone's advantage by trade. It depends, of course, on the price equilibrium (of which there may be many). Such an equilibrium is associated with "stable" states of mind, or beliefs, by the participants (Hahn, 1973). A more abstract idea of an equilibrium, but one which does not involve prices, is that of the core of an economy (the set of unbeaten commodity allocations). Under certain assumptions, the core of an exchange economy will be nonempty (and will include the competitive equilibrium). Unfortunately, for more general cooperative games, such as voting, the core (the set of unbeaten outcomes) is generically empty. However, it is possible to extend the notion of the core to a more general object that I have called the *heart*.

The mathematical object, the heart, has been shown to be always nonempty and to be continuous under certain circumstances (such as "convexity" of preferences), in the rules of the "game." The framework utilized is one in which agents are characterized by preferences and there is some particular social choice rule, such as voting. It was this notion that was described in Figure 2.3, and generated by the particular voting rule in use. However, the formal construct is abstract enough to be relevant in the more general context of beliefs, and very general social choice rules. In the world, however, beliefs need not be "convex." An individual may hold two conflicting views, assigning to each differing probabilities of truth, or indeed, as Keynes noted, may be completely uncertain. Because of the failure of convexity, the heart can fail continuity at certain configurations of beliefs. By analogy with dynamic systems, the failure of continuity is called a *catastrophe*. A cascade is precisely the *catastrophic* change from one heart configuration to a completely different one. This very simple notion of a "catastrophic cascade" is adapted from Zeeman's earlier ideas (Zeeman, 1974). However, the extension of the idea that I have proposed is made in the attempt to include more general transformations than those considered by Zeeman.

The abstract object that I call a heart may not, in fact, be an "equilibrium," if by this we mean that it is associated with unchanging beliefs and constant behavior on the part of the members of the society. However, the heart is defined by certain boundaries in the domains of beliefs and actions. An important feature of the heart is that when the equilibrium or core is, in fact, nonempty, then the heart and core coincide. On the other hand, when the core is empty, then behavioral "cycles" are certainly possible inside the heart. In normal circumstances, such cycles need not prove destructive to fundamental belief coherence in the constitution. As I have throughout this book, I use the term *core belief* to refer to the set of collective beliefs that are mutually compatible within the community. Under the circumstance of a catastrophe, the core belief may disappear.

The heart of the constitution is the complex pattern of belief and actions, all of which are individually rational with respect to empirical reality, and tenable, according to the ideological attitudes of the members of the community. It is defined by certain barriers, or boundaries, to belief, cognition, and behavior. What I have termed the *chaos hypothesis* (my interpretation of Keynes' key insight), was a device by Keynes to overcome a belief barrier that prevented his understanding of the Depression. The discussion in Chapter 7 was meant to show that Keynes' insight made accessible a number of different possible "constitutional hearts." One of these eventually came into focus in the period after World War II, and the evolution of the Atlantic Constitution can generally be regarded as continuous since that time.

The fundamental problem of political economy, as I see it, is to obtain a general understanding of how a core belief, or more properly the heart of the constitution, transmutes itself through a cascade to a new configuration. The various analyses of quandaries that have been undertaken recently have provided a number of interesting examples of such cascades. The work by Margolis (1987) on the evolution of research programs, as well as insight into the interaction of shared mental models, ideologies, and institutions are obviously important (Denzau and North, 1994).

As I have suggested by the discussion of Einstein's work, a belief component of the heart may be considered to be an essential aspect of a paradigm (Kuhn, 1962). The collapse of such a component has some of the features of a scientific revolution. To escape or resolve a scientific or constitutional quandary may involve overcoming a conceptual barrier (such as the equilibrium thesis that beset Keynes or the notion of absolute space and time that Einstein rejected). Even when the barrier is overcome, it may prove difficult to construct a new core belief, because of the resistance, or "risk-aversion," of the participants, or because of the profound disagreements between the members of the society.

8.6 MODELLING BELIEFS

The human brain is, without a doubt, the most complex physical object known to us. It contains about 30 billion (30×10^9) neurons and a million billion (10^{15}) connections, or synapses. The number of "neural" states of the brain is to all intents and purposes infinite. More to the point, the structure of synapse firing is neither independent (in the sense that synapses fire without pattern) nor correlated (in that all fire together). Instead, the brain is characterized by shifting, currently mysterious, patterns of local correlations (Edelman and Tononi, 2000).

It is surprising, therefore, that economic theory has used an extremely simple model of the mind (namely, preferences and their supposed "rationality" properties of transitivity, etc.) to derive hypotheses concerning human interaction. It is even more remarkable that the theory has any predictive power at all. As we have observed above, economic theory asserts the existence of concatenations of behavior known as equilibria, at least for the limited sphere of commodity markets. An underlying assumption of economic theory is that each individual is "an autonomous end in himself" and to this extent, "somewhat mysterious and inaccessible to one another." Another way of expressing this assumption is that the acts of individuals are independent, and therefore uncorrelated.

In contrast, one interpretation of the key idea put forward by Keynes in his *General Theory* is that individual acts in certain kinds of asset markets need not be independent, but may, in fact, be highly correlated. For example, a "speculator" will value assets not by any intrinsic value that they may have, but in terms of the choices of other speculators. Such correlations may induce market chaos.

Game theory, as it is currently understood, has, in a sense, accepted the possibility of correlated individual choices. Savage's work on the axiomatic structure of preference can be seen as the basis for this theory (Savage, 1954). In this framework, fundamental preferences are indeed "mysterious and inaccessible," but secondary preferences, those that govern individual acts, are mediated by the beliefs of the agent. These beliefs can be interpreted as probability assessments over the possible states of the world, over beliefs held by other agents and so forth. Clearly, the "belief space" thus generated may be of extreme complexity (see e.g., Gribben, 2004).

Moreover, choice by the individual depends on the individual's risk posture, and this is characterized by fundamental preferences, not by secondary preferences. It is hardly surprising that secondary preferences over risky choices may appear to violate the usual axiomatic properties imputed to preference (Kahneman and Tversky, 1979).

A "Nash equilibrium" can be thought of as a collection or vector of acts by the individuals in the game, with the property that no one individual has a motivation and capability to switch to a different act. However, since secondary preferences are determined by beliefs, it obviously follows that each equilibrium (in acts) is characterized by a set of beliefs, one for each agent. These "equilibrium beliefs" reside, of course, in the belief space and may be as complex as one could imagine. It is for this reason that game theory is beset by an abundance of Nash equilibria. This problem for game theory is thus very different from the principal problem of nonexistence of equilibria in social choice theory.

A second problem for game theory arises out of this multiplicity of equilibria: Some equilibria are "unstable," since they are sustained by beliefs that, while rational in some sense, are only barely credible. To filter these out by a refinement exercise, and to construct a plausible mode of transition from one equilibrium to another, has occupied many theorists in recent years.

Perhaps an illustration to do with the story of the emperor's New Clothes would be useful. The emperor was persuaded by a gifted confidence trickster that his new clothes, while invisible to the emperor, were nonetheless superlative, and visible to everyone else. That the emperor should believe this story does, of course, require a stretch of the imagination. During the parade through the town, nearly every individual must have disbelieved the evidence of their own eyes. Nonetheless, because all the other townspeople were cheering the emperor and his new clothes, each individual gave greater credence to the particular inference that there was nothing amiss (except for that individual's hallucination). This is a Nash equilibrium in the acts of the townspeople. Of course, the "belief equilibrium" underlying this joint act was broken when a single child laughed out loud on seeing the naked emperor. The childish act led immediately to a credible inference that the emperor was indeed naked, and thus to another joint equilibrium act, the expression of derision by the townspeople. The point is that the original belief equilibrium was broken by the act of a child which, under normal circumstances, would not warrant attention. Both equilibria were associated with highly correlated acts. Almost everyone applauded in the first equilibrium, and everyone (except the Emperor) laughed in the second. The transformation from one equilibrium to another has been called an *informational cascade*, and it is true that information was provided by a child's laugh. However, what was crucial was the effect of this information (and its credibility) on the beliefs of the townspeople. For this reason, throughout this book I have used the term *belief cascade* for the correlated changes in beliefs associated with a move from one Nash equilibrium to another (Bikhchandani, Hirschleifer and Welsh, 1992). I am certainly not in a position to provide a general model of belief cascades, but I believe that the stochastic model of elections can be used to indicate how such a model may be constructed.

8.7 MODELLING ELECTIONS

Game theoretic accounts of social "acts," such as voting, have been hard-pressed, in the past, to give a plausible, individual-focused account of why individuals vote, or act altruistically, or engage in battle. In contrast, sociological accounts assume, as a matter of course (in the terminology used here), that individual acts are highly correlated through correlated beliefs called *culture* or *norms*. For example, a generally accepted "sociological" mode of analysis of elections is that voters "identify" with a particular party. The implicit idea underlying party identification (PI) is that voters with similar histories will make similar judgments early in their lifetime that one party is preferred. (Campbell et al., 1960; Butler and Stokes, 1969). Clearly PI implies that voter choice satisfies a particular "correlation structure" which is stable over time, and defined by societal cleavages. (This framework also suggests that all the electoral action resides in the choices of "independents," who perhaps base their decisions on small, indeterminate, or chaotic features of each election.)

Such a framework is very different from the "rational choice" model derived from Downs (1957), where each individual is assumed to interpret the policy implications of the parties, *de novo*, and to make a choice based on the individual's idiosyncratic preferences. In such a model, the correlation in acts of the voters must be low.

It would seem, however, that neither the pure PI model nor the pure rational choice model gives a satisfactory account of elections. On the one hand, PI in Britain and the United States appears to be on the decline (Clarke and Stewart, 1998). On the other hand, there is some evidence that the pure rational choice model needs to be modified to take account of correlations in voter perceptions and choices. For example, so-called probabilistic spatial voting models typically assume that the probability that a voter chooses a party, or candidate, is a monotonically decreasing function of "distance" from the party or candidate. The implicit errors in the model are generally assumed to be independent (Enelow and Hinich, 1984). This implies voter choice is (pairwise) statistically independent. More recent empirical work suggests that, in fact, voter choice is (pairwise) statistically correlated (Quinn, Martin, and Whitford, 1999). This work has also attempted to combine "rational choice" and "sociological" accounts of elections, by utilizing the notion of Nash (1950, 1951) equilibrium and, in the terminology used here, allowing for the possibility of correlations in voter beliefs and choices. Once the idea of correlations in voter choice is considered, then it is possible to imagine episodes where the correlation structure within the electorate dramatically changes. Such transformations would naturally be associated with "critical" elections, wherein voters' perceptions of the parties, and the resulting electoral choices, change suddenly. Burnham (1970), for example, posits that the elections of 1800, 1828, 1860, 1896, and 1932 were critical.

Mayhew (2000, 2002) has recently argued that there is no clear evidence that such elections were indeed critical, in the sense of being turning points in U.S. political history. In fact, what is missing in the earlier political historical accounts is a theory that would give some mode of analysis by which to define what is meant by "critical."

In this book I have developed the idea of a constitutional quandary, associated with profound uncertainty over the proper institutional rules of the society. As the uncertainty deepens, coalitional or political chaos intensifies. Behavioral correlations, such as party identification, collapse. Very often, a new belief or interpretation of the world, is put forward, and the society bifurcates into those who accept the belief and those who deny it. Depending on the institutional rules, one of these two groups may have the will and power to bring about a new social state, and possibly a new interpretation of the constitution. By analogy with social choice theory, I have called the resulting constitution a *core* outcome, and the belief that underpins it, a *core belief*. I have also emphasized that constitutional transformations are brought about by the resolution of a quandary intrinsic to the society. Although electoral preferences may be described within a policy space of relatively low dimension, the way these preferences are aggregated at crucial junctures depends on how uncertainty and risk are interpreted by social "architects" of the eventual decision. At these junctures, contingency may play a role in how the quandary is understood. Because the consequences of the decision can be only dimly perceived, the architect must undertake two related tasks. The first, which I have characterized by the term *expected utility calculus*, is to lay out as clearly as possible the various eventualities and the associated probabilities. The second is to acknowledge the risk associated with the decision, and to offer an argument for what seems to be the correct choice. The acceptance of this choice by the electorate not only legitimizes the eventual decision, but adds weight to the belief that it is indeed "fit."

Although the construction of a formal model of such a belief game is not possible at present, the following section offers a tentative first attempt based on an adaptation of the stochastic model of voting.

8.8 A FORMAL MODEL OF ELECTIONS

Throughout this book I have used the idea of collective decision making under risk. The notion has been to formulate the costs of the various options facing a society, together with the subjective probabilities of the eventualities. However, estimates of costs and subjective probabilities will differ across the members of the society. I propose now to adapt the standard apparatus of the spatial model of voting so that it can incorporate both *preferences* and *beliefs*. As suggested in the above discussion, beliefs are essentially subjective probability assessments. Recent formal models of voting have also made use of the Condorcetian idea that voters may form judgments about the validity of various political propositions. Unlike Condorcet's conception that these propositions are "universally true," the kind of propositions that I consider here have the form, "The South does indeed intend to extend slavery to the Pacific," and "The North is indeed based on capitalist expansion that is inimitable to the South." Evidence can be given as regarding propositions and, depending on the interests of voters, the beliefs so generated will affect the choices of voters.

The "stochastic" variant (Hinich, 1977) of the spatial model allows voters to be uncertain in their choice, and it is this model that I shall adapt.

The primitives[12] of the model are:

(i) some "policy" space X which characterizes both voter interests, and possible eventualities.

(ii) the population or "electorate," N, of size n, is described by a set $\{x_i\}$ of "ideal points," one for each "voter," $i = 1, \ldots, n$. An individual's ideal point describes the location of the voter in the space X, and represents that voter's interests.

(iii) the set of options, S, of size s, is a set $\{z_j\}$, each one being a point in X. In the situation of an election, each element of S is a declaration of intended or proposed policy. There is one for each candidate, j.

(iv) in the simplest model, the "latent utility," u_{ij}, of voter i for candidate j has the form

$$u_{ij}(x_i, z_j) = \lambda_{ij} - A_{ij}(x_i, z_j) + \theta_j^{\mathsf{T}} \eta_i. \qquad (8.1)$$

---

[12] Here I repeat the definitions given in section 1.2 of Chapter 1.

Here $\theta_j^T \eta_i$ models the effect of the sociodemographic characteristics η_i of voter i in making a political choice. That is, θ_j is a k-vector specifying how the various sociodemographic variables appear to influence the choice for party j. The term $A_{ij}(x_i, z_j)$ is a way of representing the interests of voter i. In particular, $A_{ij}(x_i, z_j)$ will be some function of the distance between x_i, the preferred position of voter i and z_j, the declared policy of candidate j, according to some appropriate metric. In Chapter 6, for example, the metric is assumed to be "ellipsoidal," assigning different valences to different axes for different individuals. In the standard electoral model, however, it is assumed that $A_{ij}(x_i, z_j) = \beta \|x_i - z_j\|^2$ is the Euclidean quadratic loss (with $\beta > 0$) associated with the difference between the two positions.

The model is stochastic because of the implicit assumption that $\lambda_{ij} = \lambda_j + \varepsilon_j$, for $j = 1, \ldots, s$. Here $\{\varepsilon_j\}$ is a set of possibly correlated disturbances and λ_j is the "valence" of candidate j. This valence is a way of modeling the nonpolicy judgment by voter i of the quality of candidate j.

The probability that voter i chooses candidate j is

$$\rho_{ij} = \Pr[u_{ij}(x_i, z_j) > u_{ij}(x_i, z_k) \text{ for all } k \neq j]. \tag{8.2}$$

Hinich (1977) assumed each candidate, j, adopted a declaration, z_j, chosen so as to maximize the expected vote share of the candidate. The vote share is given by the average

$$\frac{1}{n} \sum_{i=1}^{n} \rho_{ij}. \tag{8.3}$$

He argued that the resulting "Nash equilibrium" would be one in which both candidates adopted the same position, at the mean of the voter distribution. However, there is one proviso. If the "valences" are ranked $\lambda_s > \lambda_{s-1} > \ldots > \lambda_1$, then it is necessary for this convergence result that a "convergence coefficient"

$$c(\lambda, \beta) = 2\beta[1 - 2\rho_1]v^2 \tag{8.4}$$

be bounded above by the dimension of the space. In this expression, ρ_1 is the probability that each voter picks the lowest valence candidate when all candidates adopt the same position at the mean, while v^2 is a measure of the electoral variance. In the case the disturbances are independent and generated by a logistic distribution, then

$$\rho_1 = \left[1 + \sum_{k \neq 1} \exp\left[\lambda_k - \lambda_1\right]\right]^{-1}. \tag{8.5}$$

A similar expression can be obtained under assumptions that the errors are multivariate normal and correlated.

Obviously, if candidate s has much higher valence than candidate 1, or if the variation, ν^2, in electoral beliefs is significant, then this necessary condition will fail. The consequence is that low-valence candidates will not locate near the electoral mean.

Empirical analyses of elections in Britain, the United States, as well as of polities using proportional electoral methods such as Israel and Italy demonstrate that the empirical values obtained for the parameters imply that the necessary condition fails (Schofield, Miller and Martin, 2003; Schofield and Sened, 2005a,b, 2006).

The conclusions of this valence model suggest why convergence to an electoral center is a nongeneric phenomenon. Indeed, it is only likely to occur when the election involves such a high degree of uncertainty (or electoral variance) that policy differences are irrelevant.

This valence model can be interpreted in terms of Madison's theorem in *Federalist X*. We may view λ_j as the average electoral judgment that candidate j is a "fit choice" for the position of the Chief Magistrate. In the model outlined above, the particular weighting that i gives to j is a stochastic variable, $\lambda_{ij} = \lambda_j + \varepsilon_j$, where ε_j has some explicit stochastic distribution, either Gaussian or so-called "Type I extreme value" (see Schofield and Sened, 2006, for a full definition of the model). The logic underlying this model is that it may be, in principle, impossible to gauge precisely what weight an individual, i, gives to the arguments for the option offered by candidate j. It is clearly possible in this model for a voter to actually vote for candidate j over k even though, in terms of explicit policies, candidate k has declared an intended option that more closely matches i's interests. The fact that candidates do not converge to an electoral mean provides a reason why the candidate positions represented in Figures 6.2 through 6.5 in Chapter 6 are not convergent.

The model can be extended in the obvious way, because there is no compelling reason to assume that the stochastic component is random in the manner just specified. It is more plausible that the judgment made by i of candidate j is a function of j's stated option. Indeed, the judgment

λ_{ij} by i of j could be a function $\lambda_{ij}(x_i, z_j)$ of both the preferred point, x_i, of the voter, and the declared option z_j. In this case, the stochastic error, ε_j, associated with voter i could also depend on the preferred point, x_i, of the voter. Moreover, judgments about different candidates could move in different directions in different subsets of the population. Such a model has been proposed by Miller and Schofield (2003) and was presented in Chapter 6 in order to account for the effect of activists on candidate support. The key idea in this model is that judgments are more like infections and are subject to contagion. In other words, an increase in the positive judgment for one of the candidates by some subset of the electorate may trigger further changes in such electoral judgments—positive among some members of the electorate, and negative among others. Although the model has not been fully developed, it does seem to suggest that party positions slowly evolve over time as new activist coalitions come into being. Figures 6.3 and 6.4, in Chapter 6 for example, give hypothetical illustrations of the transformation of party positions from 1860 to 1896 and from 1896 to 1932 in the United States. Implicitly, I argue that these transformations at times of "critical" elections (Key, 1955) are brought about by the electoral belief cascades. It seems obvious that the belief cascades in the northern and southern electorates moved in opposite directions from 1858 to 1860. That is, the judgments $\lambda_{ij}(x_i, z_j)$ for $j =$ Lincoln or Breckinridge became large depending on whether i belonged to the North or South. An electoral game of this kind would induce extreme divergence. This could account for the lack of success of a moderate candidate like Bell.

While this model involving electoral judgments has some affinities to Condorcet's Jury theorem and Madison's version of it in *Federalist X*, the theorem itself cannot be used directly to argue that the selected candidate is necessarily superior. Because the probabilities ρ_{aj}, ρ_{bj} (that voters a, b choose j) depend on x_a and x_b, they will not be independent. We can interpret this to mean that the stochastic disturbances display complex correlations. Only if the electoral variation, v^2, is very small, will convergence occur. If one candidate has a clearly dominant valence then this candidate will win the election, with high probability.

To interpret this observation, suppose that β approaches zero so that, in the limit, the interests of the voters become irrelevant. Suppose further that there is information available to some subset M of the electorate which is consistent with the judgment

$$\lambda_s > \lambda_{s-1} > \ldots > \lambda_1. \tag{8.6}$$

Then it will be the case that, for every voter i in M, the probabilities will be ranked

$$\rho_{is} > \rho_{is-1} > \ldots > \rho_{i1} \qquad (8.7)$$

for these voters. From the multinomial theorem it follows that the majority rule preference within the set M will choose s with greater probability than $s - 1, s - 2, \ldots, 3, 2, 1$. If M is itself a majority under the electoral rule, then candidate s will win. (A proof of a version of the Jury theorem is given in the appendix to this chapter. It is important to note that the theorem depends on the assumption of independence of voter choice.) This is an analogue of Condorcet's Jury theorem, in the case that both interests and judgments are involved.

If there is some linkage between information available to the electorate and the individual judgments made by voters, then the stochastic spatial model just presented can be interpreted as a generalization of the Jury theorem (see also Schofield, 1972a, for an early attempt at formulating Madison's argument in terms of a version of the Jury theorem where different groups in the society have differing notions of a fit choice).

In the case where electoral interests are relatively weak, because β is small we can infer that the second aspect of the Jury theorem will also hold. In the limit, as the population size, n, becomes large, the probability of a fit choice approaches 1. Because the model can incorporate interests, which were of concern to Madison in writing *Federalist X*, we may also view the model as a method of studying the interaction of interests and judgments in a polity.

Even when interests are involved, so β is significant in magnitude, we can still draw some conclusions about the equilibrium behavior of candidates as they respond to electorate incentives. Since we can infer that the relevant necessary condition for the "mean voter theorem" will fail, it follows that candidates will adopt very different positions. If the individual judgments are correlated in some fashion, then this phenomenon will be more pronounced.

If there is a single dimension involved, as suggested by Figure 2.4 for the Jefferson election of 1800, then it is plausible that there exists only a unique vector of equilibrium positions for the candidates. Indeed, the figure is meant to suggest that this was the case from 1800 until at least 1852, and this is why I suggested that the two-party system was in balance in this period. If there are two dimensions, as I have suggested is a plausible assumption for the election of 1860, then the equilibrium will depend on the valence characteristics of the candidates.

Figure 2.5 positions the four presidential candidates for 1860 within a two-dimensional policy space, characterized by a land/capital axis and a labor/slavery axis. In a pure stochastic model for such a situation there would be multiple possible equilibria. The activist version of the model proposed by Schofield (2005a) suggests that if these activist valence functions are sufficiently concave in the candidates' positions, then there will indeed be a unique equilibrium (that is, a set of positions, one for each candidate).

It is implicit in this model, that *contention*, rather than *compromise*, is the fundamental characteristic of politics. It should also be obvious that each candidate should do everything in his (or her) power to enhance his (or her) valence.

If my argument about the importance of judgments is correct, then the kind of deterministic instability implicit in the Arrovian or chaos theorems will not occur in the election of the Chief Magistrate. Instead, such elections will be affected by changes in average societal judgments, and by the possible correlation and sectional distribution of these judgments. This may be what Beard (1913) had in mind.

I have conjectured here that the U.S. political system tends to sustain risk-taking policy options by successful presidential candidates and by influential policy makers or architects of change, such as Franklin, Madison, Jefferson, Lincoln, or Johnson. I also conjecture that risk taking by candidates is enhanced by the effects of activist interest groups. This balance between presidential risk taking and congressional risk aversion was seemingly intended by the Founders.

Clearly, the social world of beliefs is much more complex than the world of preferences. As I have suggested, the space of beliefs, regarded as a mathematical object, is extremely complex. The historical illustrations of this book suggest that dramatic transformations can occur as core beliefs in the society are transformed. It is this feature of social transformation that the notion of the heart tries to capture.

8.9 APPENDIX: CONDORCET'S JURY THEOREM

The Jury theorem formally only refers to a situation where there are just two alternatives $\{1, 0\}$, and alternative 1 is the "true" option. Further, for every individual, i, it is the case that $\rho_{i1} > \rho_{i0}$. We can assume that $\rho_{i1} + \rho_{i0} = 1$, so obviously $\rho_{i1} > \frac{1}{2}$. To simplify the proof, we can assume that ρ_{i1} is the same for every individual, thus $\rho_{i1} = \alpha > \frac{1}{2}$ for all i. We use χ_i ($= 0$ or 1) to refer to the choice of individual i, and let $\chi = \Sigma_{i=1}^{n} \chi_i$ be the number of individuals who select the true option 1. We use Pr for the probability operator, and E for the expectation operator. In the case that the electoral size, n, is odd, then a majority, m, is defined to be $m = \frac{n+1}{2}$. In the case n is even, the majority is $m = \frac{n}{2} + 1$. The probability that a majority chooses the true option is then

$$\alpha^n_{maj} = \Pr[\chi \geq m].$$

The theorem assumes that voter choice is *pairwise independent*, so that $\Pr(\chi = j)$ is simply given by the binomial expression $\binom{n}{j}\alpha^j(1-\alpha)^{n-j}$.

A version of the theorem can be proved in the case that the probabilities $\{\rho_{i1} = \alpha_i\}$ differ but satisfy the requirement that $\frac{1}{n}\Sigma^n_{i=1}\alpha_i > \frac{1}{2}$. Versions of the theorem are valid when voter choices are not pairwise independent (Ladha and Miller, 1996).

The Jury Theorem.[13] If $1 > \alpha > \frac{1}{2}$, then $\alpha^n_{maj} \geq \alpha$, and $\alpha^n_{maj} \longrightarrow 1$ as $n \longrightarrow \infty$.

Proof. Consider the case with n odd. Now

$$\Pr(\chi = j) = \binom{n}{j}\alpha^j(1-\alpha)^{n-j} = \binom{n}{n-j}\alpha^j(1-\alpha)^{n-j}.$$

Since $\alpha > \frac{1}{2}$ we see that $\alpha^{n-j}(1-\alpha)^j > \alpha^j(1-\alpha)^{n-j}$. Thus,

$$\Sigma^{m-1}_{j=0} j \Pr(\chi = n - j) > \Sigma^{m-1}_{j=0} j \Pr(\chi = j)$$

or

$$\Sigma^n_{k=m}(n-k)\Pr(\chi = k) > \Sigma^{m-1}_{k=0}k\Pr(\chi = k). \tag{8.8}$$

Thus,

$$n\Sigma^n_{k=m}\Pr(\chi = k) > \Sigma^{m-1}_{k=0}k\Pr(\chi = k) + \Sigma^n_{k=m}k\Pr(\chi = k).$$

But

$$n\alpha_{maj} = n\Sigma^n_{k=m}\Pr(\chi = k)$$

and

$$E(\chi) = \Sigma^n_{k=0}k\Pr(\chi = k) = n\alpha.$$

Thus, $\alpha_{maj} > \alpha$ when n is odd.

---

[13] This proof is adapted from Ladha (1996).

The case with n being even follows in similar fashion, taking $m = \frac{n}{2} + 1$, and using an equiprobable tie-breaking rule when $k = \frac{n}{2}$. This gives

$$\alpha_{maj} = \Sigma_{k=m}^{n} \Pr(\chi = k) + \frac{1}{2} \Pr\left(\chi = \frac{n}{2}\right).$$

For both n being even or odd, as $n \longrightarrow \infty$, the fraction of voters choosing option 1 approaches $\frac{1}{n} E(\chi) = \alpha > \frac{1}{2}$. Thus, in the limit, more than half the voters choose the true option. Hence the probability $\alpha_{maj}^n \longrightarrow 1$ as $n \longrightarrow \infty$.

Laplace also wrote on the topic of the probability of an error in the judgment of a tribunal. He was concerned with the degree to which jurors would make just decisions in a situation of asymmetric costs, where finding an innocent party guilty was to be more feared than letting the guilty party go free. As he commented on the appropriate rule for a jury of twelve, "I think that in order to give a sufficient guarantee to innocence, one ought to demand at least a plurality of nine votes in twelve" (Laplace 1951 [1814]: 139).

9

Political Change

> The essential point to grasp is that in dealing with capitalism we are dealing with an evolutionary process. ... Capitalism, then, is by nature a form or method of economic change and not only never is but never can be stationary. And this evolutionary character of the capitalist process is not merely due to the fact that economic life goes on in a social and natural environment which changes. ... The fundamental impulse that sets and keeps the capitalist engine in motion comes from the new consumers' goods, the new methods of production or transportation, the new markets, the new forms of industrial organization that capitalist enterprise creates. ... [T]he ... process of industrial mutation ... incessantly revolutionizes the economic structure from within, incessantly destroying the old one, incessantly creating a new one. This process of Creative Destruction is the essential fact about capitalism. It is what capitalism consists in and what every capitalist concern has got to live in. ...
>
> It must be seen in its role in the perennial gale of creative destruction.
>
> (Schumpeter, 1942: 82–4)

We can agree with Schumpeter that the future will be one of technological change and what is now called "globalization." We need not accept all of Schumpeter's arguments about capitalism, but we can extend his metaphor of the dynamical system of the "weather" to make some general points about the process of change in the global political economy.

Weather is a dynamical system involving the oceans and the air on the surface of the earth. Even though the local laws of motion, the "physics" of the weather are well understood, its global behavior defeats computation except in the very short run. As Lorenz (1993) has noted, this system may contain local chaotic subsystems—hurricanes and the like—but also major discontinuities, like the onset of an ice age. The theory of dynamic systems, originating in the work of Poincaré (1993 [1892–9]) and more recently of Smale (1966), would suggest that such a complex dynamic system

276

is unlikely to be structurally stable.[1] We are now sensitive to the fact that relatively small changes, induced by our own actions, can potentially induce dramatic change in the qualitative aspects of the system of weather.

If we now think of the social world as a dynamical system, driven by changes in the beliefs of its members, then we can use this metaphor of the global weather system to draw out some tentative parallels.

First, it will never be in equilibrium. There may be temporary domains of relative stability, or equilibrium, but these will in time be transformed.

Second, the interactions that can occur, and the "causes" of the transformations, may take place over extended temporal and spatial domains, and involve very subtle and unsuspected linkages.

Third, just as the weather system is "forced," by periodicities generated by the sun and the moon, and possibly by our own actions, so is the social system "forced" by technological change. Different subdomains, or political economies, may well be forced in different directions by the effects of technology. While the weather system is generally predictable, it does contain small-scale, chaotic events, like hurricanes, and on occasion very large-scale changes. We might expect the social system to exhibit the same pattern of unpredictability occurring at different levels (Stiglitz, 2002; Mandelbrot and Hudson, 2004).

While the local laws of motion of the weather system were found by studying much simpler, isolated physical systems (Gribbin, 2004), we only have very local models of subsets of the social system by which to make guesses about its true laws of motion. These local social models were discussed in Chapter 8 and include "the general equilibrium model of economics" as well as versions of Condorcetian "belief aggregation," "social choice theory," "game theory," and the models of scientific innovation discussed by Popper, Kuhn, and Feyerabend. Obviously enough, all of these are very incomplete theories, that can, at best, only give us some insight into local aspects of the social dynamic. Developing these models requires both extensions of the deductive theories of dynamic processes and of inductive techniques for perceiving patterns in the world.

It was Condorcet's belief that

the moral and political sciences are capable of the same certainty as those that comprise the system of the physical sciences, and even as those branches of physical science which like astronomy, seem to approach mathematical certainty.[2]

---

[1] Further comments on these observations are given in Schofield (2003d).
[2] Quoted in Gillespie (1972: 2). See also Gillespie (1980, 2005).

In fact, it was Condorcet's contemporary, Pierre-Simon Laplace, who contributed most to this enlightenment research program by his development of celestial mechanics, but also by his efforts to formulate a theory of induction applicable to social analysis.[3] Two centuries after Condorcet and Laplace, we have a somewhat better understanding that dynamic systems, whether physical or social, need not exhibit the certainty imputed by Condorcet. My own inclination is that it is important to continue the research program that I have associated with Condorcet and Laplace by embracing both deductive and inductive aspects of learning and of the mind. Recent developments in stochastic models of behavior of complex systems (Mumford, 2002) suggest that such a program is not impossible. However, we should be cautious and resist the inclination to jump too readily to grand conclusions about the nature of change in the global society.

In this book, I have used a version of the electoral model, and have tried to combine aspects of both preference and belief aggregation. The formal model, while fairly simple, is essentially based on Bayesian and stochastic techniques (Schofield and Sened, 2006). It can, in principle, be extended to incorporate more subtle aspects of belief, and what I have called *valence*. As I have emphasized, valence is an aspect of judgment, and can be subject to rapid change—a kind of infection, in any democratic society. The historical occasions I have considered suggest that these belief transformations may take the form of a change in a key constituent or core belief induced by the obvious need to deal with a quandary facing the society. I have also used the example of Keynes' ideas to suggest that the way to resolving such a quandary may be by overcoming a theoretical barrier associated with a core belief that has proved to be false. Chapters 5 and 6 used the examples of events in 1860 and 1964 to infer that the belief changes that were brought about were coherent or rational in some sense. At the same time, of course, these belief changes led, respectively, to the Civil War and to the unrest associated with the Vietnam War. In more developed versions of the electoral model, it would be necessary to focus on the rationalizability of the belief changes.

There are instances, of course where belief changes can be rationalized. The collapse of the Soviet Union in the early 1990s appears to have been due to a general realization that the "imperial" system of the USSR was ill

---

[3] See *Traité de mécanique céleste* (Laplace, 1798–1825) and his theories of induction in *Théorie analytique des probabilités* (1812) and in *Essai philosophique sur les probabilités* (1814).

designed to solve the quandaries resulting from increasing technological competition with the West. However, this example certainly does not imply the end of history—the universal acceptance of the superiority of capitalist democracy. As Keynes foresaw, the chaos resulting from very rapid political-economic change can induce risk-averse electorates to opt for autocracy. This may be happening now in Russia and in other countries which, for whatever reason, find themselves overwhelmed by the effects of globalization.

It is obvious that some countries will founder in a world where efficient institutions are crucial for prosperity. Indeed, there will be countries that find it impossible to construct or maintain institutions that give them hope for survival. Poverty and disorder will engender beliefs that have their bases in nationalism and religion. Because these beliefs owe their origin to social processes that are essentially chaotic, the effect will be to create very difficult and unpleasant quandaries for other societies.

In those countries that do not adapt, poverty and disorder will continue to conspire to bring autocrats to power. In many countries in Africa, for example, this will induce further economic collapse. One way to help such countries build sustainable and efficient institutions would be for the developed countries to open themselves to a greater degree of agricultural trade with the less-developed world. How this may be done in the face of protectionist pressure is just one of the quandaries associated with globalization. A deeper quandary is how best to assist the struggling polities in constructing efficient institutions and learning to deal with economic change.

Throughout this book, I have emphasized that one necessity of a democratic polity is that its leader be willing and able to take risk in the face of a fundamental quandary. However, I have also argued that risk taking should be balanced by the concerns of the sceptical, and by the calculation of reasonable guesses about the probabilities of possible outcomes. Obviously, if the outcomes are truly uncertain, then there can be no guarantee that correct choices are made.

How Al-Qaeda came about, and the origin of the beliefs that sustain it, are quite mysterious (Gray, 2003). But it does seem that while the social and moral beliefs of the members of Al-Qaeda are unintelligible to us, this has not prevented them from adapting the technology of this age, producing consequences that are completely out of proportion to their resources.

The extreme heterogeneity of beliefs that may have been triggered by the coalition invasion of Iraq and the capture of Saddam Hussein seem to be incompatible with any peaceful move to democratic institutions in that country. Although attempts are being made to create a constitutional design that will bring about some degree of political balance, this may take many years, or even be impossible. But the choices that have been made during the last few years by U.S. decision makers appear, at least in retrospect, to have ignored the real possibility that the attempt to impose order in Iraq would lead to political chaos and trigger further changes in belief throughout the Middle East. The U.S. Presidential election of 2004 turned on a core belief in the electorate that linked Al-Qaeda to Saddam Hussein. On this basis it was believed that the military strategy was a risky but appropriate response to a fundamental quandary. This belief may turn out to be a chimera.

Bibliography

Acemoglu, Daron, and James Robinson. 2000. "Why Did the West Extend the Franchise? Growth, Inequality and Democracy in Historical Perspective." *Quarterly Journal of Economics* 115: 1167–99.

Acemoglu, Daron, and James Robinson. 2005. *Economic Origins of Dictatorship and Democracy.* New York: Cambridge University Press.

Acemoglu, Daron, Simon Johnson, and James Robinson. 2002. "Reversal of Fortune: Geography and Institutions in the Making of the Modern World Income Distribution." *Quarterly Journal of Economics* 118: 1231–94.

Acemoglu, Daron, Simon Johnson, and James Robinson. 2005. "The Rise of Europe: Atlantic Trade, Institutional Change, and Economic Growth." *The American Economic Review* 95: 546–79.

Adair, Douglass G. 1943. *The Intellectual Origins of Jeffersonian Democracy: Republicanism, the Class Struggle, and the Virtuous Farmer.* Ph.D. Dissertation. Yale University.

Adair, Douglass G. 1974. *Fame and the Founding Fathers.* (Trevor Colbourn, ed.) New York: Norton.

Adair, Douglass G. 2000. *The Intellectual Origins of Jeffersonian Democracy.* Lanham, MD: Lexington Books.

Adams, Charles F. ed. 1856. *The Works of John Adams.* Boston, MA: Little Brown.

Adams, Henry. 1986 [1889]. *History of the United States during the Administrations of Thomas Jefferson* (Earl N. Harbert, ed.) New York: Library of America.

Adams, James, and Samuel Merrill. 1999. "Modeling Party Strategies and Policy Representation in Multiparty Elections: Why are Strategies So Extreme?" *American Journal of Political Science* 43: 765–91.

Aldrich, John. 1983a. "A Downsian Spatial Model with Party Activists." *American Political Science Review* 77: 974–90.

Aldrich, John. 1983b. "A Spatial Model with Party Activists: Implications for Electoral Dynamics." *Public Choice* 41: 63–100.

Aldrich, John. 1995. *Why Parties?* Chicago, IL: University of Chicago Press.

Aldrich, John, and Michael McGinnis. 1989. "A Model of Party Constraints on Optimal Candidate Positions." *Mathematical and Computer Modelling* 12: 437–50.

Allen, Robert. 1988. "The Price of Freehold Land and the Interest Rate in the Seventeenth and Eighteenth Centuries." *The Economic History Review* 41: 33–50.

Alt, James. 1979. *The Politics of Economic Decline.* Cambridge, UK: Cambridge University Press.

Anderson, Fred. 2000. *Crucible of War.* New York: Knopf.

Anderson, Fred, and Andrew Clayton. 2005. *The Dominion of War: Empire and Liberty in North America 1500–2000.* New York: Penguin.

Ansolabahere, Steve, and James Snyder. 2000. "Valence Politics and Equilibrium in Spatial Election Models." *Public Choice* 103: 327–36.

Appleby, Joyce. 1992. *Liberalism and Republicanism in the Historical Imagination.* Cambridge, MA: Harvard University Press.

Arrow, Kenneth. 1950a. "A Difficulty in the Concept of Social Welfare," *Journal of Political Economy* 58: 328–46.

Arrow, Kenneth. 1950b. "An Extension of the Basic Theorems of Classical Welfare Economics." In *Proceedings of the Second Berkeley Symposium on Mathematics, Statistics, and Probability.* Berkeley: University of California Press, edited by Jerry Neyman.

Arrow, Kenneth. 1951. *Social Choice and Individual Values.* New York: John Wiley and Sons. Rev. ed. 1963. New Haven, CT: Yale University.

Arrow, Kenneth. 1956. "Existence of an Equilibrium for a Competitive Economy." *Econometrica* 22: 265–90.

Arrow, Kenneth. 1973. "Some Ordinalist Utilitarian Notes on Rawls' Sense of Justice." *Journal of Philosophy* 70: 245–63.

Arrow, Kenneth. 1986. "Rationality of Self and of Others in an Economic System." *Journal of Business* S59: 385–390.

Arrow, Kenneth. 1988. "Workshop on the Economy as an Evolving Complex System: Summary." In *The Economy as an Evolving Complex System.* Reading, MA: Addison-Wesley, edited by Philip Anderson, Kenneth Arrow, and David Pines.

Arrow, Kenneth. 1999. "Comments on Commentaries." In *Competition and Cooperation: Conversations with Nobelists about Economics and Political Science.* New York: Russell Sage Foundation, edited by James Alt, Margaret Levi and Elinor. Ostrom.

Arrow, Kenneth, and Frank Hahn. 1971. *General Competitive Analysis.* San Francisco: Holden Day.

Arrow, Kenneth, and Gerard Debreu. 1954. "Existence of an Equilibrium for a Competitive Economy." *Econometrica* 22: 265–90.

Aumann, Robert. 1976. "Agreeing to Disagree." *Annals of Statistics* 4: 1236–39.

Aumann, Robert, and Michael Maschler. 1964. "The Bargaining Set for Cooperative Games." In *Advances in Game Theory.* Princeton, NJ: Princeton University Press, edited by Melvin Drescher, Lloyd Shapley and Albert Tucker.

Austen-Smith, David, and Jeffrey Banks. 1996. "Information Aggregation, Rationality, and the Condorcet Jury Theorem." *American Political Science Review* 90: 34–45.

Austen-Smith, David, and Jeffrey Banks. 1998. "Social Choice Theory, Game Theory and Positive Political Theory." *Annual Review of Political Science* 1: 259–87.

Austen-Smith, David, and Jeffrey Banks. 1999. *Positive Political Theory: I Collective Choice.* Ann Arbor, MI: University of Michigan Press.

Austen-Smith, David, and Jeffrey Banks. 2005. *Positive Political Theory: II Strategy and Structure.* Ann Arbor, MI: University of Michigan Press.

Axelrod, Robert. 1984. *The Evolution of Cooperation.* New York: Basic Books.

Baack, Ben. 1998. "The American Revolution: A Reinterpretation." Ohio State University. Unpublished Manuscript.

Bailyn, Bernard. 2005. *Atlantic History.* Cambridge, MA: Harvard University Press.

Baker, Keith M. 1975. *Condorcet: From Natural Philosophy to Social Mathematics.* Chicago, IL: University of Chicago Press.

Ball, Philip. 2004. *Critical Mass.* New York: Farrar, Strauss and Giroux.

Badinter, Elisabeth, and Robert Badinter. 1988. *Condorcet: Un intellectuel en Politique.* Paris, Fayard.

Banks, Jeff S. 1995. "Singularity Theory and Core Existence in the Spatial Model." *Journal of Mathematical Economics* 24: 523–36.

Banks, Jeff S., and John Duggan. 2005. "The Theory of Probabilistic Voting in the Spatial Model of Elections." In *Social Choice and Strategic Decisions.* Berlin: Springer, edited by David Austen-Smith and John Duggan.

Banks, Jeff, John Duggan, and Michel Le Breton. 2002. "Bounds for Mixed Strategy Equilibria and the Spatial Model of Elections." *Journal of Economic Theory* 103: 88–105.

Bates, Robert, Avner Greif, Margaret Levi, Jean-Laurent Rosenthal, and Barry Weingast. 1998. *Analytical Narratives.* Princeton, NJ: Princeton University Press.

Baugh, Daniel. 1994. "Maritime Strength and Atlantic Commerce: The Uses of a 'Grand Marine Empire.'" In *An Imperial State at War.* London: Routledge, edited by Lawrence Stone.

Beard, Charles. 1913. *An Economic Interpretation of the Constitution of the United States.* New York: Macmillan.

Beard, Charles. 1915. *Economic Consequences of Jeffersonian Democracy.* New York: Macmillan.

Beer, Samuel. 1982. *Britain Against Itself.* London: Faber and Faber.

Beer, Samuel. 1993. *To Make a Nation.* Cambridge, MA: Harvard University Press.

Bemis, Samuel. 1935. *The Diplomacy of the American Revolution.* Bloomington, IN: Indiana University Press.

Bemis, Samuel. 1962. *American Foreign Policy.* New Haven, CT: Yale University Press.

Bikhchandani, Sushil, David Hirschleifer, and Ivo Welch. 1992. "A Theory of Fads, Fashion, Custom and Cultural Change as Information Cascades." *Journal of Political Economy* 100: 992–1026.

Bird, Kai. 1992. *The Chairman: John McCloy and the Making of the American Establishment*. New York: Simon & Schuster.

Black, Duncan. 1958. *The Theory of Committees and Elections*. Cambridge, UK: Cambridge University Press.

Block, Fred. 1977. *The Origins of International Economic Disorder*. Berkeley, CA: University of California Press.

Block, Fred. 1996. "Controlling Global Finance." *World Policy Journal* 13: 24–34.

Boaz, Noel. 1997. *Eco Homo*. New York: Basic Books.

Bobrick, Benson. 1997. *Angel in the Whirlwind*. New York: Penguin.

Boland, Philip. 1989. "Majority Systems and the Condorcet Jury Theoreom." *The Statistician* 38: 187–9.

Bordo, Michael, and Hugh Rockoff. 1996. "The Gold Standard as a 'Good Housekeeping Seal of Approval.'" *Journal of Economic History* 56: 389–428.

Brady, David. 1988. *Critical Elections and Congressional Policy Making*. Stanford, CA: Stanford University Press.

Branch, Taylor. 1998. *Pillar of Fire*. New York: Simon & Schuster.

Brands, H. W. 2000. *The First American: The Life and Times of Benjamin Franklin*. New York: Random House.

Brewer, John. 1976. *Party Ideology and Popular Politics at the Accession of George III*. Cambridge, UK: Cambridge University Press.

Brewer, John. 1988. *The Sinews of Power*. Cambridge, MA: Harvard University Press.

Brinkley, Alan. 1998. *Liberalism and its Discontents*. Cambridge, MA: Harvard University Press.

Brittan, Samuel. 1977. *The Economic Consequences of Democracy*. London: Maurice Temple.

Brittan, Samuel. 1978. "Inflation and Democracy." In *The Political Economy of Inflation*. London: Martin Robertson, edited by Fred Hirsch and John Goldthorpe.

Brittan, Samuel. 1983. *The Role and Limits of Government*. Minneapolis, MN: University of Minnesota Press.

Brouwer, Luitzen. 1910. "Uber Abbildung von Manningfaltigkeiten." *Mathematische Annalen* 71: 97–115.

Buchan, James. 2003. *Cowded with Genius: The Scottish Enlightenment*. New York: HarperCollins.

Buchanan, James, and Gordon Tullock. 1962. *The Calculus of Consent: Logical Foundations of Constitutional Democracy*. Ann Arbor, MI: University of Michigan Press.

Burnham, Walter. 1968. "American Voting Behavior and the 1964 Election." *Midwest Journal of Political Science* 12: 1–40.

Burnham, Walter. 1970. *Critical Elections and the Mainsprings of American Politics*. New York: Norton.

Butler, David, and Donald Stokes. 1969. *Political Change in Britain*. New York: St. Martin's Press.

Byrnes, James. 1947. *Speaking Frankly*. New York: Harper.

Calaprice, Alice. 2005. *The Einstein Almanac*. Baltimore, MD: The Johns Hopkins University Press.

Califano, Joseph, Jr. 1991. *The Triumph and Tragedy of Lyndon Johnson.* New York: Simon & Schuster.

Calvert, Randall. 1985. "Robustness of the Multidimensional Voting Model: Candidates, Motivations, Uncertainty and Convergence." *American Journal of Political Science* 29: 69–85.

Calvert, Randall. 1995. "Rational Actors, Equilibrium and Social Institutions," in *Explaining Social Institutions.* Ann Arbor, MI: Michigan University Press, edited by Jack Knight and Itai Sened.

Calvin, William. 1991. *The Ascent of Mind.* New York: Bantam.

Campbell, Angus, Philip Converse, Warren Miller, and Donald Stokes. 1960. *The American Voter.* Chicago, IL: University of Chicago Press.

Campbell, James. 1999. *Recovering Benjamin Franklin.* Chicago, IL: Open Court.

Canavan, Francis. ed. 1999. *Selected Works of Edmund Burke* Volume 1. Indiananpolis, IN: Liberty Fund.

Cantillon, Richard. 1964 [1755]. *Essays on the Nature of Commerce in General.* Translated and edited by Henry Higgs. New York: Kelly.

Carmines, Edward, and James Stimson. 1989. *Issue Evolution: Race and the Transformation of American Politics.* Princeton, NJ: Princeton University Press.

Caro, Robert A. 2002. *The Years of Lyndon Johnson: Master of The Senate.* New York: Knopf.

Carter, Don. 1995. *The Politics of Rage.* New York: Simon & Schuster.

Cerami, Charles. 2003. *Jefferson's Great Gamble.* Naperville, IL: Sourcebooks.

Chernow, Ron. 2004. *Alexander Hamilton.* New York: The Penguin Press.

Chown, John. 1994. *The History of Money.* London: Routledge.

Clark, George. 1956. *The Later Stuarts 1660–1714.* Oxford: Clarendon Press.

Clarke, Harold, and Marianne Stewart. 1998. "The Decline of Parties in the Minds of Citizens." *Annual Review of Political Science* 1: 357–78.

Clubb, Jerome, William Flanigan, and Nancy Zingale. 1980. *Partisan Realignment.* Beverly Hills: Sage.

Colloway, Colin. 1995. *The American Revolution in Indian Country.* Cambridge, MA: Harvard University Press.

Commager, Henry S. 1977. *The Empire of Reason: How Europe Imagined and America Realized the Enlightenment.* Garden City, NJ: Doubleday.

Condillac, Etienne Bonnot de. 2001 [1746]. *Essay on the Origin of Human Knowledge.* New York: Cambridge University Press.

Condorcet, Nicolas. 1994 [1785]. *Essai sur l'application de l'analyse à la probabilité des décisions rendues à la pluralité des voix.* Imprimerie Royale, Paris translated in part in *Condorcet: Foundations of Social Choice and Political Theory* by Iain McLean and Fiona Hewitt, Aldershot, Edward Elgar Publishing.

Condorcet, Nicolas. 1955 [1795]. *Esquisse d'un tableau historique des progrès de l'esprit humain: Sketch for an Historical Picture of the Human Mind.* London: Weidenfeld and Nicholson, translated and edited by John Barraclough and with an introduction by Stuart Hampshire.

Connelly, Marjorie. 2000. "Who Voted: A Portrait of American Politics, 1976–2000." *New York Times* November 12: 4.

Cooper, William, Jr. 2000. *Jefferson Davis: American.* New York: Knopf.

Coughlin, Peter. 1992. *Probabilistic Voting Theory*. New York: Cambridge University Press.

Crafts, Nick. 1994. "The Industrial Revolution." In *The Economic History of Britain since 1700, Vol. 1*. Cambridge, UK: Cambridge University Press, edited by Roderick Floud and Deirde McCloskey.

Crouch, D. 1985. "Corporatism in Industrial Relations: A Formal Model." In *The Political Economy of Corporatism*. London: Macmillan, edited by William Grant.

Cziko, Gary. 1995. *Without Miracles*. Cambridge, MA: MIT Press.

Dahl, Robert A. 1956. *A Preface to Democratic Theory*. Chicago, IL: University of Chicago Press.

Dahl, Robert A. 1998. *On Democracy*. New Haven, CT: Yale University Press.

Dahl, Robert A. 2001. *How Democratic is the American Constitution?* New Haven, CT: Yale University Press.

Darnton, Robert. 1997. "Condorcet and the Craze for America in France." In *Franklin and Condorcet*. Philadelphia: American Philosophical Society, edited by J. Brown.

Davies, Godfrey. 1959. *The Early Stuarts 1603–1660*. Oxford: Clarendon Press.

Davis, L., and Douglass C. North. 1970. "Institutional Change and American Economic Growth: A First Step towards a Theory of Institutional Innovation." *Journal of Economic History* 30: 131–49.

Dawson, John. 1997. *Logical Dilemmas*. Wellesley, MA: A. K. Peters.

Debreu, Gerard. 1974. "Excess Demand Functions." *Journal of Mathematical Economics* 1: 15–23.

Dennett, Daniel. 1991. *Consciousness Explained*. Boston, MA: Little Brown.

Dennett, Daniel. 1995. *Darwin's Dangerous Idea*. New York: Simon & Schuster.

Denzau, Arthur, and Douglass C. North. 1994. "Shared Mental Models: Ideologies and Institutions." *Kyklos* 47: 3–31.

Descartes, Rene. 1968 [1637]. *Discourse on Method and Other Writings*. Edited by Frank Sutcliffe. Harmondsworth, UK: Penguin.

Destutt de Tracy, Antoine-Louis-Claude. 1798. *Commentaire sur l'ésprit des lois de Montesquieu*. Paris: Desoer.

Dickason, Olive Patricia. 1992. *Canada's First Nation*. Norman, OK: University of Oklahoma Press.

Dixon, Kim, and Norman Schofield. 2001. "The Election of Lincoln in 1860." *Homo Oeconomicus* 16: 49–67.

Donald, David. 1995. *Lincoln*. London: Cape.

Downs, Anthony. 1957. *An Economic Theory of Democracy*. New York: Harper.

Draper, Theodore. 1996. *A Struggle for Power*. New York: Random House.

Drobak, John. 1993. "The Courts and Slavery in the United States: Property Rights and Credible Commitment." In *Political Economy: Institutions: Competition and Representation*. Cambridge, UK: Cambridge University Press, edited by William Barnett, Melvin Hinich, and Norman Schofield.

Dull, Jonathan. 1985. *Diplomatic History of the American Revolution*. New Haven: Yale University Press.

Duverger, Maurice. 1954. *Political Parties: Their Organization and Activity in the Modern State*. New York: Wiley and Sons.

Duverger, Maurice. 1984. "Which is the best electoral system?" In *Choosing an Electoral System*. New York: Praeger, edited by Arendt Lijphart and Bernard Groman.

Edelman, Gerald, and Giulio Tononi. 2000. *Consciousness: How Matter Becomes Imagination*. London: Penguin Press.

Egnal, Marc. 1988. *A Mighty Empire*. Ithaca, NY: Cornell University Press.

Ehrlich, Walter. 1979. *They Have No Rights: Dred Scott's Struggle for Freedom*. Westport, CT: Greenwood Press.

Eldredge, Niels, and Steven J. Gould. 1972. "Punctuated Equilibria." In *Models of Paleobiology*. New York: Norton, edited by Thomas Schopf.

Elkins, Stanley, and Eric McKitrick. 1993. *The Age of Federalism: The Early American Republic, 1788–1800*. Oxford: Oxford University Press.

Enelow, James, and Melvin Hinich. 1984. *The Spatial Theory of Voting*. Cambridge, UK: Cambridge University Press.

Evans, Richard. 2003. *The Coming of the Third Reich*. London: Penguin Books.

Fagan, Brian. 1999. *Floods, Famines and Emperors*. New York: Basic.

Fan, Ky. 1961. "A Generalization of Tychonoff's Fixed Point Theorem." *Math Annalen* 42: 305–10.

Fedderson, Timothy, and Wolfgang Pesendorfer. 1997. "Voting Behavior and information aggregation in elections with private information." *Econometrica* 65: 1029–58.

Fehrenbacher, Dan E. 1981. *The Dred Scott Case: Its Significance in Law and Politics*. New York: Oxford University Press.

Fehrenbacher, Dan E. ed. 1989a. *Lincoln: Speeches and Writings 1832–1858, Vol. 1*. New York: Library of America.

Fehrenbacher, Dan E. ed. 1989b. *Lincoln: Speeches and Writings 1859–1865, Vol. 2*. New York: Library of America.

Fehrenbacher, Dan E. 2001. *The Slaveholding Republic*. New York: Oxford University Press.

Feingold, Mordechai. 2004. *The Newtonian Moment: Isaac Newton and the Making of Modern Culture*. New York: Oxford University Press.

Ferguson, Niall. 1999. *The Pity of War*. New York: Basic Books.

Ferguson, Niall. 2001. *The Cash Nexus: Money and Power in the Modern World, 1700–2000*. New York: Basic Books.

Ferguson, Niall. 2002. *Empire: The Rise and Demise of the British World Order*. London: Penguin Books.

Ferguson, Niall. 2003. "British Imperialism Revised." Stern School of Business, New York University. Unpublished Manuscript.

Ferguson, Niall. 2004. *Colossus: The Price of America's Empire*. New York: Penguin Books.

Ferling, John. 1992. *John Adams*. New York: Henry Holt.

Fermi, Enrico, John Pasta, and Stanislaw Ulam. 1955. "Studies in Nonlinear Problems," in *Analogies Between Analogies*. Berkeley, CA: University of California Press, edited by Stanislaw Ulam.

Feyerabend, Paul. 1970. "Consolation for the Specialist." In *Criticism and the Growth of Knowledge*. Cambridge, UK: Cambridge University Press.

Feyerabend, Paul. 1975. *Against Method*. London: Verso.

Filmer, Robert. 1949 [1632–1652]. *Patriarcha and Other Political Writings.* Oxford: Basil Blackwell, edited by Peter Laslett.

Fine, Sidney. 1976. *Laissez-Faire and the General Welfare State.* Ann Arbor, MI: University of Michigan Press.

Fink, Evelyn, and William Riker. 1989. "The Strategy of Ratification." In *The Federalist Papers and the New Institutionalism.* New York: Agathon, edited by Benard Grofman and Donald Wittman.

Fletcher, George. 2001. *Our Secret Constitution.* New York: Oxford University Press.

Floud, Roderick, and Deirdre McCloskey. eds. 1994. *The Economic History of Britain since 1700, Volume 1: 1700–1860.* Cambridge, UK: Cambridge University Press.

Fogel, Robert. 1994. *Without Consent or Contract.* New York: Norton.

Foner, Eric. 1970. *Free Soil, Free Labor, Free Men.* Oxford: Oxford University Press.

Foner, Eric. ed. 1995. *Thomas Paine: Collected Writings.* New York: Library of America.

Freeman, Joanne. 2001. [ed.] *Hamilton: Writings.* New York: Library of America.

French, A. P. 1979. *Einstein: A Centenary Volume.* Cambridge, MA: Harvard University Press.

Friedman, Milton. 1968. "The Role of Monetary Policy," *American Economic Review* 58: 1–18.

Fudenberg, Drew, and Jean Tirole. 1992. *Game Theory.* Cambridge, MA: MIT Press.

Fukuyama, Francis. 1992. *The End of History and the Last Man.* New York: The Free Press.

Galison, Peter. 1997. *Image and Logic.* Chicago, IL: University of Chicago Press.

Gallup, George. 1972. *The Gallup Poll: Public Opinion 1935–71.* New York: Random House.

Garrett, G. 1998. *Partisan Politics in the Global Economy.* Cambridge, UK: Cambridge University Press.

Gary, Kelley. 2004. "The Social Choice of Secession." *Homo Oeconomicus* 21: 355–72.

Gauthier, David. 1986. *Morals by Agreement.* Oxford: Clarendon Press.

Geanakoplos, John, and Herakles Polemarchakis. 1982. "We Can't Disagree Forever." *Journal of Economic Theory* 28: 192–200.

Gibbon, Edward. 1994 [1781]. *The History of the Decline and Fall of the Roman Empire.* Harmondsworth, UK: Penguin, edited by David Womersley.

Gillispie, Charles C. 1972. "Probability and Politics: Laplace, Condorcet and Turgot." *Proceedings of the American Philosophical Society* 116: 1–20.

Gillispie, Charles C. 1980. *Science and Polity in France: The End of the Old Regime.* Princeton, NJ: Princeton University Press.

Gillispie, Charles C. 2005. *Science and Polity in France: The Revolutionary and Napoleonic Years.* Princeton, NJ: Princeton University Press.

Gladwell, Malcolm. 2000. *The Tipping Point: How Little Things Can Make a Big Difference.* New York: Little Brown.

Gleick, James. 1987. *Chaos: Making a New Science.* New York: Viking.

Gleick, James. 2003. *Isaac Newton.* New York: Random House.

Gödel, Kurt. 1931. "Uber formal unentscheidbare Satze der Principia Mathematica und verwandter Systeme." *Monatschefte fur Mathematik und Physik* 38: 173–98. Translated as "On Formally Undecidable Propositions of *Principia Mathematica* and Related Systems." In Jean van Heijenoort, *Frege and Gödel: Two Fundamental Texts in Mathematical Logic*. Cambridge, MA: Harvard University Press.

Goldman, Eric. 1952. *Rendezvous with Destiny*. New York: Vintage Books.

Goldstein, Rebecca. 2005. *Incompleteness*. New York: Norton.

Goldsworthy, Adrian. 2000. *The Punic Wars*. London: Cassell.

Goodhart, Charles and Richard Bhansali. 1970. "Political Economy." *Political Studies* 18: 43–106.

Goodwin, Jason. 1999. *Lords of the Horizon*. New York: St. Martin's Press.

Gould, Stephen J. 1996. *The Structure of Evolutionary Theory*. Cambridge, MA: Harvard University Press.

Gray, John. 1984. *Hayek on Liberty*. Oxford: Basil Blackwell.

Gray, John. 2004. *Al-Qaeda and What It Means To Be Modern*. London: Routledge.

Greenberg, Joseph. 1979. "Consistent Majority Rules over Compact Sets of Alternatives." *Econometrica* 41: 286–97.

Greif, Avner. 1997. "On the Interrelations and Economic Implications of Economic, Social, Political, and Normative Factors: Reflections from Two Late Medieval Societies." In *The Frontiers of the New Institutional Economics*. San Diego: Academic Press, edited by John Droback and John Nye.

Gribbin, John. 2004. *Deep Simplicity: Bringing Order to Chaos and Complexity*. New York: Random House.

Groseclose, Timothy. 2001. "A Model of Candidate Location when One Candidate has a Valence Advantage." *American Journal of Political Science* 45: 862–86.

Haber, Stephen. ed. 1997. *How Latin America Fell Behind*. Stanford, CA: Stanford University Press.

Hahn, Frank. 1973. *On the Notion of Equilibrium in Economics*. Cambridge, UK: Cambridge University Press.

Hammond, Thomas H., and Gary Miller. 1987. "The Core of the Constitution." *American Political Science Review* 81:1155–74.

Hardin, Russell. 1982. *Collective Action*. Baltimore: Johns Hopkins University Press.

Hardman, John. 2000. *Louis XVI*. London: Hodder.

Harrod, Roy. 1971. *The Life of John Maynard Keynes*. New York: Avon.

Hicks, John. 1937. "Mr. Keynes and the 'Classics'; A Suggested Interpretation." *Econometrica* 5: 147–59.

Hinich, Melvin. 1977. "Equilibrium in Spatial Voting: The Median Voter Result is an Artifact." *Journal of Economic Theory* 16: 208–219.

Hobbes, Thomas. 1960 [1651]. *Leviathan; or the Matter, Forme, and Power of a Common-wealth, Ecclesiastical and Civil*. Harmondsworth, UK: Penguin, edited by Crawford MacPherson.

Hodges, Andrew. 1983. *Alan Turing: The Enigma*. New York: Simon & Schuster.

Hoffman, Philip, and Jean-Laurent Rosenthal. 1997. "The Political Economy of Warfare and Taxation in Early Modern Europe: Historical Lessons for

Economic Development." In *The Frontiers of the New Institutional Economics*. San Diego: Academic Press, edited by John Droback and John Nye.

Holland, John. 1988. "The Global Economy as an Adaptive Process." In *The Economy as an Evolving Complex System*. Reading, MA: Addison-Wesley, edited by Philip Anderson, Kenneth Arrow, and David Pine.

Holzer, Harold. ed. 1993. *The Lincoln Douglas Debates*. New York: Harper Collins.

Holzer, Harold. 2005. *Lincoln at Cooper Union*. New York: Simon and Schuster.

Hotelling, Harold J. 1929. "Stability in Competition." *Economic Journal* 39: 41–57.

Huberman, Bernardo, and Natalie Glance. 1995. "Beliefs and Cooperation." In *Chaos and Society*. Amsterdam: IOS Press, edited by Alain Albert.

Huckfeldt, Robert, and Carol Kohfeld. 1989. *Race and the Decline of Class in American Politics*. Urbana-Champaign, IL: University of Illinois Press.

Hume, David. 1985 [1752]. *A Treatise of Human Nature*. London: Collins.

Hume, David. 1985 [1742, 1748, 1777]. *Essays: Moral, Political and Literary*. Indianapolis, IN: Liberty Fund, edited by Eugene Miller.

Israel, Jonathan. 2001. *Radical Enlightenment*. Oxford: Oxford University Press.

Jaffa, Harry V. 2000. *New Birth of Freedom*. Lanham, MD: Rowman and Little-field.

Jenkins, Roy. 2001. *Churchill: A Biography*. New York: Farrar, Straus and Giroux.

Jennings, Francis. 1988. *Empire of Fortune*. New York: Norton.

Jennings, Francis. 2000. *The Creation of America: Through Revolution to Empire*. Cambridge, UK: Cambridge University Press.

Jones, Joseph. 1955. *The Fifteen Weeks: February 21–June 5, 1947*. New York: Viking.

Kahn, Richard. 1984. *The Making of Keynes' General Theory*. Cambridge, UK: Cambridge University Press.

Kahneman, Daniel, and Amos Tversky. 1979. "Prospect Theory: An Analysis of Decision under Risk." *Econometrica* 47: 263–91.

Kakutani, Shizno. 1941. "A Generalization of Brouwer's Fixed Point Theorem." *Duke Mathematics Journal* 8: 457–59.

Kapur, Devesh, John Lewis, and Richard Webb. 1977. *The World Bank: Its First Half Century*. Washington, D.C.: Brookings Institution Press.

Karol, David. 1999. "Realignment Without Replacement: Issue Evolution and Ideological Change among Members of Congress." UCLA. Unpublished manuscript.

Kauffman, Stuart. 1993. *The Origins of Order*. Oxford: Oxford University Press.

Kauffman, Stuart. 1995. *At Home in the Universe*. Oxford: Oxford University Press.

Kennan, George. 1976. *Memoirs, 1925–1950*. Boston, MA: Little Brown.

Kennedy, Paul. 1987. *The Rise and Fall of the Great Powers*. New York: Random House.

Keohane, Robert. 1984. *After Hegemony*. Princeton, NJ: Princeton University Press.

Keohane, Robert, and Joseph Nye. 1977. *Power and Interdependence*. Boston, MA: Little Brown.

Ketcham, Ralph. 1971. *James Madison: A Biography*. Charlottesville: University Press of Virginia.

Key, Vladimir Orlando. 1955. "A Theory of Critical Elections." *Journal of Politics* 17: 3–18.

Keynes, John Maynard. 1919. *Economic Consequences of The Peace*. London: Macmillan.

Keynes, John Maynard. 1921. *A Treatise on Probability, Vol 8 of Collected Writings*. London: Macmillan.

Keynes, John Maynard. 1933. "National Self-Sufficiency." *Yale Review* 26: 755–69.

Keynes, John Maynard. 1936. *The General Theory of Employment, Interest and Money*. London: Macmillan.

Keynes, John Maynard. 1937. "The General Theory of Employment." *Quarterly Journal of Economics* 51: 209–23.

Kindleberger, Charles. 1973. *The World in Depression 1929–1939*. Berkeley, CA: University of California Press.

Kirkland, Richard. 1995. "Today's GOP: The Party's Over for Big Business." *Fortune* Feb 6: 50–95.

Kirman, Alan, and Dieter Sondermann. 1972. "Arrow's Impossibility Theorem: Many Agents and Invisible Dictators." *Journal of Economic Theory* 5: 267–78.

Koford, Kenneth. 1989. "Dimensions in Congressional Voting." *American Political Science Review* 83: 949–62.

Kohler, Imke. 1998. "The Marshall Plan and the World Bank's Role in European Recovery." Washington University in St. Louis. Unpublished manuscript.

Kotz, Nick. 2005. *Judgement Days: LB Johnson, Martin Luther King Jr., and the Laws that Changed America*. New York: Houghton Mifflin.

Kramer, Gerald H. 1973. "On a Class of Equilibrium Conditions for Majority Rule." *Econometrica* 41: 285–97.

Kramnick, Isaac. 1990. *Republicanism and Bourgeois Radicalism*. Itahca, NY: Cornell University Press.

Kramnick, Isaac. 1992 [1968]. *Bolingbroke and his Circle*. Ithaca, NY: Cornell University Press.

Kreps, David, Paul Milgrom, John Roberts, and Robert Wilson. 1982. "Rational Cooperation in the Finitely Repeated Prisoner's Dilemma." *Journal of Economic Theory* 27: 245–52.

Kuhn, Thomas. 1962. *The Structure of Scientific Revolutions*. Chicago, IL: University of Chicago Press.

Ladha, Krishna. 1992. "Condorcet's Jury Theorem, Free Speech and Correlated Votes." *American Journal of Political Science* 36: 617–74.

Ladha, Krishna. 1993. "Condorcet's Jury Theorem in the Light of de Finetti's Theorem: Majority Rule with Correlated Votes." *Social Choice and Welfare* 10: 69–86.

Ladha, Krishna. 1995. "Information Pooling through Majority Rule Voting: Condorcet's Jury Theorem with Correlated Votes." *Journal of Economic Behavior and Organization* 26: 353–72.

Ladha, Krishna. 1996. "Hypothesis Testing and Collective Decision Making." In *Collective Decision Making*. Boston, MA: Kluwer, edited by Norman Schofield.

Ladha, Krishna, and Gary Miller. 1996. "Political Discourse, Factions and the General Will: Correlated Voting and Condorcet's Jury Theorem." In *Collective Decision Making*. Boston, MA: Kluwer, edited by Norman Schofield.

Landes, David. 1998. *The Wealth and Poverty of Nations*. New York, Norton.

Lange, Oskar. 1938. "On the Economic Theory of the State." In *The Economic Theory of Socialism*. Minneapolis: University of Minnesota Press, edited by Oskar Lange and Frank Taylor.

Laplace, Pierre-Simon. 1798–1825. *Traité de mécanique céleste* (5 volumes). Paris: Gauthiers-Villars.

Laplace, Pierre-Simon. 1812. *Théorie analytique des probabilités*. Paris: Gauthiers-Villars.

Laplace, Pierre-Simon. 1814. *Essai philosophique sur les probabilités*. Paris: Gauthiers-Villars. *A Philosophical Essay on Probabilities*, translated by Frederick Truscott and Frederick Emory, 1951, with an introduction by Eric Bell. New York: Dover.

Laslett, Peter. 1988. "Introduction" to *The Two Treatises of Government* by John Locke. Cambridge, UK: Cambridge University Press.

Laver, Michael, and Norman Schofield. 1998 [1990]. *Multiparty Government: The Politics of Coalition in Europe*. Oxford: Oxford University Press. Reprinted Ann Arbor, MI: University of Michigan Press.

Lehmbruch, G. 1979. "Consociational Democracy, Class Conflict and the New Corporatism." In *Trends Towards Corporatist Intermediation*. London: Sage, edited by George Lehmbruch and Philippe Schmitter.

Li, T.-Y., and J. A.Yorke, 1975. "Period Three Implies Chaos." *American Mathematical Monthly* 82: 985–92.

Lijphart, Arendt. 1969. "Consociational Democracy." *World Politics* 21: 207–25.

Lin, Tse-Min, James Enelow, and Han Dorussen. 1999. "Equilibrium in Multi-candidate Probabilistic Spatial Voting." *Public Choice* 98: 59–62.

Locke, John. 1988 [1690]. *Two Treatises of Government*. Cambridge, UK: Cambridge University Press, edited and with an introduction by Peter Laslett.

Lopez, Claude-Anne. 1966. *Mon Cher Papa: Franklin and the Ladies of Paris*. New Haven, CT: Yale University Press.

Lopez, Claude-Anne. 2000. *My Life with Benjamin Franklin*. New Haven, CT: Yale University Press.

Lorenz, Edward. 1993. *The Essence of Chaos*. Seattle, WA: University of Washington Press.

Lucaks, John. 1999. *Five Days in London*. New Haven, CT: Yale University Press.

Mackie, Gerry. 2001. "Is Democracy Impossible? Riker's mistaken account of antebellum politics." Australian National University. Unpublished manuscript.

MacPherson, Crawford. 1968. "Introduction" to *Leviathan* by Thomas Hobbes. Harmondsworth, UK: Penguin Books.

MacRae, Duncan. 1977. "A Political Model of the Business Cycle." *Journal of Political Economy* 85: 239–63.

Macmillan, Margaret. 2001. *Peacemakers*. London: John Murray.

Madison, James. 1977. *Papers Vol. 10*. Chicago, IL: University of Chicago Press, edited by Robert Rutland and Charles Hobson.

Madison, James. 1979. *Papers Vol. 12*. Charlottesville, VA: University Press of Virginia, edited by Charles Hobson, Robert Rutland, William Rachal and Jeanne Sissan.

Madison, James. 1985. *Papers Vol. 15*. Charlottesville, VA: University Press of Virginia, edited by Thomas Mason, Robert Rutland, and Jeanne Sisson.

Malthus, Thomas. 1970 [1798]. *An Essay on the Principle of Population and a Summary View of the Principle of Population*. Harmondsworth, UK: Penguin, edited and with an introduction by Anthony Flew.

Mandelbrot, Benoit, and Richard Hudson. 2004. *The (Mis) Behavior of Markets*. New York: Basic Books.

Mandeville, Bernard. 1924 [1714]. *The Fable of The Bees or Private Vices, Publick Benefits*. Oxford: Oxford University Press. Reprinted, Indianapolis, IN: Liberty Fund.

Mann, Robert. 1996. *The Walls of Jericho*. New York: Harcourt Brace.

Mantel, Rolf. 1974. "On the Characterization of Aggregate Excess Demand." *Journal of Economic Theory* 7: 197–201.

Margolis, Howard. 1987. *Patterns, Thinking and Cognition: A Theory of Judgement*. Chicago, IL: University of Chicago Press.

Margolis, Howard. 1993. *Paradigms and Barriers: How Habits of Mind Govern Scientific Beliefs*. Chicago, IL: Universityof Chicago Press.

Marshall, Alfred. 1890. *Principles of Economics*. London: Macmillan.

Martinelli, Cesar. 2003. "Would Rational Voters Acquire Costly Information?" ITAM, Mexico City. Unpublished manuscript.

MasColell, Andreu. 1985. *The Theory of General Economic Equilibrium*. Cambridge, UK: Cambridge University Press.

Mason, Edward John, and Robert Asher. 1973. *The World Bank since Bretton Woods*. Washington, D.C.: Brookings Institute Press.

Mayer, David. 1994. *The Constitutinal Thought of Thomas Jefferson*. Charlottesvile, VA: University Press of Virginia.

Mayhew, David. 2000. "Electoral Realignments." *Annual Review of Political Science* 3: 449–74.

Mayhew, David. 2002. *Electoral Realignments: A Critique of an American Genre*. New Haven, CT: Yale University Press.

McCloy, John. 1947. "International Investment of Capital." Address at the Seventh Annual Forum of Social and Economic Trends, New York City.

McCoy, Drew R. 1980a. *The Elusive Republic*. Williamsburg, VA: University of North Carolina Press.

McCoy, Drew R. 1980b. "Jefferson and Madison on Malthus." *Virginia Magazine of Historical Biography* 88: 159–76.

McCoy, Drew R. 1989. *The Last of the Fathers: James Madison and the Republican Legacy*. Cambridge, UK: Cambridge University Press.

McCracken, Paul. 1977. *Towards Full Employment and Price Stability*. Paris: OECD.

McCullough, David. 2001. *John Adams*. New York: Simon & Schuster.

McCullough, David. 2005. *1776*. New York: Simon & Schuster.

McDonald, Forrest. 2000. *States' Rights and the Union*. Lawrence, KS: University Press of Kansas.

McGrath, David. 1983. *James Madison and Social Choice Theory: The Possibility of Republicanism*. College Park, MD: University of Maryland, unpublished doctoral dissertation.

McKelvey, Richard D. 1976. "Intransitivities in Multi-Dimensional Voting Models and Some Implications for Agenda Control." *Journal of Economic Theory* 12: 472–82.

McKelvey, Richard D. 1979. "General Conditions for Global Intransitivities in Formal Voting Models." *Econometrica* 47: 1085–111.

McKelvey, Richard D. 1986. "Covering, Dominance, and Institution-Free Properties of Social Choice." *American Journal of Political Science* 30: 382–14.

McKelvey, Richard, and Norman Schofield. 1986. "Structural Instability of the Core." *Journal of Mathematical Economics* 15: 179–88.

McKelvey, Richard, and Norman Schofield. 1987. "Generalized Symmetry Conditions at a Core Point." *Econometrica* 55: 923–33.

McKelvey, Richard, and Talbot Page. 1986. "Common Knowledge, Consensus, and Aggregate Information." *Econometrica* 54: 109–27.

McKenzie, Lionel. 1959. "On the Existence of a General Equilibrium for a Competitive Economy." *Econometrica* 27: 54–71.

McLean, Iain. 2000. "Irish Potatoes, Indian Corn, and British Politics: Interests, Ideology, Heresthetic and the Repeal of the Corn Laws." In *International Trade and Political Institutions*, Cheltenham, UK: Edward Elgar, edited by Fiona McGillivray, Iain McLean, Robert Pahre, and Cheryl Schonhardt-Bailey.

McLean, Iain. 2002. *Rational Choice and British Politics*. Oxford: Oxford University Press.

McLean, Iain. 2003. "Before and After Publius: The Sources and Influence of Madison's Political Thought. " In *The Theory and Practise of Republican Government*. Stanford: Stanford University Press, edited by Samuel Kernell.

McLean, Iain. 2005. "The Eighteenth Century Revolution in Social Sciences and the dawn of Political Science in America." Nuffield College, Oxford University. Unpublished Manuscript.

McLean, Iain, and Fiona Hewitt. 1994. *Condorcet: Foundations of Social Choice and Political Theory*. Aldershot, UK: Edward Elgar.

McLean, Iain, and Arnold B. Urken. 1992. "Did Jefferson or Madison Understand Condorcet's Theory of Social Choice?" *Public Choice* 73: 445–57.

McLennan, Andrew. 1998. "Consequences of the Condorcet Jury Theorem for Beneficial Information Aggregation by Rational Agents." *American Political Science Review* 92: 413–18.

Meinig, Donald W. 1993. *The Shaping of America, Volume 1, Atlantic America, 1492–1800*. New Haven, CT: Yale University Press.

Merrill, Samuel, and Bernard Grofman. 1999. *A Unified Theory of Voting*. Cambridge, UK: Cambridge University Press.

Mershon, Carol. 2002. *The Costs of Coalition*. Stanford, CA: Stanford University Press.

Middlekauff, Robert. 1982. *The Glorious Cause*. Oxford: Oxford University Press.

Miller, Gary, and Norman Schofield. 2003. "Activists and Partisan Realignment." *American Political Science Review* 97: 245–60.

Miller, William Lee. 1995. *Arguing about Slavery.* New York: Alfred Knopf.

Minsky, Hyman. 1975. *John Maynard Keynes.* New York: Columbia University Press.

Montesquieu, Charles. 1990 [1734]. "Considerations on the Cause of the Romans' Greatness and Decline." In *Montesquieu: Selected Political Writings.* Indianapolis, IN: Hackett, edited by Melvin Richter.

Montesquieu, Charles. 1990 [1748]. "The Spirit of the Laws." In *Montesquieu: Selected Political Writings.* Indianapolis, IN: Hackett, edited by Melvin Richter.

Moore, George. 1903. *Principia Ethica.* Cambridge: Cambridge University Press.

Mumford, David. 2002. "Pattern Theory: The Mathematics of Perception. Brown University. Unpublished Manuscript.

Nachbar, John. 1997. "Prediction, Optimization, and Learning in Repeated Games." *Econometrica* 65: 275–309.

Nachbar, John. 2001. "Bayesian Learning in Repeated Games of Incomplete Information." *Social Choice and Welfare* 18: 303–26.

Nachbar, John. 2005. "Beliefs in Repeated Games." *Econometrica* 73: 459–80.

Namier, Lewis. 1957. *The Structure of Politics at the Accession of George III.* London: Macmillan.

Nakamura, Kenjiro. 1979. "The Vetoers in a Simple Game with Ordinal Preferences." *International Journal of Game Theory* 8: 55–61.

Nash, John. 1950. "Equilibrium Points in N-person Games." *Proc. National Academy of Sciences, USA* 36: 48–9.

Nash, John. 1951. "Non-cooperative Games." *Annals of Mathematics* 54: 259–95.

Nevins, Allan. 1950. *The Emergence of Lincoln.* New York: Charles Scribner's Sons.

Newberry, David, and Joseph Stiglitz. 1981. *Theory of Commodity Price Stabilisation.* Oxford: Clarendon Press.

Newton, Isaac. 1984 [1672]. "New Theory about Light and Colours." In *The Optical Papers of Isaac Newton,* Cambridge, Cambridge University Press, edited by Alan Shapiro, originally published in *The Philosophical Transactions of the Royal Society.*

Newton, Isaac. 1995 [1687]. *Philosophiae Naturalis Principia Mathematica.* Amherst, NY: Prometheus Books, translated, edited and with an introduction by Andrew Motte.

Newton, Isaac. 1704. *Opticks: Or, a Treatise of the Reflexions, Refractions, Inflexions and Colours of Light.* London: Smith and Walford.

Niskanen, William. 1971. *Bureaucracy and Representative Government.* New York: Aldine.

Norberg, Kathryn. 1994. "The French fiscal crisis of 1788 and the financial origins of the revolution of 1789." In *Fiscal Crises, Liberty and Representative Government.* Stanford, CA: Stanford University Press, edited by Philip Hoffman and Katherine Norberg.

Nordhaus, William. 1975. "The Political Business Cycle." *Review of Economic Studies* 42: 167–90.

North, Douglass C. 1961. *The Economic Growth of the United States.* New York: Norton.

North, Douglass C. 1981. *Structure and Change in Economic History.* New York: Norton.

North, Douglass C. 1990. *Institutions, Institutional Change and Economic Performance.* Cambridge, UK: Cambridge University Press.

North, Douglass C. 1993. "Institutions and Credible Commitment." *Journal of Institutional Theoretical Economics* 149: 11–23.

North, Douglass C. 1994. "Economic Performance through Time." *American Economic Review* 84: 359–68.

North, Douglass C. 2005. *Understanding the Process of Economic Change.* Princeton, NJ: Princeton University Press.

North, Douglass C., and Andrew Rutten. 1984. "The Northwest Ordinance in Historical Perspective." In *The Economy of the Old Northwest.* Athens: Ohio University Press, edited by D. Klingaman and D. Vedder.

North, Douglass C., and Robert Thomas. 1970. "An Economic Theory of Growth of the Western World." *Economic History Review* 23: 1–17.

North, Douglass C., and Robert Thomas. 1973. *The Rise of the Western World: A New Economic History.* Cambridge, UK: Cambridge University Press.

North, Douglass C., and Robert Thomas. 1977. "The First Economic Revolution." *Economic History Review* 30: 229–41.

North, Douglass C., and Barry R. Weingast. 1989. "Constitutions and Commitment: The Evolution of Institutions Governing Public Choice in Seventeenth Century England." *Journal of Economic History* 49: 803–32.

Nozick, Robert. 1974. *Anarchy, State, and Utopia.* New York: Basic Books.

Nye, John. 1991. "Revisionist Tariff History and the Theory of Hegemonic Stability." *Politics and Society* 19: 209–32.

Nye, John. 1992. "Guerre, Commerce, Guerre Commercial: L'économie politiques des échanges franco-anglais." *Annales: Economics, Societes, Civilisations* 3: 613–32.

Nye, John. 2006. *War, Wine and Taxes: The Political Economy of Anglo–French Trade 1689–1860.* Princeton, NJ: Princeton University Press, in press.

O'Brien, Conor C. 1996. *The Long Affair: Thomas Jefferson and the French Revolution, 1785–1800.* Chicago, IL: University of Chicago Press.

O'Shaughnessy, Andrew J. 2000. *An Empire Divided.* Philadelphia, PA: University of Pennsylvania Press.

Olson, Mancur. 1965. *The Logic of Collective Action.* Cambridge, MA: Harvard University Press.

Olson, Mancur. 1982a. *The Rise and Decline of Nations.* New Haven, CT: Yale University Press.

Olson, Mancur. 1982b. "The Political Economy of Comparative Growth Rates." In *The Political Economy of Growth.* New Haven, CT: Yale University Press, edited by Dennis Mueller.

Olson, Mancur. 2000. *Power and Prosperity: Outgrowing Communist and Capitalist Dictatorships.* New York: Basic.

Ordeshook, Peter, and Kenneth Shepsle. eds. 1982. *Political Equilibrium.* Boston, MA: Kluwer.

Parker, Geoffrey. 1998. *The Grand Strategy of Philip II*. New Haven, CT: Yale University Press.

Penrose, Roger. 1989. *The Emperor's New Mind*. Oxford: Oxford University Press.

Penrose, Roger. 1994. *Shadows of the Mind*. Oxford: Oxford University Press.

Penrose, Roger. 1997. *The Large, the Small, and the Human Mind*. Cambridge, UK: Cambridge University Press.

Petersen, Ivars. 1993. *Newton's Clock: Chaos in the Solar System*. New York: Freeman.

Peterson, Merril D. ed. 1984. *Thomas Jefferson: Writings*. New York: The Library of America.

Petrocik, John. 1981. *Party Coalitions: Realignment and the Decline of the New Deal Party System*. Chicago, IL: University of Chicago Press.

Phillips, Kevin. 1999. *The Cousins' War*. New York: Basic Books.

Plott, Charles. 1967. "A Notion of Equilibrium and Its Possibility Under Majority Rule." *American Economic Review* 57: 787–806.

Plumb, J. H. 1967. *The Growth of Political Stability in England: 1675–1725*. London: Macmillan.

Pocock, John. 1975. *The Machiavellian Moment*. Princeton, NJ: Princeton University Press.

Pocock, Tom. 1998. *The Battle for Empire, 1756–1763*. London: O'Mara Books.

Poincare, Henri. 1993 [1892–1899]. *New Methods of Celestial Mechanics*. New York: American Institute of Physics, edited and with an introduction by Daniel Goreff.

Polanyi, Michael. 1958. *Personal Knowledge*. Chicago, IL: University of Chicago Press.

Poole, Keith, and Howard Rosenthal. 1984. "U.S. Presidential Elections 1968–1980: A Spatial Analysis." *American Journal of Political Science* 28: 283–312.

Poole, Keith, and Howard Rosenthal. 1997. *Congress: A Political Economic History of Roll Call Voting*. New York: Oxford University Press.

Popper, Karl. 1992 [1935]. *The Logic of Scientific Discovery*. London: Routledge & Kegan Paul.

Popper, Karl 1945. *The Open Society and Its Enemies*. London: Routledge & Kegan Paul.

Popper, Karl. 1959. *The Poverty of Historicism*. London: Routledge & Kegan Paul.

Popper, Karl. 1972. *Objective Knowledge: An Evolutionary Approach*. Oxford: Oxford University Press.

Popper, Karl, and John Eccles. 1977. *The Self and the Brain*. Berlin: Springer-Verlag.

Porter, Roy. 2000. *Enlightenment: Britain and the Creation of the Modern World*. London: Penguin.

Prigogine, Ilya. 1980. *From Being to Becoming: Time and Complexity in the Physical Sciences*. San Francisco: Freeman.

Rae, Douglas. 1969. "Decision Rules and Individual Values in Constitutional Choice." *American Political Science Review* 63: 40–56.

Rakove, Jack. 1996. *Original Meanings*. New York: Alfred Knopf.

Rakove, Jack. ed. 1999. *James Madison: Writings*. New York: Library of America.

Rakove, Jack, Andrew Rutten, and Barry Weingast. 1999. "Ideas, Interests and Credible Commitments in the American Revolution." Stanford University. Unpublished Manuscript.

Randall, William S. 1993. *Thomas Jefferson: A Life.* New York: Henry Holt.

Randall, William S. 1997. *George Washington: A Life.* New York: Henry Holt.

Ransom, Roger. 1989. *Conflict and Compromise.* Cambridge, UK: Cambridge University Press.

Rawls, John. 1972. *A Theory of Justice.* Cambridge, MA: Harvard University Press.

Rehfeld, Andrew. 2000. "The Extended Republic and James Madison's *Federalist X.*" Washington University in St. Louis. Unpublished Manuscript.

Rhodehamel, John. ed. 1997. *George Washington: Writings.* New York: Library of America.

Richards, Diana. 1990. "Is Strategic Decision Making Chaotic?" *Behavioral Science* 35: 219–32.

Riker, William. 1953. *Democracy in the United States.* New York: Macmillan.

Riker, William. 1957. *Soldiers of the States.* Washington, D.C.: Public Affairs Press.

Riker, William. 1962. *The Theory of Political Coalitions.* New Haven, CT: Yale University Press.

Riker, William. 1964. *Federalism: Origin, Operation, Maintenance.* Boston, MA: Little Brown.

Riker, William. 1980. "Implications from the Disequilibrium of Majority Rule for the Study of Institutions." *American Political Science Review* 74: 432–46, reprinted in *Political Equilibrium* (1982). Boston, MA: Kluwer, edited by Peter Ordeshook and Kenneth Shepsle.

Riker, William. 1982. *Liberalism against Populism.* San Francisco: Freeman.

Riker, William. 1984. "The Heresthetics of Constitution-making: The Presidency in 1787 with Comments on Determinism and Rational Choice." *American Political Science Review* 78: 1–16.

Riker, William. 1986. *The Art of Manipulation.* New Haven, CT: Yale University Press.

Riker, William. 1987. *The Development of American Federalism.* Boston, MA: Kluwer.

Riker, William. 1991. "Why Negative Campaigning is Rational." *Studies in American Political Development* 5: 224–300.

Riker, William. 1993. "Rhetorical Interaction in the Ratification Campaign." In *Agenda Formation.* Ann Arbor, MI: University of Michigan Press, edited by William Riker.

Riker, William. 1995. "The Experience of Creating Institutions: The Framing of the U.S. Constitution." In *Explaining Social Institutions.* Ann Arbor, MI: University of Michigan Press, edited by Jack Knight and Itai Sened.

Riker, William. 1996. *The Strategy of Rhetoric: Campaigning for the Ratification of the Constitution.* New Haven, CT: Yale University Press.

Riker, William H., and Peter C. Ordeshook. 1973. *An Introduction to Positive Political Theory.* Englewood Cliffs, NJ: Prentice Hall.

Roche, Daniel. 1998. *France in the Enlightenment*. Cambridge, MA: Harvard University Press.

Rogow, Arnold. 1986. *Thomas Hobbes: Radical in the Service of Reaction*. New York: Norton.

Rogowski, Ronald. 1989. *Commerce and Coalitions*. Princeton, NJ: Princeton University Press.

Rohde, David, and Kenneth Shepsle. 2005. "Advising and Consenting in the 60-vote Senate: Strategic Appointments to the Supreme Court." Harvard University. Unpublished Manuscript.

Root, H. 1994. *The Fountain of Privilege*. Berkeley: University of California Press.

Rosenthal, Jean-Laurent. 1998. "The Political Economy of Absolutism Reconsidered." In *Analytical Narratives*. Princeton, NJ: Princeton University Press, edited by Robert Bates, Avner Greif, Margaret Levi, Jean-Laurent Rosenthal, and Barry Weingast.

Rossiter, Charles. ed. 1961 [1787–1788]. *The Federalist Papers*. New York: New American Library.

Rothbard, Murray. 1995. *Economic Thought before Adam Smith*. Cheltenham, UK: Edward Elgar.

Rothschild, Emma. 2001. *Economic Sentiments: Adam Smith, Condorcet and the Enlightenment*. Cambridge, MA: Harvard University Press.

Rousseau, Jean-Jacques. 1968 [1762]. *The Social Contract*. Harmondsworth, UK: Penguin, edited and with an introduction by Maurice Cranston.

Rutland, R. A., and C. F. Hobson. 1977 [eds.] *The Papers of James Madison*, *Vol. 10*. Chicago, IL: University of Chicago Press.

Saari, Donald. 1991. "Erratic Behavior in Economic Models." *Journal of Economic Behavior and Organization* 16: 3–35.

Saari, Donald. 1996. "The Generic Existence of a Core for q-Rules." *Economic Theory* 9: 219–60.

Saari, Donald. 2005. *Collisions, Rings, and Other Newtonian N-Body Problems*. University of California at Irvine. Unpublished Manuscript.

Savage, Leonard. 1954. *The Foundations of Statistics*. New York: Dover.

Scarf, Herbert. 1960. "Some Examples of Global Instability for the Competitive Equilibrium." *International Economic Review* 1: 157–72.

Schama, Simon. 1989. *Citizens: A Chronicle of the French Revolution*. New York: Knopf.

Schattschneider, E. E. 1960. *The Semi-Sovereign People*. New York: Holt, Rinehart and Winston.

Schiff, Stacy. 2005. *A Great Improvisation: Franklin, France and the Birth of America*. New York: Henry Holt.

Schlesinger, Joseph A. 1994. *Political Parties and the Winning of Office*. Chicago, IL: University of Chicago Press.

Schofield, Norman. 1972a. "Is Majority Rule Special?" In *Probability Models of Collective Decision-making*. Columbus, OH: Charles E. Merrill Publishing Co, edited by Richard G. Niemi and Herbert F. Weisberg.

Schofield, Norman. 1972b. "Ethical Decision Rules for Uncertain Voters." *British Journal of Political Science* 2: 193–207.

Schofield, Norman. 1975. "A Game Theoretic Analysis of Olson's Game of Collective Action." *Journal of Conflict Resolution* 19: 441–61.

Schofield, Norman. 1977a. "The Logic of Catastrophe." *Human Ecology* 5: 261–71.

Schofield, Norman. 1977b. "Dynamic Games of Collective Action." *Public Choice* 30: 77–105.

Schofield, Norman. 1978. "Instability of Simple Dynamic Games." *Review of Economic Studies* 45: 575–94.

Schofield, Norman. 1979. "Rationality or Chaos in Social Choice." *Greek Economic Review* 1: 61-76.

Schofield, Norman. 1980. "Generic Properties of Simple Bergson-Samuelson Welfare Functions." *Journal of Mathematical Economics* 7: 175–92.

Schofield, Norman. 1983. "Generic Instability of Majority Rule." *Review of Economic Studies* 50: 695–705.

Schofield, Norman. 1984a. "Social Equilibrium and Cycles on Compact Sets." *Journal of Economic Theory* 33: 59–71.

Schofield, Norman. ed. 1984b. *Crisis in Economic Relations Between North and South*. Aldershot, England: Gower Press.

Schofield, Norman. 1985a. *Social Choice and Democracy*. Berlin: Springer.

Schofield, Norman. 1985b. "Anarchy, Altruism and Cooperation." *Social Choice and Welfare* 2: 207–19.

Schofield Norman. 1995. "Democratic Stability." In *Explaining Social Institutions*. Ann Arbor, MI: University of Michigan Press, edited by Jack Knight and Itai Sened.

Schofield, Norman. 1996. "The Heart of a Polity." In *Collective Decision Making: Social Choice and Political Economy*. Boston: Kluwer, edited by Norman Schofield.

Schofield, Norman. 1999a. "The C^1-Topology on the Space of Smooth Preference Profiles." *Social Choice and Welfare* 16: 445–70.

Schofield, Norman. 1999b. "The Heart and the Uncovered Set." *Journal of Economics* S. 8: 79–113.

Schofield, Norman. 1999c. "The Amistad and Dred Scott Affairs: Heresthetics and Beliefs in Antebellum America, 1837–1860." *Homo Oeconomicus* 16: 49–67.

Schofield, Norman. 1999d. "The Heart of the Atlantic Constitution: International Economic Stability, 1919–1998." *Politics and Society* 27: 173–215.

Schofield, Norman. 1999e. "Equilibrium or Chaos in Preference and Belief Aggregation." In *Competition and Cooperation*. New York: Russell Sage Foundation, edited by James Alt, Margaret Levi and Elinor Ostrom.

Schofield, Norman. 2000a. "Constitutional Political Economy: Rational Choice Theory and Comparative Politics." *The Annual Review of Political Science* 3: 277–303.

Schofield, Norman. 2000b. "Institutional Innovation, Contingency and War: A Review." *Social Choice and Welfare* 17: 463–79.

Schofield, Norman. 2000c. "Core Beliefs in America at the Founding of the American Republic." *Homo Oeconomicus* 16: 433–462.

Schofield, Norman. 2002a. "Quandaries of War and of Union in North America: 1763–1861." *Politics and Society* 30: 5–49.

Schofield, Norman. 2002b. "Evolution of the Constitution." *The British Journal of Political Science* 32: 1–20.

Schofield, Norman. 2003a. "The Founding of the American Agrarian Empire and the Conflict of Land and Capital." *Homo Oeconomicus* 19: 471–505.

Schofield, Norman. 2003b. "Power, Prosperity and Social Choice: A Review." *Social Choice and Welfare* 20: 85–118.

Schofield, Norman. 2003c. "Constitutional Quandaries and Critical Elections." *Politics, Philosophy and Economics* 2: 5–36.

Schofield, Norman. 2003d. *Mathematical Models in Economics and Social Choice.* Berlin: Springer.

Schofield, Norman. 2004a. "The Probability of a Fit Choice." In *Justice and Democracy.* Cambridge: Cambridge University Press, edited by Keith Dowding, Robert Goodin, and Carole Pateman.

Schofield, Norman. 2004b. "Quandaries of Slavery and Civil War in the U.S." *Homo Oeconomicus* 21: 315–54.

Schofield, Norman. 2005a. "A Valence Model of Political Competition in Britain: 1992–1997." *Electoral Studies* 24: 347–70.

Schofield, Norman. 2005b. "Local Political Equilibria." In *Social Choice and Strategic Decisions: Essays in Honor of Jeffrey S. Banks.* Berlin: Springer, edited by David Austen-Smith and John Duggan.

Schofield, Norman. 2006. "The Mean Voter Theorem: Necessary and Sufficient Conditions for Convergence." Forthcoming in *The Review of Economic Studies.*

Schofield, Norman, Andrew Martin, Kevin Quinn, and Andrew Whitford. 1998. "Multiparty Electoral Competition in the Netherlands and Germany: A Model Based on Multinomial Probit." *Public Choice* 97: 257–93.

Schofield, Norman, Gary Miller, and Andrew Martin. 2003. "Critical Elections and Political Realignments in the USA: 1860–2000." *Political Studies* 51: 217–40.

Schofield, Norman, and Itai Sened. 2005a. "Multiparty Competition in Israel: 1988–1996." *British Journal of Political Science* 35: 635–63.

Schofield, Norman, and Itai Sened. 2005b. "Modeling the Interaction of Parties, Activists and Voters: Why is the Political Center So Empty?" *European Journal of Political Research* 44: 355–90.

Schofield, Norman, and Itai Sened. 2006. *Multiparty Democracy.* New York: Cambridge University Press.

Schom, Alan. 1997. *Napoleon Bonaparte.* New York: Harper Collins.

Schotter, Andrew. 1981. *The Economic Theory of Social Institutions.* Cambridge, UK: Cambrige University Press.

Schumpeter, Joseph. 1942. *Capitalism, Socialism, and Democracy.* New York: Harper.

Scitovksy, Tibor. 1941. "A Note on Welfare Properties in Economics." *Review of Economic Studies* 9: 77–88.

Searle, John. 1999. "I Married a Computer," *New York Review of Books* XLVI 6: 34–8.

Sen, Amartya. 1970. *Collective Choice and Social Welfare.* San Francisco: Holden Day.

Shepsle, Kenneth. 1979. "Institutional Arrangements and Equilibrium in Multidimensional Voting Bodies." *American Journal of Political Science* 23: 27–60.

Skidelsky, Robert. 1983. *John Maynard Keynes: Hopes Betrayed, 1883–1920.* London: Macmillan.

Skidelsky, Robert. 1992. *John Maynard Keynes: The Economist as Saviour, 1920–1937.* London: Macmillan.

Skidelsky, Robert. 2000. *John Maynard Keynes: Fighting for Britain, 1937–1946.* London: Macmillan.

Sloan, Herbert. 2001 [1995]. *Principle and Interest.* London: Oxford University Press and Charlottesville, VA: University Press of Virginia.

Smale, Stephen. 1966. "Structurally Stable Systems Are Not Dense." *American Journal of Mathematics* 88: 491–96.

Smale, Stephen. 1973. "Global Analysis and Economics I: Pareto Optimum and a Generalization of Morse Theory." In *Dynamical Systems.* New York: Academic Press, edited by Maurice Peixoto.

Smith, Adam. 1984 [1758]. *The Theory of Moral Sentiments.* Indianapolis, IN: Liberty Fund.

Smith, Adam. 1981 [1776]. *An Inquiry into the Nature and Causes of the Wealth of Nations.* Indianapolis, IN: Liberty Fund.

Smith, James M. ed. 1995. *The Republic of Letters* (3 volumes). New York: Norton.

Smith, Jeff. 2002. "Trading Places? The Two Parties in the Electorate from 1970–2000." Presented at the meeting of the Midwest Political Science Association, Chicago, April.

Sobel, Andrew. 1998. "Rosy Expectations, Cloudy Horizons." *Columbia Journal of European Law* 4: 453–65.

Sobel, Andrew. 1999. *State Institutions, Private Incentives, Global Capital.* Ann Arbor, MI: University of Michigan Press.

Solomon, Robert. 1977. *The International Monetary System, 1945–1976.* New York: Harper and Row.

Sonnenschein, Hugo. 1972. "Market Excess Demand Functions." *Econometrica* 40: 549–63.

Stagg, Jack. 1981a. "Anglo-Indian Relations in North America in 1763." Department of Indian Affairs, Ottawa. Unpublished Manuscript.

Stagg, Jack. 1981b. "An Analysis of the Royal Proclamation of 7 October 1763." Department of Indian Affairs, Ottawa. Unpublished Manuscript..

Stanley, Steven. 1996. *Children of the Ice Age.* New York: Harmony Books.

Stasavage, David. 2002. "Credible Commitment in Early Modern Europe: North and Weingast Revisited." *Journal of Law, Economics and Organization* 18: 155–86.

Stasavage, David. 2003. *Public Debt and the Birth of the Democratic State.* Cambridge, UK: Cambridge University Press.

Stiglitz, Joseph. 1994. *Whither Socialism.* Cambridge, MA: MIT Press.

Stiglitz, Joseph. 2002. *Globalization and Its Discontents*. New York: W. W. Norton.

Stourzh, Gerald. 1954. *Benjamin Franklin and American Foreign Policy*. Chicago, IL: University of Chicago Press.

Strnad, Jeff. 1985. "The Structure of Continuous Valued Neutral Monotonic Social Functions." *Social Choice and Welfare* 2: 181–96.

Surowiecki, James. 2004. *The Wisdom of Crowds*. New York: Doubleday.

Sugden, Robert. 1980. *The Economics of Rights, Cooperation and Welfare*. Oxford: Blackwell.

Surowsiecki, James. 2004. *The Wisdom of Crowds*. New York: Randon House.

Sundquist, James. 1983. *Dynamics of the Party System*. Washington: Brookings Institution Press.

Tattersal, Ian. 1998. *Becoming Human*. New York: Harcourt Brace.

Taylor, Michael. 1969. "Proof of a Theorem on Majority Rule." *Behavioral Science* 14: 228–31.

Taylor, Michael. 1976. *Anarchy and Cooperation*. London: Wiley.

Taylor, Michael. 1982. *Community, Anarchy, and Liberty*. Cambridge, UK: Cambridge University Press.

Thurow, Lester. 1992. *Head to Head*. New York: Morrow.

Thurow, Lester. 1996. *The Future of Capitalism*. New York: Morrow.

Tracy, Destutt. 1819 [1798]. *Commentaire sur l'esprit des lois de Montesquieu*. Paris: Desoer.

Triffin, Robert. 1960. *Gold and the Dollar Crisis*. New Haven, CT: Yale University Press.

Truman, Harry S. 1947. Address delivered before a Joint Session of the Senate and House of Representatives, March 12 (80th Congress).

Tufte, E. 1978. *Political Control of the Economy*. Princeton, NJ: Princeton University Press.

Tullock, Gordon. 1981. "Why So Much Stability?" *Public Choice* 37: 189–205.

Turgot, Anne-Robert-Jacques. 1973 [1766]. "Reflections on the Formation and Distribution of Wealth." In *Turgot on Progress, Sociology* and *Economics*. Cambridge, UK: Cambridge University Press, edited by Ronald Meek.

Turing, Alan. 1937. "On Computable Numbers with an Application to the Entscheidungs Problem." *Proceedings of the London Mathematical Society* 42: 230–65. Reprinted in Jack Copeland [ed.] *The Essential Turing*. Oxford: The Clarendon Press.

Turing, Alan. 1950. "Computing Machinery and Intelligence." *Mind* 59: 422–60. Reprinted in Jack Copeland, [ed.] *The Essential Turing*. Oxford: The Clarendon Press.

Ulam, Stanislaw, and John von Neumann. 1947. "On Combination of Stochastic and Deterministic Processes: Preliminary Report." *Bulletin of the American Mathematical Society* 53: 1120.

United States Government Printing Office. 1973. *The Long Report to the United States Senate*.

Urken, Arnold. 1991. "The Condorcet-Jefferson Connection and the Origins of Social Theory." *Public Choice* 72: 213–36.

van Doren, Carl. 1938. *Benjamin Franklin*. Harmondsworth, UK: Penguin.

Viner, Jacob. 1936. "Mr. Keynes on the Causes of Unemployment." *Quarterly Journal of Economics* 51: 147–67.

Voltaire, Francois. 1738. *The Elements of Sir Isaac Newton's Philosophy*. London: Stephen Austen, translated from the French by John Hanna.

von Hayek, Friederich. 1944. *The Road to Serfdom*. London: Routledge & Kegan Paul.

von Hayek, Friederich. 1948. *Individualism and Economic Order*. London: Routledge & Kegan Paul.

von Hayek, Friederich. 1973. *Law, Legislation, and Liberty, Volume 1, Rules and Order*. London: Routledge & Kegan Paul.

von Hayek, Friederich. 1978. *New Studies in Philosophy, Politics, Economics and the History of Ideas*. Chicago, IL: University of Chicago Press.

von Mises, Ludwig. 1935 [1920]. "Economic Calculation in the Socialist Commonwealth." In *Collectivist Economic Planning*. London: Routledge & Kegan Paul, edited by Freidrich von Hayek.

von Mises, Ludwig. 1944. *Omnipotent Government*. New Haven, CT: Yale University Press.

von Neumann, John. 1928. "Zur Theorie der Gesselschaftsspiele." *Mathematical Annals* 100: 295–20.

von Neumann, John. 1945 [1932]. "A Model of General Economic Equilibrium." *Review of Economic Studies* 13: 1–9.

von Neumann, John. 1958. *The Computer and the Brain*. New Haven, CT: Yale University Press.

von Neumann, John. 1966. *Theory of Self-reproducing Automata*. Urbana: University of Illinois Press, edited by Arthur Burks.

von Neumann, John, and Oscar Morgenstern. 1944. *Theory of Games and Economic Behavior*. Princeton, NJ: Princeton University Press.

Weingast, Barry. 1997a. "The Political Foundations of Democracy and the Rule of Law." *American Political Science Review* 2: 245–63.

Weingast, Barry. 1997b. "The Political Foundations of Limited Government: Parliament and Sovereign Debt in 17th and 18th Century England." In *The Frontiers of the New Institutional Economics*. New York: Academic Press, edited by John Drobak and John Nye.

Weingast, Barry. 1998. "Political Stability and Civil War." In *Analytical Narratives*. Princeton, NJ: Princeton University Press, edited by Robert Bates, Avner Grief, Margaret Levi, Jean-Laurent Rosenthal, and Barry Weingast.

Weintraub, Stanley. 2005. *Iron Tears: America's Battle for Freedom, Britain's Quagmire 1775–1783*. New York: Free Press.

Weisberger, Bernard A. 2000. *America Afire*. New York: Harper Collins.

Wilcox, William. ed. 1982. *The Papers of Benjamin Franklin: March 23, 1775 through October 27, 1776*. New Haven, CT: Yale University Press.

Williams, Basil. 1960. *The Whig Supremacy, 1714–1760*. Oxford: Clarendon Press.

Williams, Melissa S. 1998. *Voice, Trust and Money*. Princeton, NJ: Princeton University Press.

Wills, Gary. 1999. *A Necessary Evil*. New York: Simon & Schuster.

Wills, G. 2003a. "The Negro President." *The New York Review of Books* 50(17): 45–51.

Wills, G. 2003b. *"Negro President": Jefferson and the Slave Power.* New York: Houghton Mifflin.

Woodward, Llewellyn. 1962. *The Age of Reform 1815–1870.* Oxford: The Clarendon Press.

Womersley, David. 2002. *Gibbon and the Watchmen of the Holy City.* Oxford: Oxford University Press

Yergin, Daniel, and Joseph Stanislaw. 1998. *Commanding Heights.* New York: Simon and Schuster.

Yourgrau, Palle. 1999. *Gödel Meets Einstein: Time Travel in the Gödel Universe.* Peru, IL: Open Court Publishing Company.

Yourgrau, Palle. 2005. *A World Without Time.* New York: Basic Books.

Young, Peyton. 1998. *Individual Strategy and Social Structure: An Evolutionary Theory of Institutions.* Princeton, NJ: Princeton University Press.

Zame, William. 1987. "Competitive Equilibria in Production Economies with Infinite Dimension Commodity Spaces." *Econometrica* 55: 1075–108.

Zeeman, Christopher. 1974. "On the Unstable Behavior of Stock Exchanges." *Journal of Mathematical Economics* 1: 39–49. Reprinted in Christopher Zeeman (1977) *Catastrophe Theory.* Reading, MA: Addison-Wesley.

SUPPLEMENTARY READING

Adams, William Howard. 1997. *The Paris Years of Thomas Jefferson.* New Haven CT: Yale University Press.

Ambrose, Stephen. 1996. *Undaunted Courage.* New York: Simon & Schuster.

Bailey, Thomas. 1940. *A Diplomatic History of the American People.* New York: Meredith.

Bailyn, Bernard. 1992 [1967]. *The Ideological Origins of the American Revolution.* Cambridge, MA: Harvard University Press.

Bailyn, Bernard. ed. 1993a. *The Debate on the Constitution: Part One.* New York: Library of America.

Bailyn, Bernard. ed. 1993b. *The Debate on the Constitution, Part Two.* New York: Library of America.

Bailyn, Bernard. 2003. *To Begin The World Anew.* New York: Knopf.

Banning, Lance. 1978. *The Jeffersonian Persuasion.* Ithaca, New York: Cornell University Press.

Banning, Lance. 1995. *The Sacred Fire of Liberty.* Ithaca, New York: Cornell University Press.

Brookhiser, Richard. 1999. *Alexander Hamilton: American.* New York: Free Press.

Ellis, Joseph. 2000. *Founding Brothers.* New York: Knopf.

Ellis, Joseph. 2004. *His Excellency: George Washington.* New York: Knoff.

Farber, Daniel. 2003. *Lincoln's Constitution.* Chicago: University of Chicago Press.

Ferguson, Niall. 1995. "Keynes and the German Inflation." *The English Historical Review* 110: 368–91.

Ferling, John. 2004. *Adams vs. Jefferson.* New York: Oxford University Press.

Fiorina, Morris. 2005. *Culture War?* New York: Longmans.

Fischer, David H., and James C. Kelly. 2000. *Bound Away: Virginia and the Western Movement*. Charlottesville, VA: University Press of Virginia.

Gordon-Reed, Annette. 1992. *Thomas Jefferson and Sally Hemmings: An American Controversy*. Charlottesville, VA: University Press of Virginia.

Grant, Michael. 1998. *From Rome to Byzantium*. London: Routledge.

Harrington, James. 1992 [1656]. *The Commonwealth of Oceana,* edited with an Introduction by J. G. A. Pocock. Cambridge: Cambridge University Press.

Heidler, David S., and Jeanne T. Heidler. eds. 1997. *Encyclopedia of the War of 1812*. Santa Barbara, CA: ABC.

Hibbert, Christopher. 1998. *George III*. New York: Basic Books.

Hoffman, Philip. 1994. "Early Modern France: 1450–1700." In *Fiscal Crises, Liberty and Representative Government, 1450–1789*. Stanford, CA: Stanford University Press, edited by Philip Hoffman and Katherine Norberg.

Holt, Michael. 1992. "Abraham Lincoln and the Politics of Union." In *Political Parties and American Political Development from the Age of Jackson to the Age of Lincoln*. Baton Rouge, LA: Louisiana State University Press, edited by Michael Holt.

Holt, Michael. 1999. *The Rise and Fall of the American Whig Party*. Oxford: Oxford University Press.

Holton, Woody. 1999. *Forced Founders*. Chapel Hill: University of North Carolina Press.

Isaacson, Walter. 2003. *Benjamin Franklin: An American Life*. New York: Simon & Schuster.

Johnson, Paul. 1997. *A History of the American People*. New York: Harper.

Kaplan, Leonard. 1972. *Colonies into Nation*. New York: Macmillan.

Keane, John. 1995. *Tom Paine: A Political Life*. New York: Little Brown.

Kennedy, Roger G. 2003. *Mr. Jefferson's Lost Cause*. New York: Oxford University Press.

Kramer, Larry. 1999. "Madison's Audience." *Harvard Law Review* 112: 611–79.

Kramer, Larry. 2004. *The People Themselves*. New York: Oxford University Press.

Langley, Lester D. 1996. *The Americas in the Age of Revolution: 1750–1850*. New Haven, CT: Yale University Press.

Lemay, J. A. Leo. ed. 1987 [1782]. *Franklin: Writings*. New York: Library of America.

Madison, James. 1987 [1840]. *Notes of the Debates in the Federal Convention*. New York: Norton.

McDonald, Forrest. 1979 [1964]. *E Pluribus Unum*. Indianapolis, IN: Liberty Fund.

McDonald, Forrest. 1979. *Alexander Hamilton: A Biography*. New York: Norton.

Miller, William Lee. 2002. *Lincoln's Virtues*. New York: Alfred Knopf.

Remini, Robert V. 2001. *Andrew Jackson and His Indian Wars*. New York: Viking.

Simon, James. 2002. *What Kind of Nation*. New York: Simon & Schuster.

Sugden, John. 1997. *Tecumseh: A Life*. New York: Henry Holt.

Todd, Emmanuel. 2003. *After the Empire: The Breakdown of the American Order*. New York: Columbia University Press.

Tucker, Robert W., and David C. Hendrickson. 1990. *The Empire of Liberty: The Statecraft of Thomas Jefferson*. Oxford: Oxford University Press.

Wallace, Anthony. 1999. *Jefferson and the Indians*. Cambridge, MA: Harvard University Press.

Watson, Steven. 1960. *The Reign of George III: 1769–1815*. Oxford: Clarendon Press.

Wiencek, Henry. 2003. *An Imperfect God: George Washington, His Slaves and the Creation of America*. New York: Ferrar, Strauss and Giroux.

Wood, Gordon S. 1969. *The Creation of the American Republic*. New York: Norton.

Wood, Gordon S. 1991. *The Radicalism of the American Revolution*. New York: Knopf.

Wood, Gordon S. 2002. *The American Revolution: A History*. New York: Random House.

Wood, Gordon S. 2004. *The Americanization of Benjamin Franklin*. New York: The Penguin Press.

Index

Act of Revocation (Great Britain), 49
activism, civil rights and, 195
activism, political party, 176–178
  model for, 178–182
  public perception from, 177–178
Adams, John, 79, 96, 108
Adams, John Quincy, 137
Adams, Samuel, 96
"The Address at Cooper Institute" (Lincoln), 155
"anarchic philosophers," 208
Anne (Queen), 18, 54
apex games, 48
"architects of change," 21, 24, 233–240
  Madison as, 108
aristocracies, under social choice theory, 109
Arrow, Kenneth
  Social Choice and Individual Values, 257
Arrow-Debreu Theorem, 260
Arrow's Impossibility Theorem, 22, 244, 246, 257
  dictators under, 246
asset markets, 204
"Atlantic Constitution," 16, 200, 201, 208, 211, 214, 229
  Great Britain and, 16
  Keynes on, 206
  transformations in, 213, 222
Attila, 7

autocracies
  chaos and, 114
  under social choice theory, 109
autocrats. *See also* dictators

Ballader, Eduoard, 216
Bank of the U.S., Hamilton and, 55, 127–128, 127
Bank of England, 17, 18, 34, 52
"belief aggregation," 254
belief cascades, 85, 104, 145, 158
  in game theory, 265
  Wall Street crash as, 224
Bell, John, 158
Benton, Thomas Hart, 148
Blair, Montgomery, 148
Blow, Elizabeth, 146
Blow, Peter, 146
Blow, Taylor, 149
Bonaparte, Napoleon, 7, 36, 79
Brahe, Tycho, 230
brain, models for, 263
Breckenridge, John, 158
Bretton Woods System, 21, 31, 216, 220
  Smithsonian Agreement and, 207
Brouwer Fixed Point Theorem, 243, 256
Bryan, William Jennings, 19, 63, 164, 186
Buchanan, James, 148
Bull Moose Progressive Party, 186, 187
Bush, George W., 177, 240
Byrnes, James, 236

CAP (Common Agricultural Policy), EU and, 10